Children's
Literature
Review

Guide to Gale Literary Criticism Series

For criticism on	Consult these Gale series
Authors now living or who died after December 31, 1999	*CONTEMPORARY LITERARY CRITICISM (CLC)*
Authors who died between 1900 and 1999	*TWENTIETH-CENTURY LITERARY CRITICISM (TCLC)*
Authors who died between 1800 and 1899	*NINETEENTH-CENTURY LITERATURE CRITICISM (NCLC)*
Authors who died between 1400 and 1799	*LITERATURE CRITICISM FROM 1400 TO 1800 (LC)* *SHAKESPEAREAN CRITICISM (SC)*
Authors who died before 1400	*CLASSICAL AND MEDIEVAL LITERATURE CRITICISM (CMLC)*
Authors of books for children and young adults	*CHILDREN'S LITERATURE REVIEW (CLR)*
Dramatists	*DRAMA CRITICISM (DC)*
Poets	*POETRY CRITICISM (PC)*
Short story writers	*SHORT STORY CRITICISM (SSC)*
Black writers of the past two hundred years	*BLACK LITERATURE CRITICISM (BLC)* *BLACK LITERATURE CRITICISM SUPPLEMENT (BLCS)*
Hispanic writers of the late nineteenth and twentieth centuries	*HISPANIC LITERATURE CRITICISM (HLC)* *HISPANIC LITERATURE CRITICISM SUPPLEMENT (HLCS)*
Native North American writers and orators of the eighteenth, nineteenth, and twentieth centuries	*NATIVE NORTH AMERICAN LITERATURE (NNAL)*
Major authors from the Renaissance to the present	*WORLD LITERATURE CRITICISM, 1500 TO THE PRESENT (WLC)* *WORLD LITERATURE CRITICISM SUPPLEMENT (WLCS)*

ISSN 0362-4145

volume 68

Children's Literature Review

Excerpts from Reviews,
Criticism, and Commentary
on Books for Children
and Young People

Jennifer Baise
Editor

Thomas Ligotti
Associate Editor

GALE GROUP

Detroit
New York
San Francisco
London
Boston
Woodbridge, CT

STAFF

Lynn M. Spampinato, Janet Witalec, *Managing Editors, Literature Product*
Kathy D. Darrow, *Product Liaison*
Jennifer Baise, *Editor*
Mark W. Scott, *Publisher, Literature Product*

Rebecca J. Blanchard, Thomas Ligotti, *Associate Editors*
Mary Ruby, *Technical Training Specialist*
Deborah J. Morad, Kathleen Lopez Nolan, *Managing Editors*
Susan M. Trosky, *Director, Literature Content*

Maria L. Franklin, *Permissions Manager*
Shalice Shah-Caldwell, *Permissions Associate*

Victoria B. Cariappa, *Research Manager*
Tracie A. Richardson, *Project Coordinator*
Sarah Genik, Ron Morelli, Tamara C. Nott, *Research Associates*
Nicodemus Ford, *Research Assistant*

Dorothy Maki, *Manufacturing Manager*
Stacy L. Melson, *Buyer*

Mary Beth Trimper, *Manager, Composition and Electronic Prepress*
Carolyn Roney, *Composition Specialist*

Michael Logusz, *Graphic Artist*
Randy Bassett, *Imaging Supervisor*
Robert Duncan, Dan Newell, *Imaging Specialists*
Pamela A. Reed, *Imaging Coordinator*
Kelly A. Quin, *Editor, Image and Multimedia Content*

Library of Congress Catalog Card Number 76-643301
ISBN 0-7876-4574-5
ISSN 0362-4145
Printed in the United States of America

10 9 8 7 6 5 4 3 2 1

Contents

Preface

Literature for children and young adults has evolved into both a respected branch of creative writing and a successful industry. Currently, books for young readers are considered among the most popular segments of publishing. Criticism of juvenile literature is instrumental in recording the literary or artistic development of the creators of children's books as well as the trends and controversies that result from changing values or attitudes about young people and their literature. Designed to provide a permanent, accessible record of this ongoing scholarship, *Children's Literature Review* (*CLR*) presents parents, teachers, and librarians—those responsible for bringing children and books together—with the opportunity to make informed choices when selecting reading materials for the young. In addition, *CLR* provides researchers of children's literature with easy access to a wide variety of critical information from English-language sources in the field. Users will find balanced overviews of the careers of the authors and illustrators of the books that children and young adults are reading; these entries, which contain excerpts from published criticism in books and periodicals, assist users by sparking ideas for papers and assignments and suggesting supplementary and classroom reading. Ann L. Kalkhoff, president and editor of *Children's Book Review Service Inc.*, writes that "*CLR* has filled a gap in the field of children's books, and it is one series that will never lose its validity or importance."

Scope of the Series

Each volume of *CLR* profiles the careers of a selection of authors and illustrators of books for children and young adults from preschool through high school. Author lists in each volume reflect:

- an international scope

- representation of authors of all eras

- the variety of genres covered by children's and/or YA literature: picture books, fiction, nonfiction, poetry, folklore, and drama

Although the focus of the series is on authors new to *CLR,* entries will be updated as the need arises.

Organization of the Book

A *CLR* entry consists of the following elements:

- The **Author Heading** consists of the author's name followed by birth and death dates. The portion of the name outside the parentheses denotes the form under which the author is most frequently published. If the author wrote consistently under a pseudonym, the pseudonym will be listed in the author heading and the author's actual name given in parentheses on the first line of the biographical and critical information. Also located here are any name variations under which an author wrote, including transliterated forms for authors whose native languages use non-roman alphabets. Uncertain birth or death dates are indicated by question marks.

- A **Portrait of the Author** is included when available.

- The **Author Introduction** contains information designed to introduce an author to *CLR* users by presenting an overview of the author's themes and styles, biographical facts that relate to the author's literary career or critical responses to the author's works, and information about major awards and prizes the author has received. The introduction begins by identifying the nationality of the author and by listing genres in which s/he has written for children and young adults. Introductions also list a group of representative titles for which the author or illustrator being profiled is best known; this section, which begins with the words "major works include," follows the genre line of the introduction. For seminal figures, a listing of major works about the author follows when appropriate, highlighting important biographies about the author or illustrator that are not excerpted in the entry. The centered heading "Introduction" announces the body of the text.

- ■ **Criticism** is located in three sections: **Author Commentary** (when available) **General Commentary** (when available), and **Title Commentary** (commentary on specific titles).

  The **Author Commentary** presents background material written by the author or by an interviewer. This commentary may cover a specific work or several works. Author commentary on more than one work appears after the author introduction, while commentary on an individual book follows the title entry heading.

  The **General Commentary** consists of critical excerpts that consider more than one work by the author or illustrator being profiled. General commentary is preceded by the critic's name in boldface type or, in the case of unsigned criticism, by the title of the journal. *CLR* also features entries that emphasize general criticism on the oeuvre of an author or illustrator. When appropriate, a selection of reviews is included to supplement the general commentary.

  The **Title Commentary** begins with the title entry headings, which precede the criticism on a title and cite publication information on the work being reviewed. Title headings list the title of the work as it appeared in its first English-language edition. The first English-language publication date of each work (unless otherwise noted) is listed in parentheses following the title. Differing U.S. and British titles follow the publication date within parentheses. When a work is written by an individual other than the one being profiled, as is the case when illustrators are featured, the parenthetical material following the title cites the author of the work before listing its publication date.

Entries in each title commentary section consist of critical excerpts on the author's individual works, arranged chronologically by publication date. The entries generally contain two to seven reviews per title, depending on the stature of the book and the amount of criticism it has generated. The editors select titles that reflect the entire scope of the author's literary contribution, covering each genre and subject. An effort is made to reprint criticism that represents the full range of each title's reception, from the year of its initial publication to current assessments. Thus, the reader is provided with a record of the author's critical history. Publication information (such as publisher names and book prices) and parenthetical numerical references (such as footnotes or page and line references to specific editions of works) have been deleted at the discretion of the editors to provide smoother reading of the text.

- ■ A complete **Bibliographical Citation** of the original essay or book precedes each piece of criticism.

- ■ Selected excerpts are preceded by brief **Annotations,** which provide information on the critic or work of criticism to enhance the reader's understanding of the excerpt.

- ■ Numerous **Illustrations** are featured in *CLR*. For entries on illustrators, an effort has been made to include illustrations that reflect the characteristics discussed in the criticism. Entries on authors who do not illustrate their own works my include photographs and other illustrative material pertinent to their careers.

Special Features: Entries on Illustrators

Entries on authors who are also illustrators will occasionally feature commentary on selected works illustrated but not written by the author being profiled. These works are strongly associated with the illustrator and have received critical acclaim for their art. By including critical comment on works of this type, the editors wish to provide a more complete representation of the artist's career. Criticism on these works has been chosen to stress artistic, rather than literary, contributions. Title entry headings for works illustrated by the author being profiled are arranged chronologically within the entry by date of publication and include notes identifying the author of the illustrated work. In order to provide easier access for users, all titles illustrated by the subject of the entry are boldfaced.

CLR also includes entries on prominent illustrators who have contributed to the field of children's literature. These entries are designed to represent the development of the illustrator as an artist rather than as a literary stylist. The illustrator's section is organized like that of an author, with two exceptions: the introduction presents an overview of the illustrator's styles and techniques rather than outlining his or her literary background, and the commentary written by the illustrator on his or her works is called "Illustrator's Commentary" rather than "Author's Commentary." All titles of books containing illustrations by the artist being profiled are highlighted in boldface type.

Indexes

A **Cumulative Author Index** lists all of the authors who have appeared in *CLR* with cross-references to the biographical, autobiographical, and literary criticism series published by the Gale Group. A complete list of these sources is found facing the first page of the Author Index. The index also includes birth and death dates and cross-references between pseudonyms and actual names.

A **Cumulative Nationality Index** lists all authors featured in *CLR* by nationality, followed by the number of the *CLR* volume in which their entry appears.

A **Cumulative Title Index** lists all author titles covered in *CLR*. Each title is followed by the author's name and corresponding volume and page numbers where commentary on the work is located.

Citing *Children's Literature Review*

When writing papers, students who quote directly from any volume in the Literary Criticism Series may use the following general format to footnote reprinted criticism. The first example pertains to material drawn from periodicals, the second to material reprinted from books.

Cynthia Zarin, "It's Easy Being Green," *The New York Times Book Review* (November 14, 1993): 48; excerpted and reprinted in *Children's Literature Review,* vol. 58, ed. Deborah J. Morad (Farmington Hills, Mich: The Gale Group, 2000), 57.

Paul Walker, *Speaking of Science Fiction: The Paul Walker Interviews,* (Luna Publications, 1978), 108-20; excerpted and reprinted in *Children's Literature Review,* vol. 58, ed. Deborah J. Morad (Farmington Hills, Mich: The Gale Group, 2000), 3-8.

Suggestions are Welcome

In response to various suggestions, several features have been added to *CLR* since the beginning of the series, including author entries on retellers of traditional literature as well as those who have been the first to record oral tales and other folklore; entries on prominent illustrators featuring commentary on their styles and techniques; entries on authors whose works are considered controversial; occasional entries devoted to criticism on a single work or a series of works; sections in author introductions that list major works by and about the author or illustrator being profiled; explanatory notes that provide information on the critic or work of criticism to enhance the usefulness of the excerpt; more extensive illustrative material, such as holographs of manuscript pages and photographs of people and places pertinent to the careers of the authors and artists; a cumulative nationality index for easy access to authors by nationality; and occasional guest essays written specifically for *CLR* by prominent critics on subjects of their choice.

Readers who wish to suggest new features, topics, or authors to appear in future volumes, or who have other suggestions or comments are cordially invited to call, write, or fax the Managing Editor:

Managing Editor, Literary Criticism Series
The Gale Group
27500 Drake Road
Farmington Hills, MI 48331-3535
1-800-347-4253 (GALE)
Fax: 248-699-8054

Acknowledgments

The editors wish to thank the copyright holders of the excerpted criticism included in this volume and the permissions managers of many book and magazine publishing companies for assisting us in securing reproduction rights. We are also grateful to the staffs of the Detroit Public Library, the Library of Congress, the University of Detroit Mercy Library, Wayne State University Purdy/Kresge Library Complex, and the University of Michigan Libraries for making their resources available to us. Following is a list of the copyright holders who have granted us permission to reproduce material in this volume of *CLR*. Every effort has been made to trace copyright, but if omissions have been made, please let us know.

COPYRIGHTED EXCERPTS IN *CLR*, VOLUME 68, WERE REPRODUCED FROM THE FOLLOWING BOOKS:

PHOTOGRAPHS APPEARING IN *CLR*, VOLUME 68, WERE RECEIVED FROM THE FOLLOWING SOURCES:

Avi
1937-

(Full name Avi Wortis) American author of novels and short stories.

Major works include *The Fighting Ground* (1984), *The True Confessions of Charlotte Doyle* (1990), *Nothing but the Truth* (1991), *Poppy* (1995), *Beyond the Western Sea, Book One: The Escape from Home* (1996).

Major works about the author include *Avi* (Lois Markham, 1996), *Presenting Avi* (Susan P. Bloom and Cathryn M. Mercier, 1997).

For further information on Avi's career, see *CLR*, Volume 24.

INTRODUCTION

Considered one of the most popular and versatile writers of fiction for young people, Avi is lauded for successfully contributing to a variety of genres for the early, middle, and upper grades. Many of his works are historical fiction, but Avi has also written contemporary coming-of-age stories, mysteries, fantasies, psychological thrillers, and adventure stories. Critics have praised Avi for investing his works with spirited plots, believable characters, vivid atmosphere, accurate historical detail, and considerable irony and wit. Writing in a literary style that ranges from terse to richly textured, Avi is admired for addressing complex issues with sensitivity and skill. His works explore the thoughts and feelings of young people in difficult or troubling situations, and through his characters' choices he encourages his readers to question conventional values. Although several of his books explore the darker sides of both the natural and supernatural worlds, Avi is also the author of a number of comic stories and parodies. Regardless of the genre or style of his works, critics consistently note Avi's fast-paced and inventive plots and his ability to tell a compelling story. Avi has summarized his goals as a writer for young people, saying: "I want my readers to feel, to think, sometimes to laugh. But most of all I want them to enjoy a good read."

BIOGRAPHICAL INFORMATION

Born in Manhattan in 1937 and raised in Brooklyn, Avi grew up in an artistic environment. Several members of his family, including his parents, were writ-

ers. As a child Avi read a great deal, though a learning disability made writing difficult. In spite of his problems with writing, Avi decided at a young age that he wanted to be an author. As a student at Antioch University, he enrolled in playwriting classes. One of his plays won a contest and was published in a magazine. He later earned a master's degree in library science and became a librarian, a career that lasted twenty-five years. Avi continued writing after becoming a librarian, and after his two sons were born he began writing children's books. He submitted some of his stories to publishers, and in 1970 his story *Things That Sometimes Happen* was published by Doubleday.

MAJOR WORKS

While Avi has garnered praise for writing in a variety of genres, he is primarily known for writing historical fiction. Several of his works, including *Captain Grey* (1977), *Night Journeys* (1979) and its sequel

Encounter at Easton (1980), and *The Fighting Ground,* take place in colonial America. The award-winning *Fighting Ground* presents one eventful day in the life of Jonathan, a thirteen-year-old boy caught up in the Revolutionary War. At the beginning of the novel Jonathan looks forward to the chance to experience the glory of battle, but as the novel progresses and Jonathan does in fact get the chance to fight, he discovers the painful and unpleasant reality of war. Critics have praised Avi's ability to transform a distant historical event into what Zena Sutherland describes as "personal and immediate: not history or event, but experience; near and within oneself, and horrible."

Avi again achieved success in the historical fiction genre with *The True Confessions of Charlotte Doyle,* which tells the story of an aristocratic thirteen-year-old girl who finds herself involved in a mutiny on a transatlantic ship in 1832. Charlotte begins the voyage as a girl with conventional values about social class and gender roles, but her experiences at sea lead her to question—and discard—those values. *Charlotte Doyle* has earned accolades from critics for its suspense, its evocation of life at sea, and particularly for the rich and believable narrative of its protagonist as she undergoes a tremendous change in outlook. Also taking place on the high seas during the nineteenth century, *Beyond the Western Sea, Book One: The Escape from Home* received considerable praise from critics for its adventurous, fast-paced story and colorful characters. The story begins in 1850s Ireland during the potato famine, with two children, Maura and Patrick O'Connell, left to fend for themselves on a voyage to America. They've been forced from their home in Ireland by an unscrupulous landlord, Lord Kirkle, and their mother sends the children to join their father in the United States. While in Liverpool on the first part of their journey Maura and Patrick encounter young Laurence, the eleven-year-old son of Lord Kirkle, who has run away from his father. At the novel's end readers are left in suspense as to the fate of Laurence, suspense that is resolved in book two of the series, *Beyond the Western Sea, Book Two: Lord Kirkle's Money* (1996). While readers of the second installment discover that Laurence is safe, they also learn about the harsh realities and discrimination faced by the Irish immigrants in the United States.

In addition to historical fiction, Avi is also the author of several contemporary coming-of-age novels, including *A Place Called Ugly* (1981), *Sometimes I Think I Hear My Name* (1982), and *Nothing but the Truth,* all of which tell the stories of boys enduring the alienation and confusion of adolescence. *Nothing but the Truth* is the story of Philip Malloy and his battle with an English teacher, Miss Narwin. Philip is suspended from school for repeatedly breaking school rules by humming the national anthem along with the public address system in home room. At the time, the school is in the midst of elections, and some candidates for public office exploit Philip's experience, charging that Philip was punished for his patriotism. The incident attracts national media attention, and in the storm of patriotic rhetoric that follows, the truth of the matter is obscured. The story of *Nothing but the Truth* is related through school memos, diary entries, letters, dialogues, newspaper articles, and radio talk show scripts. Presented without narrative bias, the story takes into account the differing points of view surrounding the incident, leaving the reader to root out the real problems leading to Philip's suspension. Critics have commended the creative and skillful structure of the novel, the realistic portrayal of the incident's negative impact on characters' lives, and Avi's wry commentary on the tendency of the media to distort the truth.

Highly regarded for his fantasy writing, Avi has written several books in a series set in the animal kingdom, beginning with the award-winning *Poppy* and followed by *Poppy and Rye* (1998), *Ragweed* (1999), and *Ereth's Birthday* (2000). In the first book of the series, a community of deer mice, including the title character, live under the tyrannical rule of an owl named Mr. Ocax, who has promised them protection from other animals if they agree to live under his leadership. The timid Poppy realizes that to save her family she must overcome her fears—of Mr. Ocax, of her supposed enemies in the forest, and of her strict father. Reviewers have applauded the book's rich characterizations and its lively and suspenseful plot. The latest entry in the series, *Ereth's Birthday,* features Poppy's ill-humored friend, a porcupine named Ereth. In a foul mood because he believes Poppy has forgotten his birthday, Ereth walks off by himself and comes across a fox dying in a trap. He reluctantly promises the fox that he will look after her three kits. In spite of his attempts to distance himself from complicated relationships, Ereth forms an attachment to his charges, becoming a devoted foster parent to the young foxes. In a review of *Ereth's Birthday, Publishers Weekly* states: "Avi has delivered another crackling good read, one shot through with memorable descriptions . . . and crisp, credible dialogue."

AWARDS

Avi's works have received numerous awards and citations. Three of Avi's works were runners-up for the

Edgar Allan Poe Award: *No More Magic* in 1975, *Emily Upham's Revenge* in 1979, and *Shadrach's Crossing* in 1984. He also received the Christopher Award for *Encounter at Easton* in 1981 and the Scott O'Dell Award for *The Fighting Ground* in 1984. Both *The True Confessions of Charlotte Doyle* and *Nothing but the Truth* were named Newbery Medal honor books in 1991 and 1992, respectively. *Charlotte Doyle* also won a Golden Kite Award in 1990. In 1996 *Poppy* received the *Boston Globe/Horn Book* Award.

AUTHOR COMMENTARY

Avi

SOURCE: "The Child in Children's Literature," in *The Horn Book Magazine*, Vol. 69, No. 1, January-February, 1993, pp. 40-1, 50.

What is this thing—on which we adults spend so much time—that we call children's literature?

It would be interesting to compile a survey regarding the circumstances as well as the motivations which bring people to the world of writing for children. I believe the popular vision of the criteria for writing for young people is contained in this description of a children's literature course given at a local Rhode Island university. "Writing for children," it says, "requires three things: knowing what children read. Knowing the elements of good prose and poetry. Feeling like a child again."

I first want to consider that last requirement. One night my wife and I were visiting a couple, colleagues of hers from the university where she teaches. These people have two children, ages three and five. We were there for dinner, and these two boys were not happy about it. After all, they were going to have to go to bed earlier than usual. In any case, they were being reminded that they were not the center of the universe. On the contrary, they were about to be shunted aside by adults. As a result, they were unhappy and grumpy.

To placate their sense of being excluded, the eldest boy, Nicholas, was allowed to go around and ask the adults what drinks they would like. And Nicholas did it with a deeply serious look on his face, an unconscious imitation, I suspect, of the adult world. Anyway, he made his rounds. One adult requested sherry.

Another, wine. And so forth. When it came my turn, I leaned forward and whispered, "Please, Nicholas, I'd like a glass of spit."

"What?" said Nicholas, his eyes suddenly very large.

"A glass of spit, please."

Those deep, dark eyes gazed at me intently for a moment. Then across that angelic face spread a wicked grin. Turning, Nicholas cried out at the top of his voice, "He wants a glass of spit!"

What happened next was extraordinary. The two boys reacted as if a cage had been opened, their handcuffs removed. They began running about the room, whooping and hollering. And, indeed, as justice would have it, I got my glass of spit. On the rocks. The primacy of infantile desire had been restored to its rightful, central place. At which point the mother of these children turned to me and said, "Now I know why you write for children."

What she was suggesting, I believe, is that my talent for being childish—my ability to feel like a child—was an indication of my insight into children. So, logically, I *should* be writing for children.

But the logic of this view is played out in another anecdote. My wife and I were at yet another academic gathering. A learned astronomy professor said to me, "Tell me something which I've never been able to grasp. How can you, an adult"—he paused to fuss pretentiously with his pipe—"How can you, with an adult's mind, think *down* to a child's level?"

I told the professor that I did not think like a child, much less think "down." "If anything," I assured him, "I'm more often than not reminded of my complexity."

"But your books," he said—not that he had read any of them, and I was fairly certain he never would—"*are* for kids, and they are not adults." Children, he might as well have said right out, are not smart.

"You are an astronomy professor," I said. "You teach freshmen. Do you teach those freshman astronomy students the accepted facts, principles, and concepts of your science?"

"Of course," he said. "A fact is a fact."

"Yes, but do you teach your freshmen in the same way you teach your graduate students?"

"Not at all."

"In other words," I reminded him, "the substance of your course is essentially the same, but your means of presentation does change."

"Ah," he said, "now I understand. Everything is simple in kids' books."

"No," I said. "Simplicity has nothing to do with it. The facts—if you will—are presented so they have meaning within the context of children's experience."

"Kids have no experience," he insisted. "That's what makes them kids."

I changed the subject.

Let's turn now to that second requirement for writing for children: knowing what children read. What *are* children reading? The Center for the Learning and Teaching of Literature, in its 1989 "Study of Book-Length Works Taught in High School English Courses," indicated that Shakespeare is far and away the most widely read required author in schools.

My experience, based on country-wide school visits, is that the one author young people ask me about most is Stephen King. A few years ago it was V. C. Andrews. These authors write what Jerry Weiss calls "underground children's literature." But I don't think anyone would describe these writers as creators of what we call children's literature. By the same token, I'm sure we would all agree that *Alice in Wonderland* is a work of children's literature. But it is not currently being read much by children today.

Consider what a course in children's literature would cover if it treated only materials actually read by masses of children. Ask yourself this: if you placed a volume by your favorite writer of children's literature on a table next to a volume of Garfield the Cat, or the Baby-Sitters Club, or Sweet Valley High, and said, "Pick one," which book would today's child pick?

In my view, of the three criteria cited above, only "knowing the elements of good prose and poetry" contributes meaningfully to an understanding of what is children's literature. But if children's literature is not about being childish, if it is not about simplifying, or writing down, what is it? Let's start by asking a basic question: Who and what is this child for whom this literature is written? Is it the twelve-year-old toting a gun on the streets of the inner city? Or is it the American college graduate who comes home weekly to ask mom to wash his clothes? A history of childhood I've been reading suggests that childhood

is far less a biological construct than an economic one. For although we talk of childhood as some universally understood period of time, in fact each culture, each historical period, each socioeconomic group has its own definition of childhood. There is no universal understanding of what constitutes childhood. In other words, the "child" of children's literature is not specific.

Today, urban areas are full of children who are killers. But these killers are only children in terms of age. Why do they act this way? Let me give you some reasons. Our culture has rejected them as children. It allows them no childhood. To survive, these young people act like adults. They kill people. So that when one talks of children's literature, it is important to ask, *which* child? One of the interesting things about children's literature is that it *is* different according to time, place, and even ethnic group.

Not long ago I was reading an excerpt from my ghost tale, **Something Upstairs,** to a group of children, something I had been doing that spring with much success. But after this reading, the librarian informed me that one large group of my listeners was deeply offended because in their Southeast Asian culture, ghosts—or spirits—were to be treated as sacred. Here was a reminder that one person's children's literature is another's sacred text.

Consider that curious form of picture-book literature called comic books. When I was a child, in the 1940s, my friends and I read them by the ton. Childhood literature, to be sure. In that standard history of the literature, Meigs's *Critical History of Children's Literature* (Macmillan), comic books are not even mentioned. But look at this irony: chapbooks—those eighteenth-century comic books—are! In 1991 no children are reading chapbooks, though I read recently of an attempt to revive Classic Comics. What is children's literature? What is not?

To help solve the puzzle, let's consider the role of the child in children's literature. I write the book. I give it to my agent, who gives it to a publisher. They then make the decision to publish it or not. If published, it is designed by adults, edited by adults, physically made by adults, promoted by adults, evaluated by adults, and even given awards by adults. Finally, these books are purchased by adults and placed on shelves by adults.

Then, and only then, do children get their eyes and hands on the book. Then, and only then, do they come into the complex world of children's literature. Thus, in regard to children and what we call children's literature, children are at the end of the line. They are the readers. They are the consumers. They are not the creators.

Is this a crucial distinction to make? I believe so. Because if we make it, we acknowledge that the entire world of children's literature is hedged about by adult choices. To the extent that children buy children's books, it is usually paperback titles, but these are books that have usually already been issued in hard cover. And, after all, the way children select books indicates that a selection process has been imposed on them by schools, parents, and, of course, television—all controlled by adults. Anyone who writes for children has had a suggestion for revision put to him or her by an editor with the introductory phrase, "Your story may be true, but kids today don't like . . . "

Let me then be blunt in making this reality clear: children's literature has very much more to do with adults than with children. While that may appear contradictory, it is the case. It is affirmed historically. Children did not demand what came to be known as children's books. Children's literature was created by adults who were troubled about the kind of texts children were reading, works which were considered unsuitable from a political or religious point of view. Indeed, the idea of a distinct children's literature came about when the religious-educational establishments of the day felt the need to control what kids read, to shape the child's image of the world. So Plato wrote in his *Republic*.

> Shall we permit our children without scruple to hear any fables composed by any authors indifferently, and so receive into their minds opinions generally the reverse of those which, when they are grown to manhood, we shall think they ought to entertain? . . . Our first duty will be to exercise a superintendence over the authors of fables, selecting their good productions, and rejecting the bad. And the selected fables we shall advise our nurses and mothers to repeat to their children, that they may thus mould their minds with the fables, even more than they shape their bodies with the hand.

And here is what Sarah Trimmer—considered to be the first true critic of children's literature—had to say in the 1780s in her "Essay on Christian Education":

> Novels . . . however abridged, and however excellent, should not be read by young persons, till they are in some measure acquainted with real life; but under this denomination we do not mean to include those exemplary tales which inculcate the duties of childhood and youth, without working too powerfully upon the feelings of the mind, or giving false pictures of life and manners.

Given the vast array of adult choice, we adults select what constitutes the relevant experience for children and express it in children's literature. Crucially, in what we write, *we* define childhood for *them*. Children's literature has become one of the important ways the adult world defines childhood, or, as Plato said it, so as to "mould their minds" with the fables. Or as Mrs. Trimmer had it, "inculcate the duties of childhood and youth."

But what are the implications if everything we express in our children's books is filtered through our adult beings? First of all, we are never adults being children. It is impossible to be a child once one becomes an adult. We are adults writing for children, adults who write these books out of adult desire and experience. Even if we remember our childhood, it is memory based on the adult vantage point. The best that we can do is represent children in our books as we adults perceive them.

So to fully grasp what is happening in the writing of children's books, we must look, not to childhood itself, but to adult conceptions of childhood. I think this is easier to see in the field of nonfiction. The facts presented in nonfiction are, at least to the best of our abilities, objective. We do not alter our knowledge of reality to conform to children's views; rather, we alter our means of communicating that reality.

Take a children's book on astronomy. The child's empirical observation may be that the sun travels around the earth. But we adults know otherwise. Or do we? It's not beside the point to mention that I'm not sure how I know this fact. I never checked myself. I can't give the proof of it. But I do know it is the proper adult view.

Some years ago I was told by a Texas librarian that a parent had come to the school objecting to a book on astronomy. Why? Because some of the constellations were named after pagan gods! And this violated the parent's perception of true religion. Of course, whereas stars are real, the visual arrangement of stars into constellations is artificial. That arrangement is—if you will—art. So that parent was not objecting to stars, only to the way we perceive them.

In the same way, our children's book of astronomy does not give a child's view of the universe. We present the adult understanding of astronomy, but in terms that a child can understand.

In children's fiction, we present our complex experiences in narrative terms that will be understandable to the child. We do not alter our adult experience of reality. We shape it so that it has meaning to a child. That's not simplicity. Rather, it is a system of representing reality so as to be grasped by people who have had less experience than adults do—who have new constellations of reality.

Children have a full range of experience even before they learn to read. They are capable of love, hate, and anger. But two things differentiate them from adults. First, because they have not lived as long as adults, they do not have the passage of time by which to judge experience. Second, and as a result of the first, they focus intensely on their own lives and beings, which, after all, constitute their primary experience. Even as the earth is perceived as the center of the universe, the child believes that he or she is the center of the social universe. Growing up is, to a large degree, the process of finding one's place in the social structure as a whole, as well as gaining a sense of mortality. Growing up means learning two key things: our possibilities and our limitations.

Even as the book of astronomy seeks to present reality, the fiction we write is equally an attempt to present reality in adult or grown-up terms to children.

In teaching the writing of children's literature, I find two kinds of would-be authors. The majority of writers come to the field because their association with children is the primary factor of their lives. Often excluded from the world of adults—you may read that as the world of white male adults—these people are often forced to identify exclusively with children. They make the sad presumption that if one is childlike, one can write well for children. This notion fails—fails miserably, embarrassingly. It fails because these people often *are* childlike. In fact, it is difficult for children to create literature because they are, naturally, self-centered. Children are quite capable of producing images. In terms of literature they do produce good poems, most of them images of self. But children only very rarely produce more complex works of art. Indeed, the typical progress of children's writing is instructive. Poems first. Then the short story. Then the novel. And they are written in radically diminishing numbers. I once tried to track down the number of teenagers who had published novels. I came up with something like twenty-four. But there is a second group of writers—they are in the minority—and they see the field as a form of literature. They write from an adult perspective. And, in my view, they write far better than the first group.

So to be most effective in writing for children, one must be effective first in being an adult. Yet, ironically, it must be acknowledged that we see in the stereotypical artist a certain childishness. What kind of childishness? A refusal to go along with authority. Indeed, if adults do not conform to social structures, we say of them that they are immature, childlike. The child is held up as a metaphor for unsocial behavior. The artist, as a person, is thus childlike; but the artist as a creator is a fusion of opposites, of child and adult. In other words, there is a certain childlike way of being that becomes a means of adult liberation. By using children as our protagonists to fight our adult battles, we are on safer ground. But if we do this in the adult world, we are viewed critically. After all, when I asked for a glass of spit, it was only acceptable because I asked it of a child. Can you imagine what would happen if I were to ask for such a thing in an adult social situation? At best I would be thought odd. Do it for children, and I gain a measure of acceptability. The point is, the reason I was able to get away with antisocial behavior was because those children were protecting me.

Notice that those works of children's literature which seem to last the longest appear to do so precisely because they appeal simultaneously to both adults' and children's culture. They strike a chord in both. A singular harmony of opposites is created in the art form itself. But when the harmony of opposites is not there, we have an explanation for the split in the field, where those books judged best by adults are often not read by children. Simultaneously, often the children's choice—the Garfields, the Stephen Kings—we pronounce the worst forms of children's literature.

Who is in charge? Central to our present culture is the idea expressed by the poet Wordsworth that the child is the parent of the adult. Later that idea was extended into an entire system of psychology by Freud. Wordsworth's concept was presented at the historical moment when the idea of childhood was taking on new shape and form. There was an increased conviction that the child was different from the adult, a break from the previous view. The first English novel about childhood *per se,* Dickens's *Oliver Twist,* appeared in 1836, roughly at the same time Wordsworth offered his image.

I believe we write about the child to get back to beginnings, as a means to start afresh. But that begs the question: start *what* afresh?

Look closely at the novel in children's literature. Is it life itself? No. It is merely a representation, representing life in certain patterns even as we arrange the stars in visually defined constellations. Consider then the typical protagonist in children's literature: the child alone, resolving issues of control—more often than not adult authority. Asserting self. Being self. Determining who is in charge. Getting back home. You could not think of two more different books in form, in style, in ideas than Dr. Seuss's *The Cat in the Hat* (Random) and Paula Fox's *One-Eyed Cat* (Bradbury). But both books are energized by the tensions brought on by parental control or lack of it. Indeed, the question of control—parents, teachers, police—is absolutely fundamental to children's literature.

Now, if we look at the children's novel that way, the question we are led to is: Why do writers of children's books so often write about questions of control? I believe that it is not out of concern about childhood, but from a profound feeling of unease about the adult world.

What is it that makes us uneasy? Although children do have the full range of emotions, what they don't have yet is the ability to compromise. I suspect that it is just that passionate consistency, that almost defiant integrity, which makes children so attractive a subject. It is my view that in children's literature we adults are writing stories that inform the child of our being uneasy with adult society at the very point where idealism and social control clash. Things are wrong in the adult world. Our childhood ideals did not come true. Children's literature allows us, as adults, to change this if we go back to the beginning. The child shall set it right. Therefore, we write books about children because they represent the ideal of relative freedom from constraint, a constraint we feel in our adult world. In other words, we mask our anxiety about confronting this issue in an adult world by writing about and for children. And we call this writing children's literature.

Fiction in children's literature is about unfairness, inconsistency, and lack of justice in the adult world. The constant struggle to adjust good with bad. Save us, we are saying to the children, save us from what you are becoming. Save us from what we are teaching you to become. The ultimate irony is that the plots of children's literature fiction are more often than not about the passage into adulthood. So, children's literature is a cry for help from adults to children.

Look at the endings of so many children's novels. The end of narcissism. The need to leave childhood. These endings are presented as triumph. A commitment to real self-knowledge. Things which spell out adulthood. But, at the same time, with that knowledge, with that success, comes a profound sense of loss, creating that element of nostalgia that is so pervasive in the literature.

What is this story we are telling? It's one of the oldest stories of our culture, a metaphor for the transition from childhood to adulthood. It is the story of Eden and of being driven from Eden.

At random, I picked some novels from my shelves. I looked at the endings. I noticed how often there is a return to home, but I noticed, too, that home often looks different to the child protagonist. This is from Paula Fox's *A Place Apart* (Farrar).

> I felt a great swoop of regret as though my heart, like the kite that morning, had fallen through space to the ground. I didn't want to feel that way anymore. I hurried on toward home. But I looked back. Just once.

And *The Wizard of Oz.*

> "My darling child!" [Aunt Em] cried, folding the little girl in her arms and covering her face with kisses; "where in the world did you come from?" "From the Land of Oz," said Dorothy gravely. "And here is Toto, too. And oh, Aunt Em! I'm so glad to be at home again!"

Children's literature, in the deepest sense, most often tells the tale of the acquisition of knowledge, but it is knowledge which in itself brings about—by fact or metaphor—the end of childhood. These triumphant endings, by virtue of the fact that they usher the child into adulthood, are, ironically, a kind of defeat. This is because, more often than not, these endings constitute an end to idealism. Children's literature often seems to be saying to children, "Don't do what we have done. Do better. Please make the world into what I, like you, once believed it capable of becoming. Don't make the mistake I made. Don't grow up."

And yet, at the same time we seem to be saying that growing up is the sad fate of humankind. You are doomed to it. Like travelers who learn most about home by visiting foreign shores, we discover Eden by leaving it.

But wait! There is a "subversive" children's literature, a literature in which the protagonist does not go back home, but rather leaves home. *Escapes* might be the better word. Generally speaking, these are the books the adult world of children's literature find most disturbing.

Which books are these? Starting with older titles, there is *Huckleberry Finn.* And, interestingly enough, *Little Women,* if you remember that it is in reality two books, the second half, *Good Wives,* having been urged on by Alcott's publisher because of the success of the first book. *Little Women* ends, for its day, on a radical note: Jo is not married!

What about modern titles? *Catcher in the Rye* is our classic. There are others, like *Harriet the Spy* (Harper), Robert Cormier's books, and some of Paul Zindel's. Notice how these kinds of books end. Here's the ending from Jenny Davis's first novel, *Good-bye and Keep Cold* (Orchard).

> Mama walked off from the people who raised her and never looked back. I don't want to do that. But I do want to be free of them, want them in perspective, want myself apart. I need to shake them loose, let go. Charlie says everybody has to raise their parents. Is that true? He says the time comes for all of us when we have to kiss them good-bye and trust them to be okay on their own. I've done the best I could with mine. Good-bye, you all, and good luck. Good-bye and keep cold.

In these kinds of books our protagonists are leaving Eden, and not looking back. And we who write these endings are troubling the adults. Are we troubling the children? I don't think so. I think we're challenging them to leave home, a metaphor for changing the world. Thus, those of us who write this way seem to be trying to say, "Good-bye, Eden. Hello, world. Here comes the millennium."

Avi

SOURCE: "I Can Read, I Can Read," in *The Horn Book Magazine,* Vol. 70, No. 2, March-April, 1994, pp. 166-69.

When I was five years old—or so the family legend has it—I appeared at the dinner table screaming, "I can read, I can read!" Alas, the legend makes no reference to what it was I read. True or not, that this story was told with pride and amusement suggests how important books were to me—and my family.

Books are in my blood. Two of my great-grandfathers were writers. My grandmother was a playwright. One aunt was a journalist. My parents wanted to be novelists. My twin sister is a writer. My wife writes literary criticism. And of my three sons, one is a journalist and the other two write rock lyrics.

When I was a kid my parents rented rooms in our house, and one of the tenants was Millicent Selsam. My fourth grade was the class portrayed in Bette Bao

Lord's *In the Year of the Boar and Jackie Robinson.* (In the book she calls me Irvie, a kid in the back of the room who remains silent until the end of the class, when he raises his hand and inevitably says something useless.) Walter Dean Myers was a fellow student at the first high school I went to, though we never met and I flunked out before he dropped out. In my next high school Norma Klein was a classmate. Our English teacher said she was the best writer he ever had. He told my parents I was the worst.

No birthday or Christmas passed without my receiving at least one book. No Friday came without a quick trip to the local public library. Why quick? Great selection of books. No public toilet. But by saving my allowance I could go to a bookstore each month and purchase one book to create my own library.

I received my most memorable gift on my sixteenth birthday when my father took me to the Strand Book Store in New York City—then on lower Fourth Avenue, a used bookstore area which I haunted—and said to me, "Buy all the books you want up to thirty-five dollars." I still have a few of those books.

So you see, a bookstore is the true north of my private cultural compass. I can never be in any city without quickly finding my way to one. Though my carpentry skills are slight, I build a mean book case. It should come as no surprise, then, when I insist that it's impossible to overstate the importance of the book in our culture. From the fifteenth century on, the freedom and growth of independent writing, publishing, selling, and reading has been, I believe, the marker that indicates the state of human freedom.

When books and bookstores are under censorship attack—as they always have been—it is vital to remember that these attacks occur because books matter, matter enormously. Books threaten demagogues, moral bullies, and those who hate diversity. When any one of us—seller, publisher, writer—is under attack, we are all under attack. No book I write is ever going to be crucial to anyone's life. But my freedom to write, publish, and sell my books *is* crucial to everyone's life.

Moreover, free access to books—the right to privacy in choosing what one reads—whether it be for information or pleasure, is not a privilege to be ranked with sports or television. Free access to the widest selection of books is a basic right in a truly democratic society.

We must not be fooled into thinking that current budgetary restraints on schools and libraries are simply a matter of shared woe in a period of hard times. Somehow we find billions for busted banks, while brains go bankrupt. This occurs in the face of a Federal Department of Education report that tells us that nearly half of the nation's adult citizens cannot read.

The undermining of schools and libraries through underfunding is part of a political agenda to control the minds of the young. Recently, I visited a city where right-wing fundamentalists succeeded in taking over a local school board. The first day after the election, the leader of that new board talked about the need to examine children's books for proper morality.

In a recent *New York Times* article, these morality cops were willing to expose themselves as people "who are dogmatic on how [we] feel about some things. When I say dogmatic, I mean that when it is the word of God you are talking about, you don't compromise."

Not long ago, a major publisher who wanted to edit one of my previously published books for a new textbook series told me she was not engaged in censorship, but explained, "We need to protect the children."

These censors, skinheads with hair, are the scrubbed faces of American Fascism. Yes, it is right to be outraged by "ethnic cleansings" in the Balkans. But we need to be aggressively resistant to "moral cleansings" right in our own country. Travel around our country; tales of censorship will fill your ears.

Censorship matters, particularly for the young. Why? Because there are two stages to becoming a reader. First comes the skill of learning to read, which emerges as the young person seeks and finds what pleases. The second stage is the evolving skill of making judgments about what we read. But if the judgment of books comes first—which is the goal of dogmatists—then children are not free to seek the pleasure. Yet they will not read unless they have that delight. How do they find it? From diversity on the shelves.

It is only when a young person is able to select a book privately from a wide range of titles, then read that book privately, enjoy and think about it privately, that the life-long reader is created. But tragically, some libraries have stopped buying new books altogether. All too many have radically reduced the new titles they can make available.

That's why the children's bookstore is one of the crucial institutions in our country today, and I believe its importance will increase. Those of you who own

and run these stores constitute a vital source of free choice. Quite simply, nothing combines the highest ideals of our culture—an open market for free and independent thinking, and sheer pleasure—as well as a bookstore. It alone can be counted upon to provide young readers with the greatest possible range of new books and old. Those who offer children a free choice of books constitute the catalyst in the chemistry that turns them into life-long and free readers.

Here I need to remind us all of something important. I am thrilled when young people turn to the fiction of, say, Walter Dean Myers, Paula Fox, Robert Cormier, and naturally, to my own. But the process by which children become readers is one in which they are allowed to read anything and everything. They are not, generally, sophisticated in their choices. When children become readers, they don't just select books; they devour them. I can only hope they are not pushed into sophistication.

I'm not a writer of so-called junk books, but I have rarely met a writer, who, when young, did not read such books. Comic books, the Hardy Boys, the Boy Inventors, Cowboy Jack—whatever the titles, I read them. Do I remember any single one of them? Absolutely not. Do I remember reading them with pleasure? Absolutely yes.

My mother was a devoted reader of Jane Austen and Charles Dickens. She hated "*trash*," to use her word. But I came to care about Dickens and Austen only after I read a million comic books on the front stoop (where they were allowed), only after I read every Freddy the Pig book, only after I consumed each monthly issue of *Popular Science.*

I've long held that what is popular may not be—by my standards—a work of quality. But a popular work is always important and must always be noted—and learned from. I feel that art can be at its best—and reach a wider audience—when there is a cross-fertilization of popular forms with new ideas. I believe it was the great French writer Flaubert who said that style is a way of seeing.

Friends, we are born with eyes. That is biology. But it is culture that teaches us how to see. The human who sees but one thing, be it creed, faith, or ideology, sees nothing—tragically, not even the self.

Those of you who run the bookstores of this land provide a multitude of ways of seeing. Democracy needs that multitude of visions to flourish. To accept limitations on our vision is to accept the hooded darkness of demagoguery and tyranny. We as a nation, and as individuals, must keep our eyes open. There is no better way to do that than by supporting the right of children to read with freedom and privacy—with all the loud pride and fury we can muster.

Yes, history teaches us that this is an unceasing struggle. Happily, history also reminds us that, though it is never easy, the struggle for diversity is a struggle we can keep winning.

Thank you, booksellers, for who you are, for what you do, and for all you have done for the children— and that includes me. May "I can read, I can read!" be heard throughout the land.

Avi

SOURCE: "Poppy," in *The Horn Book Magazine,* Vol. LXXIII, No. 1, January-February, 1997, pp. 40-2.

With this award you have been kind enough to honor a book I have written. It is with the greatest pleasure that I accept it.

Yet, even as I feel honored, I have a nagging sense of embarrassment. Consider our young readers. The notion of *best* may apply to sports teams and foot races, but when it comes to literature, I confess to having serious doubts as to whether any piece of writing is ever best for any one child. Better, yes; best, no. I worry that the child who is handed a "best" book and finds it wanting may believe *he* is wanting.

For while I am truly honored that three judges with, collectively, a vast knowledge of children's books found **Poppy** to be pleasing, there will be plenty of young readers who—we must acknowledge—will take greater pleasure in Eloise McGraw's *The Moorchild* and/or Ruth White's *Belle Prater's Boy* (this year's Boston Globe-Horn Book Honor Books). More power to these kids. They should enjoy these books. They are fine ones, in no way less than mine.

The truth is, my friends, our young readers may find different pleasures in each of these books, in none of them, or in others not cited here. And yet—make no mistake about it—if this award is meant to honor the literature we all hold so dear, if it says, Here, notice this, then I am thrice honored, for my writing, for the fellowship of all writers, for the enterprise of writing books for kids.

Whatever the myths, no writer works alone. In the case of this particular book, I have special debts to acknowledge. There is, of course, my good friend and editor, Richard Jackson, who is always there to collaborate in the creation of the best of books. He brings great intuitive insights and an actor's eye and ear for the small gesture, as well as a keen director's hand in shaping the big production. But what I think we have going for us—as collaborators—is that most of all Dick and I find great pleasure in the making of good books. That may seem a modest goal, but it is, in my view, the only goal. And indeed, it is the only thing we try to do.

In regard to this particular book, I have had the singular privilege of having the pages graced by the talent, humor, and hard work of illustrator Brian Floca. This is not the first project I have had enhanced by Brian's work. I hope it won't be the last. What I admire most about Brian and his work is that it is never passive. He adds immeasurably to whatever text I have been able to provide, fulfilling the ideal set forth by Arthur Rackham that the illustrator of a book must see and capture what the author has not noticed. To do that takes a great talent. Brian has endowed my efforts with just such vision, meaning, and wit. Brian, thank you.

My third debt is perhaps the most important one to honor. Anyone who looks at the origins of writers in this field of ours will see again and again that great souls in small bodies with receptive ears and hearts, thirsting for stories, have motivated many a writer. So with me.

At the age of seventeen I made up my mind to be a writer. It was not until some twenty-odd years later that the direction I should take (books for kids) was made clear to me by a singularly sweet and persuasive voice—the voice of my son, Shaun.

The stories in my first book were told to him, on his demand. Later on, it was I who demanded that he listen to what I wrote. No greater criticism could be made when, in the middle of a chapter, came his or his brother Kevin's request, "Can I go out and play now?" No greater approval could be had when, at the end of a chapter, I might hear, "Keep reading."

Not every child gives his father his profession. Not every father is given the opportunity to publicly acknowledge the debt. Happily for me, he is here today. So Shaun, with much love and gratitude, I thank you.

Finally, I believe we who are given honors gain two great gifts. We gain the capacity to be more patient with the inherent frustrations of the writing process. Or, as I like to say, success gives us the courage to accept our failures. Just as important, it gives us the place and time to say thanks to those who care so much about the stories and books we offer to our young people.

So let me again say thank you. The best I can do to return the favor is to keep writing. Here's hoping that what comes in the future will allow us to meet again. I would like that.

Avi with Diana L. Winarski

SOURCE: "Avi on Fiction," in *Teaching PreK-8*, Vol. 28, September, 1997, p. 62-4.

Epiphany may seem an awfully strong word, but no other one so aptly describes what happened to Avi after he failed at New York's Stuyvesant High School and began heading down the same path at a small private school in Manhattan.

"The English teacher called my folks and told them I was truly the worst student he had ever had," Avi told me over coffee in his publisher's office. "So, the summer I was 16, they got me a tutor who worked with me every day.

"I was a typical shy boy, and the tutor began by telling me, 'You know, you're really very interesting. If you wrote better, people would know about it." Avi grinned. "She changed my whole view of writing. From then on, I wanted to write."

What he didn't know at the time—and what he wouldn't find out until adulthood—was that he has dysgraphia, a writing dysfunction that manifests itself in extremely bad spelling, word omissions and substitutions, and right and left confusion.

"My parents knew about the dysgraphia, and, for better or for worse, they didn't tell me. They just actively tried to discourage me from writing because of it. They weren't saying I wasn't smart or that I couldn't be a sculptor or a lawyer, or whatever, but clearly, writing wasn't the right thing for me to pursue. It became very important at that point to prove I could write."

Avi attacked his goal head-on. His first published piece was in a college literary journal. He kept writing as he studied theater and history, and continued throughout his 25-year-long career as a university librarian. Avi's two sons "finally" left home (they're now 30-ish rock musicians and lyricists), and he began to write full time.

Anticipating the question, Avi grinned warmly when I asked him about his unusual name. "My twin sister, Emily, gave me the nickname Avi when I was a child. I honestly don't even know where it came from." And yes, he does have a real first name (we promised not to publish it) and a last name, which he purposely chose not to use when his first book was published in 1970.

"I resented my parents so much for not telling me about the dysgraphia earlier in my life," he admitted almost sheepishly, "that I didn't want to put their name on my books."

If you saw Avi's unedited work today, you'd find words missing and sentences reversed, evidence of his dysgraphia. "It's just something that's in me. But now that I know about it, I can work with it.

"One of the great moments in my life was when I learned to use the computer's spell checker," he laughed. "Before that, I would write on a typewriter and ask someone to proofread my work. Then, I'd retype the document and make half again as many mistakes. The computer has been a lifesaver." It helps him conquer what he calls his "dysfunction."

The word conquer is an understatement. Avi's roughly 35 books have won numerous prestigious awards, including Newbery Honors for *The True Confessions of Charlotte Doyle* and *Nothing But the Truth.*

Rather than stick with one particular winning formula, Avi finds energy in exploring innovative styles. His repertoire includes a novel-length comic book, *City of Light, City of Dark,* a novel entirely in unattributed dialogue *"Who Was That Masked Man, Anyway?",* a collection of memos, newspaper articles, journal entries and dialogue in *Nothing But the Truth* and most recently, a newspaper serial titled *Keep Your Eye on Amanda.*

Avi cut his teeth on the serial approach in his two-part Victorian-style novel *Beyond the Western Sea,* a tome divided into 193 four or five-page chapters. "That book gave me confidence to know I could do the newspaper project I had in mind.

The Amanda project is the same kind of writing style. "Each 700-word chapter brings the story forward, establishes character and ends in a cliffhanger. It's a rigorous process. If I added a sentence, I took one out. It's a very journalistic approach."

Initially, Avi approached some newspapers himself, proposing that one chapter of Amanda appear in a section of the paper each week for 21 weeks. "They were baffled at first. They just didn't know what to make of this idea. Curiously, there's nothing new about it, yet it seems peculiarly radical to people today".

Until the 1950's, children's stories did run in newspapers regularly. Radio programs and comic books—which Avi loved—employed the serial formula, too. Today, Avi points out, serials only exist in television soap operas. "The serial is such an important educational tool. When you don't know what's going to happen and you're caught up in the story, you write the story forward (in your mind). It's the process that's important in relation to how kids respond to story and think about it."

Teachers using **Amanda** in their classrooms tell Avi the students constantly ask, "Don't you know what's going to happen next?" They're amazed when the teacher doesn't know.

"This project doesn't provide the immediate gratification that exists in so much of our culture today," he mused. "Kids have very little understanding of continuity; the notion of waiting another week to find out what happens is quite unusual to them. They're puzzled, fascinated and frustrated by it.".

The Amanda project has progressed far beyond anything Avi originally conceived. "It's a contemporary, funny, hip animal story—we're not talking *War and Peace* here," he explained, "but it's absolutely fascinating to see what's happening."

Beginning with the *Colorado Springs Gazette,* more than 25 papers nationwide have contracted to run the story. In Colorado Springs, the local chapter of the International Reading Association has developed questions and a teacher guide for each chapter.

"Working with local public libraries and teacher-parent groups helps get it into newspapers. It's becoming a community event."

More accurately, Avi would agree that his project returns reading to the community. "When you watch the way kids learn to read, you see that it's a spoken event. They don't learn to read silently. Reading silently, as most of us do now, is actually relatively recent in cultural history. We use terms like 'writer's voice' and say, 'let me tell you what the author is trying to say.' It's oral.

"When I write, I hear the voices of my characters and I simply record what I hear. I'm recording rather than inventing. To the extent that I hear and see what's happening with the characters, I'm inventing the truth.

"The best definition of fiction I've ever heard," Avi continued, "was from the writer Paula Fox who said, 'The writer's job is to imagine the truth.' That's what I do."

GENERAL COMMENTARY

Michael Cart

SOURCE: *Booklist,* Vol. 95, Nos. 9-10, January 1, 1999, p. 846.

Avi has an insatiable appetite for creative challenges. From historical fiction to stories told entirely in dialogue, from graphic novels to documentary fiction, the work of this two-time Newbery Honor-winning author is informed by experimentation and envelope pushing. So what's whetting his writer's appetite now? Breakfast serials! No, not Cheerios but, instead, the serialization of kids' stories in our nation's daily newspapers.

"It's an old idea and a very American one," he told me in a recent telephone interview. "We tend to look to England for its origins but, in fact, the first serialized fiction there—Charles Dickens' *Pickwick Papers*—appeared in a magazine, not a newspaper. The reasons were economic and political. British newspapers were heavily taxed to make them too expensive for mass readership."

"It was a different story in this country," Avi continued, pointing out that as early as 1729, a Philadelphia newspaper, *The Pennsylvania Gazette,* was serializing the Daniel Defoe novel *A Religious Courtship.*

"The point is clear," he stated. "Serialized fiction has long had its place in the American newspaper world and in our literary culture." (The point might parenthetically be made that America's children's magazines were also rich repositories of serialized fiction. Serendipitously I just found on my shelves a bound run of *Our Young Folks* for 1869, the year in which the magazine published George Peck's *Story of a Bad Boy* in 12 installments!) Avi traces his own interest in serialized fiction to his childhood experience of reading Thronton W. Burgess' *Bedtime Story Books* in the *New York Herald Tribune,* "Not only did I read these tales," Avi told me, "but they also became the first books I bought with my own money."

From the earliest days of his writing career, Avi nursed the idea of writing a serial of his own. But it wasn't until he moved to Colorado in 1996 and had a midnight visit from a pair of raccoons that inspiration and timing came together. The result was **Keep Your Eye on Amanda.** The first chapter of this story appeared in the *Colorado Springs Gazette Tribune* on October 3, 1996, and continued for 21 weeks. And then something interesting happened: the *Denver Post* asked to look at it. "And they took it," Avi told me, "and then, one after another, other papers joined in."

Before he knew it, the author had turned into a one-man syndicate. "This was all serendipity," he told me, sounding a bit bewildered by his success, "I certainly didn't think this through when I started it."

The demand quickly grew so great that he wrote a second story about Amanda, the raccoon: **Amanda Joins the Circus!** Together, he told me, the two serials appeared in some 100 U.S. and Canadian newspapers boasting a combined circulation of nine and one-half million readers! The two stories will be published as books next February by Avon. Meanwhile, Avi has formed a nonprofit foundation called Breakfast Serials to handle distribution of these and future stories. As of last month, a total of 126 newspapers from Juneau to Miami, from Canada to Texas, from Maine to California were running the stories. Avi is no longer writing them himself. The current story, *Orphan Journey Home,* is by Liza Ketchum; soon to come is *Field of Dogs* by Katherine Paterson.

"Be sure to tell them about the illustrations," Avi urged me. And so . . . Breakfast Serials provides newspapers not only with text but also with illustrations by such artists as Janet Stevens and David Wisniewski (who illustrated the Amanda books), by C. B. Mordan who is illustrating *Orphan Journey* (the technique he's employing, scratchboard, is appropriately a technique that was developed in the nineteenth century for use in newspaper illustration), and by Emily Arnold McCully, who will illustrate *Field of Dogs.* What about the text, though? Each story, aimed at readers in upper-elementary/lower-middle school, is 15 to 17 chapters in length. The chapters are short, only three manuscript pages. "Each chapter," Avi explained, "needs to end with sufficient energy to bring readers back for more."

Yes, it's a demanding form, and Avi told me that he rejects far more submissions than he accepts. "Not every writer can do this," he said. Why has this project been so spectacularly successful? "We're offering quality," Avi answered without a pause. "And people love free stuff."

To my mind, another reason for the project's success is that the participating newspapers—in an act of enlightened self-interest—are promoting the daylights out of the series. Newspaper readership is declining after all, and publishers obviously hope to capture the attention—and interest—of a new generation of potential subscribers. When the *Sacramento Bee* (my own hometown newspaper) recently launched the Liza Ketchum story, it devoted the entire first page of the "Scene" section to the story, to its illustrations, and to a sidebar feature about Ketchum and her book. The story and sidebar also occupied half of page eight. The *Bee,* thus, devoted an astonishing page and a half of an eight-page section to the serialization. Such attention is paying off in dramatic increases in newspaper circulation. The *Bee's* sister paper, the *Fresno Bee,* for example, reports an astounding 62 percent increase in circulation on days when one of the stories is published. Avi acknowledged that, yes, there are other factors involved here, but, nevertheless, "they give a large measure of credit to the serial."

For me, the most exciting thing about the entire project is that serialization—with its built-in cliffhanger endings—has got kids talking about books, speculating about what will happen next, and waiting anxiously to read the next installment. And research consistently shows that one way to excite the interest of reluctant readers in books is to start them talking about the reading they're doing. "I understand Dickens now," Avi enthused, "here are ten million kids talking."

But not only kids. Anecdotal evidence supports the notion that adults are also reading the serials—many for their own pleasure but many more are also reading the stories with or to their kids and grandkids. Thanks to Avi's inspired project, we seem to be embarked on bringing back what poet Donald Hall has called "the out-loud culture," the culture that once thrived in an America where family entertainment was reciting works of literature.

"My grandpa and I read your story in the morning before I go to school," a boy named John wrote in a letter to Avi. "We drink coffee and hot chocolate when we read the paper. My grandpa likes your story a lot."

Is it any wonder that other newspapers are becoming interested in this phenomenon? I recently received a phone call from an editor at the *Los Angeles Times,* telling me of their plans to begin serializing stories of their own and asking me to recommend authors who might be interested in writing for them. Delighted by such interest, Avi feels that in four or five years "children's literature in daily newspapers will be restored to its old place—but better."

Clearly, this is another story that will be continued, and the ending promises to be a happy one. (If you're interested in learning more about Breakfast Serials, you can reach Avi by calling 303-777-0538.)

TITLE COMMENTARY

WINDCATCHER (1991)

Kirkus Reviews

SOURCE: A review of *Windcatcher*, in *Kirkus Reviews*, Vol. 59, February 15, 1991, p. 244.

A contrived but exciting adventure in which a summer vacation on the Connecticut coast becomes a hunt for sunken treasure. Impelled by a sudden enthusiasm, 11-year-old Tony invests all his savings in a small sailboat before leaving for his Portuguese grandma's and the small town of Swallows Bay. There, while taking sailing lessons and learning about the vagaries of weather firsthand, he discovers a mysterious couple in a motorboat, who seem to be searching for something. The town is associated with a vague shipwreck story; after uncovering some clues in an old ship model, Tony follows the couple into a foggy storm that leaves him stranded on a small island. During a desperate swim, he sights the centuries-old wreck and is then rescued by the couple, who try to buy his silence concerning their illegal activities. Though very fond of money, Tony, without hesitation, opts to turn them in. Avi expertly captures the pleasures of small-boat sailing while building suspense and putting Tony in enough danger to keep the story moving. Lighter fare than *The True Confessions of Charlotte Doyle* (1990, Newbery Honor Book); still, fine, low-violence mystery.

Hazel Rochman

SOURCE: A review of *Windcatcher*, in *Booklist*, Vol. 87, No. 13, March 1, 1991, pp. 1382-83.

Gr. 4-7. Like the girl in Adler's *Mismatched Summer* . . . the boy in this story dreads the thought of a dull summer by the sea. But where Adler's girl finds friendship, Avi's 11-year-old Tony finds sailing adventure, complete with treasure, a couple of crooks, and a survival ordeal; and all of it right near Grandma's home on the Connecticut shore. The search for

the treasure (buried somewhere in the bay since a shipwreck in revolutionary times) is hardly convincing, and Tony's never in grave danger, but the understated suspense is appealing—it could almost happen to you. As always, Avi writes snappy, realistic dialogue (Tony's Grandma tells him when he goes out sailing alone, "You must not get lost. . . . Or sink or be back later than five o'clock." No wonder he grins and agrees.). The sailing lore will attract readers, as will the good humor of the story, the characters, and the moral conflict. Tony would do a lot for money, but when he's offered the chance, he refuses to get treasure by dishonest means.

Barbara Chatton

SOURCE: A review of *Windcatcher*, in *School Library Journal*, Vol. 37, No. 4, April, 1991, p. 116.

Gr 4-6—Tony Souza, 11, uses his paper route earnings to buy a 12-foot sailboat that he takes with him when he spends part of the summer with his grandmother on the Connecticut shore. During his stay, he learns to sail and becomes intrigued by tales of buried treasure in the area. He and his grandmother learn more about the treasure, and he begins to piece together clues to its whereabouts. As he hunts, Tony encounters a couple who are illegally diving for the treasure, and they warn him away from their boat with an attack on his sailboat. After being lost in a storm, he puts together the final clues only to be captured by the villains and then, predictably, rescued in the nick of time. While this brief novel begins with a 1777 shipwreck that precipitates the modern story, the events of past and present are too neatly drawn together. The characterization and suspense of Avi's *The True Confessions of Charlotte Doyle* (Orchard, 1990) are absent here. Even so, for readers in search of an accessible adventure story, this will provide satisfaction.

Nancy Vasilakis

SOURCE: A review of *Windcatcher*, in *The Horn Book Magazine*, Vol. 67, No. 3, May-June, 1991, pp. 329-30.

An introductory flashback describing a violent storm at sea and resultant shipwreck quickly sets the tone for this bracing mystery adventure. Eleven-year-old Tony is spending the summer with his grandmother at her Long Island Sound home, learning to sail his new boat. A few tantalizing bits of local lore from his teenage instructor and the suspicious behavior of a couple—who roar off in their motorboat each day laden down with digging equipment —are enough to convince a curious and imaginative Tony that there is treasure to be had. Ample and judiciously spaced clues will keep mystery lovers engaged, while the narrative is laced with enough dramatic action and cliffhanging chapter endings to hold the attention of readers inclined toward adventure stories. Although the characterizations are in the main perfunctory, Tony is a believable child. His single-minded pursuit of the hidden treasure causes him to make some foolhardy decisions that leave him stranded on an outlying island on one occasion and adrift in his boat without a compass on another. The treasure is discovered as much by accident as by deduction, adding a further touch of realism to this solid, neatly plotted, and fast-moving yarn.

NOTHING BUT THE TRUTH (1991)

Ellen Fader

SOURCE: A review of *Nothing but the Truth,* in *School Library Journal,* Vol. 37, No. 9, September, 1991, p. 277.

Gr 6-9—Ninth grader Philip Malloy finds himself unable to participate on the track team because of his failing grade in English. Convinced the teacher, Margaret Narwin, dislikes him, he concocts a scheme to get transferred from her homeroom: instead of standing "at respectful, silent attention" during the national anthem, Philip hums. Throughout the ensuing disciplinary problems at school, his parents take his side, ignore the fact that he is breaking a school rule, and concentrate on issues of patriotism. The conflict between Philip and his school escalates, and he quickly finds the situation out of his control; local community leaders, as well as the national news media, become involved. At this point, the novel surges forward to a heartbreaking, but totally believable, conclusion. Avi carefully sets forth the events in the story, advancing the plot through conversations between students, Philip's parents, school personnel, and community politicians, while Philip's point of view is revealed through his diary entries, and Margaret Narwin's through letters to her sister. Also enriching the narrative are copies of school memos and newspaper articles, transcripts of speeches delivered, and copies of letters received by both Philip and his teacher; each document provides another perspective on the conflict and illuminates the many themes that beg to be discussed—most notably the irony of lives destroyed because of the misuse of power and the failure of people to communicate. Admirably well crafted and thought provoking.

Publishers Weekly

SOURCE: A review of *Nothing but the Truth,* in *Publishers Weekly,* Vol. 238, No. 40, September 6, 1991, p. 105.

Structured as a series of journal entries, memos, letters and dialogues, this highly original novel emerges as a witty satire of high school politics, revealing how truth can easily become distorted. After Philip Malloy, a clownish, rather unmotivated freshman, is punished for causing a disturbance (humming "The Star Spangled Banner"), facts about the incident become exaggerated until a minor school infraction turns into a national scandal.

Philip's parents, several reporters and a neighbor (who happens to be running for the school board) accuse the school of being unpatriotic. Philip gains fame as a martyr for freedom; his homeroom teacher, Miss Narwin, however, faces dismissal from her job. After gleaning the points of view of many characters, readers will side with Miss Narwin and will recognize the hollowness of Philip's eventual victory. It is clear that Avi (**The True Confessions of Charlotte Doyle**) is attuned to the modern high school scene.

With frankness and remarkable insight, he conveys the flaws of the systems while creating a story that is both entertaining and profound. Ages 11-up.

Stephanie Zvirin

SOURCE: A review of *Nothing but the Truth,* in *Booklist,* Vol. 88, No. 2, September 15, 1991, p. 136.

Gr, 7-12. Every word counts in Avi's newest book, which plunges readers into a series of skillfully orchestrated incidents that fuse into tense drama. Like a theatrical performance in its economy of description and phrase, the novel combines diary entries, phone conversations, discussions, and high school faculty memos into a provocative exploration of the way emotions and preconceptions define and distort truth. Philip Malloy desperately wants to be on the track team, but his low grade in English class prevents him from even trying out. He blames his teacher, Miss Narwin, and when she reprimands him for humming the national anthem during homeroom (school rules dictate "respectful, silent attention"), he defies her. Eventually he's sent to the assistant principal, who, unable to convince Philip to alter his behavior, invokes a suspension. A simple rules infraction neatly resolved? Not quite. After a newspaper reporter prints a blased, inflammatory version of the story, Phil's expulsion takes on patriotic overtones and becomes a local political hot potato that causes major problems for everyone concerned. Irony infuses the cleverly structured plot: Phil couldn't care less that he's headline news—he just wants a different English teacher; Miss Narwin's request for a stipend to further her education becomes "proof" she can't do the job instead of "proof" she's a good teacher trying to become better. And there's much, much more. The implications of what occurs are as intriguing as the novel's cynicism. Patriotism, is, of course, not Avi's real concern. He's writing about self-expression in a larger sense, and he's sharply critical of human behavior with regard to it. None of his characters triumphs. All share blame for what happens, and no one escapes consequences—not the perfidious school superintendent concerned about an upcoming budget vote; not self-absorbed Phil; not even Miss Narwin, who learns the hardest lesson of all. Avi levels the harshest denunciation, though, on the media, suggesting purposeful irresponsibility on their part.

Pessimistic and somber, the book fascinates as much as it disturbs. It challenges us to reexamine our ethical standards and to set aside kindergarten concepts of truth and falsity in determining the conduct of our lives. Is the principal being honest when she describes Phil's vocalizing as "loud and raucous"? The answer, according to Avi, is not a simple yes or no. There's no question that the book sets out to make a point. It succeeds. That makes it ideal material for the whole-language curriculum, bound to foster debate on a wide range of issues—from parent-child communication to media accountability to personal values. But the deceptively simple story also stands up as riveting entertainment, and like the best in YA literature, it will be talked about and read again and again.

Kirkus Reviews

SOURCE: A review of *Nothing but the Truth,* in *Kirkus Reviews,* Vol. 59, October 1, 1991, p. 1284.

Ninth-grader Philip has never been in trouble, but he's upset because his English grade is keeping him off the track team. Meanwhile, though the rule is "respectful, silent attention," he hums along with the daily playing of the national anthem—a habit ignored by his jocular homeroom teacher. Then he's moved to the homeroom of Miss Narwin, his English teacher—well-liked because she's fair but rigid, humorless, and out of touch with modern kids. When she tries to enforce the silence rule, Philip responds with offhand rudeness borne of his distress about track plus his chronic tongue-tied style; the ensuing confrontation escalates into a two-day suspension followed by national media attention based on the erroneous belief that Philip has been denied the right to express his patriotism. Skillfully composing his story from school memos, news clips, dialogues, and Philip's diary, Avi shows how well-meaning people can generate misinformation through a combination of interrupting or simply not listening, shaping facts to suit their own goals, letting preconceptions muddy thought, or just lacking the will and the skill to get things straight. The garbled conversations here are all too believable; only one reporter makes an intelligent effort to find out what really happened, and his story is never printed. Nobody wins: Philip transfers to a school that doesn't have track, and Miss Narwin is forced to take leave. Wryly satirical: nothing but the deplorable truth about our increasingly inarticulate, media-driven society. Starred Review.

Elizabeth S. Watson

SOURCE: A review of *Nothing but the Truth,* in *The Horn Book Magazine,* Vol. 68, No. 1, January-February, 1992, p. 78.

Freshman Philip Malloy wants to be on the track team and is sure of winning a place, but a failing grade in English makes him ineligible. A personality conflict with his English teacher—also his homeroom teacher—seems to Philip to be the root of the problem. He determines to find a way out of her class. Whether by accident or design, his persistent humming of the National Anthem, played at the start of each school day, supposedly "to respectful silence," is the vehicle that gets him out—so far out that he is suspended from school. From that point on, emotions become tangled, communication is broken, and the action surges along out of everyone's control. The book is effectively set entirely in monologue or dialogue; conversations, memos, letters, diary entries, talk-radio transcripts, and newspaper articles are all interwoven to present an uninterrupted plot. The construction is nearly flawless; the characters seem painfully human and typically ordinary. Philip's inability to communicate with anyone is bleakly real. The tragedy moves inexorably to an ironic conclusion that raises gooseflesh. A powerful, explosive novel that involves the reader from start to finish.

English Journal

SOURCE: A review of *Nothing but the Truth,* in *English Journal,* Vol. 81, No. 5, September, 1992, p. 95.

Ninth grader Philip Malloy hums along with the playing of the "Star-Spangled Banner" daily during the homeroom period. Margaret Narwin, teacher of English and Philip's homeroom teacher, sends Philip to the vice-principal for breaking a faculty rule that requires students at Harrison High School to stand at "respectful, silent attention" during the presentation of the national anthem. These two statements of fact might lead the reader to respond, "So what?" However, after reading the first few pages, one begins to experience the carefully crafted "truth" from each character's point of view. What seems to be a simple breaking of the rule, mushrooms into charges and countercharges regarding respect, freedom, and patriotism involving students, parents, teachers, administrators, and the national media. *Nothing but the Truth* is written in documentary style, providing a quick and easy read for middle- and high-school students, but after the reading, the truth that may come will take more time and may not be as easy to attain.

English Journal

SOURCE: A review of *Nothing but the Truth,* in *English Journal,* Vol. 81, No. 7, November, 1992, pp. 91-2.

Avi's name has graced so many excellent YA books in the last few years that it's hardly a surprise to discover yet another fine Avi book. But it's surprising that his books differ so much in subject matter. Last year's *The True Confessions of Charlotte Doyle* was a remarkable adventure of a thirteen-year-old girl caught up in a story of the sea and murder. *Romeo and Juliet—Together (and Alive!) at Last* was funny. *A Place Called Ugly* told of the environment and roots. *Devil's Race* was scary. Avi's books have only one thing in common, something common to many other YA authors—the need to survive no matter what.

And we have a survivor of sorts and a victim of sorts in *Nothing but the Truth.* Miss Narwin wants ninth-grader Philip Malloy to care about literature, and Philip wants Miss Narwin to leave him alone and to pass him so he'll be eligible to go out for track. Neither gets what either one wants, and worse yet, he's transferred out of the homeroom of the chief-teacher-clown of the school into Miss Narwin's home room. There what was already miserable for both becomes

far worse. Students at Harrison High School are expected to "stand at respectful, silent attention for the playing of our national anthem," but Philip, who's been a smart-ass in Narwin's English classes, decides to hum along with the music during the national anthem. Narwin quietly asks him not to hum, he persists, she sends him to the assistant principal, and he (over her objection) boots Philip out of school for two days. The word leaks out that a Harrison High student has been disciplined because he was patriotic and wanted to sing along. Patriotic groups and individuals and newspapers across America defend Philip—one paper headlines the story, "Suspended for Patriotism"—and attack the unpatriotic and cruel English teacher. A local talk show host engages in a brief dialogue with a caller.

Steve (caller): Look—about that kid.

Jake Barlow (host): The one kicked out of school for singing "The Star-Spangled Banner?"

Steve: Yeah. Hey, you know, that gripes me. Really does. Things may be different. But, come off it!

Jake Barlow: Right! What are schools for, anyway?

Steve: People might call me a—a—

Jake Barlow: Jerk?

Steve: Yeah, maybe. But like they used to say, America, love it or leave it. And that school—

Jack Barlow: It was a teacher.

Steve: Yeah, teacher. She shouldn't be allowed to teach. That's my opinion.

Jake Barlow: Right, I'm with you there, Steve. I mean, there are the three R's—reading, 'riting, and 'rithmetic—and the three P's—prayer, patriotism, and parents.

We wonder what kids will think of this book if they read it. Presumably they would sympathize with Philip even though other kids in the book weren't all that sympathetic. Teachers are likely to sympathize with Miss Narwin though she didn't seem to us to be a model of professionalism or talent. The administrators protect themselves at all times and squirm out of the tight spots. School board members come across even worse. So do newspaper reporters. In other words, this is an honest and realistic book—more like real life than most of us want to encounter in a book.

It's subtitled "A Documentary Novel" because it's told through documents—memos, stenographic records of conversations, letters, newspaper stories, and the like. Such pseudo-objectivity doesn't make the reader any more comfortable. Nor does the concluding line in the book, which is an O'Henry-type kicker.

BLUE HERON (1992)

Hazel Rochman

SOURCE: A review of *Blue Heron*, in *Booklist*, Vol. 88, No. 10, January 15, 1992, p. 930.

When you read the lyrical nature descriptions in the quiet parts of this story, it's hard to believe that they're by the writer of books like the tight thriller *Wolf Rider*, or the raucous comedy *S.O.R. Losers*, or the jumpy, brilliant school story *Nothing but the Truth*. Then, as this novel continues and the scenes of stillness and solitude contrast with raging family confrontation, you realize that Avi is drawing on everything he's written, and more. The telling has the best kind of surprise, reversal that then appears inevitable. There's a rich ambiguity, a yoking of opposites in character, language, mood, pace, and viewpoint that's rare in YA fiction. It doesn't always work. But then, Avi's never been afraid to take risks, to try something new.

At first, the nature symbolism and the family dynamics seem like coming-of-age clichés. Maggie, nearly 13, flies in from her home on the West Coast to spend August with her divorced father, his young wife, and their new baby in a rented cabin on a pond at the New England shore. Early every morning, alone in the mist, Maggie watches an enormous blue heron on the marsh. Quiet, solitary, dogged, patient, she's obsessed with its beauty, its infinite slowness.

Avi builds each chapter with tight emotion, ending on a hanging note that leaves you wondering and yet pulls you to read on. Maggie soon realizes that her father is ill and that his new marriage is troubled. She's surprised at how much she likes her stepmother, even as she sees that the father she loves is a bully, that he's cruel and also deeply hurt. The message is spelled out ("The people I love—sometimes—I don't like them"), but the story does show that things are confused, complicated, changing—and connected. There's a double climax: one of yelling, explosive fury when Maggie discovers her father's seething secret, what he's been talking about all vacation in those intense, private business calls on his cellular phone; the other, an infinitely fragile moment when Maggie finally gets close enough to touch the heron "hardly more than a breath of finger to feather."

Through the most private experience, Maggie connects with nature and with people. Watching the bird, she doesn't know she's being watched by Tucker, a sad, lonely boy who's trying to shoot the heron. The scenes between these two very different kids are moving and funny (he calls her Big Bird), with a contemporary dialogue that's casual and intense. It turns out they're not as different as they seem. She's horrified to see his father slap Tucker's face in public, but soon after, her own father yells abuse at her when he breaks down in a crowded restaurant. Maggie and Tucker are joined in trouble and, finally, in their feeling for something beyond themselves. In contrast to that slap, there's another exquisite moment of contact: when Maggie begs Tucker not to kill the heron she loves, she "touched fingers to his cheek."

To Maggie's father, all herons look the same, and the pond is "pretty as a picture." But she looks close enough and hard enough to get beyond that stereotype, and she finds "a different way of seeing . . . what else is there."

Kirkus Reviews

SOURCE: A review of *Blue Heron*, in *Kirkus Reviews*, Vol. 60, January 15, 1992, p. 66.

A versatile author whose popular books include rousing historical adventures (*The True Confessions of Charlotte Doyle*, 1990, Newbery Honor) and sparkling satire (*Nothing But the Truth*, 1991) portrays a contemporary family under unusual stress. Flying in for her annual visit with her 50-ish father, his young wife Joanna, and their new baby, Maggie (12) hopes that "nothing about her father [has] changed." Not so: Dad is unaccountably snappish and unreasonable. As the vacation on a Connecticut lake progresses, it develops that he's at odds with Joanna and has heart trouble, while even Joanna doesn't know that he lost his job just after the baby's birth and isn't taking his medication. Maggie's plea that he do so precipitates an angry outburst during which Dad nearly dies in an accident. Though sadly credible, Dad's behavior, as observed by Maggie, makes him unsympathetic and hard to like. Meanwhile, Avi draws other relationships with exceptional subtlety, especially Maggie's growing affection for her nice, intelligent stepmother, who in her need reaches out to her like a sister; and Maggie's delicate negotiation with a neighborhood bully, Tucker, who has been stalking a noble great blue heron. The heron, a potent symbol (Dad says it can mean life or death), has been Maggie's preoccupation and solace; in the end, though Dad's adult problems may defy solution, she manages to transform the belligerent Tucker's perception of the awe-inspiring bird. A thoughtful, beautifully crafted story.

Publishers Weekly

SOURCE: A review of *Blue Heron,* in *Publishers Weekly,* Vol. 239, No. 4, January 20, 1992, p. 66.

Maggie Lavchek, a great believer in magic, makes a wish that nothing about her father will ever change. But when she spends three weeks in a vacation cabin with him and his new family, Maggie cannot deny that things are already different. The presence of a new baby has caused a rift in her father's second marriage, and Mr. Lavchek has developed a heart condition but refuses to treat it. Outside the cabin, however, Maggie rediscovers magic in the misty marsh and endangered blue heron, whose vulnerability parallels her father's own mortality. Despite its rather obvious symbolism, this story remains quietly intriguing up to its hard-hitting climax. As he does in **Nothing but the Truth** and **The True Confessions of Charlotte Doyle,** Avi reveals an uncanny understanding of human nature. Although Maggie's workaholic father is somewhat stereotyped, his despair and regret are painfully realistic. Maggie emerges as a sensitive heroine whose perceptions are genuine as well as compelling. Reflecting the complexity of people and their emotions, this novel explores rather then solves the conflicts introduced. Ages 10-14.

Marjorie Lewis

SOURCE: A review of *Blue Heron,* in *School Library Journal,* Vol. 38, No. 4, April, 1992, p. 112.

Gr 5-8—Almost-13-year-old Maggie has a loving mother, a terrific young stepmother, and a father whose delight in seeing her each summer is apparent. This year, there's an infant half-sister for Maggie to meet. The status quo is perfect. But even before her arrival at the rented marsh-side cottage, the girl senses that something isn't right. Her father's anger is barely under control; the relationship between him and his wife is rapidly deteriorating; and Maggie is too young to understand fully the troubles that are destroying them. When she learns that her father's health is poor, and he confesses that he has lost his job and hasn't told his wife, she feels mired in a marsh of complex adult emotions. As she tries to sort things out, she sees a blue heron. It becomes a symbol in her life, especially when she discovers that someone is trying to kill it with a bow and arrow. This is a complex novel, and it is needlessly compli-

cated by symbolism. An overburdened story line about the heron's would-be killer, a lonely boy, is never fully explored and serves to muddle rather than enrich and enhance. The important thread, that of a happy family coming apart because of events seemingly beyond their control—depression, poor health, unemployment—is poignant enough without further intricacies.

WHO WAS THAT MASKED MAN, ANYWAY? (1992)

Publishers Weekly

SOURCE: A review of *Who Was That Masked Man, Anyway?,* in *Publishers Weekly,* Vol. 239, No. 31, July 13, 1992, p. 56.

As expertly crafted as Avi's **Nothing But the Truth**, this lightning-paced satire set during WW II shows how Franklin D. Wattleson, a superhero fan, creates his own brand of adventure when taking on the identity of "Chet Barker, master spy." With best friend Mario, 12-year-old Frankie stirs up considerable excitement and trouble carrying out his plot to dispose of evil scientist Mr. Swerdlow (the Wattlesons' upstairs boarder) and marrying off brother Tom (a wounded vet) to sixth-grade teacher Miss Gomez (whose fiance was recently killed in action). Ignoring continual reprimands for neglecting homework and snooping into other people's affairs, Frankie manages to complete his mission successfully. Nostalgia buffs in particular will be drawn to this book, which contains segments of old-time radio serials and commercials. Besides providing much hilarity, this ingeniously structured montage of broadcasts, fantasies and conversations exposes many ironies of heroism and war. Ages 9-up.

Hazel Rochman

SOURCE: A review of *Who Was That Masked Man, Anyway?,* in *Booklist,* Vol. 88, No. 22, August, 1992, p. 2012.

Gr. 5-7. With his glasses perched over his mask, sixth-grader Frankie Wattleson of Brooklyn, New York, tries to be a Master Spy, "ruthless, clear-eyed, brave, and smartly dressed." In the last chaotic months of World War II, Frankie's brother has come home wounded and depressed, school's a bore, and a lodger has taken Frankie's room. Only Frankie's beloved radio serials make any sense. He tries to transform his life into a script from "Captain Midnight," "Superman," and "The Lone Ranger." The whole future of the free world depends on the outcome of his adventures, which he embarks on with his trusty sidekick, Mario, from across the street. Their crucial quest is to get rid of the Evil Scientist (that is, the lodger) so that Frankie can get his room back and have his own radio. Then, in a grim outburst that counterpoints all the Superman fun and games, Frankie's brother tells him what war was really like: mess, slaughter, and babble.

Avi tells the whole story through dialogue. There's not even a "he said" to show who's speaking, though a different typeface sets off the radio excerpts. Yet, the characters and the parody are so sharp, the fast-paced scenes so dramatic, that readers will have no trouble following what's going on. In fact, they might enjoy acting out parts or making up their own contemporary scripts. Avi has tuned into the way kids play. The joy of the story is that he both mocks heroic stereotypes and celebrates our common dreams. Even while Frankie faces the truth about heroes, the farce of his ordinary life outdoes his make-believe adventures.

Kirkus Reviews

SOURCE: A review of *Who Was That Masked Man, Anyway?*, in *Kirkus Reviews*, Vol. 60, August 1, 1992, p. 986.

Gorged on an excess of radio drama, "Chet Barker, Master Spy" (a.k.a. sixth-grader Frankie Wattleston) drags "Skipper O'malley" (Mario Calvino), his "faithful but brilliant sidekick," into a series of hilarious misadventures. Banished to the basement when his brother Tom returns, wounded and shell-shocked, from WWII, Frankie vows to get his room back by driving out the family boarder (a humorless medical student) and to introduce Torn to his luscious teacher—the very image, he thinks, of Veronica Lake. Reading this is like listening to an old radio show; interspersing episodes about the Green Hornet, Lone Ranger, and other masked heroes, Avi writes entirely in dialogue (a tricky device that succeeds here because each character has such a distinct voice), making for a breathless pace and rich, imaginative comedy. Despite setbacks—including literal and figurative skeletons in the closet—Frankie's schemes are wildly successful; and though he pays the price for his obsession with radio by being left back, six months later he has his room back and a new sister-in-law. A characteristically multilayered tour-de-force (cf. Avi's 1992 Newbery honor book): an entertaining farce; an

outspoken satire on the mesmerizing effects of the media; and a thought-provoking contrast between the heroic fantasies of a boy deprived of his busy parents' attention and the horrors of real war. Starred Review.

Michael Cart

SOURCE: A review of *Who Was That Masked Man, Anyway?*, in *School Library Journal*, Vol. 38, No. 10, October, 1992, p. 112.

Gr 4-6—Return with us now to those thrilling days of yesteryear when radio was king and kids were its loyal subjects. The most loyal of them all may well be Frankie (Franklin Delano) Wattleson who—to his presidential namesake's Four Freedoms—would fervently add a fifth: the freedom to listen to the radio! But even in those long-ago days of World War II, the tyranny of parents and homework kept interferring. Trying to find a radio to listen to is only one of the boy's problems. His parents have rented a room to a mad scientist (actually he's a medical student), and his brother is wounded in combat; sent home to recover, he takes Frankie's room, sending the boy to the basement—without benefit of a radio. But Frankie has a plan. Several plans actually, for in reality, he is (ta da!) Chet Barker, Master Spy! The happy ending is hard-won but consistent with both the cheerful tone of the book and the tradition of period radio dramas, excerpts from which are interspersed within the narrative. What turns this delightful book into a tour de force is Avi's choice—to tell his incident—and character rich narrative entirely through dialogue. And unattributed dialogue at that. Yet so sure is his grasp of his characters and the unique sounds of their individual voices that readers will never doubt who is speaking or wonder what is happening. Avi's skill and obvious affection for the golden age of radio shine through, and are sure to keep readers tuned in for another episode.

Maeve Visser Knoth

SOURCE: A review of *Who Was That Masked Man, Anyway?*, in *The Horn Book Magazine*, Vol. 69, No. 2, March-April, 1993, p. 205.

The most recent novel from award-winning author Avi is an experiment in fiction writing. The historical drama is written entirely in dialogue, a feature sure to attract readers who complain to teachers about long, boring, descriptive passages. The story takes place in Brooklyn in 1945, and the protagonist, Frankie Wattleson, is enamored with radio adventure programs. Frankie involves his best friend, Mario, in his scheme to conquer the injustices of the world, including his parents' refusal to buy him his own radio. The two boys set out to prove that the family boarder, a medical student who keeps a skeleton in his room, is in fact an evil scientist. They also hope to rescue their teacher from sadness since her fiance was killed in the war and hope to create a romantic attachment between her and Frankie's wounded older brother. Their schemes all come to satisfying, if unrealistic, conclusions. Avi's drama is filled with action and hilarious conversations and events. Frankie is an irrepressible boy whose response to the excitement of radio stories is similar to modern children's response to Ninja Turtles and Batman. The novel is structured much like a radio drama and punctuated with brief episodes from "Superman" and "Captain Midnight." Because the novel is written entirely in dialogue, there are weaknesses as well as strengths. Peripheral characters, particularly Frankie's brother, and subplots are revealed very slowly, and there is virtually no setting. The reader is given little information about characters beyond their actions and responses to each other. In spite of the humorous, contrived nature of the story, Avi does develop a serious theme about the nature of heroism and the contrast between fictional heroes and real people who face a war with fear and humanity. Readers who enjoyed Avi's **Romeo and Juliet—Together (and Alive!) at Last** will revel in his new farce. The strong humor, mystery, and quick pace of the story, along with the alluring cover, will guarantee a wide readership.

PUNCH WITH JUDY (1993)

Ilene Cooper

SOURCE: A review of *Punch with Judy*, in *Booklist*, Vol. 89, No. 14, March 15, 1993, p. 1312.

Gr. 6-8. A starving, ragtag orphan does a jerky dance for pennies and is hired by Joe McSneed, owner of a traveling medicine show. Named Punch by McSneed, the boy doesn't mind that he's a servant rather than a performer. All he really cares about is having the chance to gaze upon McSneed's daughter, the lovely Judy. But when McSneed dies, all hell breaks loose. The show is going broke, some of the troupe members take off, and an ornery sheriff is trailing the rest of them across the county to arrest them as thieves. Despite the travails, Judy decides to hang on to the show and restructure it around comedy. Her centerpiece is to be Punch, but there's just one problem— Punch is the saddest excuse for a comedian anyone

has ever seen. Avi, as usual, tries something new here and meets with mixed results. Perhaps the intention is to have the reader experience the story as an audience would a medicine show, for both characters and action seem at a distance from the reader, as if this story were being played out on a stage. This leaves the reader with entertaining enough fare, but no personal involvement with any of the characters, who are, in any case, sketched very broadly. The blurring of tragedy and comedy is also one of the underpinnings of the story, and this aspect works much better, with Punch personifying the blending. A sad sack who takes an unintentional but powerful beating in a real-life Punch and Judy show at the book's conclusion, young Punch is also the comedic element that forces the sheriff to give in to his hilarity and leave the troupe alone. An interesting effort, punctuated by Lisker's small ink drawings that appear here and there within the text.

Publishers Weekly

SOURCE: A review of *Punch with Judy*, in *Publishers Weekly*, Vol. 240, No. 14, April 5, 1993, p. 79.

"One raw day in 1870," the owner of a touring medicine show takes in an eight-year-old orphan as "company servant" and dubs him Punch, a whimsical tribute to his beloved daughter, Judy. Four years later, the owner is dead, and a sanctimonious clergyman in a neighboring village calls upon the sheriff to arrest the showfolk: laughter, claims Parson Cuthwhip, "is the voice of the devil." Following the troupe's unsuccessful run for the state border, a bet is waged: if they can make the sheriff laugh, their freedom is assured. Avi (**The True Confessions of Charlotte Doyle**) creates a dark, eerie world as backdrop for his somber narrative; while the story starts slowly, it eventually becomes an absorbing tale centered around Punch's unrequited love for Judy. This beleaguered protagonist engenders such sympathy that readers will cheer him on through his many predicaments. Lisker's stark black-and-white spot illustrations suit the novel's melancholy tone. Ages 11-14.

Kirkus Reviews

SOURCE: A review of *Punch with Judy*, in *Kirkus Reviews*, Vol. 61, April 15, 1993, p. 523.

In a dark tale like the verso of one of Sid Fleischman's comic adventures of traveling performers, Avi explores the idea that great clowns derive power from a profound sense of the tragic. Impresario Joe

McSneed has died, leaving Mrs. McSneed, an acrobat who imagines herself to be "The King of Tipperary's Widow"; her daughter Judy, 15, now in charge; a dispirited crew of other performers; and dogsbody Punch, 12, taken in by McSneed in hope that his barely glimpsed talent might blossom. But now the group's performances are devoid of humor, a lack intensified by their loss, and they're outraged when Punch and his beloved pig inadvertently provoke the kind of laughter Judy now suggests may restore their fortunes. She's proved right; but before most of the men desert, Judy betrays Punch's timid affection by marrying another, and the group is hounded by a grim sheriff trying to take him into custody as an orphan. He agress to let Punch go free if the group can make him laugh, which they manage to do with a live Punch-and-Judy show—in which Punch nearly dies when Judy's slap-stick begins to deliver blows that are all too real. Midway, one character clearly outlines the varieties of humor, but, curiously, despite a cast and setting proclaiming farce, there's little here. Rather, it's a touching but somber tale, enlivened by idiosyncratic characters and pungent descriptions, of an undervalued, overly modest boy finding his talent and his true friends. Lisker's incisively sketched figures lighten the format.

Sally Margolls

SOURCE: A review of *Punch with Judy,* in *School Library Journal,* Vol. 39, No. 6, June, 1993, p. 102.

Gr 5-7—Avi's style here doesn't work well, and this offering won't be among his popular works. After the Civil War, a young street performer is taken in by a traveling showman with an acrobatic wife (sort of a show biz Mr. and Mrs. Macawber), their daughter Judy, and an assortment of ragtag entertainers. The boy, dubbed Punch, becomes general servant to the rest, tries to please everyone, but is constantly abused and berated. When her father dies and her mother loses touch with reality, Judy tries to run the operation. As the troupe struggles to survive, Punch tries to establish himself. He also struggles with his love for Judy, a futile crush, he being 12 years old and she old enough to marry. As in a Punch and Judy show or *commedia dell'arte,* the tale is cast with stock characters. There is a cruel streak present here that's made all the more chilling because the voice is so objective, so removed from any involvement, any sense of a warm presence. Punch, as is his puppet forbear, is pounded on, emotionally and, finally, physically. Illustrated with black-and-white heavy ink drawings in a naive style, this book keeps readers at a distance. Perhaps the aimlessness of the performers

is a metaphor for the state of the country post-war. Other than that, there's little sense of time or place, and events occur without much preparation. There is minimal character development, and in spite of the stated action and conflict, there is no tension. Instead, the book is a stark outline of a story within a stylistic exercise. Are readers expected to provide the human context? If so, it seems likely that few will be interested.

CITY OF LIGHT, CITY OF DARK (1993)

Publishers Weekly

SOURCE: A review of *City of Light, City of Dark,* in *Publishers Weekly,* Vol. 240, No. 33, August 16, 1993, p. 105.

One of the most versatile YA novelists of the day teams up with first-time illustrator Floca to produce first-rate science fiction in comic-book form. After outlining an altered version of New York City's history, the elaborately plotted saga shows how, through courage and cunning, two preteens, Carlos and Estella, and Estella's clairvoyant mother thwart a power-hungry villain and thereby prevent Manhattan from turning to ice. Against backdrops of neon lights, circling pigeons, abandoned subway stations and storefronts, Avi and Floca dynamically convey a timeless tale of good versus evil. Brilliantly parodying the superhero cartoons of old, this myth conceived in the same spirit as *Who Was That Masked Man Anyway?* is sure to be a hit with reluctant and advanced readers alike. Ages 9-up.

John Peters

SOURCE: A review of *City of Light, City of Dark,* in *School Library Journal,* Vol. 39, No. 9, September, 1993, p. 228.

Gr 4-7—Avi continues his series of experiments in children's fiction with this graphic-novel send-up that features a convoluted plot, bad guys both natural and supernatural, and a rainbow cast of New Yorkers. The real owners of Manhattan are the disembodied, irascible Kurbs. According to an ancient agreement, unless a human finds their hidden Power each year and puts it in a designated safe place, the Kurbs will freeze the island and reclaim it. The current searcher is Asterel, a young African-American woman wandering the streets disguised as a bag lady; the Power is invested in a certain subway token, and to track it down she enlists the aid of two children, Carlos and Estella (who is actually her long-lost daughter). The token is also being sought by Underton, a ruthless blind man with sinister plans and a flock of trained pigeons to help him do his dirty work, and one human minion: Estella's father. Driven by huge contrivances, the plot takes readers over and under city streets, from a cavern deep beneath a spooky abandoned subway station, to the climatic confrontation high atop the Statue of Liberty. Floca's comic-book pen-and-ink art makes for crowded pages, but also for effective action sequences and easily recognizable character types. Text and illustrations work well together, each supporting and adding detail to the other. Asterel and her young companions charge into their task with an earnest nobility that contrasts comically with Underton's crazed mumbling and exaggerated nastiness—but though Avi's fans have learned by now to expect the unexpected from him, only inveterate comic-book or graphic-novel readers are likely to appreciate this tongue-in-cheek escapade.

Janice Del Negro

SOURCE: A review of *City of Light, City of Dark*, in *Booklist*, Vol. 90, No. 2, September 15, 1993, p. 142.

Gr. 6-9. This story, created in comic-strip style, is about Sarah Stubbs, about her father's secret, and about saving Manhattan from the Kurbs, the creatures who really own the island. Sarah's mother, Asterell, is the keeper of a token that must be offered each year to the Kurbs to renew humanity's lease on the island. Carlos, a classmate of Sarah's, accidentally finds the token. Amid a flurry of chases, mistaken identities, and confusion, the children manage to save Sarah's father from the villainous Underton, Asterell is able to pass her powers to her daughter, and the Kurbs receive their tribute in time to save the island from freezing. The black-and-white illustrations move the action along at a fast clip, though Floca's unsophisticated style of cartooning lacks the kind of definition that would have added to the text. This will not, however, discourage readers attracted by the comic-book format, and with strong women as heroes and an action-packed plot, the book should prove popular across both gender and genre lines.

Kirkus Reviews

SOURCE: A review of *City of Light, City of Dark*, in *Kirkus Reviews*, Vol. 61, October 1, 1993, p. 1268.

Complications abound in a graphic novel related in brief narrative boxes plus dialogue (some of it in both Spanish and English) in hundreds of b&w comic-book frames. Sarah has been told (falsely) that her mother died; Carlos can't understand why an old blind man is so interested in a subway token he's found. The two kids team up and eventually learn the truth: the evil Mr. Underton was blinded by Sarah's mother 11 years ago when he tried to steal the token that's the source of power for the metropolis (N.Y.C.), which will freeze if the token isn't delivered to safekeeping each December 21 by Sarah's mother (and, someday, by Sarah). With neat feats of derring-do but uncharacteristically lumpy plotting and motives (Stubbs hides from his wife for 11 years, fearing she'll hate him—to keep her love, he leaves her?), this isn't quite fish or fowl. Still, robust spirits run appealingly amok until the expected triumph of good. Author (and publisher) get high marks for experimenting with a new genre, though this may not be the book to make it fashionable. A bold venture that will probably entertain the young more than their elders.

THE BIRD, THE FROG, AND THE LIGHT (1994)

Publishers Weekly

SOURCE: A review of *The Bird, the Frog, and the Light*, in *Publishers Weekly*, Vol.. 241, No. 3, January 17, 1994, p. 432.

A pretty bird opens each day by singing: although her song is "nothing very special," it nonetheless causes the sun to beam. This bucolic routine is interrupted one day by a pompous, bossy frog, who leads the bird to his underground kingdom and directs her to the many signs of his greatness—marble palace, ancient throne, massive army. Because his kingdom is pitch black, these things can be only felt, not seen. At the frog's insistence, the bird illuminates the underworld with a ray from her friend the sun, revealing the "kingdom" to be no more than a collection of dingy leavings—a stone, a box, a tin can—and forcing the frog, however grudgingly, to renounce his grandiosity. Avi's dry wit leads to a pungent telling, with lessons about the power and pitfalls of delusion kept humorous and light. In an impressive picture-book debut, Henry adds finely textured paintings that aptly evoke both the airy, sun-bathed earth and the ambiguous darkness of the frog's lair. His frog king—dour, imperious, literally inflated with his own importance—is a comic masterstroke. A deceptively simple tale packed with clever verbal and visual details. Ages 5-7.

Shirley Wilton

SOURCE: A review of *The Bird, the Frog, and the Light,* in *School Library Journal,* Vol. 40, No. 4, April, 1994, p. 95.

K-Gr 3—One day the bird who wakes the sun with song is captured by a pompous, puffed-up frog who thinks himself king of the underground world. When, at the frog's command, the bird brings a single sun ray to his dark kingdom, his possessions and subjects are shown to be nothing but bits of trash. He has been deceived in his wealth, his subjects, and even his library, which is only a scrap from a telephone book. The frog, humbled by knowledge of his error, asks the bird to teach him to read from the tattered "R" page of the phone book. The message of the value of reading seems tacked on to this curious tale of enlightenment. The moral of the fable is the necessity of seeing one's situation truly, informed by the light of truth and/or understanding. The frog, in the end, suddenly sees a connection between learning to read and seeing the light, but it will not be clear to readers. The bird, as the bearer of truth and the one who greets the sun, is never explained. The story is elaborately and handsomely illustrated with full-page, bordered paintings.

Julie Corsaro

SOURCE: A review of *The Bird, the Frog, and the Light,* in *Booklist,* Vol. 90, No. 16, April 15, 1994, p. 1538.

Ages 5-8. In this picture-book fable, the emperor not only has no clothes, he's also illiterate. When a bombastic Frog King forces a singing Bird to bring sunlight into his dark underground kingdom, both creatures are in for a shock. The Frog's "marble palace" turns out to be a small, smooth rock. His "throne" is nothing more than a roosting box, his "treasure" a single penny. While the moral comes through, the final message about reading (the sovereign can't) feels tacked onto an otherwise streamlined tale. Moreover, if the Frog King can't read, how does he know that "R is for ridiculous," as he says near the conclusion? The polished, airbrushed compositions by debuting illustrator Henry are definitely the best part of the book. The art ably contrasts the benign world above and the menacing one below the ground and intriguingly illustrates the nature of reality.

THE BARN (1994)

Hazel Rochman

SOURCE: A review of *The Barn,* in *Booklist,* Vol. 91, No. 1, September 1, 1994, p. 40.

Rooted in a one-room family cabin in Oregon Territory in the 1850s, this is a classic survival story of kids who suddenly find themselves on their own without adults to care for them.

The terror is there from the first line: "Your father has met with an accident," nine-year-old Ben is told at boarding school. He must go home to help his 13-year-old brother, Harrison, and 15-year-old sister, Nettie. Mother died the year before of diphtheria; another brother died on the trail coming west. Now Ben, Harrison, and Nettie stand uncertainly in front of the cabin: "We hardly knew what or how to be." Not only must they farm the family claim and bring in the crop, but they must also care for their father, who is paralyzed. He's as helpless as a baby, unable to speak or move his body or control his bowels.

At first Ben is "mortified" at having to feed and clean his father. But then it becomes routine. in fact, "his filth proved that Father still lived. . . . in this way did I begin to learn how heaven and earth do mingle."

Ben's spare, first-person narrative tells of the special relationship he had with his father—their own private mischief." Now, his father can't talk to him. in a chapter of almost unbearable intensity, Ben does finally get his silent father to communicate. Ben asks a question and screams in anger, "If you mean yes, you must close your eyes!" And then, his father does close his eyes. Is it an accident? Or does he mean yes?

The question Ben asked was whether Father wanted his children to build the barn he had been hoping to build himself. Ben persuades Harrison and Nettie that they must build it to give Father a reason to live and that they must build it alone, without the help of neighbors, as a gift to their father. Nettie tries to make Ben see that Father is dying anyway, but Ben denies it. With Father propped up in a barrow, they mark fell the trees. They use the oxen to haul the logs, then they cut, strip, and split them. While Father wastes away, they pile rocks for the foundation, and raise the walls and roof. When the barn is finally done, it is nothing much to look at and probably not truly square, yet it holds them there. And Father is dead. Did Ben build the barn for Father? Did Father get Ben to build it?

That yoking of opposites is in every scene, almost in every sentence, of this plain-spoken novel. The name Ben means "son of." The story shows that the child is father of the man: that dying and building are one cycle; that silence can be eloquent language. Nothing is certain. Every statement opens out, even the Lord's Prayer: "Our father" is dead, and he's in heaven, and he's in the barn. Heaven and earth do mingle.

The characters have the same complexity. Ben is very smart—that's why he was the one sent to school—yet he hates being special, and he envies his brother's size and strength. Through Ben's memories, the character of his beloved father emerges as far from perfect. Father never quite built a home; he said he never had much "luck," moving his family from Vermont to Illinois to Missouri before coming to Oregon. Father didn't build the barn himself. It's ironic that he now helps Ben find the self-reliance to do it for them both.

The writing is understated, almost monosyllabic, with a casual tone and concrete imagery reminiscent of the poetry of Robert Frost. It's interesting that the most detailed part of the story is the mechanics of the barn building. Work, especially manual work, is getting more attention in children's books. Here Avi particularizes the struggle to make a place that is home.

Avi is one of our most versatile and prolific children's writers. He never does the same thing twice, always experimenting with form and theme and setting, from realistic fiction to radio play and graphic novel. This small, beautiful historical novel has a timeless simplicity. It's the best thing he's done. Like MacLachlan's *Sarah, Plain and Tall* (1985), the story reaches from home to the universe.

Publishers Weekly

SOURCE: A review of *The Barn,* in *Publishers Weekly,* Vol. 241, No. 36, September 5, 1994, p. 112.

A departure from Avi's recent sweeping adventure stories *(City of Light, City of Dark; Who Was That Masked Man, Anyway?),* this austere tale set in 1855 tells how the children of Oregon settlers are left to fend for themselves on the frontier. Nine-year-old Ben, the scholar of the family and the narrator here, leaves his Portland boarding school after his widowed father is paralyzed by an attack of palsy. While his older brother and sister work the fields of their farm, Ben looks after his stricken father and laments that his father will not be able to realize his dream of

building a barn on their property. As the days go by, Ben becomes more and more convinced that he and his siblings must build the barn themselves. Much of the book (which is illustrated with a few diagrams) recounts the children's step-by-step process of raising a structure that will make their father proud. Only after the enormous undertaking is completed does Ben question the meaning of his labor. Easily read in one sitting, this unembellished story proves to be as intimate as a diary, gracefully revealing its protagonist's keen intelligence, strong determination and secret fear of being separated from his loved ones. Although the novella may not draw as wide an audience as many of the author's previous works, it will gratify those who seek a quiet, contemplative read. Ages 9-11.

Steven Engelfried

SOURCE: A review of *The Barn,* in *School Library Journal,* Vol. 40, No. 10, October, 1994, p. 118.

Gr 3-6—After their father suffers a "fit of palsy," three motherless children try to keep their struggling farm going in 1855 Oregon. Although nine-year-old Benjamin is the youngest, he is the cleverest of the three, and also the one who truly believes that the man can recover. His sister Nettie wants to marry and start her own life, but agrees to help the family for as long as she can. Harrison is much bigger and stronger than his younger brother, but not quite as quick thinking. After Benjamin figures out a way to communicate with his father, he convinces the others that if they can build the barn that the man had been planning, he will somehow find a reason to live. The family relationships are well drawn, as the siblings react to each situation in their own way, though Benjamin's obsession with curing his father makes him a hard character to empathize with at times. Ultimately, the boy is forced to question his own additional motives for building the barn. While focusing mainly on his characters, Avi presents a vivid picture of the time and place, including fairly involved details about how the barn is constructed. This novel may not have the wide appeal of some of Avi's earlier titles, but it is a thought-provoking and engaging piece of historical fiction.

Kirkus Reviews

SOURCE: A review of *The Barn,* in *Kirkus Reviews,* Vol. 62, October 15, 1994, p. 1404.

Once again, the ever-resourceful Avi (*The Bird, the Frog, and the Light,* etc.) explores new ground. Ben is nine when his teenage sister, Nettie, fetches him from school, where he'd been sent to honor his dead mother's wishes. Their father has had a "palsy" (a stroke), and Ben's help is needed on the 300-acre family claim in Oregon Territory. Ben, intellectually gifted and a natural leader, soon determines the most efficient division of labor: He'll care for Father while Harrison, 13, and Nettie farm. (Some of this stretches credulity: Paralyzed and incontinent, Father requires more lifting than a nine-year-old could credibly manage; and, although Avi suggests the difficulties in one poignant scene, dealing with the necessary laundry is never mentioned.) Desperate to reclaim Father, Ben pins his hopes on the idea that if they can build a barn, as Father had planned, then he will recover. The three children do build a sizable, sturdy barn (without even the traditional help of neighbors, stretching credulity still more). Though the effect of the barn's completion doesn't literally match Ben's dream, it's a gift from the three to their dying father and enables him to give them a gift as well: understanding. Ben's spare narrative is lovingly honed, the interaction of the characters drawn with sensitivity and skill. A small, quiet book that may appeal to perceptive readers.

Roger Sutton

SOURCE: A review of *The Barn,* in *Bulletin of the Center for Children's Books,* Vol. 48, No. 4, December, 1994, p. 120.

In this short novel set in 1850s Oregon, nine-year-old Ben is sent from boarding school back to his family's farm when his father suffers a completely incapacitating stroke. Ben's father cannot talk or move; it falls upon Ben, after discussion with his older brother and sister, to care for their father, feeding him and changing his soiled clothing. After some days of this, Ben becomes convinced that his father can blink his eyes to mean *yes*; Ben then becomes convinced that Father wants them to build a barn, a difficult task and probably pointless, too, as each of the children has expressed a desire to leave the homestead. The theme here is hermeneutical as well as spiritual: how do we know what we hear? does affirmation come from response, or from within? These are hard and subtle questions, but Avi asks them in terms of a taut, untheoretical story, told with spare economy and action that moves with the ideas. Although the novel—and the words—are short and to the point, the style is sometimes over-deliberate, too apparently controlled. Even given his relatively expansive education and native intelligence, Ben is not entirely convincing as

a nine-year-old—at least today's nine-year-old won't find him so—and his closing conversation with his siblings (after Father has died, never seeing the now-finished barn) has a taste of the late twentieth century about it. Still, there's a sharp and unadorned picture of the harshness of homestead pioneer life, and an immediacy of pain that transcends setting.

Ellen Fader

SOURCE: A review of *The Barn,* in *The Horn Book Magazine,* Vol. 71, No. 1, January-February, 1995, p. 57.

The last time nine-year-old Ben had seen his father was seven months before, on the journey to boarding school in Portland, Oregon, late in 1854. Now, their father has been taken ill, and Ben's fifteen-year-old sister Nettie has come to take him home. During the two-day, thirty-mile ride to their Yamhill County claim, Nettie attempts to explain their father's dire condition after his recent attack. At his father's bedside, Ben is shocked to discover the reality of having a totally disabled parent who cannot feed or toilet himself, move from his bed, or speak. Because Nettie and their brother Harrison are older and stonger, and therefore better suited to heavy field work, Ben takes on the burden of their father's daily care. He becomes convinced that their father can communicate through eye blinks and that his fervent wish is for a barn to replace their leaky lean-to. Ben, sure that giving the barn to their father as a gift will cure him, persuades his brother and sister to help him design and build it. It takes the siblings over three months to assemble the materials and construct the barn. On the night they finish, Ben tells their father, who seems to be asleep, that they have completed the project. But their father dies during the night, apparently without ever hearing the news. Nevertheless, the three young people all feel their father's spirit in the barn after his death. Ben, telling this story seventy years later, expresses the importance of the barn in his life: "Every morning when I get up, the first thing I do is look at the barn. Like Father promised: it's something fine to come home to. Still standing. Still strong." Deceptively easy to read, this novel offers much to the reflective reader. Although most of the children's books about the Oregon Trail recount the tremendous physical obstacles that the pioneers surmounted, *The Barn* is a contemplative survival novel of a different sort. Ben's drive to bring his project to fruition stands as a testament to hope and to belief in the continuity of life and the human spirit.

📖 *TOM, BABETTE, AND SIMON: THREE TALES OF TRANSFORMATION* (1995)

Carolyn Phelan

SOURCE: A review of *Tom, Babette, and Simon: Three Tales of Transformation*, in *Booklist*, v. 91, No. 18, May 15, 1995, p. 1643.

Gr. 4-6. Bored with home and school, Tom wishes he could sleep all day like his cat. With help from a wizard, Tom and his cat switch places, but soon Tom decides that he wants to be a boy again. At this point, readers might expect Tom to go back to his old life, but Avi's conclusion is more unsettling. The second story involves a princess who was born flawless, as her mother had insisted, but invisible. When she realizes that no one can see her, the haughty princess undergoes trials to discover how to become visible. The third tale concerns a spoiled lad who grows into a vain man. Transformed into a bird from the neck up, he endures the scorn of men and birds until a selfless act sets him free. Although the first tale has a modern setting and tone and the others are closer to fairy tales, the stories share themes of the outward and inward transformation of the main characters. Reminiscent of Joan Aiken's short stories, these brief tales will intrigue young readers.

Cheri Estes

SOURCE: A review of *Tom, Babette, and Simon: Three Tales of Transformation*, in *School Library Journal*, Vol. 41, No. 6, June, 1995, p. 108.

Gr 3-6—In the first and most successful of these quirky tales, a bored boy envies his cat Charley, who sleeps all day, and wishes he could do the same. The neighborhood wizard-cat transforms human into cat and cat into human, and, in a truly Hitchcockian twist, Charley refuses to change back into a feline when Tom is ready to be a boy again. It seems that all over the world, bored children agree to be turned into cats, and the only way out of the enchantment is to trick another child into switching. Babette gives new meaning to the phrase "self-made woman." Her mother will accept only a flawless child, and so the princess is born invisible. Everyone in the kingdom convinces themselves of her beauty, and without mirrors to contradict, Babette believes them. She is horrified to learn the truth, but she finds a place where she may choose her own eyes, feet, thumbs, etc., and becomes a person of her own making. In the parable of Simon, even a thoroughly unlikable character receives grace. The young man's greed leads him in pursuit of the Golden Bird, and when he kills her, he is changed into a bird from the neck up. Captured and put on display, he is eventually cast out. He returns to the forest filled with self-pity, but when the Golden Bird reappears, Simon is remorseful. She transforms all of him into a majestic bird, and he flies away forgiven. These sophisticated short stories are witty if a bit odd. Read them aloud or share with a child who enjoys something out of the ordinary.

Kirkus Reviews

SOURCE: A review of *Tom, Babette, and Simon: Three Tales of Transformation*, in *Kirkus Reviews*, Vol. 63, June 1, 1995, p. 776.

Shape-shifting adventures in a grand tradition. Tom, who is bored with life, becomes his cat, Charley, and Charley becomes the boy; when Tom grows tired of being a cat and wants to change back, he learns Charley himself was once a bored boy who underwent a similar transformation, and has no intention of giving up his new life. Babette's mother is a stuck-up queen who wants a daughter without any visible flaws; when the baby is born, she is invisible. Simon hunts down the Golden Bird who, as she dies, turns him into a bird from the neck up. Avi (*The Barn*, 1994, etc.) has a confident sense of the possibilities of fiction; his stories are rich amalgamations of magic, suspense, horror, and philosophy. The text doesn't have a polished feel, but these plots don't need it— they keep readers glued to the page simply to find out what happens next. With scratchy b&w illustrations.

Roger Sutton

SOURCE: A review of *Tom, Babette, and Simon: Three Tales of Transformation*, in *Bulletin of the Center for Children's Books*, Vol. 48, No. 11, July-August, 1995, pp. 376-77.

Taking a break from his more ambitious works such *The Barn*, Avi here offers three ironic fantasy turns on the old be-careful-what-you-wish-for theme. Tom is lazy, and happily trades bodies with a cat; princess Babette is born without a blemish—and without a face; Simon wants everyone to notice him, and after he's turned into a bird-man, they do. **"Tom"** is the most tightly structured while **"Simon"** offers the most drama; **"Babette"** begins with more promise than it eventually fulfills. While the stories aren't very substantial, they're easy to read and wear their morals relatively lightly. Natchev supplies each story with a raffish ink sketch.

POPPY (1995)

Kirkus Reviews

SOURCE: A review of *Poppy,* in *Kirkus Reviews,* Vol. 63, September 15, 1995, p. 1346.

An adolescent mouse named Poppy is off on a romantic tryst with her rebel boyfriend when they are attacked by Mr. Ocax, the owl who rules over the area. He kills the boyfriend, but Poppy escapes and Mr. Ocax vows to catch her. Mr. Ocax has convinced all the mice that he is their protector when, in fact, he preys on them mercilessly. When the mice ask his permission to move to a new house, he refuses, blaming Poppy for his decision. Poppy suspects that there is another reason Mr. Ocax doesn't want them to move and investigates to clear her name. With the help of a prickly old porcupine and her quick wits, Poppy defeats her nemesis and her own fears, saving her family in the bargain. The book is a cute, but rather standard offering from Avi (*Tom, Babette, and Simon,* etc.).

Publishers Weekly

SOURCE: A review of *Poppy* in *Publishers Weekly,* Vol. 92, No. 4, 15 October 1995, p. 402.

Newbery Honor author Avi (*Tom, Babette and Simon,* turns out another winner with this fanciful tale featuring a cast of woodland creatures. As ruler of Dimwood Forest, Ocax the hoot owl has promised to protect the mice occupying an abandoned farmhouse as long as they ask permission before "moving about." Poppy, a timid dormouse, is a loyal, obedient subject—until she sees Ocax devour her fiance and hears the owl deny her father's request to seek new living quarters. To prove that the intimidating ruler is really a phony, Poppy embarks on a dangerous and eye-opening quest, which ends with her one-on-one battle with Ocax. While the themes about tyranny and heroism are timeless, Avi leavens his treatment with such 20th-century touches as Poppy's jive-talking boyfriend and Poppy's own romantic vision of herself as Ginger Rogers. An engaging blend of romance, suspense and parody, this fantasy is well-nigh irresistible . . . Ages 9-11.

Carolyn Phelan

SOURCE: A review of *Poppy,* in *Booklist,* Vol. 92, No. 4, October 15, 1995, p. 402.

Gr. 4-6. a good old-fashioned story with an exciting plot, well-drawn characters, and a satisfying ending, Avi's latest novel will please readers on many levels.

Mr. Ocax the owl rules the territory where Poppy, a young deer mouse, lives with her large, extended family. The mice have agreed to obey Mr. Ocax, and, in exchange, he has promised to protect them from porcupines, animals that the mice know only from the owl's alarming description. Although warned by her officious father not to leave home without the owl's permission, Poppy sneaks one night with her boyfriend, Ragweed. Poppy listens to Ragweed's goading about her tearful submissiveness, then watches in horror as Mr. Ocax pounces on Ragweed, killing him instantly. Poppy soon finds her own way from cowardice to courage when she sets out on a quest to find her family a new home. As an adventure story, the book combines action, suspense, and humor. As a novel of character, it convincingly portrays growth as Poppy faces her fears and finds her way. Older children may recognize the politics of power played out through the three figures who initially dominate Poppy: Mr. Ocax, who cleverly coaxes, rules by fear, and despises those he oppresses; Poppy's father, who hides his cowardly stance behind his bluster; and Ragweed, who puts down Poppy for her cautious ways. For reading alone or reading aloud.

Marie Orlando

SOURCE: A review of *Poppy,* in *School Library Journal,* Vol. 41, No. 12, December, 1995, p. 102.

Gr 3-5—A fast-paced, allegorical animal story. Mr. Ocax is a great horned owl who rules the mice who live around Dimwood Forest, preying on their fears by promising protection from the dreaded porcupine in exchange for unconditional obedience. Challenging his despotic authority is the smart-talking, earring-sporting golden mouse Ragweed, whose refusal to obey turns him into a meal for the owl. His timid sweetheart Poppy returns home, where she learns that a delegation must go to request permission from Mr. Ocax to relocate half of the mouse family as they have outgrown their present quarters. When he refuses, Poppy, inspired by Ragweed's independent thinking, decides to undertake the scouting journey to the proposed new home anyway, encountering along the way an irreverent porcupine who explains that he and his ilk are no threat to mice. Armed with Ragweed's earring, a quill sword, and the awareness of the owl's deception, she plans to expose Ocax as a cowardly bully. She finds herself in a fierce battle with him, resulting in his death and allowing for the mice's liberation. This exciting story is richly visual, subtly humorous, and skillfully laden with natural-history lessons. The anthropomorphism is believable and the characters are memorable. The underlying messages, to challenge unjust authority and to rely on logic and belief in oneself, are palatably blended with action and suspense. Black-and-white illustrations are in keeping with the changing moods and forest locale. A thoroughly enjoyable book.

Roger Sutton

SOURCE: A review of *Poppy,* in *Bulletin of the Center for Children's Books,* Vol. 49, No. 5, January, 1996, p. 154.

Poppy, a mouse, knew she was doing the wrong thing when she went with her boyfriend Ragweed to Bannock Hill without the permission of Mr. Ocax, the owl who has styled himself the ruler of Dimwood Forest. Ragweed, an Angry Young Mouse, scorned the rules set down by the owl for the community of Dimwood Forest mice, and for his rebellion he is eaten by the owl, who unsuccessfully attacks Poppy as well. Although this mouse fantasy is fiercer than, say, Dick King-Smith's *The School Mouse,* reviewed below, it hasn't the gore of Jacques' *Redwall* books, and the owl-and-mouse chase that ensues as a vengeful Ocax contrives to destroy Poppy is cozied by the woodsy atmosphere (and Brian Floca's personable and realistic pencil illustrations), leavened by the humor of Poppy's unlikely prickly helper (a grouchy porcupine), and ennobled by Poppy's own fumbling yet valiant heroism. The fate of her people depends upon Poppy's ability to stay out of Ocax's talons and find the mice a new home on the other side of the forest, and her quest holds both peril and adventure. Sprightly but un-cute dialogue, suspenseful chapter endings, and swift shifts of perspective between Ocax and Poppy will make chapter-a-day readalouds cause for anticipation, rewarded by a fight-to-the-death conclusion.

Ann A. Flowers

SOURCE: A review of *Poppy,* in *The Horn Book Magazine,* Vol. 72, No. 1, January-February, 1996, p. 70.

Illustrated by Brian Floca. This story of bravery, persistence, and an overthrown tyrant features the heroine Poppy, a small deer mouse with beautiful orange-brown fur, dark round eyes, and pink toes. She and her family live under the protection of Mr. Ocax, a great horned owl. The mice cannot leave their terri-

tory without the permission of Mr. Ocax, at the risk of being eaten as punishment; in return, he promises to protect them from other dangers, especially porcupines. Poppy's friend Ragweed is an iconoclast; he asks inconvenient questions, such as whether any of the mice has ever actually seen a porcupine. One night, he persuades Poppy to go out in the moonlight without asking Mr. Ocax's permission. Although Ragweed is an original thinker, he is not a careful mouse, and Mr. Ocax catches him and eats him. The horrified Poppy barely escapes with her life. When she makes it back home, she finds her bombastic father, Lungwort, delivering a speech to the assembled mice about moving to a new home—aptly called New House—where there is more food. He insists that Poppy accompany him on a mission to seek Mr. Ocax's permission, and when Mr. Ocax refuses, the mice blame Poppy. Terrified but resolute, Poppy travels to see New House for herself and enters Dimwood, where Mr. Ocax and many other horrors reside. There she blunders into a porcupine's den, only to find him grumpy and smelly with a great talent for rough language such as "slug slop" and "bat bilge," but a decided vegetarian. This revelation confirms her growing suspicion about the benevolence of Mr. Ocax's rule. Poppy taunts Ocax and finally defeats him with a porcupine quill in a battle of epic dimensions. The wonderful characterizations—Poppy and her slowly growing awareness, the evil Mr. Ocax, the pompous Lungwort, and Ragweed the rebel—will remind readers of Robert Lawson's *Rabbit Hill* and Robert C. O'Brien's *Mrs. Frisby and the Rats of NIMH.* A splendid read-aloud, and a tribute to the inquiring mind and the stout heart.

BEYOND THE WESTERN SEA, BOOK ONE: THE ESCAPE FROM HOME (1996)

Roger Sutton

SOURCE: A review of *Beyond the Western Sea, Book One: The Escape From Home,* in *Bulletin of the Center for Children's Books,* Vol. 49, No. 6, February, 1996, p. 183.

While you actually do have to turn the pages for yourself here, the task soon feels like it's out of your hands as Avi's tense, twisting storytelling takes over. It is 1851, and brother and sister Patrick and Maura are escaping poverty and the landlord's destruction of their wretched Irish hovel; Laurence, son to an English lord, is running away from abuse and his own guilty conscience. All three young people are—hope to be—on their way to America, with trouble and intrigue pursuing them every step of the way. Although the book has the harum-scarum action of melodrama, it never becomes pastiche; instead, Maura, Patrick, and Laurence seem like real people in really dangerous straits as various villains, for various and conflicting reasons, try to keep them from boarding the *Robert Peel,* set to sail on Friday, January 24. (The book essentially begins on the Monday of the same week, so you can see that things move thick and fast.) The suspense and the shifting among various points of view are expertly deployed but do become slightly mechanical towards the last pages; you still won't be able to stop reading. More of a problem is the cliff-hanging ending: the three kids are all on the boat but they're still up to their necks in it, and you feel like you've only read half a book. Which you have—and the next installment, *Lord Kirkle's Money,* won't be published until the fall. Libraries may want to wait and purchase both volumes at once.

Hazel Rochman

SOURCE: A review of *Beyond the Western Sea, Book One: The Escape From Home,* in *Booklist,* Vol. 92, No. 11, February 1, 1996, p. 930.

Gr. 6-10. Avi's last historical novel, *The Barn* (1994), was a spare story about a boy at home. Nothing could be more different than this pulsing 1850s emigrant adventure (at 300 pages, it's only book 1), packed with action and with a huge cast of villains and heroes. The first chapter grabs you: poor Irish peasants Maura O'Connell, 15, and her brother, Patrick, 12, see their home destroyed. They leave for Liverpool to board a ship for America. Their father has sent money from New York, but their mother is too broken to go, and they must make the journey alone. Interwoven with their story is that of their English landlord's son, 11-year-old Sir Laurence Kirkle, who, hotly pursued by friend and foe, has run away from his unhappy home. Although the historical research is never obtrusive, there's an authentic sense of the Liverpool dockside slums, with the desperate pressed together in a foul, teeming hell. The young lord's story is not as compelling as that of the O'Connells, especially since it's not easy to keep straight which schemer is pursuing him and why, but every chapter ends with a cliffhanger, and the suspense builds as they all converge on the same ship sailing for America. At the climax, Laurence is a stowaway in deadly danger. Great for reading aloud, the vivid scenes and larger-than-life characters also lend themselves to readers' theater. The comedy is both grotesque and sinister. As in Dickens' works, coinci-

dence is not just a plot surprise but a revelation that those who appear to be far apart—the powerful and the "failures"—are, in fact, intimately connected. Now we have to wait for book 2.

Publishers Weekly

SOURCE: A review of *Beyond the Western Sea, Book One: The Escape From Home,* in *Publishers Weekly,* Vol. 243, No. 14, April 1, 1996, p. 77.

Devotees of historical novels will quickly become absorbed in this drama set in 19th-century England, about the misadventures of an Irish peasant and the young son of an English lord who cross paths before boarding a ship bound for America. The biting irony present in Avi's contemporary novels (*Nothing but the Truth*; *City of Light, City of Dark*) surfaces here in portrayals of the sharp contrasts between the upper and lower classes. Although the plot does tend to meander (the emigrants do not actually set sail until the last few pages), the author provides so many enticing side attractions in the form of unsavory villains and extraordinary twists of fate that readers will stay hooked. Full of tongue-in-cheek contrivances, this voluminous, Dickensian-style novel offers surprises around every corner. Fittingly, the book ends *in medias res,* so readers must await the September '96 publication of the second, and final installment, *Lord Kirkle's Money,* to discover the destinies of Patrick and Laurence, the two unlikely traveling companions. Ages 11-14.

Margaret Cole

SOURCE: A review of *Beyond the Western Sea, Book One: The Escape From Home,* in *School Library Journal,* Vol. 42, No. 6, June, 1996, p. 150.

Gr 6-9—A suspense-filled adventure. Among the masses abandoning their Irish homes to escape famine, disease, and poverty in 1851 are 12-year-old Patrick and his older sister, Maura, who are joining their father in America. As they pass through the port city of Liverpool, they join an assortment of England's own unfortunates and malcontents. Among them is 11-year-old Laurence, penniless and hopelessly confused, who regrets having fled his wealthy home in London in a fit of rage. Patrick and Laurence meet only briefly, but long enough to seal their fate. As the dank, dirty back alleys of Liverpool come alive through the struggles of the three children, the scenes shift rapidly, challenging readers to keep track of a tangle of Dickensian characters ranging from the misguided to the malevolent. At its best, this book resembles Avi's much loved *The True Confessions of Charlotte Doyle* (Orchard, 1990), but is far weaker in character development and focus. The paradox of a fine novel is that it satisfies completely yet leaves readers thirsting for more. The clear intention of this book, however, is to introduce a two-part series. It is an engrossing read, worthy of purchase, but only if you fully intend to go for the yet-to-be-published sequel. Michael Morpurgo's well-done *Twist of Gold* (Viking, 1993; o.p.) covers strikingly similar territory for an only slightly younger audience.

Mary M Burns

SOURCE: A review of *Beyond the Western Sea, Book One: The Escape From Home,* in *The Horn Book Magazine,* Vol. 72, No. 4, July-August, 1996, p. 461.

Like a rip-roaring rollercoaster ride, this picaresque adventure careens from one escapade to another, ending at a precipitous pause. The action begins in Ireland during the disastrous potato famine as hirelings of Lord Kirkle, a rackrent landlord, destroy the wretched cottages of a small village. Among his victims are Maura and Patrick O'Connell, who, with their mother, have been sent sufficient funds to join their father in America. No stalwart example of Irish womanhood, the mother succumbs to despair, leaving her two children to pursue their quest alone. In Liverpool, where ships embark for the journey west, their paths intersect with that of Laurence Kirkle, younger son of the landowner who had evicted them. He, thanks to the machinations of a conniving older brother, has run away from his London home to seek asylum, like the O'Connells, in the land of opportunity. Similar to many stories in this genre, the emphasis is on plot and action with refrences to historical events setting it in time and place. Shifting back and forth between converging stories, the narrative, with its short, snappy chapters and unremitting suspense, is a real page turner. Personalities representing all tones from virtue to villainy add color and intrigue. The characters, types rather than unique, include a spinoff of Dickens's Fagin, an unemployed actor, and a conniving proprietess of a derelict boarding house. Maura and Patrick, particularly in their dialogue, come perilously close to stage-Irish stock, but the audacious use of coincidence and dazzling pace disguises these shortcomings. Warning: The ending leaves one of the main characters "in dire straits," as the old-fashioned melodramas used to say, insuring that readers will be eagerly awaiting the promised sequel.

Diane Broughton

SOURCE: A review of *Beyond the Western Sea, Book One: The Escape From Home,* in *School Librarian,* Vol. 45, No. 4, November, 1997, p. 211.

This is part one of a two-part saga, set in England and Ireland of 1851, which recounts the hazardous journey of two Irish children in their attempts to escape the gruelling poverty of their homeland and join their father in the land of opportunity that is America. Running parallel with their story is that of poor little rich boy, Sir Laurence Kirkle, who runs away from the harsh treatment he receives at the hands of a scheming elder brother and misguided father and finds himself contemplating emigration as the only option. Inevitably, their paths gradually interwine.

This is an old-fashioned romping good read, full of Dickensian-style characters with names such as Mr Pickler and Sergeant Rumpkin. It is rich in historical detail, painting a vivid picture of life in this period, particularly in its descriptions of the old port of Liverpool. It is no surprise to learn that the author visited Cork, London and Liverpool in the course of his research.

An excellent adventure story that is somewhat out of vogue at the moment. Unfortunately, the all-important cover does little to promote it.

BEYOND THE WESTERN SEA, BOOK TWO: LORD KIRKLE'S MONEY (1996)

Publishers Weekly

SOURCE: A review of *Beyond the Western Sea, Book Two: Lord Kirkle's Money,* in *Publishers Weekly,* Vol. 243, No. 35, August 26, 1996, p. 98.

It is no small feat replicating the narrative style, character types and intricate plotting of a 19th-century serial novel, but Avi continues to accomplish the task with panache in Book Two of his ongoing saga about a family of poor Irish immigrants and the runaway son of an English lord. Just as good as its predecessor, *The Escape from Home,* this story begins where that book left off. Siblings Patrick and Maura O'Connell, aboard the *Robert Peel* on their way to meet their father in the U.S., are sharing cramped quarters with hundreds of other travelers. Lord Laurence Kirkle, robbed of his fortune, is a stowaway, while his two enemies, Mr. Clemspool and Mr. Grout, enjoy the comforts of first class accommodation. The stew of trouble that begins to simmer on ship comes to full boil when Patrick, Maura and Laurence finally set foot on land and discover just what kind of opportunity awaits them in America. Poverty, wretched working conditions, anti-Irish sentiments and news of Mr. O'Connell's death are only a few of the obstacles crossing the youngsters' paths. The future holds some promise for the characters by the time this book ends, but plenty of loose ends remain to whet appetites for another installment. Adventure lovers should not be intimidated by the thickness of this volume. Its short chapters full of clever narrative hooks and fast-paced adventure will keep most readers on the edge of their seats. Ages 11-14.

Wendy D. Caldiero

SOURCE: A review of *Beyond the Western Sea, Book Two: Lord Kirkle's Money,* in *School Library Journal,* Vol. 42, No. 10, October, 1996, p. 144.

Gr 6-9—This sequel to ***Beyond the Western Sea, Book One*** (Orchard, 1996) continues the adventures of Patrick and Maura O'Connell and their friends Mr. Horatio Drabble and Laurence Kirkle as they sail to America. This book begins with the four on board ship, with Laurence a stowaway and Maura, Patrick, and Mr. Drabble traveling in steerage. True to its Dickensian flavor, the villains are also on board. On arrival in Boston, all end up in the mill city of Lowell, MA. Patrick and Maura's father has died and the children find themselves facing anti-Irish sentiment, a greedy mill owner, poverty, inhuman working conditions, and, of course, all the villains. The action jumps back and forth from one person to another as their paths cross and recross. All characters "coincidentally" come together at the climax and the villains are vanquished. This is a well-written, but overly ambitious work that suffers from an overabundance of characters. The lack of a major hero and a primary villain fragments the work. Character development is minimal and the many different plots stop and start so often that the focus is lost. Avi's ability to use words and dialogue to develop a strong sense of time and place is evident and his theme that all people are created equal and that evil cannot be blamed on anything but evil individuals is strongly and clearly presented. For that reader who enjoys a well-written historical novel and who will not be deterred by the two-volume length or the complexity of the plots, this will satisfy if not excite.

Mary M. Burns

SOURCE: A review of *Beyond the Western Sea, Book Two: Lord Kirkle's Money,* in *The Horn Book Magazine,* Vol. 72, No. 6, November-December, 1996, p. 731.

Blockbuster epics are seldom found in books for children, but with this two-volume production, totaling 675 pages, Avi becomes a serious contender in the James Michener sweepstakes. For a precis of the eventful Book One, see the July/August 1996 Horn Book, page 461. The action resumes in Book Two as Patrick searches the hold where Laurence has stowed away; Maura fends off the love-smitten Mr. Drabble; Messrs. Clemspool and Grout find themselves again searching for Laurence Kirkle; and two new principals—eight-year-old Bridy Faherty and Ambrose Shagwell, an American mill owner—are added to the mix. Once more shifting scenes in a series of short, pithy chapters, Avi re-creates the horrendous conditions of the steerage quarters aboard the emigrant ships as well as the numbing environment of the nineteenth-century mills in Lowell, Massachusetts. Unaware that animosity against the Irish, fueled by the Know-Nothings, will threaten their dreams, Maura and Patrick land in America only to learn that their father is dead. With no other sanctuary, they, plus Bridy, head for Lowell. Eventually, Laurence, Mr. Drabble, and the newly penitent Mr. Grout join them as all elements are resolved, partly through the machinations of the embittered Mr. Jenkins, intent on destroying the Irish in general and one James Hamlyn in particular. Pacing and Dickensian characters add color and substance to a bravura performance, clearly the product of empathy and research. The virtuous, except for one tragic figure, are rewarded and the villains punished; the whole concludes on a hopeful note. An adventure in the grand style, the story benefits from its historical foundation and skillful plotting.

Elizabeth Bush

SOURCE: A review of *Beyond the Western Sea, Book Two: Lord Kirkle's Money,* in *Bulletin of the Center for Children's Books,* Vol. 50, No. 4, December, 1996, p. 128.

At the conclusion of Book One, exhausted emigrants Patrick and Maura were awaiting their steerage berth assignments, errant Sir Laurence was stowed away in a crate in the *Robert Peel's* hold, and readers were clenching their teeth firmly on their fingernails. Scarcely skipping a heartbeat between volumes, Avi lashes the action along, setting old enemies on the trio's trail and new obstacles in their path, most formidable of which is the Order of the Star-spangled Banner, an anti-immigrant organization lying in ambush in the children's promised land of Lowell, Massachusetts. Luckily, new allies join the side of the angels: Nathaniel, Da's teenaged roommate; the Hamlyns, kindly boarding house owners; even the once-treacherous Mr. Grout, now repentant and zealously atoning for past misdeeds. Taut and ingenious plotting, breakneck pacing, and meticulously timed shifts among story lines easily counter the Dickensian heft of the saga, and readers can expect to put their own lives on hold until the last villain is punished, all heroes and heroines are rewarded, and the back cover is slapped shut with a sigh of relief.

Donald R. Gallo

SOURCE: A review of *Beyond the Western Sea, Book Two: Lord Kirkle's Money,* in *The ALAN Review,* Vol. 24, No. 3, Spring, 1997, p. 380.

Adventure on the high seas, intrigue on the back streets, and a motley cast of characters propel this second half of Avi's lengthy two-part story focusing on poor Irish immigrants seeking a better life in the mill town of Lowell, Massachusetts, in 1851 and the prejudice that greets them there. If "yet be" attracted by novels like Pullman's *Ruby in the Smoke* and Avi's *The True Confessions of Charlotte Doyle,* then *Beyond the Western Sea* will suit "yer fancy." The books are filled with mysterious doings, with villains aplenty, and enough historical details to make the 1850s come alive for readers of any age. Although there is enough action in Book Two to carry it on its own, interested readers should start with Book One to fully understand the motivations of the characters, young and old, and the value of Lord Kirkle's money.

(Another clue is that Book Two begins with chapter 75.)

Janet Fisher

SOURCE: A review of *Beyond the Western Sea, Book Two: Lord Kirkle's Money,* in *School Librarian,* Vol. 45, No. 4, November, 1997, p. 211.

1. This is the sequel to *The Escape from Home* and judging by the ending there are more to come. Maura and Patrick are on their way to join their father in Lowell, Massachusetts, under the illusion he is rich, Helped by Mr Drabble, they survive the voyage across the Atlantic in steerage. Patrick is helping his friend Laurence to stow away and on board also are Mr Grout and Mr Clemspool who were instrumental in Laurence's flight. The complicated plot gets even more so but does at least settle down in Lowell, where anti-Irish fever is being fermented by Jeremiah Jenkins. The story wavers between farce and a good straight narrative and Avi needs to make his mind up which he wants this series to be. The scenes below deck have an authentic and tragic feel but then the narrative jumps to Grout and Clemspool and loses its way. This is a long book and unless the first one has been read, readers of 12 upwards might give up; but it is a good romp with moments of emotion and drama.

FINDING PROVIDENCE: THE STORY OF ROGER WILLIAMS (1997)

Kirkus Reviews

SOURCE: A review of *Finding Providence: The Story of Roger Williams,* in *Kirkus Reviews,* Vol. 65, January 1, 1997, p. 56.

Avi's first entry in the I Can Read chapter-book series tells the true story of Roger Williams's 1635 flight from arrest for "preaching dangerous new ideas." He heads into the wilds of colonial New England, eventually sending for his family to join him in founding a new settlement where religious freedom is allowed, which his daughter, the narrator, names Providence. The story covers only his decision to flee and the highlights of his subsequent journey, an odd time frame that leaves out the events leading up to Williams's trial, his life with the Indians, the rigors of founding a new settlement, or even much detail about the Puritan intolerance from which he fled. During the trial, only the gasps of spectators indicate the contrast between their views and his, the latter of which will seem right and just to contemporary readers, and therefore unfathomable as the basis for prosecution. The illustrations are soft and pale, lacking drama; many of the characters share the same expression, looking as if they are whistling. A complement to other sources on Williams's life—this is neither interesting enough for general readers, nor specific enough for those not already grounded in the facts.

Hazel Rochman

SOURCE: A review of *Finding Providence: The Story of Roger Williams,* in *Booklist,* Vol. 93, no. 11 February 1, 1997, p. 949.

Gr. 2-3. With powerful simplicity, Avi tells the story of Roger Williams, the devout Puritan preacher who was driven from the Massachusetts Bay Colony in 1635 because he stood up for the separation of church and state. This biography in the I Can Read Chapter Book series is told through the slightly fictionalized first-person narrative of Williams' young daughter, who witnesses the court case in Boston where Williams is accused of preaching for religious freedom and against the Europeans' right to Indian land. New readers will be caught by the drama of the court case and then by the historical adventure of Williams' escape into the wilderness, where he survives with the help of his Narraganset Indian friends and goes on to found the settlement of Providence, Rhode Island. Watling's glowing illustrations on every page create a strong sense of the period, though at times they almost overpower the spare text.

Elizabeth Bush

SOURCE: A review of *Finding Providence: The Story of Roger Williams,* in *Bulletin of the Center for Children's Books,* Vol. 50, No. 7, March, 1997, p. 240.

Among the more challenging entries in the I Can Read series, this tale of the man who defied Puritan leaders to defend religious liberty offers readers an introductory course in colonial political theory as well as an exciting story of escape and survival. Williams' daughter Mary narrates five brief chapters covering her father's Massachusetts trial, the warning of his impending deportation, the decision to flee, his survival in the wilderness, and his settlement among the Narragansetts in what would become Providence, Rhode Island. Plentiful dialogue speeds the action along, and even the philosophical issues are cogently presented for young readers in the form of Williams' interrogation at the trial. Watling's watercolors have a rough-hewn quality appropriate to the early colonies, and his grave figures are charged with tension. Students will find this a strong choice for beginner history reports, but an ambitious social-studies teacher might also consider converting the conversations and limited settings into a play, bringing everyone into the act.

Maeve Visser Knoth

SOURCE: A review of *Finding Providence: The Story of Roger Williams,* in *The Horn Book Magazine,* Vol. 73, No. 3, May-June, 1997, p. 313.

Avi's foray into the beginning-reader genre is a fictional account of Roger Williams's escape from Massachusetts and his settlement of Providence, Rhode Island. The historical chronicle is told by Williams's daughter and covers a few brief episodes in Colonial history. While Roger Williams is on trial in the Massachusetts Bay Colony for his belief in the separation of church and state, he is warned that he is to be sent back to England. Rather than be captured, Williams leaves his family to journey through the wilderness to find a new place to settle. Though his success is never in doubt (both the title and the choice of narrator guarantee that), this account of how he achieves it is acceptable history and a good story. Watercolor illustrations in shades of brown and green contribute to this portrait of Williams as a serious man driven by strong beliefs. An author's note provides a larger historical context in which to place the story.

WHAT DO FISH HAVE TO DO WITH ANYTHING?, AND OTHER STORIES (1997)

Deborah Stevenson

SOURCE: A review of *What Do Fish Have to Do with Anything?, and Other Stories,* in *Bulletin of the Center for Children's Books,* Vol. 51, No. 2, October, 1997, p. 43.

The seven stories here all seem to focus on kids in quandaries who are trying to find a way out. In **"The Goodness of Matt Kaizer,"** a troublemaking preacher's kid is mistaken for an angel by a dying man; Gregory aims to become a **"Teacher Tamer"** when Mrs. Wessex picks on him unjustly once too often; Eve is alarmed when her beloved cats refuse to leave her alone after their death in **"Pets."** The stories are direct and explanatory, without the vignettish subtleties that sometimes go over the heads of younger readers, and the points will be clear even to the literarily inexperienced. If anything, Avi errs a bit too much in the direction of clarity, contriving his plot packages too tidily and writing with more smoothness than excitement or energy. Kids with aims for loftier stuff than Paul Jennings (see *Unbearable,* and others) but not quite ready for Tim Wynne-Jones (*Some of the Kinder Planets,* will appreciate the approachable entries here. A new-wavy black-and-white print decorates each story.

Publishers Weekly

SOURCE: A review of *What Do Fish Have to Do with Anything?, and Other Stories,* in *Publishers Weekly,* Vol. 244, No. 44, October 27, 1997, p. 77.

Avi (*City of Light, City of Dark*) is in top form constructing these seven surprising stories. Seemingly ordinary events (offering a handout, getting a series of hang-ups on the telephone, eating Chinese food) take unexpected turns, leading Avi's middle-school heroes and heroines (and readers) to profound, often disturbing truths. Will, the protagonist of the title story, gains insight into his newly separated mother's unhappiness after talking with a philosophical beggar outside his apartment building. In **"Talk to Me,"** Maria O'Sullivan comes to grips with the disappearance of her brother, who left home at 16, during a series of one-sided conversations with a mysterious, silent caller. Parker, the narrator of **"Fortune Cookie,"** thinks his birthday "belongs to [him], like writing your own fortune cookie," and, for a present, asks his recently divorced parents if they will both take him to dinner. The outing proves disastrous, but he leaves the restaurant with a clearer understanding of his feelings about his mother, father and himself. Each of the selections, characterized by a sharp and often dark ironic twist, is like a carefully packaged parcel. The process of unwrapping its layers is almost as exciting as finding the pearl of wisdom inside. Ages 10-14.

Kirkus Reviews

SOURCE: A review of *What Do Fish Have to Do with Anything?, and Other Stories,* in *Kirkus Reviews,* Vol. 65, November 1, 1997, p. 1640.

Avi (*Finding Providence,* etc.) has experimented with virtually every literary form; here the versatile veteran returns to short fiction with seven thoughtful tales. In the title story a sixth grader's melancholy in the wake of his father's departure breaks when a street person offers a cure for unhappiness; the light tone of the following tale, **"The Goodness of Matt Kaizer,"** in which a daredevil minister's son learns, to his regret, that he's fundamentally a decent sort, gives way to the eeriness of **"Talk To Me,"** about a telephone that takes to ringing at exactly 4:00—but no one is on the line. In other episodes, Eve's dead **"Pets"** return to rescue her from two demanding ghost cats, a seventh grader finds out **"What's Inside"** when he narrowly thwarts an older cousin's

suicide, and Gregory realizes that a compliment makes a better **"Teacher Tamer"** than a stink bomb. Mitchell contributes small black-and-white chapter openers, mostly portraits, to each story. Appealingly varied in tone and narrative voice, rich in character insights, and replete with imaginatively presented ideas, these tales offer something to please almost everyone.

Time for Kids

SOURCE: A review of *What Do Fish Have to Do with Anything?, and Other Stories,* in *Time for Kids,* Vol. 3, No. 9, November 14, 1997, p. 8.

Which author has one name, two Newbery Honors and seven new short stories for kids? If you guessed AVI (Ah-vee), you must be one of thousands of fans who gobble up his vivid, realistic books about capable, thoughtful kids. "A girl wrote to me, 'Please write a sequel to *The True Confessions of Charlotte Doyle.* I've read it 16 times, and my mother won't let me read it anymore!'" says the Boulder, Colorado, author.

His new book of stories, *What Do Fish Have to Do with Anything?* was harder to write than a long book that tells a single story. The less space there is to tell a story, he says, the more each word counts: "Short stories have to be perfect. You read each one all in one gulp."

Michael Cart

SOURCE: A review of *What Do Fish Have to Do with Anything?, and Other Stories,* in *Booklist,* Vol. 94, No. 6, November 15, 1997, p. 557.

Gr. 5-8. The ever-versatile Avi serves up a collection of seven stories about kids teetering on the brink of adolescence. Happily, angst is less the order of the day here than irony, which takes the form of some pretty nifty plot twists. In **"The Goodness of Matt Kalzer,"** for example, the baddest kid in town (the eponymous Matt) is mistaken for an angel and turns into the bestest—er, best! But it's authentic emotional insights that provide the surprises and right-on rites of passage in the most successful of the stories—the title tale and **"Fortune Cookie,"** which is further enhanced by a character-defining first-person voice. Another solid performance by an important writer.

Marilyn Bousquin

SOURCE: A review of *What Do Fish Have to Do with Anything?, and Other Stories,* in *The Horn Book Magazine,* Vol. 73, No. 6, November-December, 1997, p. 676.

In these seven stories Avi's taut style and snip-snap dialogue zero in on a variety of ways in which adolescents realize their own power to effect a course of action. **"What's Inside"** provides the most obvious example when an unnamed thirteen-year-old boy makes a quick-witted, albeit risky, decision that prevents his fifteen-year-old cousin from committing suicide. In other stories, Eve rescues herself from being victimized by the ghosts of her dead cats; Matt, whose reputation hinges on his being "bad," confronts the disheartening possibility that he may actually want to be "good"; and Gregory, set to avenge his teacher for falsely indicting him, changes his mind after hearing (and taking to heart) her side of the story. While Avi's endings are not tidy, they are effective: each story brings its protagonist beyond childhood self-absorption to the realization that one is an integral part of a bigger picture.

Carol A. Edwards

SOURCE: A review of *What Do Fish Have to Do with Anything?, and Other Stories,* in *School Library Journal,* Vol. 43, No. 12, December, 1997, p. 120.

Gr 4-8—These short stories affirm the ability of their main characters to choose their fate. In the title story, Willie bravely searches for the cure for unhappiness. It, and the other stories, show readers the resilience and power of kids using their eyes and minds over accepting conventional adult wisdom. In **"Pets,"** Eve comes up with a solution to the ghost cats who want her to join them, even though she is desperately ill. In **"Teacher Tamer,"** Gregory sneaks into the house of his teacher to seek revenge for her persecution of him; instead, he comes to understand her. Whether facing a domineering mother, divorced parents, or a reputation as a bad guy, the protagonists take positive steps forward. It is this constant of taking action, of choosing the halo over the pitchfork, that make these stories inspiring. Some characters are crass and brash; others are introspective and quiet. Danger lurks in guns, ghosts, strangers, and unjust adults. It's a rare treat to be so surprised so consistently in a collection of stories that still adheres to its theme. Unpredictable and fun, these selections stand out for their inventiveness in dealing with difficult issues in a positive way without sacrificing the honest voices of real kids.

Donna Scanlon

SOURCE: A review of *What Do Fish Have to Do with Anything?, and Other Stories,* in *Voice of Youth Advocates,* Vol. 21, No. 1, April, 1998, p. 44.

Once again, Avi demonstrates his versatility and insight in this collection of seven short stories that take aim at the heart of familiar adolescent emotional storms. The main characters in each story face a personal transformation, one which affects that individual alone. Each faces a choice and makes a decision; no outside intervention directly affects the outcome as much as the action, or lack of action, of the protagonist. In the title story, a boy asserts his independence and individuality, while in **"Talk to Me,"** Maria exorcises some of her pain over her runaway brother. In **"The Goodness of Matt Kaizer,"** a minister's son accepts a dare to be good and is dismayed to discover his true nature. Eve's love for her cats is tested in **"Pets,"** while Gregory and his teacher test each other in **"Teacher Tamer."** A boy draws on both ingenuity and courage to save his cousin's life in **"What's Inside,"** and another boy comes to terms with his family's circumstances in **"Fortune Cookie."** Each character is at once unique and recognizable; for many teens, reading the stories will be like looking in a mirror. By turns funny, poignant, and thought provoking, these stories continue to confirm Avi's reputation for writing inventive, on-target tales for young adults.

POPPY AND RYE (1998)

Sally Estes

SOURCE: A review of *Poppy and Rye,* in Booklist, Vol. 94, No. 18, May 15, 1998, p. 1625.

Gr. 4-6. In this sequel to *Poppy,* a Youth Editors' Choice '95, the intrepid deer mouse Poppy persuades her curmudgeonly porcupine friend Ereth to accompany her on a trek to tell Ragweed's family how her beloved golden mouse had met an untimely death. Although Ereth grumbles his way west, the pair eventually reach "The Brook," where the golden mouse family lives, only to discover that the family has been forced to move because the brook has been dammed by beavers ("Canad and Co. 'Progress Without Pain,' that's our motto"), and the mouse family's home has been flooded. With Poppy's planning and help, the golden mice manage to defeat the beavers, driving them away and breaking the dam. In the process, Poppy and Rye, Ragweed's brother, fall in love.

The battle against the beavers is exciting. Rye is captured sneaking into the beavers' lodge and held prisoner; Poppy makes her way by raft to the lodge and enters through a vent hole and almost drowns as she escapes. As he took on the politics of power in *Poppy*, Avi here tackles the advance of progress for the sake of progress, no matter the consequences. With the exception of Poppy and Ereth, characters lack the fine development of those in the first book, but Poppy's fans will welcome her return and cheer her on in her new adventure.

Beth Wright

SOURCE: A review of *Poppy and Rye,* in *School Library Journal,* Vol. 44, No. 6, June, 1998, p. 94.

Gr 3-6—This novel tells the story, as promised in the final pages of *Poppy* (Orchard, 1995), of how the courageous deer mouse met and married her husband Rye. Picking up Poppy's story after her victory over Mr. Ocax the owl, Avi chronicles her quest to find her late fiance's family and tell them of his death in Mr. Ocax's claws. The couple meet early in her journey, but their growing love is temporarily thwarted by Rye's imprisonment within the lodge of cliche-spouting, indefatigably eager beavers. He is also hindered by his fears that he can't live up to Poppy's memories of Ragweed, who was Rye's sometimes admired, sometimes despised older brother. Unfortunately, the mouse's conflicting feelings about his brother are never clearly resolved, and Rye remains a less-developed character than Poppy, whose growth from timid to brave is one of the previous book's chief delights. *Poppy and Rye* also loses steam during a distracting subplot featuring Ereth the porcupine's cranky (and unrequited) love for Poppy, but it will still appeal to fans of the first book.

Kirkus Reviews

SOURCE: A review of *Poppy and Rye,* in *Kirkus Reviews,* Vol. 66, June 1, 1998, p. 808.

Still grieving over the loss of her beau Ragweed of *Poppy* (1995), the intrepid deer mouse decides to bring the sad news to his family in this uneven, heavy-handed sequel. Setting out from Dimwood Forest with her hopelessly infatuated porcupine friend, Ereth, Poppy arrives just in time to help Ragweed's parents and numerous siblings avert eviction. Led by ruthless Caster P. Canad, a crew of beavers has dammed up the nearby brook in preparation for a housing project. The mice have already been flooded out of one home, and their new one is about to be threatened. Saddened—but also secretly relieved to be out from under his brother's shadow—dreamy Rye dashes out to see what he can do against the beavers, and is quickly captured. Having fallen in love with him at first sight, Poppy organizes a rescue, urging the meek mice to fight back; they do. The bad guys silently depart, and Poppy and Rye set a date. Avi develops his characters to a level of complexity that provides a distracting contrast with the simplistic story, an obvious take on human land-use disputes, and easily distinguishable victims and villains. In language more ugly than colorful, Ereth chews over his feelings for Poppy in several plot-stopping passages, and is last seen accompanying the happy couple back to Dimwood. Readers may wonder who to root for in this disappointing follow-up to one of the best animal stories in years.

Publishers Weekly

SOURCE: A review of *Poppy and Rye,* in *Publishers Weekly,* Vol. 245, No. 24, June 15, 1998, p. 60.

The spirited mouse star from *Poppy* must now face life after Ragweed (her fiancé who was killed by an owl). Poppy and her curmudgeonly porcupine friend Ereth leave Dimwood Forest in search of Ragweed's parents to tell them the sad news so that Poppy can "get on with her life." When they finally reach their destination, they discover it's hardly the "dullsville" that Ragweed had described. In fact, his family has been forced to leave their comfortable nest and move to higher ground: a clan of development-mad beavers are flooding out the residents in their efforts to turn the pastoral backwater into "Canad's Cute Condos." Along the way, Poppy encounters Ragweed's dreamy, poetic brother Rye, and before long the two mice are head over paws in love. When a showdown between the scheming beavers and the reluctantly heroic mice puts Rye in danger, Poppy risks everything to save him. Of course, all's well that ends well in this rollicking tale, which Avi infuses with generous helpings of adventure, romance and humor. He juggles multiple story lines effortlessly, and his characterizations are particularly engaging, from the blustering Caster P. Canad ("Bless my teeth and smooth my tail!"), head of the beaver coterie, to the smart-mouthed Ereth ("Look here, you pickle-tailed fur booger"). This thoroughly enjoyable sequel is sure to please old fans and will likely win some new ones. Ages 8-12.

Ann A. Flowers

SOURCE: A review of *Poppy and Rye,* in *The Horn Book Magazine,* Vol. 74, No. 4, July-August, 1998, p. 482.

In *Poppy* the eponymous mouse heroine lost her first love, Ragweed, and now she is journeying to tell his family of his unfortunate fate. Accompanying Poppy on her expedition is Ereth the porcupine—grumpy, smelly, foul-mouthed, and hostile to change, but a good friend under duress. Poppy meets a charming golden mouse who looks like Ragweed, and who in fact is later revealed to be his younger brother, Rye. When Poppy finds Ragweed's family, they are in the midst of a crisis: beavers have flooded their brook, forcing them to move, and even their new home is under threat. The beavers are led by Mr. Caster B. Canad, a sly takeoff on the slick-talking, amoral businessman, the master of cliché who promises everything but gives nothing ("a stranger is just a friend you haven't met. And I mean that, sincerely"). After Rye is captured by the beavers and trapped inside their lodge, Poppy leads an expedition to save him, and his family, galvanized by Poppy's bravery, plans to destroy the dam. The final desperate and one-sided battle of mice vs. beavers is decided by the sudden appearance of Ereth, whose quills even the beavers fear. The happy ending has a slight undertone of sadness, as Ereth, a misanthropist to the core, realizes that he loves Poppy, a thought so distasteful that he complains bitterly, "Love . . . Nothing but slug splat stew and toad jam. Phooey." The anthropomorphic characterization is spot-on: Ereth; Rye, chafing in the shadow of his older brother; Valerian, Rye's father, who will remind some readers of Father in Robert Lawson's *Rabbit Hill.* Accompanied once again by Brian Floca's witty yet pastoral pencil drawings, this is a sequel worthy of its predecessor.

Maura Bresnahan

SOURCE: A review of *Poppy and Rye,* in *Voice of Youth Advocates,* Vol. 21, No. 5, December, 1998, p. 362.

Fans of Avi's *Poppy* (Orchard, 1995) will find this sequel an entertaining read. As readers of the first story will remember, Poppy was determined to find the family of her deceased fiance Ragweed and let them know of his death. *Poppy and Rye* details Poppy's journey to the home of Ragweed's parents with her irascible porcupine friend Ereth. Avi delivers a romantic adventure to his audience when Poppy finds herself falling in love with Ragweed's younger brother Rye while at the same time helping his family survive the encroachment of a band of industrious beavers. The beavers are led by Caster P. Canad, who tosses mottoes and slogans around in the same manner that Ereth spews his opinions. Canad's "progress without pain" campaign to dam The Brook where the golden mice live leaves Rye's family fighting to survive as their home and resources are flooded. Poppy and Rye use their wits and bravely defend the rights of the golden mice to maintain their home against the more powerful beaver population. The fast-paced and dramatic fight for survival against the beavers provides a climax young readers will enjoy. Fans of Ereth's alliterative mutterings will not be disappointed either as Avi, once again, has the porcupine spouting some hilarious expressions. Readers waiting for the answers as to how Poppy and Rye met will be satisfied here.

PERLOO THE BOLD (1998)

Kirkus Reviews

SOURCE: A review of *Perloo the Bold,* in *Kirkus Reviews,* Vol. 66, October 15, 1998, p. 1528.

Fans of Brian Jacques's Redwall doorstoppers will hear echoes in this animal fantasy, although Avi (*Poppy and Rye,* etc.) not only has the vegetarians attacking the carnivores, but throws in other clever twists too. A mild-mannered, rabbit-like Montmer, Perloo is drawn away from his books when the dying Montmer "granter" dubs him her successor. When the seat of power is instantly usurped by the granter's son Berwig the Big and his greasy advisor Senyous the Sly, Perloo is forced to flee to the coyote-like Felbarts, traditional enemies against whom Berwig has proclaimed a war to cement his position. Amid a welter of captures and escapes, Perloo's doughty ally Lucabara gathers her friends for an uprising at home, Berwig and Senyous reveal the depths of their stupidity and villainy, and Perloo discovers that the Felbarts aren't so bad. When the rival armies finally meet, Perloo faces Senyous in single combat. Drawing on his one martial skill, Perloo defeats Senyous with a barrage of snowballs, after which the cowardly Berwig renounces his grantership, and Perloo, declaring that henceforth all Montmer decisions will be made collectively, does too. For all the soldiers and warlike behavior here, the story is free of bloodshed, and if the characters are less robust than Redwall's stars, they're also less typecast. Perhaps inevitably, there are plenty of loose ends to tie up in a sequel.

Janice M. Del Negro

SOURCE: A review of *Perloo the Bold,* in *Bulletin of the Center for Children's Books,* Vol. 52, No. 3, November, 1998, p. 87.

This political fantasy pits the Montmers ("a mix of jackrabbits, prairie dogs, and humans") against the Felbarts ("an alarming mix of human and coyote") in a battle for domination of snowy Rocky Mountain terrain. On her deathbed, Granter Jolaine chooses Perloo (the Unwilling) over her vile son Berwig to be the next granter, the new leader of the Montmers. Berwig furiously attempts to cover up Jolaine's choice by accusing Perloo and Lucabara, Jolaine's first assistant, of murdering Jolaine. Perloo and Lucabara escape, Perloo finding unexpected assistance among their Felbart enemies and Lucabara leading the rebel resistance against Berwig. In a confrontation between the Montmers and the Felbarts, Perloo defeats Berwig's slimy challenger with the help of some well-aimed snowballs. The fantasy environment here is tightly controlled if relatively slight, featuring the insides of warrens and burrows, with the occasional venture onto snowy slopes. There is little characterization outside of that which is necessary to the plot, but the physical descriptions of the villains double easily as character development. The scattering throughout of the sayings of the philosopher Mogwat the Magpie acts as a unifying element and leads readers painlessly to conclusions about power corrupting individuals, fascism being bad, and democracy being good. Perloo's decision to abdicate his role as granter in favor of Montmer self-rule is seen as an indication of his modesty and wisdom, but as all he's done throughout is regret Jolaine's choice of him as granter, it seems more self-serving than anything else. Still, the action is quick, and those pre-Redwall readers who have a yen for animal fantasy will be happy to come along.

Jennifer A. Fakolt

SOURCE: A review of *Perloo the Bold,* in *School Library Journal,* Vol. 44, No. 11, November, 1998, p. 116.

Gr 4-6—In this mildly whimsical fantasy, Avi introduces the Montmers, a race of creatures that are part jackrabbit, part prairie dog, and part human. Jolaine, the elderly chief Granter of the tribe, takes ill and dies, but not before she bestows her leadership on Perloo, a bookish loner who prefers history to reality, instead of on her pompous son, Berwig. Perloo is aghast at this new title and is immediately thrown into conflict with Berwig, who institutes martial law and accuses his rival of murdering Jolaine. Political subterfuge flourishes as Berwig's counselor plots against him. Still trying to resist his responsibility, Perloo is taken captive by the Montmers' archenemies, the Felbarts, part human, part coyote, who are preparing to defend themselves against Berwig's declaration of war. Perloo rises to the occasion in an ending reminiscent of David and Goliath, and learns some valuable lessons about courage. Unfortunately, the action lacks suspense, and the Montmers themselves fail to elicit sympathy. The story is sprinkled with words of wisdom from the creatures' philosopher, Mogwat the Magpie, who preaches peace, unity, courage, truth, and democracy; although these are admirable values, they become burdensome in the thin text. Though this tale is geared for a younger audience, it invites comparison to Brian Jacques's "Redwall" series (Philomel), and there it falls short, lacking the depth of characterization and spirit, and the rich detail of those books. A light read.

Publishers Weekly

SOURCE: A review of *Perloo the Bold,* in *Publishers Weekly,* November 23, 1998, p. 67.

Avi (*The True Confessions of Charlotte Doyle*) flexes his creative muscles again, this time with a book that "fits in the 'fun' category" as he comments in a publicity letter. Featuring endearing creatures called Montmers—a combination of jackrabbit, prairie dog and human—this fantasy/adventure also offers a sharp satire on political greed. Mild-mannered Perloo enjoys a quiet life in the Rock Mountains, reading Montmer history and mythology, until his tribe's dying "granter" or leader, Jolaine, names him her successor. But before he even has a chance to accept the honor, he is ousted by Jolaine's scheming son, Berwig, who is eager to declare war against the neighboring Felbarts (they are half-coyote, half-human). Perloo flees for his life, ends up with the Felbarts, negotiates with their leader and single-handedly prevents Berwig's advancing troops from attacking. While keeping bloodshed and violence to a minimum, Avi produces an exciting, suspenseful and witty tale of conspiracy and warfare strategy, pitting Perloo's knowledge and high morality against Berwig's lust for glory. Perloo retains his position as granter just long enough to relinquish it and award the Montmers complete freedom to rule themselves. Formation of a new Montmer government should provide plenty of material for a sequel. Ages 10-up.

Diane Tuccillo

SOURCE: A review of *Perloo the Bold,* in *Voice of Youth Advocates,* Vol. 21, No. 5, December, 1998, p. 362.

Avi has created a whole new world in his latest novel, a fantasy involving Montmers (part jackrabbit, part prairie dog, part human) and their assumed enemies, the Felbarts (part coyote, part human). Perloo, a Montmer well-versed in history, is disturbed in his cozy burrow one day, much like Bilbo Baggins is disturbed in *The Hobbit.* As Bilbo was summoned to go on an adventure, so too is Perloo summoned by Lucabara, a fellow Montmer, who demands he accompany her to see their dying leader, Granter Jolaine. Jolaine has decided that Perloo, "learned but modest," shall be the next Granter—and not her pompous, inept son, Berwig, who wishes to start a war. After Jolaine's death, Perloo finds himself tossed into a struggle for power he never wanted. Perloo's fight against Berwig and his cohorts takes him to the very caves of the Felbarts, where he comes to terms with the Felbart leader and finds the fate of both societies in his hands. Perloo manages to save the day through his use of very unorthodox weapons—snowballs! Avi has brought these creatures and their world to life in a fast-paced, compelling read that will keep middle schoolers turning pages. The wise sayings of the Montmer and Felbart guru, Mogwat the Magpie, are effectively integrated into the tale. They reinforce the underlying messages that people are more alike than they are different and that happiness lies in upstanding living. Younger fans of Brian Jacques's Redwall series will especially enjoy this story.

Sally Estes

SOURCE: A review of *Perloo the Bold,* in *Booklist,* Vol. 95, No. 8, December 15, 1998, p. 749.

Gr. 4-7. In a departure even from *Poppy* (1995), Avi offers a gentle animal fantasy involving an unlikely hero and the threat of war between longtime enemies, the Montmer tribe and the Felbart pack. The Montmers are jackrabbitlike creatures, the Felbarts, coyotelike. Perloo, an unassuming Montmer scholar who lives alone in an isolated burrow, is summoned to the death-bed of Granter Jolaine, the Montmer leader. She wants to put aside her brutish son, Berwig the Big, and name Perloo the next Granter. Berwig, however, with the help of Senyous the Sly, seizes power when Jolaine dies, claiming that Perloo murdered her. Perloo escapes, along with Lucabara, Jolaine's first assistant, only to fall into the Felbarts' cave, where he discovers that Berwig has already declared war. The plot follows various threads: Berwig, Senyous, and their double-dealing spy as they scheme against one another, each planning to do in the others, all the while waging war; Lucabara's efforts to start a rebellion and free Berwig's many prisoners; and Perloo's experiences among the Felbarts, as he tries to work with them and ends up being their reluctant champion when the Montmer army arrives. It is Perloo's modesty and honesty, as well as his knowledge of history, that win the day and that underlie the message of the story. Try this tale with your younger Redwall fans.

Nicholas J. Karolides

SOURCE: A review of *Perloo the Bold,* in *The ALAN Review,* Vol. 26, No. 2, Winter, 1999, p. 225.

Perloo, a reclusive scholar, is ensnared in the intrigue of Granter Jolene's death when she names him as her successor. Dubbed "Perloo the Unwilling" when he resists this honor, he is forced by the situation to act despite his fears and trepidation. Berwig, the self-proclaimed granter, jails Perloo while planning a war to gain glory and promote his claim to the succession. Perloo, however, escapes with Lubcabra, Jolene's first assistant; they are captured by the enemy. A satisfactory resolution is achieved many twists, travails, and surprises later, after which Perloo receives his new appellation. Within this adventure among anthropomorphic creatures, issues of greed/power and freedom/personal identity are explored. Interspersed in the text are pithy statements attributed to the great teacher Mogwat, such as, "Of all challenges, the greatest is to be yourself." This engaging fantasy will ensnare young readers immediately; Perloo, atypically devoid of heroics, will captivate them.

The Horn Book Magazine

SOURCE: A review of *Perloo the Bold,* in *The Horn Book Magazine,* Vol. 75, No. 1, January, 1999, p. 58.

Perloo is apprehensive when a fellow Montmer comes to his burrow with an urgent appeal from Jolaine the Good, "granter" of the Montmers, a jackrabbitish folk who have lived in peace and contentment for many years. Until now: Jolaine is dying, and she does not want her war-mongering (and stupid) son Berwig the Big to succeed her. She wants—of all Montmers!—the bookish and reclusive Perloo instead. The story goes pretty much the way you would expect it to, with a torn-in-two proclamation confusing Jolaine's intentions; Berwig assuming the throne with the help of the treacherous, double-dealing Senyous; and Perloo and his ally Lucabara captured and escaping a number of times until they foil the evil-doers and restore honor to the Montmer throne. The conclusion is more whimsical than it has a right to be: suffice it to say that no blood is spilled. Easier-going than the Redwall books, not as richly developed as Avi's own Poppy, Perloo the Bold is a Disneyesque animal fantasy, with theatrical dialogue, good guys (and a girl) to root for, a high-minded but firm-footed theme, and tons of action. Walt, you listening?

📖 *ABIGAIL TAKES THE WHEEL* (1999)

Marilyn Bousquin

SOURCE: A review of *Abigail Takes the Wheel*, in *The Horn Book Magazine*, Vol. 75, No. 2, March, 1999, p. 206.

The day this story takes place—sometime in the late nineteenth century—begins ordinarily enough: Tom and Abigail Bates watch vegetables being loaded onto the freight boat Neptune. Their father, Captain Bates, transports the vegetables from New Jersey to New York City, where Abigail and Tom disembark for school. They are barely out of the harbor when a string of action-packed circumstances finds Abigail not only at the wheel of the Neptune (which she has steered with her father often) but towing a large, disabled sailing ship up the Hudson River to Pier Forty-two. Avi discloses (in an appended author's note) that he based this voyage on a story which appeared in an 1881 copy of St. Nicholas magazine where it was "presented as neither fiction nor nonfiction, simply as an account of something heroic that happened." As in his debut I Can Read book, *Finding Providence* (rev. 5/97), Avi's generous dose of adventure and suspense, combined with his straightforward yet compelling story-telling style, custom-fit this revived tale for new chapter-book readers. Don Bolognese creates a turn-of-the-century nautical atmosphere with subdued watercolors that never overwhelm the text.

Hazel Rochman

SOURCE: A review of *Abigail Takes the Wheel*, in *Booklist*, Vol. 95, No. 15, April 1, 1999, p. 1424.

Gr. 2-4, younger for reading aloud. A young girl takes over the wheel, proves herself a hero, and saves the day in two stories set a century ago.

Avi's simple chapter book in the I Can Read series takes place on a boat in the waterways between New Jersey and New York in the 1880s. The first mate gets sick, and schoolgirl Abigail must step into his place and take over steering their small freight boat with a sailing ship in tow up the crowded Hudson River and through the harbor in New York City. The action-packed pictures in line and watercolor are an integral part of the story, and new readers will be caught by the exciting details of Abigail's maneuvers as she handles her task with the help of her younger brother, and narrowly avoids a series of collisions with the steam-driven ships and the sailing ships in the busy thoroughfare. Avi says in an afterword that the story (which he guesses is true) is based on an account published in a children's magazine of the time.

Kirkus Reviews

SOURCE: *A review of Abigail Takes the Wheel*, in *Kirkus Reviews*, Vol. 67, April 15, 1999, p. 626.

In the I Can Read Chapter Book series, Avi returns to some surefire ingredients—a girl and the boat she eventually pilots—though for a far younger audience than that for **The True Confessions of Charlotte Doyle**. Every day, Abigail Bates, brother Tom, and their father, Captain Bates, leave Old Port, in New Jersey, in their paddle wheel freight boat and home, the Neptune. On board is a load of fresh vegetables intended for buyers in New York City, 20 miles up the Hudson. One morning, as they leave Old Port, two sailing ships collide; Captain Bates offers to tow one of them to New York, but under harbor law, he has to take her wheel. He leaves first mate Mr. Oliver to pilot the Neptune, but Mr. Oliver becomes ill and hands the wheel over to Abigail. Scared but game, Abigail navigates the two ships through the busy river traffic, barely escaping another collision and ingeniously maneuvering the stricken sailing ship to safe berth. Predictably, for her courage and skill, she is made an honorary captain. Abigail is a spunky heroine cast in a sturdy story; the suspense will hold readers just ready for chapter books. The surprise in the competent illustrations, which conjure the late 19th-century setting, is the insertion of some unexpected diversity in the casting of the first mate.

Faith Brautigan

SOURCE: A review of *Abigail Takes the Wheel*, in *School Library Journal*, Vol. 45, No. 5, May, 1999, p. 85.

Gr 2-3—An easy-reader set in the 1880s. Abigail and Tom have made the 20-mile trip from Old Port, NJ, to New York City on their family's freight boat hundreds of times. Things take a surprising turn, though, when their father takes the helm of a damaged sailing ship they are towing into harbor and Abigail must take charge of the *Neptune* when the first mate falls ill. She navigates the freighter safely through to its final destination where she is lauded by the crews of both vessels. An author's note states that the tale is based on a story that appeared in *St. Nicholas* magazine in 1881. The setting is eastablished largely through the illustrations, from the characters' suspenders, aprons, and lace-up boots to the engine being stoked. Muted colors and a predominance of earth tones add to the atmosphere. Although the dialogue and third-person narrative have no particular period flavor, the boat signals and maneuvers are vividly described. The child-saves-the-day story line will appeal to youngsters whose daydreams tend to feature themselves as the heroic protagonists. With minimal characterization, this is a carefully illustrated, plot-driven adventure for transitional readers.

Deborah Stevenson

SOURCE: A review of *Abigail Takes the Wheel*, in *Bulletin of the Center for Children's Books,* Vol. 52, No. 10, June, 1999, p. 343.

Abigail is an old hand on her father's frieght boat, the *Neptune*, which plies the waters between the family's New Jersey home and the New York harbor. On an ordinary boat-trip to school, the *Neptune* assists a wounded three-master by giving her a tow, which requires Abigail's father to handle the towed boat while his first mate handles the *Neptune*. First Mate Mr. Oliver falls ill, however, and it suddenly becomes Abigail's job to take the *Neptune* into the busy port without harming her or the vessel she tows. The text is easy and adventurous, with an appealing capable heroine and nautical twist. An author's note states that he based the book on a story from an 1881 *St. Nicholas,* and it has an old-fashioned flair appropriate to that old classic; Avi has also managed to keep the events in their original period without cluttering them up with self-consciousness about that era's since becoming history. Bolognese's line-and-watercolor art is a bit blandly overtidy, especially in the human figures, but his line-festooned ships and sharp bows slicing through the green waves convey the milieu effectively. Readers who wish they were ready for *The True Confessions of Charlotte Doyle* will find this a pleasing stand-in.

RAGWEED: A TALE FROM DIMWOOD FOREST (1999)

Kirkus Reviews

SOURCE: A review of *Ragweed: A Tale from Dimwood Forest, Kirkus Reviews* Vol. 67, April 15, 1999, p. 626.

Avi elaborates on the "city mouse, country mouse" theme in this rousing prequel to *Poppy* (1995), starring Poppy's ill-fated beau. Impelled by wanderlust to hop a train to who-knows-where, Ragweed ends up in the rundown part of Amperville, where the local mice (all named after car parts) are being terrorized by Felines Enraged About Rodents (F.E.A.R.), a two-cat extermination squad led by evil-tempered Silversides. After several brushes with death, Ragweed defiantly teams up with Clutch, green-furred lead guitarist for the B-Flat Tires, to open a dance club for mice only, then in the climax organizes a devastating counterattack that sends F.E.A.R. scurrying out of town. In the end, though, Ragweed opts for the country life (little knowing that it's going to be sweet but short). A colorful cast in which even the ferocious Silversides comes in for a dash or two of sympathy, plus a plot replete with, of course, narrow squeaks will keep readers turning the pages, while Floca's scenes of tiny mice fleeing looming, toothy predators add more than a touch of drama.

Publishers Weekly

SOURCE: A review of *Ragweed: A Tale from Dimwood Forest,* in *Publishers Weekly,* Vol. 246, No. 19, May 10, 1999, p. 68.

Consummate storyteller Avi outdoes himself in this prequel to *Poppy* and *Poppy and Rye*, cutting loose with a crackerjack tale that's pure delight from start to finish. Here Ragweed, the adventurous mouse with whom Poppy is destined for a tragic romance, hops a train and heads for the bright lights of the big city. The hip urban setting hops with adventure and memorable characters, from the punk-haired mouse Clutch, who plays lead guitar for the Be-Flat Tires at the Cheese Squeeze Club, to Silversides, the malevolent puss president of F.E.A.R. ("Felines Enraged About Rodents"). Ragweed is wowed by the excitement of Amperville, with its abundance of "human nests," and quickly evolves from bumpkin to city slicker, picking up the lingo and mastering the "high four" paw slap. But cat-mouse hostilities escalate, with the cats destroying the Cheese Squeeze Club (the mice set up a new hang-out in an abandoned building once known as The Last Independent Bookstore). Ragweed rallies his fellow mice to lead a revolt against F.E.A.R. in a triumphant ending that finds the cats literally all washed up. Fueled with a mixture of outrageous puns and sly witticisms, this is, as Clutch would say, one totally awesome tale. High four! Final art not seen by *PW*. Ages 8-12.

Sally Estes

SOURCE: A review of *Ragweed: A Tale from Dimwood Forest,* in *Booklist,* Vol. 95, No. 18, May 15, 1999, p. 1690.

Gr. 4-6. "A mouse has to do what a mouse has to do," states young Ragweed, leaving his family to see more of the world. We first met Ragweed, albeit extremely briefly, in *Poppy* (a *Booklist* Editors' Choice 1995), in which he is snatched up and eaten by the terrifying owl, Mr. Ocax. Here, we learn what a stalwart mouse Ragweed is as he hops a freight train, lands in the rundown town of Amperville, and barely escapes the clutches of Silversides, a very angry white cat, the founder of F.E.A.R. (Felines Enraged about Rodents). Ragweed takes up with hipster mice band members Clutch, Dipstick, and Lugnut. "You cool enough to hang with me, due?" asks Clutch. When Silversides and her sidekick, Graybar, destroy the Cheese Squeeze Club, killing many mice, Ragweed not only leads the town mice to transform an abandoned bookstore into the cool Café Independent but also directs the battle against the opening night invasion by F.E.A.R. And like an old-time hero, Ragweed rides off into the sunset—aboard another freight train. Fans of *Poppy* and *Poppy and Rye* (1998) will relish the humor and the adventure, but they also may be glad they didn't know Ragweed so well before he was offed in the first story.

Eva Mitnick

SOURCE: A review of *Ragweed: A Tale from Dimwood Forest,* in *School Library Journal,* Vol. 75, No. 7, July, 1999, p. 92.

Gr 3-6—Ragweed, the golden mouse who appeared briefly in *Poppy* (Orchard, 1995) before being devoured by an owl, gets an entire book to himself in this prequel. At an early age, he sets off to explore the world beyond the Brook, so he hitches a train and ends up in the town of Amperville. Unfortunately, a fierce house cat named Silversides has created an organization called Felines Enraged About Rodents (F.E.A.R.), and is trying to rid the town of all mice. Ragweed is saved from Silversides's claws by Clutch, a streetwise young mouse who dyes her head fur green, wears an earring, and plays in a rock band. As F.E.A.R. becomes more and more of a threat, Ragweed and Clutch hatch a plan to unite the town mice at their new club, the Café Independent, where they stand up against the cats and win. After this victory, however, Ragweed's wanderlust compels him to leave Amperville and travel onward . . . to Dimwood Forest, Fun and breezy, this adventure should appeal to fans of the series and newcomers as well. It does bog down whenever the focus goes from Ragweed and his friends to the bitter Silversides, and kids probably won't be interested in Clutch's stereotypically bohemian parents (an artist and a poet). The constant slangy jive-talking of Clutch and her pals ("Look, when I say cool, I mean, you know, like, it's good") will either irritate or amuse readers, but the thrilling climax at the Café Independent will leave them breathless.

Kathleen Beck

SOURCE: A review of *Ragweed: A Tale from Dimwood Forest,* in *Voice of Youth Advocates,* Vol. 22, No. 3, August, 1999, p. 178.

In this prequel to *Poppy* (Orchard, 1995), Avi's protagonist is a country mouse who discovers the big city. Hopping a freight train near his woodland home, adventurous Ragweed precipitously bails out when a big white cat jumps into his boxcar. Alone on the streets of Amperville, he is rescued by a green-haired, skateboard-riding mouse named Clutch. She introduces him to the hip, underground mouse culture of the town, and warns him to watch out for Silversides, the white cat, and her sidekick, Greybar, whose mission is to rid the town of mice. But Ragweed is not prepared to live in fear of F.E.A.R. (Felines Enraged Against Rodents) and soon conceives a plan to turn the tables on the cats. The main young adult audience for this book will be readers who enjoyed *Poppy* and its sequel, *Poppy and Rye* (Avon Camelot, 1998). There is a certain comfort in post-childhood nostalgia and this is a classic tale of the weak triumphing over the bullies. It does not have the resonance of Poppy's archetypal, heroic journey to confront the owl but is a satisfying if undemanding story in its own right. To an adult reader, the persistent use of dude-speak ("It's like, hey, whatever") quickly becomes irritating. It may also cause the book to seem dated once slang moves on. But it is quite possible the author never intended to write a classic to appeal to all ages, simply a good story for younger readers. Buy where the first two volumes are popular.

◫ *MIDNIGHT MAGIC* (1999)

Ilene Cooper

SOURCE: A review of *Midnight Magic,* in *Booklist,* Vol. 96, No. 2, September 15, 1999, p. 256.

Gr. 5-8. Avi continues to write across genres, this time offering a medieval mystery that will keep readers guessing to the very end. Fabrizio, the servant boy of the magician Mangus, gets embroiled in palace intrigue when Mangus is called to the castle to ascertain whether 10-year-old Princess Teresina has truly seen a ghost as she claims. Count Scarazoni, the king's closest advisor and Teresina's intended, wants the ghost to be a fiction; Teresina wants the king and others to believe that the ghost is that of her missing brother. Both the unwilling Mangus and the meddling Fabrizio become entangled in a conspiracy that could lead to their deaths. Avi provides as many twists and turns as there are secret corridors and hidden rooms in Teresina's massive palace. Most of the time these bends in the plot heighten the tension, once even providing some heart-stopping action. However, especially at the book's conclusion, some of the explanations of previous actions get a bit convoluted, and kids may have to read the ending more than once before everything makes sense. They may not mind too much, though, because the combination of magic and mystery is pretty irresistible.

Steven Engelfried

SOURCE: A review of *Midnight Magic,* in *School Library Journal,* Vol. 45, No. 10, October, 1999, p. 144.

Gr 5-9—Avi takes readers to 15th-century Italy in this entertaining tale of mystery and intrigue. Twelve-year-old Fabrizio is the servant of Mangus the Magician. When the king's daughter claims to have seen a ghost, the magician and the boy are summoned to the castle. The evil Count Scarazoni wants to prove the ghost is not real so that his wedding to the princess will not be postponed. Young Fabrizio uses trickery, recklessness, and bravado to ferret out clues, spying in castle halls and secret passages. His master, meanwhile, relies on pure reason to reach the truth. Between the two of them, they are able to unveil a web of plots and deceptions, and then find a way to thwart the count and save their own skins. The quick pace and several plot twists will keep readers turning pages. The mystery will keep them guessing, but it never becomes too complicated to follow. Fabrizio makes an appealing hero. His cleverness is often outdone by the schemes of others involved, but his courage and curiosity make up the difference. The boy often injects witty aphorisms into his conversation, and his enthusiasm and energy contrast entertainingly with the calm wisdom of his master. The villainous count is less fully drawn, as is the king, but the queen and the princess develop entertainingly as the story progresses. Most of the tale takes place within the *"castello,"* and descriptions of the dark hallways, hidden staircases, and gloomy dungeon make a delightfully atmospheric setting for this historical mystery.

Publishers Weekly

SOURCE: A review of *Midnight Magic,* in *Publishers Weekly,* Vol. 246, No. 45, November 8, 1999, p. 68.

Taut and suspenseful, this vivid mystery set in an imaginary kingdom of Renaissance Italy is vintage Avi. The story starts with a bang as an unmarked coach arrives one stormy night at the home of Mangus the magician, who is under house arrest for his knowledge of the dark arts. Mangus, as readers quickly learn, is no wizard but a former entertainer, and he in fact scoffs at the notion of magic. He protests vigorously when he is summoned to the castle (along with his 12-year-old servant, Fabrizio) and ordered to help free the princess from her visions of a terrifying ghost. All is not as it seems, however, as the pair discover a court intrigue involving a missing prince, a murder, hidden passageways and the king's Machiavellian adviser, Count Scarazoni. Weaving in the age-old clash between superstition and reason, Avi creates a sort of 15th-century Holmes and Watson in the characters of Mangus and Fabrizio, who continually trade aphorisms ("'Fabrizio, if you buy with ignorance, you will be paid with the same coin.' 'But, Master, you know what people say, False gold often buys more than iron'"). With snappy dialogue, nonstop action and lavishly embroidered period backdrops, this will please Avi's fans and may well win over some new ones. Ages 10-14.

Roxy Ekstrom

SOURCE: A review of *Midnight Magic,* in *Voice of Youth Advocates,* Vol. 22, No. 5, December, 1999, p. 249.

Tarot cards, a magician, the conniving advisor, and the beautiful, clever, haunted princess. It is all there, waiting to draw the reader into Avi's latest fantasy/ adventure/ghost story. Mangus the Magician has been tried by the evil Count Scarazoni and found guilty of practicing his now illegal craft. On a sweltering, stormy August night, Fabrizio, Mangus's only servant, surreptitiously casts the Tarot cards. Just as the Death card is cast, a violent knocking summons Mangus to the door. Fabrizio and Mangus are summarily swept off to the castello, where Princess Teresina has been haunted nightly by the specter of her missing brother. Intrigue permeates the castello. The King is ineffectual, his wife turns a blind eye, the Prince has disappeared on a mission to the Pope, and Teresina has been betrothed to Count Scarazoni. Under penalty of death, Mangus must exorcise the ghost that Teresina swears is her dead brother. Mangus, master of illusion, uses cool logic and a great deal of help from Fabrizio and the princess to unmask the power-hungry Scarazoni. All ends well, the prince is really alive, the King reclaims power, and Mangus and Fabrizio return home, ready to cast the Tarot cards once more. Avi, the established craftsman, has done it again. He carries the story through all the twists and turns that the hidden passages of the castello conjure up. Some of the events are a bit far-fetched, but this is a fantasy, after all—a great light read for the middle schoolers.

Anne Sherrill

SOURCE: A review of *Midnight Magic,* in *The ALAN Review,* Vol. 27, No. 2, Winter, 2000, p. 249.

In fifteenth-century Pergamontio, twelve-year-old Fabrizio plays with some tarot cards against the advice of his master, Mangus the Magician. Mangus is trying to get out of magic and devote himself to being a good Christian. However, Fabrizio and Mangus are soon involved in a request by King Claudio to free his daughter, ten-year-old Princess Teresina, of a ghost who visits her. The Princess suspects it is her murdered brother, heir to the throne of their father, King Claudio. Lurking in the shadows, though, is Count Scarazoni—who also wants to be king. So, young Fabrizio and Mangus must use magic to thwart Count Scarazoni, free the Princess, and save the

throne. Early adolescents will revel in this story filled with secret passages, mysterious mishaps, and eerie moments. Chapters ending in cliff hangers and a parade of characters with strange names embellish a story where truth is revealed and good prevails. A fun read for younger readers.

ERETH'S BIRTHDAY: A TALE FROM DIMWOOD FOREST (2000)

Carolyn Phelan

SOURCE: A review of *Ereth's Birthday: A Tale from Dimwood Forest,* in *Booklist,* Vol. 96, No. 15, April 1, 2000, p. 1401.

Gr. 3-5. Ereth, the curmudgeonly old porcupine who first appeared in *Poppy* (1995), is now a neighbor and dear friend of Poppy, Rye, and their family of 11 little deer mice. As the story begins, Ereth feels annoyed because everyone seems to have forgotten his birthday. He rambles through Dimwood Forest and finds a vixen caught in a trap and dying. Promising to look after her three little foxes, he finds that the job taxes his patience to the limit. Throughout the book, a fisher secretly stalks Ereth and, in the end almost kills him, Young readers will feel satisfaction when goodness is rewarded and justice prevails. Avi does a fine job of presenting the animals' varied points of view, from the thoughtless young foxes to their arrogant father to the prickly but good-hearted porcupine. Ereth, however, may prove to be a difficult hero for young readers to warm up to. His colorful speech is riddled with original and creative curses, such as "Pulsating puppy pimples" and "toe jam on a toothbrush," but the humorous effect tends to wear thin after a little while. Still, a must-read for fans of the series.

The Horn Book Magazine

SOURCE: A review of *Ereth's Birthday: A Tale from Dimwood Forest,* in *The Horn Book Magazine,* Vol. 76, No. 3, May, 2000, p. 306.

Ereth the porcupine, Poppy's curmudgeonly companion in *Poppy and Rye,* remains true to his prickly nature in this fourth Dimwood Forest tale. Unlike his brave and heroic mouse friend Poppy, Ereth is a much more down-to-earth (and perhaps more sympathetic) character. Although he tries hard to avoid becoming ensnared in relationships, Ereth finds himself foster parent to three motherless fox kits. The ornery porcupine's transformation from cranky—"Phooey on all children with a squashed boll weevil on top"—to caring (if still a little cranky) unfolds naturally. When, eventually, the kits' errant father appears and tells Ereth to leave, his overwhelming sadness, barely masked by anger, is poignantly realistic. Avi adds another level of tension to the narrative in the character of Marty the Fisher, a cold killer who methodically stalks unsuspecting Ereth throughout the book. Well-developed suspense, humor, and vivid characterization make this installment a satisfying and touching continuation of the series.

Publishers Weekly

SOURCE: A review of *Ereth's Birthday: A Tale from Dimwood Forest*, in *Publishers Weekly*, Vol. 247, No. 19, May 8, 2000, p. 222.

Avi's (*Poppy; Poppy and Rye; Ragweed*) Dimwood Forest tales continue with this story—equal parts humor and suspense—that puts a non-mouse character in the limelight for the first time. Convinced that his best friend Poppy and her family have overlooked his birthday, Ereth, a curmudgeonly porcupine, wanders off in search of his favorite treat—salt. What he finds instead is an adventure he hadn't counted on: surrogate parenthood. He promises a female fox dying in a hunter's trap that he will look after her three kits until their father returns. Keeping the trio fed and out of trouble proves a Herculean task, one that teaches Ereth much about the ties that bind even as it softens some of his rough edges. His steadfast if grumpy devotion is rewarded when the three save him from an attack by a cunning fisher (a furry, four-legged creature with a hankering for porcupines). Avi delivers another crackling good read, one shot through with memorable descriptions (snow "sleeved tree branches in white") and crisp, credible dialogue. Above all, showcasing Ereth allows the author free range with his cantankerous character's trademark asides ("Babies. Nothing but poop and puke, puke and poop") and outbursts ("Sour snake sauce on spaghetti!"), many of which will have readers chuckling. Ages 8-12.

Peter Catalanotto
1959-

American illustrator and author.

Major works include *Dylan's Day Out* (1989), Cynthia Rylant, *An Angel for Solomon Singer* (1992), George Ella Lyon, *Who Came Down That Road?* (1992), *The Painter* (1995), *Dad & Me* (1999).

INTRODUCTION

Catalanotto is an author and illustrator whose works include picture books and early readers featuring his vivid and highly detailed watercolor paintings. In such self-illustrated works as *The Painter* and *Dad & Me,* Catalanotto uses detailed imagery to expand the story and often experiments with traditional formats, including placing the title page at the end of the book or including symbolic details in his illustrations. His collaborations with such authors as Cynthia Rylant and George Ella Lyon have been among his most successful works and include *Soda Jerk, Cecil's Story,* and *Who Came Down That Road?*

BIOGRAPHICAL INFORMATION

Catalanotto was the second of five children born to Anthony and Ella Virginia Catalanotto. His parents fostered an appreciation for art in their children, painting one of the basement walls white and allowing the children to cover it with their own designs. Catalanotto's mother was, in his words, "a Sunday painter," and his father was a printer who provided his family with plenty of scrap paper for drawing. Four of the five children later went to art college. Growing up in Long Island, New York, Catalanotto was always the "class artist" in school but by high school had become disillusioned and bored with art classes that were often geared to less advanced students. He attended a six-week summer course at the Parsons School of Art and Design in New York City following his junior year of high school and after graduation enrolled in the Pratt Institute in Brooklyn. At Pratt Catalanotto grew frustrated by his difficulty in finding a medium that suited him. Eventually a roommate suggested liquid watercolor, which Catal-

anotto has used ever since. According to Catalanotto, "it suits both my approach and style of painting. Also my work habits. I like to work late into the night and the last thing I feel like doing at 4 a.m. is cleaning out brushes. . . . I also do not like to sit for long stretches of time when I paint. . . . Sometimes I get lost in a painting and many hours will pass like minutes, but usually I'm up and down from my desk a lot when I work. Watercolors allow me to stop and start without a lot of cleanup or preparation."

After graduating from Pratt, Catalanotto worked at an advertising agency while pursuing freelance assignments, including magazine illustration and painting book covers for New York publishing firms. He later worked variously as a bicycle messenger, a bartender, and an elementary school custodian to supplement his income. In 1987 he came into contact with Richard Jackson of Orchard Books, who asked Catalanotto to illustrate Cynthia Rylant's *All I See* (1988). Since that collaboration, Catalanotto has written and illustrated more than fifteen titles. In 1989 Catalanotto married Jo-Ann Carrie Maynard, a photographer, and they have one child. The Catalanottos live in Doylestown, Pennsylvania.

MAJOR WORKS

Catalanotto's works may be divided into two categories, those titles that he has both written and illustrated and those for which he has provided the illustrations for a text written by another author. *Dylan's Day Out,* Catalanatto's first book as an author/illustrator, focuses on an adventure-filled day for a dog. His second book, *Mr. Mumble* (1990) depicts a man who unknowingly swallows a bird in his sleep and is misunderstood in a series of comic encounters during the following day. It was Catalanotto's own daughter who inspired his self-illustrated book *The Painter.* His art studio was off-limits to the little girl because of its numerous dangers until she reached the age of four. When he finally allowed his daughter to enter the room under careful supervision, the child was almost too excited to move. This experience led to his story of a fictional girl whose artist father is too busy working to play with her and who also forbids her to visit his studio. In the story, the pair works out a solution that a *Publishers Weekly* reviewer called credible and "uplifting," adding that Catalanotto's "book subtly attests to the joy inherent in the creation of both life and art."

Catalanotto's 1999 work *Dad & Me* describes the relationship between a father and his young son at the time of the first moon landing in July 1969. According Kay Weisman in *Booklist,* "Catalanotto's creative story speaks to the importance of both imaginative play and the relationship between fathers and sons. His bold watercolors include many details of suburbia during the 1960s and successfully meld fantasy and reality." Though intended for readers ages five to eight, the book was considered somewhat difficult by a *Publishers Weekly* reviewer who commented that "Catalanotto's watercolors are breathtaking, but so abstruse that even adult readers may be confused. . . . [*Dad & Me*] succeeds in representing a boy's imaginary play world as well as his changing moods, but the forced exposition at the beginning, the complexity of the visual images and the heavy handed symbolism may make the book difficult for young readers to understand."

Describing his collaborative titles, Catalanotto believes "the illustrations for a text have to be more than just beautiful paintings. They should add new dimensions to the text, not merely repeat in pictures what the writer has said in words." In 1989 Catalanotto illustrated Rylant's *Soda Jerk,* a collection of poems for young adults set at a soda fountain in a small-town pharmacy. *An Angel for Solomon Singer,* another volume with Cynthia Rylant, focuses on a poor, lonely man whose life is transformed by his friendship with a kind waiter. It was a story that touched a nerve in Catalanotto, who has noted "I was very poor for several years in New York City and understand the coldness Solomon experiences as well as his longing for familiar times and loved ones. I often found myself examining my life, wondering if I made the right choices. In hard times, I think this is quite common to do. This thinking gave me the idea of using a lot of reflections in my paintings—looking at our lives and examining our choices." According to *Publishers Weekly,* "Catalanotto's paintings, each a blend of realism and keen imagination, capture and reflect the idea of transformative vision—the city's streets really do seem to shimmer like fields of wheat, the buildings' lights to twinkle like stars."

George Ella Lyon has been another of Catalanotto's frequent collaborators. Their first effort together was *Cecil's Story* (1991), a poem about a boy whose father is away fighting in the Civil War. In Catalanotto's words, "The poem speaks of his hopes and fears, leaving all the imagery up to me to create. The images her words evoked in my mind were endless, and I spent many nights editing and altering to create what I felt were the right ones." Lyon is also the author of Catalanotto's *Who Came Down That Road?*, in which a curious boy and his mother discover a pathway in the woods. The mother explains who uses the path nowadays, then goes on to describe the people who have walked there in days past. A *Publishers Weekly* reviewer called Catalanotto's work in the volume "stunning and evocative watercolors that are filled with light and beauty." Catalanotto also illustrated Lyon's 1993 book *Dreamplace,* a poem about the Anasazi cliff dwellers of the southwestern United States. A *Publishers Weekly* reviewer remarked, "Lyon and Catalanotto here offer an atmospheric, shimmering glance backwards. . . . Catalanotto's extraordinary watercolors clarify this journey through time." Another collaboration with Lyon resulted in *Mama Is a Miner,* for which the author and illustrator did onsite research at a modern-day coal mine in Kentucky. In 1999 the pair teamed again for *Book.* Geared for the preschool audience, the text and pictures combine to express the imaginative possibilities inherent in reading.

Catalanotto has also illustrated books by several other authors. One *Publishers Weekly* reviewer called the illustrations in SuAnn Kiser's *The Catspring Somersault Flying One-Handed Flip-Flop* "sun-drenched watercolors, as lush and complex as ever," and *Horn Book* critic Nancy Vasilakis praised the "distinctive, impressionistic paintings" of a "tomboy whose facial expressions reveal her temperament." Vasilakis reported, again in *the Horn Book,* that Catalanotto's paintings for Susan Patron's *Dark Cloud Strong Breeze* "really capture attention," especially "the winsome informality of subjects caught off-guard" and the artist's use of "an unusual three-dimensional effect." Catalanotto's illustrations for Susan Marie Swanson's 1998 title for preschoolers *Letter to the Lake* won the praises of both Shelle Rosenfeld of *Booklist,* who called the work "a fine and visually astonishing book about the power of dreaming and memories," and a *Publishers Weekly* reviewer, who commented, "the inventive perspectives and splashes of color in Catalanotto's impressionistic watercolors visually capture the complicated relationship between one's memory and experience."

Catalanotto told *Contemporary Authors*: "I think writing and illustrating picture books suits my personality much more than simply illustrating book jackets and magazine articles. I can be quiet and subtle with my work while trying to catch someone's eye. A book jacket yells at you to take it off the shelf. An entire picture book slowly unfolds before you, almost inviting you to stay."

AWARDS

Catalanotto was named "Most Promising New Artist," by *Publishers Weekly* in 1989. *Soda Jerk* (by Cynthia Rylant) was named an American Library Association "Best Book for Teens" in 1990. *Cecil's Story* (George Ella Lyon) was honored as a "Keystone Book" for Pennsylvania in 1991; *All I See* (Rylant) and *Dylan's Day Out* both received Junior Literary Guild citations.

AUTHOR COMMENTARY

Peter Catalanotto with Cyndi Giorgis

SOURCE: An interview with Peter Catalanotto, *The New Advocate,* Vol. 9, No. 2, Spring, 1996, pp. 97-105.

Over the past nine years, Richard Jackson has been the editor for all thirteen books written and/or illustrated by Peter Catalanotto. The working relationship between this editor and author is not one to be taken lightly. A degree of mutual trust and respect has developed through the years, resulting in a highly successful partnership. In the following interview, Peter Catalanotto discusses his process in writing and illustrating books for children and the influence Dick Jackson has had on his work. Peter also reflects on the role libraries and books have played in his life and how these experiences influenced his thinking in creating the current cover illustration of The New Advocate.

Cyndi: What is it like to work with Dick Jackson?

Peter: Dick Jackson is really supportive. The strongest trait I think he has and the reason why I work with him is because he's not purely a writer's editor. A lot of editors are used to working with authors, but aren't as supportive of illustrators. Dick is really an illustrator's editor. It's equal with him. I think his main objective is to do what's best for the book. When he looks at my artwork, I trust him not to nitpick and want changes made for the sake of his control or his vision. He and I are both thinking of the book, the story first and foremost, and I trust that the changes he makes are purely for the benefit of the story. The up side of this is the trust he has in me, because he doesn't tell me how to make the changes. The strongest part of our relationship is that trust and that we are both doing what's best for the story. We are not interested in gimmicks. I can also honestly say that book sales are not our number one concern.

How did you get started working with Dick?

I was doing young adult book covers at the time and I did one for Orchard. Dick saw the painting and inquired about the illustrator. After painting three book covers for Orchard, Dick gave me a picture book manuscript to illustrate. I was a little hesitant at first because I was picturing *Clifford the Big Red Dog* and *Curious George,* because that's the kind of picture book I remember as a kid. The last time I had looked at a picture book was when I was eight years old. Dick suggested I go to the bookstores and libraries and take a look at what has happened to picture books. When I saw them, I was completely amazed by what was going on and I loved the idea of illustrating a picture book. After I painted *All I See,* Dick found out I kept a journal and that I had some ideas for stories. He encouraged me to start writing and *Dylan's Day Out* came from those conversations and encouragement.

Do you work differently with Dick when you write and illustrate as opposed to only illustrating a book?

I work differently with myself. I don't know that I work differently with Dick. That's pretty much the same. I find that it's easier to illustrate someone else's manuscript than it is to illustrate my own. I am constantly trying to figure out what is going to work better on a particualr page—are the words or the pictures going to have more impact? There is this constant battle in my head between words and pictures. When you illustrate the story you don't have that battle because the words are already there and you are free to illustrate. When I write and illustrate a book, I show Dick the words and the pictures together. With my first three books, I showed him the pictures and the story because the pictures really told the story as much as the words did. *The Painter,* the fourth book that I wrote, was the first time that I mailed Dick the manuscript without any pictures. In that sense it was probably different from the way we normally work. I can't separate the words and the pictures when I work with them. Every word is an image. I don't separate them myself and I don't separate them when I work with Dick. The conversations we have about the writing are very similar to the ones that we have about the paintings. It's strange because I had never even thought, until this moment, that there would be a difference or if there should be a difference. Logically it sounds like there should be a difference, but to me there isn't. The process is pretty much the same.

So when you send him your ideas have you already developed them into a "dummy"?

The first three books I sent him were in a dummy form with pencil sketches. For *The Painter* I basically sent him two pieces of paper stapled together with the manuscript written on it. In 1988, Dick published a book and I told him it was a beautiful story. He said he thought the pacing was really nice. I smiled and said, "That was your job, right?" He looked at me and said, "No, I really only had to change one or two words." I thought about the first three manuscripts I gave Dick and I know the original manuscripts are nothing like the final manuscripts—maybe because I was showing him much earlier drafts. I usually show him my manuscript from conception and we bang the ideas around for awhile. I then go back and rewrite the story. Dick has been a big part of the rewriting, so the final manuscript is quite different from the original. I had this fantasy that one day I would turn in a manuscript to him and he would just have to change one or two words. I never thought that would happen, but that is exactly what occurred with *The Painter.* I sent him the manuscript and he mailed it back with two changes. He changed the tense on one word and added a comma. I thought it was quite amusing that this fantasy actually came true for me.

Does that show your evolution as a writer?

I don't know. I think that may have a lot to do with that particular story. *The Painter* was such a personal story. With the first three books I showed him much earlier drafts. I think he saw the second or third draft for *Dylan's Day Out, Mr. Mumble,* and *Christmas Always.* But with *The Painter* I didn't show the manuscript to him until I had written it twelve or thirteen times. Maybe it's not my development as a writer but that I showed him a more refined manuscript. I think I am becoming more confident and am at the point where I don't feel I have to let him in so early. I could do it on my own and get closer to that final draft. Maybe it's a sign of my confidence as a writer. I think my confidence may have come from writing about my daughter and my life with my daughter and it just felt right to me. I had thirteen drafts of that book. I just found the original draft and read it. It's amazing, it was nothing like the final draft. Five years ago, that's probably what I would have shown Dick. This time I did most of the work. I didn't bring him into the process as early as I used to. It will probably break his heart to hear that but I think he'll be happy for me at the same time.

Do you think that because **The Painter** *is such a personal book it would have been more difficult if Dick would have wanted to change things?*

I was really holding my breath when I sent him the manuscript. I was terrified that he would change things that would take away from what I thought the book was about. It was the first book that I felt I knew what it was about. It was a part of me. The other books were ideas that I built on, but *The Painter* just came out of me. It came from a different place. I think I was afraid of tempering with that place. The book felt so right, so natural that I was afraid to go back and have to reexamine it from another perspective if Dick wanted to make serious changes. I was very nervous about that.

Do you think that is part of your writing process but also part of the process of building a relationship between an author and an editor? Would Dick's comments be different because this book is so personal?

Ultimately I think it would be important to him on a personal but not on a professional level because of his focus on what's best for the story. If he thought something needed work he would not say, "I can't change that because it's personal to Pete." Dick would do what's best for the book and I would want him to do that. I expect him to do that. I would be disappointed in Dick if ten years from now he told me, "There were a couple of changes I wanted to make in **The Painter** but I didn't because I knew it was personal to you." My trust in him is that he has always done what's best for the book.

Has he always been right?

I don't think it's a matter of right. He'll just think something needs work. Something in the book needs to be qualified or is needed to mend the flow of the story. That something might affect the rhythm of the story. It's a matter of a gut feeling for something the story needs.

Do you always go with Dick's gut feelings?

No. I have gut feelings of my own that he also respects. Sometimes I'll see a change and I'll work with other parts to make that part work. If I believe in a part that really needs to be in a story and Dick thinks it needs to be changed, then I can work with other parts of the story to make that part work. I think we both trust each other's gut feelings and our beliefs. I don't have the experience that he has in making a story work, so I will always consider and really think about his changes because I have tremendous respect for his experience and knowledge. Sometimes we end up not making the change. I'll show him why I'm doing something and he'll say, "Oh, now that I understand, I know how to help make this better." People would be amazed at how much goes back and forth. An editor does more than just fix the grammar. My favorite parts of making a book are those sessions where we just bang the story around. We figure out how to make the story work and how to make the painting work with the story. That's why I only work with one editor. I couldn't imagine having that relationship with more than one person. It's a process and you are exposing things about your life, your feelings, and your emotions. I just couldn't imagine saying, "I'll see you next time we work together." I need to know that when I work with somebody, I'm doing it for my career.

There is a point when you show Dick the paintings. Will he ask you to change something?

I have done thirteen picture books with Orchard so far and each picture book has eighteen paintings in it. So you are looking at close to 200 paintings. I've had to make changes on three of those paintings. We work with the dummy so much that by the time I get to the paintings there's really no question about what

Unpublished sketch for All I see, *written and illustrated by Peter Catalanotto, 1987.*

to do. Two of those three changes came from the writer after seeing the paintings. It was technical stuff. The writer does not see the dummy or the paintings until they are all finished. When I showed Dick the first dummy for **All I See,** the sketches were very tight pencil renderings. Now when I show him a dummy I will make a circle and say that's a boy and I'll make an oval and say that's a dog. He might ask what kind of dog and I'll say it's a German Shepherd. The sketches now look more like basketballs than sketches, but that's the part of working with one editor that I enjoy. He understands my doodles, he understands my inflections. Sometimes when you do a sketch too tight it's like doing the painting twice. Part of what I like about watercolors is the spontaneity. So I don't want to do my sketches too tight because I want all the spontaneity of a watercolor painting. I don't know any other editor who would allow me to show them four circles on a page and say that's a family sitting around the dinner table. That's not a putdown of editors; it's just that I would have to work with an editor five or six years before that could happen.

Is there any point at which the author has input?

In **Who Came Down That Road,** I wanted to move the title page. A third of the way through the story, there's a line "Who came down that road, Mama? Who came down that road?" Since the second line is the title itself, I wanted to put the title page in the middle of the story. That would tamper with the rhythm of writing, so I felt we should run this idea by George Ella [Lyon] to see how she felt about it. Fortunately, she loved the idea. That's one time when the writer was consulted. In our latest book, **A Day at Damp Camp,** the whole story has 54 words in it, with nine stanzas of six words each. This is wonderful for me because it allows me to extend the story and the writing. I also wanted to add a friendship to the story, but some of George Ella's writing wasn't working with that idea. She liked the idea of the friendship and was more than happy to change some of the words. She actually changed two lines in the book to accommodate the story line. This is a real testimony to George Ella and why the three of us work together. She also wants to do what's truly best for the story. She is not one of those writers who says "How dare you tamper with my writing." She was listening and it amazed me how quickly her mind worked in coming up with those new lines. George Ella is my favorite writer to illustrate because of her ability to create so much in so few words, leaving me so much to paint. George Ella and I have become very close friends. But we still do not work on the book together. If there are any questions or situations that arise about the story, we call Dick. We want him to be part of the process.

Why do you work in watercolor?

Watercolor is completely unforgivable when you first start working with it, but there are certain techniques you can apply that actually make it quite flexible. It's a very versatile medium. You can use thin washes to create transparent, luminous paintings or you can layer. For example, in **Cecil's Story,** when I wanted to show the passage of time, I used the watercolor very lightly and got a transparent feeling to the images. In a book like **An Angel for Solomon Singer,** I wanted a more dense, gritty feeling of New York City so I layered the paint. In **Cecil's Story,** there were five or six layers of paints, where in **An Angel for Solomon** Singer there might be ten or eleven layers of paint. The more you layer watercolor, the richer and more intense the color gets, so that it almost looks like oil paints. I've had people look at **An Angel for Solomon Singer** and they are surprised that it is watercolor because of how dark and rich the colors are, but one of the things I like about watercolors is that you can make them look different ways. It also suits my personality. If I worked in oil paints I would have to spend a fortune in brushes because most of the time I like painting late into the night, and when

I finish the last thing I want to do is spend any time cleaning out brushes. With watercolor, you just lay the brushes down and in the morning you pick them up and rinse them out. I not only like the look of watercolor but also the process is a lot more spontaneous because you can stop and start a lot simpler than you can with other kinds of paint. It's amazing I get any work done at all. I'll paint for forty-five minutes and then I'll get up and I'll check the mail, then I'll go back and I'll paint for another hour and then I'll take the dog out. I'll end up working a sixteen-hour day but spread out all over the day. That's why I love watercolors, because oil paints dry and then you have to start all over again. I find it hard to sit at a desk for a long period of time, so I work in spurts in which I take fifteen- or twenty-minute breaks between the sixty-minute blocks of time that I work. I think I'm a kinetic learner. I can't sit for long periods of time. The next medium I want to work with that will allow me to do that is oil sticks. It has all the look of oils without all the process, all the clean-up.

You incorporate unique ideas into your books. How does this come about?

Every story is different. Each book deserves a unique approach. It is getting harder because, in the first couple of books, I was trying to do something different in the industry. Now that I'm working on my thirteenth or fourteenth picture book, I'm trying to come up with things that are different from what I've done already. It's more difficult to give each book a different look. If you are going to do something different or unique, it has to work for that story. If it doesn't, it becomes a gimmick. Four years ago, I wanted to put the title on the back of a book, but there was no book that was right for it at the time. It would have just been a gimmick. Why would the title be on the back of **Mr. Mumble?** But with **The Painter,** I felt it was right, because the story is about painting so it should only have a painting on the cover. For years, ever since I was a kid, I have loved those movies that start and then after ten minutes they show you the title for the movie. When I started picture books, I had never seen that in a picture book, but I didn't want to use that in the first picture book I was working on. I wanted to use it for the book where it made sense, and for **Who Came Down That Road?** it was perfect. The title was right in the middle of the story. Why not use it for that book? Plus the book was about history and the beginning of the book was about a modern-day parent and child and then a third of the way in the book the story went back in time. To have the title in the middle of the book created this wonderful pause for this transition from modern time to the past. It really worked for that book. That is the difference between a gimmick and a nice idea for a book. The creator made sure that it worked for the book. He wasn't just doing it because it was something different to do.

Where do you come up with these ideas?

After I showed Dick the layout for **My House Has Stars,** he asked me, "How many of these ideas do you have left?" And I said, "Well, right now, none." Dick smiled and he understood completely what I meant. I won't know until I read the next manuscript what I'm going to do with it. It's not like I have a bunch of ideas saved up that I tack onto the stories as they come. I don't know what I'm going to do with a book until after I read the manuscript. I don't know where these ideas come from. I don't really want to know. I don't want to examine it too closely. I think if I figure out my process it might go away or it might not work anymore.

When you get a manuscript, how long do you have to sit with it until the ideas come?

I will read a manuscript anywhere from ten to thirty times, then I'll put it away for a few weeks. Then I'll read it some more. I've had manuscripts for years before I illustrate them. I've had the manuscript for **My House Has Stars** about a year and a half now. When I get a manuscript, I'll read it and if I see imagery for every page, I have no desire to do that manuscript. If I read a manuscript and I put it down and go, "Wow, I love that story, but I have no idea what I'm going to do with it," then that's the kind of manuscript I want to illustrate. I'm not interested in my initial imagery. I want to have to work to come up with something. For me, the most fun in the whole process is figuring out what to do with a manuscript.

I know you do a lot of school visits. How does that impact your work?

School visits are a wonderful gauge for what I've done and for learning about my painting. Nobody reads paintings like children do. I am looking to extend the story by the writer and the kids are extending the paintings by saying all these things I didn't think about. For example, in **Cecil's Story,** a story about a boy waiting for his parents to come home from the Civil War, one painting shows an egg turning into a chick to represent the three weeks that had passed while the child waits for his parents to come home. A first grader told me he liked the way the chick came out of the egg because the chick was now looking for his mother, just like the boy. I was so completely stunned by that because it worked so well for the story, and I didn't even do it on purpose; I didn't even know I did it. This was something that a first grader added to my painting. The most wonderful thing about school visits is that children see things in a painting that astound and amaze me and it keeps me on my toes for what I'm doing next. I don't think about what children like when I am making a book, I think about what I liked as a child and what I like now. So many people think childhood is different from being an adult, but it's not. You are the same person and what you saw as sad, interesting, and funny as a child still affects you as an adult. One of the nicest things about picture books is that you are always exploring your childhood. It's almost like getting paid to go to therapy. I am forever digging up things about my past, then having to deal with them. I have been writing a book called **Dad and Me** for the past four years. It's about my childhood and my relationship with my father, and I think I haven't resolved it in my real life and that's why I am having problems resolving it in this story. When I was doing illustrations for magazine and book covers, it was never really an issue. Illustrating picture books and writing picture books has really forced me to look at my life. I have always had the tendency to overanalyze and overexamine everything. Picture books have allowed me to deal with my past instead of things that are just happening to me on a day-to-day basis.

Let's talk about the wonderful cover illustration you did for Volume 9 of The New Advocate. *Where did you get the idea for the cover?*

I'm not sure really where my ideas come from. I started by thinking about a library and what books and libraries mean to me. I went back to my childhood and remembered being amazed and completely overwhelmed that you could walk into a library and find information about anything. It seemed like the center of the universe because it had everything you needed. Anything you wanted to know you could find in this place. I loved libraries as a kid and I still love libraries as an adult. They have always been the center of my world. So picturing that, I got the idea of turning a library into a galaxy, this Milky Way, where the library was the center and all the kids were being drawn into this vortex. The imagery started coming and I thought since the library itself was surreal I needed to do more surreal things around it. That's where I got the idea of turning the books into trees. The images in the windows are just a sampling of the information you can find in a library—science, sports, music, art, politics, etc. I tried to represent a lot of different things in that one painting.

How did painting this cover differ from illustrating a picture book?

Covers are very different than picture books because you have to say a lot in one painting. It's a whole different way of working. The illustrations for a picture book manuscript can be subtle, you can use foreshadowing, you can tell a story. When I illustrate a picture book manuscript I image in my head a movie of the story. I have to connect the imagery and make it flow. A cover has to hit the person immediately. You can't be subtle on the cover because you want to attract attention. I have always compared the two in this way: a cover is screaming at you, "Pick me up. Look at me," while a picture book slowly unfolds and invites you in to stay awhile. When you paint a cover for anything—a book, a journal—it's like a poster for the product. A poster really has to catch someone's eye and make them want to pick up the product. It's quite a different approach than illustrating a picture book manuscript.

TITLE COMMENTARY

ALL I SEE (1988)

Publishers Weekly

SOURCE: A review of *All I See* in *Publishers Weekly,* Vol. 234, No. 7, August 12, 1988, p. 458.

The gradual friendship between a shy boy named Charlie and Gregory, a paint-splattered artist, is handsomely illustrated by newcomer Catalanotto in watercolors that are full of shadows and brilliant patches of light. Although both Charlie and Gregory look across the same shimmering blue-green lake, Gregory, the artist, paints only whales because, he says, "It is all I see." Charlie, the apprentice, paints "everything he [sees], there on the lake," and knows that "something [is] waiting for him, waiting to be seen and to be painted." The sunlight etching blades of lemon-colored grass or caressing the lake at sunset is as beautiful as the deceptively simple story in which Rylant investigates the complicated difference for the artist between verisimilitude and vision. A Richard Jackson Book. Ages 5-7.

Karen Litton

SOURCE: A review of *All I See,* in *School Library Journal,* Vol. 35, No. 1, September, 1988, p. 173.

Gr 1-4—A dreamy piece about a young boy's awakening to artistic vision through his friendship with a lakeside painter. At first, shy Charlie watches from a

distance as Gregory paints, then drifts awhile in his canoe. The two communicate next through messages on the artist's canvas, and then, painting side-by-side, through sharing the process of creative expression, as Gregory paints his singular vision and Charles discovers his own. The developing relationship parallels Charlie's inner process of getting to know the private, creative part of himself. Soft-focus, soft-color illustrations—double-page watercolors—are full of sun and shadow, leaves and water, and gentle peace punctuated by bursts of energy, as when Gregory's cat springs while geese take flight. The pictures carry a sense of the mystery of art. This is romantic, but not sentimental. It is eloquently done, and the whole—words and pictures—speaks and lingers.

DYLAN'S DAY OUT (1989)

Publishers Weekly

SOURCE: A review of *Dylan's Day Out,* in *Publishers Weekly,* Vol. 236, No. 13, September 29, 1989, p. 65.

Dylan the Dalmatian spends day after day home alone, dreaming of the world beyond his black-and-white kitchen. One day he finds the door open and escapes for adventures in the colorful outdoors. Not far away, Dylan happens upon a soccer game of penguins vs. skunks, coached by nuns in black-and-white habits. Waiting spectators play dominoes and work on crossword puzzles. The penguins recruit Dylan into the game after an Oreo cookie feast incapacitates their goalie. Dylan contributes ably to the team's victory and even makes the front page of the newspaper. An aerial view (complete with arrows) depicts how Dylan helps score that winning goal. The minimal text serves as a bridge into an autumnal landscape where Dylan's (and the reader's) imagination can run free. Catalanotto employs a vivid palette and, often, unusual perspectives; his offbeat, amusing story of doggy mischief is a refreshing addition to the canine canon. Ages 3-6.

Ellen Mandel

SOURCE: A review of *Dylan's Day Out,* in *Booklist,* Vol. 86, No. 3, October 1, 1989, p. 346.

Ages 3-6. Left home alone day after day, Dylan, a bored dalmatian, steals outside to freedom one morning when the door is left open. While galloping toward country meadows, he is upended by a soccer ball that rolls over the hill and under his legs. The dog recovers his composure and finds a soccer game between skunks and penguins beginning on the other side of the hill. Though he doesn't sport high-top shoes like his teammates and opponents, Dylan tends goal for the penguins and leads them to victory before returning home, smugly contented. The jovial characters, all painted in black and white (including the sneaker-clad nun with "COACH" emblazoned on her habit), leap from the soft, multicolored background scenes, inviting readers to fill in the story of this sparsely worded, amusingly playful picture book. Catalanotto is a talent on the rise.

Patricia Dooley

SOURCE: A review of *Dylan's Day Out*, in *School Library Journal*, Vol. 35, No. 15, November, 1989, p. 76.

PreS-Gr 1—Shut in alone, Dylan—a Dalmatian—romps in a dream world of black-and-white animals (panda, zebra, egrets). One day he gets out, and, after some typical dog mischief, finds himself goalie in a soccer game played by penguins against skunks. The coach is a nun; dominoes, crossword squares, and black-and-white sneakers also feature. The ref's shirt, the soccer ball, Dylan—get it yet? The color scheme isn't a clue to fantasy: the landscape and some man-made objects have color, while animals and some man-made objects do not. Catalanotto provides good, snapshotlike pictures of Dylan in action; very little text; but no plot. Paired with Cynthia Rylant's words in *All I See* (Orchard, 1988), this artist's work was dynamite—but a picture book needs more than a graphic-design conceit.

📖 *SODA JERK* (1990)

Diane Roback

SOURCE: A review of *Soda Jerk*, in *Publishers Weekly*, Vol. 237, No. 3, January 19, 1990, p. 112.

Although this unique collaboration by Rylant and Catalanotto is in the format of a 48-page picture book, it is intended for young adult readers. The 28 untitled, resonant poems are an extended dramatic monologue by the book's title character, a sensitive boy who works as a soda jerk in a small Virginia town. "Living in Cheston," he tells the reader, "is

like living in a dream / somebody else is having," and it is through the boy's eyes that the reader sees the characters who live in Rylant's southern Spoon River. None are more vividly rendered than the observant narrator himself who, even if he never manages to leave town, consoles himself that at least he "never slept through the whole show." Catalanotto's six richly textured paintings of the drugstore, panoramas evocative of smalltown life, are placed like a gallery display at the beginning and middle of the book. Rylant's text is characteristically lyrical and thoughtful. Ages 12-up.

Kay E. Vandergrift

SOURCE: A review of *Soda Jerk*, in *School Library Journal*, Vol. 36, No. 4, April, 1990, p. 150.

Gr 7 Up—In poems that stir the senses and (for older readers) the memory, an adolescent "everyman" observes his small Virginia town and reflects upon his own life from across the counter at Maywell's Drugstore in a manner reminiscent of Wilder's *Our Town*. The visual imagery in these poems is so vivid that older readers will be able to see this small town and will recognize the cross-section of those who live there. Moreover, they will see into not only this soda jerk's life but also into the lives of the jocks who "walk with their arms sticking out some five inches," the hunters for whom "a deer corpse / is cause for joy among men," and the "old ladies / who've been somebody's mom / for so long, / they have come begging / for a person to take an interest." The first poem ends, "Tips are okay. / But the secrets are better." Each poem that follows reveals the narrator's perceptions of the secrets of the people he encounters, from the sheriff to his own father. This book is one of celebration and resignation by an average adolescent who wants to impress the popular girl and watches to see if anyone buys "sexual aids," but who also cares about people in his town. Catalanotto's watercolor paintings evoke small town life without defining it too specifically and are appropriately grouped so that all but the last poem stand on stark white pages, evoking their own images. The illustrations have an old-fashioned aura, yet combined with the contemporary references in the text, the book may give readers the sense that they are caught up in a time warp rather than in nostalgic reverie. Also, the size, format, and dust jacket indicate that this is a picture book. It will take some effort to get it into the hands of the older audience who will find themselves and their feelings captured in the poems.

MR. MUMBLE (1990)

Publishers Weekly

SOURCE: A review of *Mr. Mumble,* in *Publishers Weekly,* Vol. 237, No. 28, July 13, 1990, p. 53.

Catalanotto *(Dylan's Day Out)* offers up lifelike paintings whose realism is offset by striking, gently surreal perspectives and laconic expressions. They are a happy complement to this story in which puns and absurdity reign. A persistent tickle in the throat one day leaves Mr. Mumby prey to egregious misunderstandings. The baker gives him a "dozing beagle" instead of a "dozen bagels," the grocer a "panda bear" instead of a "pound of pears." His menagerie grows rapidly, until a doctor remedies the problem and Mr. Mumby and company head to the pet shop for provisions. Especially in his incarnation as "Mr. Mumble," Mr. Mumby inhabits a world in which the bizarre is met with unblinking equanimity: his strange requests are matter-of-factly accommodated, and his troupe causes nary a disruption in his rounds. A view of the animals solemnly testing scales and blood-pressure cuff in the physician's office is particularly memorable, and encapsulates the drollery used to rousing effect throughout. Ages 4-7.

Susan Powers

SOURCE: A review of *Mr. Mumble,* in *School Library Journal,* Vol. 36, No. 9, September, 1990, p. 196.

K-Gr 3—The success of this book hinges on the element of surprise and the humor readers find in Mr. Mumby's strange predicament: he awakens one morning with a mysterious throat complaint that results in a series of miscommunications and unbidden results. Intending to buy a dozen bagels he receives a dozing beagle, a panda bear instead of a pound of pears, etc. When he consults a doctor, the "problem" emerges—a bird had been lodged in his throat. Catalanotto's watercolors are arresting with their interesting color combinations, pliancy, and comic visual detail. The paintings loom large, perspective ever changing, edges melting; they give a sense of unbalance, of life being a bit out of focus and unpredictable. Perhaps because the tone of the story does not initially seem playful—and the portrayal of Mr. Mumby awakens not only curiosity but pathos—readers may be unprepared for the zany happenings to follow, but will willingly toss logic aside because of the cleverly executed illustrations. The text is not so strong or convincing. The wordplays are contriv-

ances, remaining narrative explanations rather than the garbled requests of Mr. Mumby himself. And so, in the end, this is a perplexing book, entertaining but not as funny as it could be, interesting despite its shortcomings, impressive for it strengths.

CECIL'S STORY (1991)

Diane Roback and Richard Donahue

SOURCE: A review of *Cecil's Story,* in *Publishers Weekly,* Vol. 238, No. 13, March 15, 1991, p. 58.

History buffs will welcome this unusual and timely picture book about a boy during the Civil War. Cecil's is not a single story, but a succession of pretended situations. "What if," Cecil wonders, his father "went off to war" and his mother had to follow him? The reader is asked to imagine Cecil in a variety of possible futures, making the complex time-sequence of the narrative confusing. Catalanotto's richly textured, evocative paintings ameliorate but do not entirely explain the convoluted historical perspective of the text. For example, a series of pictures depicting the hatching of an egg decorates a spread in which Cecil sits by a fence, waiting "for weeks"; in another, Cecil is shown as he plows in eight varying poses to simulate the passage of time. Although the tender relationships between characters and the warm assurance of the ending are laudable, Cecil's imaginary stories about the war are difficult to follow—as when the boy is pictured being reunited with his mother on the verso page, and being comforted about her absence on the right. Ages 5-7.

Lee Bock

SOURCE: A review of *Cecil's Story,* in *School Library Journal,* Vol. 37, No. 4, April, 1991, p. 98.

Gr 1-3—The trauma of separation is sensitively explored in a Civil War setting in this evocative picture book. A child worries and waits at a neighbor's farm for his mother to return with his wounded father. Each page has a simple line or two of text, complemented dramatically by double-page watercolor paintings of extraordinary quality. The passage of time is shown visually and subtly in the movement of the sun across the page, in the development of a chicken embryo, and in the changing of seasons. Movement is translated visually by repeated images, as in the wild circling of the dog when Papa returns. Today, many children are experiencing separation fears as parents go to war. This book addresses those fears honestly and feelingly, with a believable and reassuring conclusion. Life and life's work continue—the chickens must be fed, the fields plowed—even if drastically altered by outside events, and Papa is still Papa, even with one arm missing. Whether or not children are verbalizing their own thoughts about the current Gulf situation, this book provides a safe distance for looking at another child's fears. *Cecil's Story* is well worth serious consideration.

CHRISTMAS ALWAYS (1991)

Stephanie Zvirin

SOURCE: A review of *Christmas Always,* in *Booklist,* Vol. 88, September 15, 1991, p. 156.

Ages 4-7. Lying in bed on Christmas Eve, wiggling a loose tooth, and listening to party sounds coming from downstairs, Katie awaits Santa. To her surprise, it's not Santa who comes. It's the Sandman, tiny and magical, ready to sprinkle his sleeper's dust. Before he can, though, Jack Frost arrives (with icicles on his beard), followed by the dainty Tooth Fairy in a beam of shimmery light. The tiny visitors play and soar around the room, until jingling bells tell them it's time for the most wondrous visitor of all. Catalanotto combines fairy-tale charm with realistic details in his colorful, double-page spreads. Awash with hazy light and filled with movement, energy, and a child's wonder and delight, they demand more than a quick glance. Brown-eyed Katie firmly links children to the real world while the whimsical trio stretches imaginations. Katie's black-and-white cat looks on in humorous dismay.

School Library Journal

SOURCE: A review of *Christmas Always,* in *School Library Journal,* Vol. 37, No. 10, October, 1991, pp. 27-8.

PreS-Gr 2—Unique perspectives and palette are used to tell the story of a girl's reluctance to go to bed on Christmas Eve. In a fanciful turn, the Sandman, Jack Frost, and the Tooth Fairy all visit Katie to attend to their appointed tasks. But footsteps on the stairs outside her room and the sound of jingling bells warn everyone of an important visitor, and with help from the Sandman, Katie is safely asleep—just in the nick of time. Dramatic, full-page paintings showing the

evening's events compensate somewhat for the stilted text. Katie and her cat are seen cavorting with her magical visitors with almost photographic clarity, even though an impressionistic, dreamlike quality is achieved through muted watercolor hues of blue, gray, and brown, enlivened at times by splashes of bright green and red. Catalanotto's dependance on photographic models, however, clashes with his imaginary figures, resulting in an uneasy blend of realism and fantasy. More artist than poet, Catalanotto's uneven narrative is not as haunting or evocative as Van Allsburg's *The Polar Express,* (Houghton, 1985). Nevertheless, this fantastical bedtime story will delight and intrigue readers.

Publishers Weekly

SOURCE: A review of *Christmas Always,* in *Publishers Weekly,* Vol. 238, No. 38, 1991, p. 61.

Like all children, Katie complains when bedtime signals her early departure from the festivities on Christmas Eve. Tucked in but restless, Katie wiggles loose a tooth that eventually falls onto the floor. Trying to retrieve her treasure, Katie discovers the Sandman under her bed. Still amazed by this encounter, Katie watches Jack Frost blow into the room, followed a few moments later by the Tooth Fairy, who appears dancing on "a shimmer of light." Katie's bedroom visitors cause plenty of ruckus as they must perform their respective duties and make way for Santa, the man of the evening. Catalanotto's (*Dylan's Day Out*) velvety paintings sparkle, depicting twinkling holiday lights and the magical glitter of nocturnal guests. Katie's face is particularly expressive as it glows with anticipation and excitement. Offering a pleasant mix of family warmth and the enchanting dreams of childhood, this tale can be enjoyed in any season. Ages 3-6.

AN ANGEL FOR SOLOMON SINGER (1992)

Publishers Weekly

SOURCE: A review of *An Angel for Solomon Singer,* in *Publishers Weekly,* Vol. 239, No. 4, January 20, 1992, p. 64.

Solomon Singer lives a lonely life in a New York City hotel for men, but after he discovers the Westway Cafe, where the waiter, Angel, is warm and friendly, he is able to find beauty in even the bleakest surroundings. Catalanotto's paintings, each a blend of realism and keen imagination, capture and reflect the idea of transformative vision—the city's streets really do seem to shimmer like fields of wheat, the buildings' lights to twinkle like stars. Rylant's text is somewhat less persuasive, relying, alternately, on blunt, deliberate statements of emotion ("He didn't feel happy as he wandered") and sentimental formulations that ultimately seem forced—"Solomon Singer . . . ordered a bowl of tomato soup, a cup of coffee, and a balcony (but he didn't say the balcony out loud)." Compared with these gifted collaborators' earlier effort, *All I See,* this work falls somewhat short. All ages.

Kate McClelland

SOURCE: A review of *An Angel for Solomon Singer,* in *School Library Journal,* Vol. 38, No. 3, March, 1992, p. 241.

Gr 3 Up—Solomon Singer is a middle-aged man who lives in a hotel for men in New York City. One night his solitary wanderings take him into a restaurant where he reads these words on the menu: *"The Westway Cafe—where all your dreams come true."* A soft-voiced waiter (metaphorically named Angel) welcomes him and invites him back. Each night Singer returns, ordering food and, silently, ordering his wishes for the things he remembers from an Indiana boyhood. Rylant has sketched a spare portrait, in flawless, graceful prose, of a man weighted down by hopelessness. Readers do not know the details of his circumstances, but they will feel his forlornness acutely. There is a symbolic and ambiguous quality to this book, which, despite its uplifting ending, is heightened by the illustrations. Catalanotto's signature watercolors have never been more affecting. He captures the smudgy nighttime murkiness of urban streets illuminated by artificial lights that float upward to become stars and bleed downward onto wet pavements to become a vision of midwestern wheat fields. This can be read as a familiar allegory in which the mysterious stranger represents the wish giver—the angel. It also works as a straightforward reminder that, in the face of staggering social problems, a smile in chance encounters has power. Not for the average story-hour crowd, but this title will be of great value to libraries in which whole language demands new creative uses for picture books for older readers, writers, and thinkers.

WHO CAME DOWN THAT ROAD? (1992)

Publishers Weekly

SOURCE: A review of *Who Came Down That Road?,* in *Publishers Weekly,* Vol. 239, No. 29, June 29, 1992, p. 62.

The creators of **Cecil's Story** here offer a lean, lyrical text and shimmering, luminous paintings to produce an extraordinary picture book that both clarifies but doesn't oversimplify the difficult concept of historical time and evolution. A boy and his mother walk down "an old, old, old, old road" leading through the woods. "Who came down that road, Mama?" asks the child, and each turn of the page brings a time further back—the mother's "great-grandma and great-grandpa, / just married and looking to farm, / they came down that road," and before that "soldiers in blue coats," settlers, Native Americans, animals, prehistoric creatures, fish and finally—accompanied by a particularly dramatic painting—"questions crowded like a bed of stars" allude to the mysteries of creation. Each spread complements Lyon's line or two of poetic text with stunning and evocative watercolors that are filled with light and beauty. Ages 4-7.

Ellen Fader

SOURCE: A review of *Who Came Down That Road?,* in *School Library Journal,* Vol. 38, No. 10, October, 1992, p. 92.

PreS-Gr 3—Lyon tackles the difficult subject of historical continuity and evolution. The spare and elegant text creates a poetic yet childlike mood as a young boy poses a series of questions, beginning with the one in the title, concerning a road he and his mother are exploring. Her explanations carry them in reverse chronology past the time of her great-grandparents, westward settlers, Indians and buffalo, to mammoths and the period when the area was under water. The book comes to a somewhat vague conclusion in response to the boy wondering what came before: " . . . questions came before sea and ice, before mastadon and grizzly bear / before Indian and pioneer, before soldiers and newlyweds / the mystery of the making place—that came before this road." Children may have a hard time with the ending, although they will likely find the rest intriguing. Nevertheless, this is a book that will be most successful in the hands of an adult who can introduce the concepts and answer the inevitable additional questions. Catalanotto's double-page watercolor paintings, which make extensive use of light and shadow for dramatic effect, are dreamy, romanticized representations of each scenario; if laid end to end, they would create a mural that would help young readers understand the continuum.

📖 *DREAMPLACE* (1993)

Publishers Weekly

SOURCE: A review of *Dreamplace,* in *Publishers Weekly,* Vol. 240, No. 4, January 25, 1993, p. 86.

As in their previous collaboration **Who Came Down That Road?,** Lyon and Catalanotto here offer an atmospheric, shimmering glance backwards—this time at the Anasazi pueblos at Mesa Verde. Although Lyon's poem is told from the point of view and in the tone of a reflective adult, Catalanotto wisely focuses the story through his luminous paintings on the experiences of a girl who visits the canyon as a tourist. She imagines—as if she were dreaming, seeing through the scrim of historical time the Pueblo people who 800 years before "plaited sandals, wove baskets / coiled clay into pots." Then, "one day / when even trees were hungry / [they] turned their backs" on their cliff dwellings "leaving us / far in the future" standing "amazed / at the people / who built this dream / who lit its walls / with fire and stories." In both style and content, the lyrical text may be a bit sophisticated for young readers, but Catalanotto's extraordinary watercolors clarify this journey through time. Ages 4-7.

Lisa Dennis

SOURCE: A review of *Dreamplace,* in *School Library Journal,* Vol. 39, No. 3, March, 1993, p. 182.

K Up—An evocative text and exquisite illustrations lead readers on another magical journey with poet Lyon and painter Catalanotto. Once again, children are treated to a vision of the past, this time among the ruins of an Anasazi village. A young girl is the guide, and as surely as the park ranger leads her small group up the path to the ruins, this nameless narrator brings to vivid life the people who once lived in these "towers and courtyards," this "sand-castle" without water. As she imagines the details of their lives, the Anasazi appear, laughing, working, creating . . . and then, finally and inexplicably, dying,

leaving behind their homes and vanishing from history. Just as Lyon's brief text shifts effortlessly from present to past, Catalanotto's stunning paintings move from panoramic views of present-day ruins to compelling visions of everyday life in ancient times. Readers of this powerful picture book will not only feel as if they have traveled to the Southwest; seen eagles soaring; and smelled the hot, dry air; but will also believe wholeheartedly that they have truly glimpsed another time, another place, a vanished people. This book is both art and literature of a quality that is rarely seen and should be cherished. The fact that it also fits in well with today's emphasis on multicultural education and may serve to stimulate children's interest in history is just icing on the cake.

Ilene Cooper

SOURCE: A review of *Dreamplace,* in *Booklist,* Vol. 89, No. 14 March 15, 1993, p. 1321.

Ages 5-9. Joining other tourists, a young girl sees the 800-year-old site of the Anasazi as it is today, dreams of the place as it was when the tribe lived there long ago, and imagines their suffering when drought forced them to leave their home. Simple and direct, Lyon's poetic text sketches the main ideas, while the illustrations define and defy places, people, and times. Sometimes the art portrays modern-day visitors, sometimes, the ancient inhabitants, and in one scene, the place seems to exist in both times at once, the shadowy shapes of the Anasazi coexisting with the more defined figures of contemporary visitors. Rich with atmosphere, delicate with sensitivity, and dream-like in its evocation of dual realities, this would be an imaginative choice to read before a class trip to any historic site. For a more traditional look at the Anasazi, see Ayers' *The Anasazi*

📖 *THE CATSPRING SOMERSAULT FLYING ONE-HANDED FLIP-FLOP* (1993)

Publishers Weekly

SOURCE: A review of *The Catspring Somersault Flying One-Handed Flip-Flop,* in *Publishers Weekly,* Vol. 240, No. July 26, 1993, p. 70.

The heroine of this tale, who "liked doing 'boy things' so much more than she liked doing 'girl things' that everyone called her Willy," invents an amazing gymnastic move which she dubs the Catspring Somersault Flying One-Handed Flip-flop.

When her parents and 11 siblings are too busy with farm chores to watch her trick, Willy runs away in a fruitless search for a more appreciative audience. She returns home, grumpy and convinced that no one even noticed she was gone, but her family takes turns telling "the silliest story" she's ever heard, all about the rowdy farmyard melee caused by her absence. Although the text implies that the topsy-turvy goings-on were merely imaginary, the artwork suggests that these events may have actually occurred, a tension lessening the book's impact.

Catalanotto's (*All I See; Who Came Down That Road?*) sun-drenched watercolors, as lush and complex as ever, upstage first-time author Kiser's rather muddled narrative. Ages 4-7.

Nancy Vasilakis

SOURCE: A review of *The Catspring Somersault Flying One-Handed Flip-Flop,* in *The Horn Book Magazine,* Vol. 69, No. 5, September-October, 1993, p. 586.

Inspired by her grandmother's stories, the author gives a diverting account of Willy's attempts to impress her family with the acrobatics described in the title. Although Willy's situation as one of twelve children living on a family-run farm is something of an anomaly these days, her predicament will be easily understood by any child who has ever tried to get the attention of busy family members. Brothers and sisters are baking bread, feeding babies, helping Mama with the laundry or Papa with the livestock. Willy evades suggestions to lend a hand, preferring to search farther afield for an audience. She tries Grandpa down the road, but he is sound asleep on the porch. Even her best friend is away helping neighbors. Catalanotto's distinctive, impressionistic paintings depict a curly-haired, overall-clad tomboy whose facial expressions reveal her temperament and wiliness. A mumbled complaint about being ignored—"'I bet if I ran away, none of you would even know I was gone'"—expressed at the dinner table that evening brings the full force of family support down on her as each sibling describes an escalating series of disasters that would occur should Willy suddenly disappear. With her family's full attention on her at last, Willy performs her spectacular stunt right there in the dining room, and cleans up the resultant mess with a smile. This book has great read-aloud possibilities—but be sure to leave time and space for little bodies to try out their own versions of the flying one-handed flip-flop.

Alexandra Marris

SOURCE: A review of *The Catspring Somersault Flying One-Handed Flip-Flop,* in *School Library Journal,* Vol. 39, No. 10, October, 1993, pp. 101-2.

K-Gr 2—Willy (short for Wilma Letitia) lives on a farm with her mama, papa, and 11 brothers and sisters. And that's just fine with her. One day she discovers that she can do something truly amazing, but no one has time to watch—and that is not fine with Willy. By the end of the day, she's convinced that if she were to run away, her absence would not even be noticed. With warmth and humor, her family assures her that they would miss her indeed, so she demonstrates The Catspring Somersault Flying One-Handed Flip-Flop. Catalanotto's exuberant watercolor illustrations depict a spirited and mischievous girl surrounded by a loving family. Dynamic angles of the figures and unusual perspectives add to the bouncy and joyful flow of pictures and text. Expressive faces convey emotion and are highly individualized. Judging by the hairstyles and other visual clues, the scenes depicted are from the past, but could easily pass as contemporary episodes. The text flows smoothly and, although the story is a bit on the slender side, it does give a sense of familial affection and fun.

Hazel Rochman

SOURCE: A review of *The Catspring Somersault Flying One-Handed Flip-Flop,* in *Booklist,* Vol. 90, No. 7, December 1, 1993, p. 698.

Ages 3-6. The warmth of a large, busy farm family is at the center of this exuberant picture book, which is also about the difficulty of getting any personal attention in such a family. Willy's mama and papa and her 11 brothers and sisters are too busy with all their chores to watch her do her great Catspring Somersault Flying One-Handed Flip-Flop. She tries running away, but she still can't find anyone interested. Finally, at the quiet of the family dinner table, Willy says that if she ran away, no one would even miss her. "You would lose that bet, Willy," Papa says, and then everyone imagines the chaos, shouting, chasing, and excitement that would happen if the whole farm were looking for her. Catalanotto's sunlit, double-spread watercolors capture the movement and dancing energy of the country place and the determined small girl who is part of it all.

📖 *DARK CLOUD STRONG BREEZE* (1994)

Publishers Weekly

SOURCE: A review of *Dark Cloud Strong Breeze,* in *Publishers Weekly,* Vol. 241, No. 5, January 31, 1994, p. 88.

An insistently rhythmic rhyme and Catalanotto's splendid paintings describe what happens on a rainy day in a small town when a girl's father locks his keys in the car. As the father tries to jimmy the door with a coat hanger, his daughter makes friends with nearby shopkeepers and animals: "Dark cloud brisk breeze / 'Hey, Mister Locksmith, will you help us, please?' / 'Yes,' says Locksmith, clicka-me-clong / 'If you get me a guard, both brave and strong.'" The make-up, onomatopoeic phrases in Patron's (*Burgoo Stew*) bouncy couplets become a bit cloying; the book demands, somewhat too forcefully, to be read aloud. Overlaid on each black-and-white spread of the street activities is a full-color closeup that zooms in on the girl's endeavors to help, which result in the participation of dog, grocer, cat and butterfly. Despite Catalanotto's (*Mr. Mumble*) unique design, the sequential connections in the verse do not always make clear the connections between the plot and the disparate characters. The ending comes full circle as the pair returns home: the father has lost his house key. Ages 3-6.

Kay Weisman

SOURCE: A review of *Dark Cloud Strong Breeze,* in *Booklist,* Vol. 90, No. 14, March 15, 1994, p. 1374.

Ages 3-6. Strong, rhythmic verses combine with exuberant watercolor illustrations in this cumulative tale of a young girl and her father who are locked out of their car. Darkening sky and a brisk wind signal an approaching rain storm, but Dad seems unable to cope with the sight of his keys locked inside the car. Meanwhile, his resourceful young daughter sets off to find a locksmith, Unfortunately the locksmith can't leave his shop unguarded, and the girl finds herself eliciting the help of a dog, a cat, a butterfly, and a grocer to solve their predicament. Although reminiscent of "The Old Woman and Her Pig," this is a thoroughly modern story with a contemporary problem addressed in jazzy, rhymed couplets ("Dark cloud brisk breeze / 'Hey, Mister Locksmith, will you help us, please?' / 'Yes,' says Locksmith, clicka-me-clong / 'if you get me a guard, both brave and strong'"). Small, full-color illustrations depicting the daughter's activities) have been superimposed over black-and-white double-page spreads (showing Dad's unsuccessful efforts). The result is both aesthetically pleasing and vital to an understanding of the story. Patron's distinctive language makes this an obvious choice for a spring story hour; Catalanotto's expressive faces and intriguing details will bring children back for repeat viewings.

Vanessa Elder

SOURCE: A review of *Dark Cloud Strong Breeze,* in *School Library Journal,* Vol. 40, No. 5, May, 1994, pp. 102-3.

PreS-Gr 1—A rhyming, cumulative story told by a little girl whose hapless father has locked his keys in the car. As he struggles with a wire hanger and the sky threatens to storm, she comes up with a singing-in-the-rain plan of action. With the help of a friendly German Shepherd, a grocer, a white cat, a butterfly, and a locksmith, "the car gets unlocked, jangle-me jome / The car gets unlocked, and we drive home." Fortunately, the girl has her house key, because her father has lost his. Catalanotto's double-page watercolors realistically and sensitively capture expressions and scenes and complement Patron's whimsical, alliterative text. The adult's predicament and the suburban storefronts are depicted in shades of black and white; the child (wearing foul-weather gear and carrying a colorful umbrella) and her adventures are painted in vibrant color. A sunny book about getting caught in the rain on a spring day.

Nancy Vasilakis

SOURCE: A review of *Dark Cloud Strong Breeze,* in *The Horn Book Magazine,* Vol. 70, No. 3, May-June, 1994, p. 318.

In this rhyming circular tale a quick-thinking little girl comes to her father's rescue when they return from shopping to discover that he has locked the keys inside the car. She runs across the street to a locksmith, who agrees to help, "clicka-me-clong / If you get me a guard, both brave and strong." Thereupon the girl asks a dog, who leads her to a grocer, then to a cat, and finally to a butterfly. Reversing her steps, she satisfies each request until the locksmith opens the car door. Once home, father fumbles for his house keys, but his resourceful daughter proudly produces her own, hanging from a chain around her neck. The jingle is catchy; allusions to a hovering storm adding a mite more tension to the slight narrative line; but it is Catalanotto's paintings that really capture attention. The expressive features of the little girl and the befuddled look of the helpless dad as he presses his nose to the car window have the winsome informality of subjects caught off-guard in candid snapshots. An unusual three-dimensional effect is achieved by superimposing large inset pictures that portray action in full color over a background painted in subtle gray tones. An enticing read-aloud for pre-school story hour.

MAMA IS A MINER (1994)

Hazel Rochman

SOURCE: A review of *Mama Is a Miner,* in *Booklist,* Vol. 90, No. 19-20, June 1, 1994, p. 1810.

Age 4-8. Mama is a coal miner in Appalachia. From the warmth of the family kitchen, a child thinks about her mother's job, and words and pictures set the worlds of home and work side by side. While the child settles on the bus to school, Mama rides two miles in a low car headed for Black Mountain's heart. Deep underground, she bends and sweats with her work team, shoveling coal or keeping watch on the working face, her cap light bobbing in the glittery dark. Children will hear the poetry that leaps from the particulars of the workplace, both in the child's simple narrative and in the miners' rhymes ("Mountain gold, black as night. / Some big city's heat and light"). Catalanotto's double-page-spread watercolors focus on the loving bond between the child and her mother, when they're together in the light-filled house, and when they're thinking of each other above and below ground. This mother never seems to get tired or cross, but there's no idealization of her work: mining is hard and dirty and dangerous; you do it because it pays the bills in hard times ("Son of a quarter / daughter of a dime, / shoveling soup / on the old belt line"). There's drudgery underground and drama and powerful technology that "roars at the rock and rips coal from the seam." Set against that is the family dinner table, orderly and beautiful. Even when Mama is deep down the mine, she's "digging for home."

Publishers Weekly

SOURCE: A review of *Mama Is a Miner,* in *Publishers Weekly,* Vol. 241, No. 28, July 11, 1994, p. 78.

"When I'm settled on Bus 34 / Mama's crowded into a low car / cap light off, dozing, swaying / headed for Black Mountain's heart," says the narrator, who describes in detail her mother's job as a coal miner. Unfortunately, the warmth and originality of this family story are undermined by a needlessly complicated format and structure. Lyon poetically juxtaposes informative sections about mining with the story of the mother "digging for home"; but, in a voice detached from the rest of the fact-filled narrative, she interjects bewildering, if colorful, quatrains ("Firedamp, blackdamp, / Fire Boss checks the air / Bad top, kettle bottom: / don't go there"). Catalanotto (Lyon's collaborator on *Cecil's Story* and *Who Came Down That Road?*) alternates affectionate portraits of the family above ground with dark scenes of the "miles deep" mine, but the relation of his superb watercolors to the text is not always clear. Underneath a painting of a tea kettle on a kitchen stove, for example, the text reads, "Screak and ring, rail wheels sing. / Back into black. Battery pack." An interesting miss. Ages 5-8.

Lee Bock

SOURCE: A review of *Mama Is a Miner,* in *School Library Journal,* Vol. 40, No. 9, September, 1994, p. 189.

K-Gr 3—A child is drawing and thinking at the kitchen table as her mother prepares the evening meal. The room is warm, and light is all around them—in the windows, on the toaster, stovetop, teapot, and calendar. The reflections are identical to those made by her mother's head lamp that she wears deep in the dark earth. The woman is a miner. Lyon's prose is rhythmic, authentic, and strong, using the first-person narrative of a child effectively. The result is a picture of a young girl who is at once proud, awed, and worried about her mother. Dialogue is spare but significant, consisting mainly of Mama's oft-repeated phrases: "Hard work for hard times" and "I'm digging for home." The satisfying ending shows the child inside a light-flooded mountain made of blankets, revealing what she has been drawing all evening: a picture of her mother in work gear. Visually, the book is breathtaking, intertwining elements from the mine and home, child and parent, family chores and work for money. Mama brings light—into the mine and into the home—and Catalanotto's full-page, luminous watercolor illustrations vibrate with this energy. Muted shapes, soft edges, creative perspectives, and blending of scenes all come together to enhance the story of a youngster's complicated thoughts and emotions. This book packs a lot into its 32 pages and is far more than a simple "I'm so proud of my Mama" career-exploration story.

THE PAINTER (1995)

Publishers Weekly

SOURCE: A review of *The Painter,* in *Publishers Weekly,* Vol. 242, No. 34, August 21, 1995, p. 64.

Childlike narration and diffused, impressionistic watercolors seamlessly stitch together a heartwarming celebration of family love. As in Fred Marcellino's *Puss in Boots,* the main characters appear in an arresting joint portrait on the front cover of the book, with the title and credits relegated to the back. The text, like a quiet voice-over in a film, begins before the title page: "My daddy's a painter," says the narrator. Father and daughter meet mostly at mealtimes—reading the comics, cooking, doing magic tricks—while the mother looks on and comments. "We're very good dancers," the girl announces as the father strikes a flamboyant pose, gripping a rose in his teeth. "'Silly,' says Mommy. 'Funny,' says me." Because she patiently gives her father time to work, the girl is rewarded after dinner with admittance to his studio, where she paints a cheerful family portrait that is reproduced at the end of the story. In realistically acknowledging that children frequently desire more attention than their parents can give them, Catalanotto adds credibility to the uplifting resolution. His book subtly attests to the joy inherent in the creation of both life and art. Ages 4-7.

Lisa Dennis

SOURCE: A review of *The Painter,* in *School Library Journal,* Vol. 41, No. 9, September, 1995, p. 168.

PreS-Gr 2—This joyous celebration of creativity and connection combines luminous watercolors with a succinct, convincing first-person narrative to capture the love between parent and child and the pleasure of self-expression. Catalanotto's light-filled paintings create a sunny world inhabited by a bearded artist-father, a loving mother, their exuberant daughter, and a most engaging German Shepherd. The child's description of her relationship with her father begins even before the title page and reveals their enjoyment of one another whether they are cooking breakfast, reading the comics, or dancing. Sometimes, of course, he is too busy working to spend time with her. The story ends on a high note, however, for after a long day without his company, she is permitted to join him in his studio and try her hand at painting, too. The gloriously childlike result is displayed on the final pages, with the girl's cheerfully self-

confident assertion: "I'm a painter now." The book's originality is immediately apparent in the unusual cover and in the multilayered levels of reality in the illustrations. The pictures expand the brief text, injecting it with humor and adding depth of meaning. This delightful work of art deserves a place in every collection.

A DAY AT DAMP CAMP (1996)

Ruth Semrau

SOURCE: A review of *A Day at Damp Camp,* in *School Library Journal,* Vol. 42, No. 4, April, 1996, p. 114.

K-Gr 3—Megan and Sarah begin their camp experience as loners and end it as supportive friends. The journey takes them through craft classes, swimming, hiking, and campfires. Told in three pairs of words per spread—"HIGH SKY / BACK PACK / SNAIL TRAIL"—the text is both spare and lyrical. Catalanotto's innovative style layers watercolor paintings on top of one another, three scenes to a page, so that only the top one is fully visible. They are planned so carefully, however, that viewers may imagine what is hidden from sight. Extraordinary work is what we've come to expect from these collaborators, and the promise is once again delivered

Susan Dove Lempke

SOURCE: A review of *A Day at Damp Camp,* in *Booklist,* Vol. 92, No. 17, May 1, 1996, p. 1512.

Ages 6-8. The end papers help tell the story in this picture book, beginning with an array of camp clothing spread out, each item neatly labeled "Megan." Next we see a girl wearing the labeled flip-flops heading to the outhouse, followed by the first of the book's double-page spreads. On each spread, a picture is within a picture with in a picture, each labeled with a rhyming pair of words, each following a group of girl campers through their day, as they see things on a hike ("frog log / bugtug / snakeshake") and set up tents for the night. Without close observation, readers will enjoy a mundane but colorful series of camp activities, but keen observation is rewarded with a gradually unfolding story of friendship, culminating in a joint trip to the spooky outhouse. The closing end papers show Megan's once-tidy wardrobe in satisfyingly mud-spattered disarray, mixed in with more clothes labeled "Sarah." Catalanotto's sun-dappled, joyful pictures will have both adult and child readers longing for camp to start. Be sure to point this title out to scout leaders.

MY HOUSE HAS STARS (1996)

Publishers Weekly

SOURCE: A review of *My House Has Stars,* in *Publishers Weekly,* Vol. 243, No. 35, August 26, 1996, p. 97.

McDonald (*Is This a House for Hermit Crab?*) turns to geography here, showing vastly different houses from around the world which all have one feature in common: the "roof" of stars that hangs over them. Eight colorful, dense vignettes feature a child describing his or her home ("My house has walls made of sheep's wool and a real door in the front of the tent that squeaks like a crybaby"). The "tour" of each dwelling, be it houseboat, igloo, skyscraper, yurt, etc., concludes with a reference to the stars above; for example, a child in a pueblo says, "I see stars, like tiny handprints, where Coyote scattered the mica dust and stars were born!" Unexplained facts and referents abound, tantalizing readers but also likely to frustrate them: What is a jeepney? Why does the Weaver Princess star go to meet the Ox Boy star? Catalanotto's (*Who Came Down That Road?*) diffused watercolors show the children in their environments. Facing art, beneath the blocks of text, clues readers into the characters' locations: a hazy map of the world, with the child's homeland circled. The impressionistic style of the pictures suggests as much as it represents. Unfortunately, this approach exacerbates the gaps left in the vignettes. At best this is a lyrical invitation to a scavenger hunt on the reference shelf; otherwise it is essentially a cliff-hanger. Ages 5-8.

Sally R. Dow

SOURCE: A review of *My House Has Stars,* in *School Library Journal,* Vol. 42, No. 10, October, 1996, pp. 102-3.

K-Gr 4—Children from widely different cultures have one thing in common—all of their homes have a view of the night sky. From the roof of his mud-walled house in Nepal, Akam sees stars; Carmen watches them from her houseboat in the Philippines; Abu sees the night sky from his village in Ghana; Mariko looks out of paper windows from her house in Japan. In an

adobe pueblo, Chili can see the stars when he climbs to his flat rooftop; Oyun sees the heavens above her yurt in the Mongolian desert; Sergio goes out on the roof of his Brazilian city skyscraper to see the night sky, and Mattie views the winter night from her igloo in Alaska. The concept of one earth, one sky unfolds in poetic imagery embracing the universality of people everywhere: "Our house, the earth. Our roof, the sky." Full-page watercolor paintings in soft, misty colors reflect the awesome quality of the universe as viewed by youngsters throughout the world.

Carolyn Phelan

SOURCE: A review of *My House Has Stars,* in *Booklist,* Vol. 93, No. 5, November 1, 1996, p. 508.

Ages 5-8. In the framework story, a mother tells her daughter that "night is falling somewhere. And now. And now again. Night is coming to this sky. To houses everywhere. This house. / And there are stars." In the pages that follow, eight children around the world tell about their homes at night: a houseboat in the Philippines, a mud house in Nepal, a group of round huts in Ghana, a Japanese house, an adobe pueblo, a Mongolian yurt, a skyscraper apartment in Brazil, and a house on the Alaskan tundra. Each child, each culture views the night sky and the stars in a slightly different way, yet as the book's point of view pulls back visually in the last pages, it is clear that earth is home to all, and the roof above our heads is the same sky. Catalanotto's impressionistic watercolor paintings capture each culture's individuality yet maintain the same soft-focus view of the world after darkness falls. Although the scenes take place at night, each is full of light: firelight, starlight, moonlight, city lights, the northern lights, and even the light of glowing silkworms. All add to the sense of wonder created by the well-crafted words and art in this purposeful yet impressive picture book.

THE ROLLING STORE (1997)

Stephanie Zvirin

SOURCE: A review of *The Rolling Store,* in *Booklist,* Vol. 93, No. 12, February 15, 1997, p. 1026.

Ages 5-8. There's much to like about this book—a quiet nostalgia, an almost lyrical text, and wistfully realistic paintings washed in a golden haze. But this is a complicated book, in both the telling and the art, and the positioning of the title page at the back of the book is confusing despite the flap-copy note. The narrative is less a story than a pleasant memory delivered secondhand. While working industriously to make colorful strings of beads, cookies, and the like, a little girl tells her friend about the goods-laden red truck that visited rural African American communities during her grand father's childhood days. The accompanying watercolors sweep readers along, blending present and past—the grandfather appears as a little boy in a hat)—until the book comes full circle to focus on the friends, who, it seems, have been working on goods for a rolling store of their own. A sweet, upbeat story, but best for lapsharing.

Publishers Weekly

SOURCE: A review of *The Rolling Store,* in *Publishers Weekly,* Vol. 244, No. 11, March 17, 1997, p. 82.

A nostalgic look at old-time peddlers inspires two enterprising youngsters in Johnson's (*When I Am Old with You*) tender story. An African American girl tells her friend about her grandfather's fond memory of the Rowing Store that came, "with all its wonders" to "the crossroads by the pine woods" so people could buy "what they needed and didn't need." And while the two kids imagine what shopping was like in Granddaddy's day, they are busy preparing some Rolling Store magic of their own. Catalanotto's **(Who Came Down That Road?)** sun-splashed watercolor-and-pencil paintings simultaneously depict the breezy summer scenes of Granddaddy's country childhood and those of the two contemporary children baking the cookies, squeezing the lemonade, painting the rocks and stringing bead necklaces that they will sell from their red-wagon rolling store. The girl's careful recollection—and imitation—of her grandfather's descriptions subtly demonstrate the warm respect and love she has for him. The girl and her pal also exhibit a lively sense of fun and of teamwork. Ages 4-7.

📖 *LETTER TO THE LAKE* (1998)

Shelle Rosenfeld

SOURCE: A review of *Letter of the Lake,* in *Booklist,* Vol. 94, No. 16, April 15, 1998, p. 1454.

Ages 6-8. On a gray, cold winter's day, so cold the car won't start, Rosie warms herself with memories of summer at the lake, her wonderful times there and her anticipation of returning. As Rosie and her mother wait for a friend to jump-start the car, Rosie thinks of the things she loves best at the lake: the blue water and sky, the beautiful herons and dragonflies, skipping stones on the lake's smooth surface. This simple, quiet tale is enhanced by fantastic, innovative illustrations in which we view what Rosie both sees and imagines, her perspective of both the gray winter scenes and her bright, colorful remembrances juxtaposed among and above them. Unusual details invite a closer look on each page, and color is used sparingly to distinguish the dark wintertime from the summer light and life at the lake. A fine and visually astonishing book about the power of dreaming and memories.

Publishers Weekly

SOURCE: A review of *Letter of the Lake,* in *Publishers Weekly,* Vol. 245, No. 16, April 20, 1998, p. 65.

Despite Catalanotto's **(Dylan's Day Out)** exquisite paintings, this exploration of a child's winter memories of her summer at the lake seems too self-consciously contrived to be compelling. "Dear Lake," writes Rosie, "When I think of you, I think of rocks hiding under the waves, like secrets. Remember me, your friend Rosie?" Catalanotto intersperses visibly frigid black-and-white illustrations of Rosie and her mother in winter with full-color paintings of Rosie's memories of warm days at the lake. Occasionally, the two worlds overlap in the girl's imagination: a black-and-white painting of the kitchen table shows a glimpse of Rosie's face in the reflection of the toaster, alongside a tray that contains just a hint of the lake's blue and purple landscape. Rosie's random reminiscences are sometimes poetic ("Our windows rattle, trying to get warm" or "I want to row all the way to summer, where you float the water lilies, . . . ") and other times less involving ("I'm having toast for breakfast, with lots of raspberry jam. The kitchen window is covered over with frost. I keep some rocks from last summer on the windowsill"), but Swanson's (*Getting Used to the Dark*) epistolary style sounds too adult in tone to be convincing. On the other hand, the inventive perspectives and splashes of color in Catalanotto's impressionistic watercolors visually capture the complicated relationship between one's memory and experience. Ages 4-7.

Tana Elias

SOURCE: A review of *Letter of the Lake,* in *School Library Journal,* Vol. 44, No. 5, May, 1998, pp. 126-27.

K-Gr 1—In the middle of a cold and snowy winter, Rosie composes an imaginary letter to the lake where she spends summer vacations. She carries a rock that reminds her of her time there, and the paintings envision similar touchstones—a small school of fish floating on the ceiling of Rosie's room, a patch of water weeds visible in the kitchen, etc. Words and images alternate seamlessly between the carefree summer remembrances and the grimmer winter realities—a harried-looking mother fretting over her checkbook and a car that won't start. All morning, the child carries her rock, but once she and her mother have gotten the car started, she slips the rock into her mother's pocket, hoping that it will cheer her. Rosie's powerful imagination helps her through the dreary day, and her point of view is consistently conveyed through both the text and the artwork. Nearly black-and-white illustrations (with the briefest touch of summer superimposed on them) indicate a sober, winter-clothed child and her mother, interspersed with full-color pictures representing the lake in summer. One stunning full-page spread combines the two in an image of Rosie shedding her winter clothes in the same manner geese take flight as she rows past them on the lake. An excellent book for reading to one or more children who will enjoy picking out the seasonal differences in the art and will identify with the yearning for the uncomplicated times of summer.

CIRCLE OF THANKS (1998)

Shelle Rosenfeld

SOURCE: A review of *Circle to Thanks,* in *Booklist,* Vol. 95, No. 2, September 15, 1998, p. 236.

Ages 4-7. As the seasons are cyclical, so are good deeds, in this mystical tale of the tundra. When a young boy's mother rescues an otter pup, the action sets off a chain of other brave, benevolent acts among animals in the wild. The otter gives his fish dinner to an injured raven; the raven uses his flock to call a mother caribou's attention to her lost calf; the caribou springs an arctic fox from a trap. When the boy becomes injured, the arctic fox plays a hand in his rescue and return to his mother. Beautiful watercolor illustrations dramatically portray the ever-changing landscape of the Far North, from snowy winters to the vibrant, bloom-filled springs, as well as expressive, appealing renditions of the humans and animals that populate this fascinating environment. Although some would dispute the idea that animals are capable of compassion toward other species, this picture book effectively illustrates the concept of the importance of helping others—the favor may one day be returned.

Publishers Weekly

SOURCE: A review of *Circle to Thanks,* in *Publishers Weekly,* October 19, 1998, p. 79.

The drama and interconnectedness of the natural world swirl through this luminous picture book set on the Alaskan tundra. An unnamed boy and his mother venture into the spring sunshine, gorgeously depicted as bands of color in Catalanotto's (*The Painter*) striking watercolors. When Mama rescues an otter pup that has fallen into icy water, the otter seemingly responds by later performing a good deed for an injured raven. Thus, a chain of kind acts is set in motion, from animal to animal, throughout each season of the year. In the end, an arctic fox plays a role when the boy injures himself and cannot get home as a snowstorm approaches. In evocative language, Fowler (*I'll See You When the Moon Is Full*) introduces a somewhat exotic, isolated region of wide-open spaces, where humans are completely in tune with and responsive to nature; a gentle humor keeps the tone from being earnest or precious. She also effectively relays bits of information about the wildlife and flora indigenous to Alaska as well as basic animal behavior. Catalanotto's delicately lit art fluidly renders the beauty of a rugged wilderness in both summer bloom and winter snow. Thanks to imaginative perspectives, the interactions between his animals seem spontaneous and dynamic. Ages 4-7.

Pam Gosner

SOURCE: A review of *Circle to Thanks,* in *School Library Journal,* Vol. 44, No. 12, December, 1998, p. 82.

K-Gr 3—Alaska is the setting for this satisfying circular tale. A Yupik mother's rescue of an otter pup in the spring sets in motion a chain of kindness from one animal to another over the seasons. The circle is complete as winter approaches and the mother is led to her injured son by an arctic fox. In spite of their active participation in acts of charity, the animals are not otherwise anthropomorphized. The focus is on the natural world and the interrelatedness of all living things (although romanticized). Catalanotto's realistic yet poetic watercolors, similar to his paintings in George Ella Lyon's *Dreamplace* (Orchard, 1993), wonderfully capture the sweep of the tundra. The artist uses unusual points of view to increase the drama of the encounters between animals, or animals and people, and beautifully captures the warmth of the cozy cabin and the love shared by the boy and his mother. Pair this with Virginia L. Kroll's *The Seasons and Someone* (Harcourt, 1994), which is also set in Alaska, and James Magdanz's *Go Home, River* (Alaska Northwest, 1996), which gives a picture of native life before European contact.

THE LONGEST WAIT (1998)

Publishers Weekly

SOURCE: A review of *The Longest Wait,* in *Publishers Weekly,* Vol. 245, No. 38, September 21, 1998, p. 83.

A snowstorm in a time of wooden sleds and horse-drawn wagons is the setting for this picture-book slice of life. Although Thomas's mother warns that "a man's not fit" for "strong wind and deep snow," not even the driving blizzard outside their door keeps Thomas's mailman father from his charge. Catalanotto's (*Letter to the Lake*) full-spread watercolors not only portray the family's anxiety as they wait for the father's return, but in dreamlike line drawings behind or beside the contemporaneous action, he suggests both past and future events. The illustrations convey, for instance, the fun Thomas imagines he will have in the snow when Daddy comes home; then later, as Thomas listens to his feverish father's account of the day, the artist portrays the hardships the father suffered in the blinding snow. The paintings supply the emotional moods absent from the text. While Bradby's (*More Than Anything Else*) first-person narration through Thomas's eyes is sprinkled with poetic images (e.g., "a sea of snow rolled and sprayed the air thick with white sparkles"; Daniel sits in a rocking chair "rocking the time away"), readers rarely witness the protagonist's reactions. His father recounts a catastrophic day that puts his health at risk, but only Catalanotto's portraits convey the boy's responses. Ages 4-7.

Irene Symons

SOURCE: A review of *The Longest Wait,* in *School Library Journal,* Vol. 44, No. 12, December, 1998, p. 81.

K-Gr 3—Readers will be immediately drawn into this episode from the lives of a close-knit African-American family somewhere in rural America. The book begins with dramatic watercolor paintings of a blizzard and the simple phrase, "Daddy went out in the snow." Thomas's father is a mailman setting out on horseback to deliver the mail despite the terrible storm. The children are sure he'll be fine because "Daddy can do anything," but their mother is worried. While waiting, Thomas thinks about all of the things he'll do with his father when he returns. However, when supper time has passed and the man is still not home, the boy's confidence turns to anxiety. Suspense builds subtly. Even when the child sees the horse come back, through the snow it isn't clear whether or not it has a rider. Children may be confused by the placement of the title page, which comes after the first few pages of text and breaks the mood created in the opening pages. Still, this is a fine book for units on the family or courage and makes an appealing readaloud. A comforting story with a poetic style and evocative artwork.

Linda Perkins

SOURCE: A review of *The Longest Wait,* in *Booklist,* Vol. 95, No. 7, December 1, 1998, p. 669.

Ages 4-8. Determined to deliver the mail, Thomas' father sets off on horseback in a blinding snowstorm. As they wait for his return, his wife "worries up two batches of rolls," but a confident Thomas makes plans for sledding and snowball fights. Nearly frozen, Daddy returns and describes the effects of the blizzard on the town. When his father comes down with a raging fever, Thomas almost wishes it had never snowed, but the fever breaks, the storm subsides, and the boy goes out to play in the snow. Compressed to fit the picturebook format, the "wait" does not seem a long one, but the spare narrative convincingly portrays the boy's shift from excitement to anxiety to relief. The watercolor illustrations are most effective when contrasting warm, glowing interiors with the white, blinding snowstorm. Distant human figures and profiles are more expressive than some of the awkwardly rendered faces. Based on an actual event, this is a natural introduction to family stories.

📖 *CELEBRATE!: STORIES OF THE JEWISH HOLIDAYS* (1998)

Publishers Weekly

SOURCE: A review of *Celebrate!: Stories of the Jewish Holidays,* in *Publishers Weekly,* Vol. September 28, 1998, p. 95.

Berger's lively, detailed and all-around enjoyable collection is indeed something to celebrate. Gathered here are explanations of the major holidays of the Jewish faith, which, according to the author, are part of a tradition more than three thousand years old. From the Sabbath through Rosh Hashanah, Purim, Passover and Shavuot, Berger explores the historical significance of each holiday, the story from the Bible that reinforces it, the season of its celebration and the customs that make these days special as well as fun. Following each Bible story, Berger includes sections on "What We Celebrate," "How We Celebrate" and "Crafts and Food." For example, on Sukkot, a family can share the story of Moses leading his people through the desert (from Exodus and Leviticus), read about building a sukkah shelter/hut and enjoy a harvest casserole (recipe provided). Catalanotto's dramatic watercolors illustrate such legendary scenes as Jonah being pursued by the great whale, a Hanukkah lamp burning bright and Queen Esther saving her people from King Ahasuerus. This volume is sure to receive much use throughout the year and become a treasured family favorite. Ages 4-up.

📖 *BOOK* (1999)

Susan Dove Lempke

SOURCE: A review of *Book,* in *Booklist,* Vol. 95, No. 18, May 15, 1999, p. 1693.

Gr. 2-5, younger for reading aloud. Frequent collaborators Lyon and Catalanotto pair up again to evoke in words and pictures the magic of a book: "A BOOK is a HOUSE / that is all windows and doors." During the course of the story, Lyon uses the metaphors of a tree, a chest, and a farm, and turns the reader into the weather and the writer into the farmer: "Now you meet / as the gate of the book / swings wide." A blonde little girl in red pajamas opens the cover (or is it a door?) of a giant book and steps into the book's world, which is depicted in richly intense watercolors. The writer/farmer is shown with arms outspread, his words shooting out in all directions and curling to wrap around the little gift in a celebration of the con-nection between author and reader. This will be an especially good choice for using in the classroom to teach writing.

Miriam Lang Budin

SOURCE: A review of *Book,* in *School Library Journal,* Vol. 45, No. 6, June, 1999, p. 119.

K-Gr 4—In this short poem, Lyon presents metaphors about books: "A BOOK is a HOUSE / that is all windows and doors" or " . . . a CHEST / that keeps the heart's treasure" or " . . . a FARM, / its fields sown with words." Catalanotto's watercolors show a blond-haired girl moving through the scenarios evoked by the text. Many of the words from the poem are incorporated into the pictures; they swirl around the girl and appear strewn across the sky or floating in the air. This is an earnest effort, but the overall effect is pretentious and unlikely to engage readers of any age. We are better off reading good books to children than trying to describe their effect in picture-book format.

📖 *DAD & ME* (1999)

Publishers Weekly

SOURCE: A review of *Dad & Me,* in *Publishers Weekly,* Vol. 246, No. 32, August 9, 1999, p. 351.

"Today the first American is going to walk in space," begins this tale of a father and son's reconciliation. Tommy is looking forward to telling his father about the spaceship blastoff he's seen on TV at school, but his father pulls up to the driveway and "growls, 'move your bike. Now!'" Tommy is devastated, "A million stars burst in my body. Hot and cold." The language may be strong, but Tommy's feelings of rejection are believable, and when Dad finally understands Tommy's distress, he comes to the small astronaut's rescue. Catalanotto's (*Mr. Mumble*; *The Painter*) watercolors are breathtaking, but so abstruse that even adult readers may be confused. Each spread shimmers with light, brims with intriguing designs and details that reinforce the period setting, and the faces seem alive with energy and emotion. But the conceit of having the father and his car represent the father himself is cumbersome. For example, paired with the text "Maybe Dad doesn't care about spacewalking" is an illustration of Tommy watching his father drive the car through the living room, as if the man had just blown through the patio doors. When

Dad orders Tommy to remove his colander / space helmet, "Dad beeps, 'No helmets at the table'" and the father and his car are pictured tableside. The book succeeds in representing a boy's imaginary play world as well as his changing moods, but the forced exposition at the beginning, the complexity of the visual images and the heavy-handed symbolism may make the book difficult for young readers to understand. Ages 5-8.

Margaret Jennings

SOURCE: A review of *Dad & Me,* in *School Library Journal,* Vol. 46, No. 1, January, 2000, p. 93.

Gr 1-2-Tommy has a very active imagination. His favorite fantasy involves pretending he is exploring outer space while his father flies his spaceship. So June 3, 1965, the day the first American walks in space, is a very big day for him. His excitement builds over the course of his day and he can hardly wait to share it with his father. When dad gets home, however, he is in a bad mood. He yells at Tommy and sends him to his room. Feeling that his father doesn't care about him, the child acts out by pasting a picture of his face on the body of the astronaut in the newspaper. When dad sees the paper, he changes his attitude and calls Tommy on his walkie-talkie for another imaginary adventure in space. The watercolor illustrations lend a nostalgic feel to the story. Period details abound and the composition is inventive, if at times, bizarre. Dad is always depicted behind the wheel of his sedan even in the living room and at the dinner table. The surreal elements may confuse and even frighten literal-minded youngsters and there isn't enough of a story for more sophisticated picture-book readers. Anyone looking for a lighthearted look at fathers or space adventure will want to explore further.

Additional coverage of Catalanotto's life and work is contained in the following sources published by The Gale Group: *Contemporary Authors,* Vol. 138; *Contemporary Authors New Revision Series,* Vol. 68; *Something about the Author Autobiography Series,* Vol. 25; *Something about the Author,* Vols. 70, 113, 114.

Christopher Paul Curtis
1954-

American novelist.

Major works include *The Watsons Go to Birmingham—1963* (1995) and *Bud, Not Buddy* (1999).

INTRODUCTION

Curtis is the author of two highly praised novels for intermediate readers, *The Watsons Go to Birmingham—1963* and *Bud, Not Buddy,* the tale of an orphan in search of his father during the Great Depression, which won both the Newbery Medal and the Coretta Scott King Award for fiction in 2000. A former auto factory worker from Flint, Michigan, Curtis began writing during breaks on the assembly line and eventually left that job to pursue a career as an author. His first novel, the comic coming-of-age story *The Watsons Go to Birmingham—1963,* also won numerous honors, including being named an American Library Association Best Book for Young Adults, a Newbery and King honor book, and the winner of a Golden Kite Award.

BIOGRAPHICAL INFORMATION

Curtis was the second of five children born to Herman Curtis, a chiropodist who later worked as an auto worker, and Leslie Curtis, a homemaker. Raised in Flint, Michigan, he worked at the Fisher Body assembly plant there for more than a decade after graduating from high school and put his dreams of a college education on hold for several years. He began attending classes at the University of Michigan part time while holding down another job and finally graduated in 1996. During that time, encouraged by winning the university's Hopwood prize for a rough draft of his story, Curtis agreed with his wife's suggestion that he take a year off to see what he could do as a writer. Curtis, who now lives in Windsor, Ontario, wrote *The Watsons* longhand in the children's section of the Windsor Public Library and completed the story by the end of 1993. He entered his manuscript in a national writing contest, where it came to the attention of Delacorte editors. Although his story did not meet the contest's content guidelines, Delacorte editor Wendy Lamb responded favorably to the novel and began making arrangements to publish it.

MAJOR WORKS

Curtis's debut novel, *The Watsons Go to Birmingham—1963* is a coming-of-age tale focusing on ten-year-old Kenny Watson, who lives with his family in a predominately black neighborhood in Flint. The novel follows the close-knit "Weird Watsons," as they travel to the racially divided South during the Civil Rights Movement of the 1960s. *The Watsons Go to Birmingham* has been praised for its warmly drawn characters and its vivid settings. The entertaining tale includes Curtis's memories of his own childhood, as well as a historic event—the bombing of Birmingham's Sixteenth Avenue Baptist Church in September 1963.

During the summer of 1963, Kenny's parents decide to take a vacation to Birmingham, Alabama, the home of Grandma Sands, to see if she can discipline Kenny's obstinate and unruly thirteen-year-old brother, Byron. After packing, everyone piles into the family car, the "Brown Bomber," to begin the long journey. In Birmingham, the mood of the novel shifts—the lighthearted hijinks of the Watson brood suddenly become overshadowed by the racial tensions of the era. Kenny and his family experience racial violence first-hand when four girls are killed after a bomb explodes in the Sunday school classroom where Kenny's little sister Joetta has been. Although Joetta is physically unharmed, she and the rest of her family return to Michigan transformed by their experiences.

Remarking on the shift between the humorous first part of Curtis's novel and its tragic ending, Betsy Hearne wrote in the *Bulletin of the Center for Children's Books*: "The contrast is startling, innovative, and effective . . . showing how—and why—the Civil Rights movement affected individual African Americans." *Horn Book* reviewer Martha V. Parravano similarly asserted that "Curtis's control of his material is superb as he unconventionally shifts tone and mood, as he depicts the changing relationship between the two brothers, and as he incorporates a factual event into his fictional story." "Evoking a full spectrum of emotions, this exceptional first novel is certain to reverberate within the reader's psyche," according to a reviewer for *Publishers Weekly*.

Described by *Horn Book* reviewer Roger Sutton as "a story that's as far-fetched as it is irresistible, and as classic as it is immediate," Curtis's second novel *Bud, Not Buddy* was an even greater success than his first. Set during the Great Depression, the story is told from the perspective of a ten-year-old who flees a foster home and travels across Michigan in search of his father. In and out of temporary homes since his mother died when he was six, Bud Caldwell believes his father is the bandleader Herman E. Calloway and sets out on foot from Flint to Grand Rapids to find him. Along his journey he meets a variety of characters; the narrative is rich with plot twists in a manner that more than one critic deemed Dickensian.

The character of Bud himself has drawn much critical favor and many devoted readers, particularly for his list of "Rules and Things for Having a Funner Life and Making a Better Liar Out of Yourself," including Number 83, the universal insight that "If an Adult Tells You Not to Worry, and You Weren't Worried Before, You Better Hurry Up and Start 'Cause You're Already Running Late." According to a *Publishers Weekly* reviewer, "While the grim conditions of the times and the harshness of Bud's circumstances are authentically depicted, Curtis shines on them an aura of hope and optimism." Curtis's editor Wendy Lamb noted that each of his books "is carried along by the exaggerated tone and the heightened childlike energy of the voice, and by the tension created when

[Curtis] sets each boy up against a great, dark force: the bombing; the Depression; racism. In *Bud, Not Buddy* the rules are funny and to the point, but they also show us what inspired them—Bud's hard, hard life in the hands of strangers." Michael Cart concluded in *Booklist*, that "in dramatizing Bud's experience, Curtis turns his novel into a celebration of the human capacity for simple goodness. Bud is, throughout, an altogether engaging character, and his search for a father—and the extended family that he finds instead—will warm readers' hearts and refresh their spirits."

AWARDS

The Watsons Go to Birmingham—1963 was named a Coretta Scott King Honor Book and a Newbery Honor Book in 1996. In addition it was selected as a "Best Book" by both *Publishers Weekly* and the *New York Times Book Review,* given a Golden Kite award from the Society of Children's Book Writers and Illustrators, and named a Best Book for Young Adults by the American Library Association (ALA). In 2000, *Bud, Not Buddy* won both the John Newbery Medal and the Coretta Scott King award given by the ALA.

AUTHOR COMMENTARY

Christopher Paul Curtis and Teri Lesesne

SOURCE: An interview with Christopher Paul Curtis, in *Teacher Librarian*, Vol. 26, No. 4, March, 1999, p. 54.

We all have special books in our lives, books which have moved us to laughter or to tears, books with characters so memorable we expect to meet them on the streets of our neighborhoods, books which leave a permanent mark on our lives as readers. That was certainly my experience when I read *The Watsons Go to Birmingham—1963* by Christopher Paul Curtis. I know I am not alone, for as I visit schools and do booktalks, this one book flies off the shelves and stays in circulation. Once students meet Kenny, Byron, and the rest of the "weird" Watson family, they are hooked. I have had the great good fortune to meet Christopher Paul Curtis and hear him speak and wanted to give all of you a chance to know more about this remarkable author. So, sit back and enjoy a few moments with the creator of the Watsons, Christopher Paul Curtis.

[Teri Lesesne]: So, does your heart still beat a bit faster when someone introduces you as a Newbery winner? (Or a Coretta Scott King winner? Or a Golden Kite winner?)

[Christopher Paul Curtis]: I still have a moment of disbelief when I am introduced as a Newbery or Coretta Scott King Honor winner. Not only do the awards make it possible for the book to get much wider recognition and placement, they also help immeasurably in boosting one's self confidence, something writers are always in need of. Strangely enough I was sitting in the public library writing when I got word to call home because the book had just been given the awards. I leave home early in the morning to go and write, so I was hard at work when one of the librarians came over to me with an enormous smile and gave me a huge hug. I knew something special was up for, though the librarians at this library are warm and friendly, they had not shown it to this extent before.

Your first book won numerous awards. Did that make writing the second book more or less difficult?

I actively tried not to think about the reception of **The Watsons** while I was working on number two. I love the whole writing process and simply got back into the joy of writing. The success of **The Watsons** shows what can happen when many things come together at the right time.

You came to writing after a career outside of children's literature. Was the story "brewing" all those years? Did you have an inkling that you would one day find it possible to put it down on paper for others to read?

I believe people are a lot like geese in that we are imprinted early in our lives as to what we will be and how we will look at ourselves. I spent my first 13 years after high school working on the line in an automobile factory in Flint. I think I am imprinted in that way. Though I have had other jobs, I have always thought of myself as an autoworker/whatever: autoworker/campaign worker, autoworker/warehouse clerk and autoworker/author. I never thought it would be possible to make a living as a writer, but my wife Kay had more faith in me and gave me the courage and opportunity to take a chance. I do believe we all have stories brewing inside of us, that it takes just the right amount of maturity, skill, dedication and luck to get them down into a published book.

Kids must ask you this question, and I admit I cannot resist it either: are you more like Kenny or Byron?

I am asked this question a lot and I always answer that it depends on who in my family you ask. I like to think I have Kenny's sensitivity and understanding, but I have a brother four years younger than I am who swears that Byron is pure autobiography. All of the characters in my stories are composites: that is one of the things that is so much fun about writing. The author has the god-like ability to create, to destroy, to reap deep and abiding revenge! No one character is based on one particular person; they all have bits of me, bits of relatives, bits of friends.

The historical significance of the setting of the Watson family shenanigans never gets in the way of the story. As a matter of fact, the tragic occurrence in Birmingham is made all the more shocking because it comes as almost an affront after the chapters of the deliciously humorous adventures of the weird Watsons. How could you be sure that the humorous tone of the novel would not take away from the emotional impact of that awful historical event?

I don't think an author is ever really aware of what impact their story is having on the reader, which is probably the way it should be. In retrospect, I feel the humor of the story adds to the emotional impact of the bombing. The reader comes to know the family and hopefully has an emotional involvement in them by the time the story goes to Birmingham. In that way, the victims of the act become more than names in a book—the reader says, "Wow, I know them."

What kinds of responses have you received from the kids who read your books?

Student responses have been all over the board. Some focus on the hijinx of Byron and Buphead, some are deeply touched by the bombing and some analyze and understand in ways that would never have occurred to me at their age. If the book has an effect on readers, I hope that first they have fun with it and then want to know more about the Civil Rights Movement, a time in American history unlike any before or since.

What can we expect to see from you in the future? What books are in the works still?

My next book **Bud, not Buddy,** will be out in October 1999. It is the story of a ten-year-old orphan from Flint who believes there is a man on the other side of the state who is his father. It is set in the 1930s and deals with Bud's journey to see if the man is indeed his dad.

You have done a few school visits I would guess. How do these trips into the classrooms affect your work?

I have made many school visits and love them. Yes, I am asked the same questions over and over (and sometimes simultaneously) and the traveling can sometimes be difficult, but I love it nonetheless.

What can teachers and librarians do to help awaken readers to the important lessons of history?

I feel so unqualified and inadequate to give teachers and librarians suggestions about encouraging readers. I have become an admirer of the job that so many educators do and can only hope I can contribute books that young people enjoy reading. I think a lot of the onus rests with publishers and authors. I think it is possible to have books that entertain and inform and that students will seek these books out. I guess I would say to teachers and librarians: keep doing what you are doing to encourage readers and we will give you strong material with which to work.

Despite the success of Walter Dean Myers, you, and others, there is still a shortage of writers of color, especially in the juvenile field. How can teachers and librarians encourage kids, all kids, to consider a career in writing?

You are so right. When I attend conferences with other authors, there is a real dearth of African-American, Hispanic and other writers of color. Putting my unqualified, inadequate hat on once again, I would try to let young people know what a wonderful, empowering, fun act writing is. If young people knew the almost criminal enjoyment I get out of writing, they would be so jealous. I can only suggest that librarians and teachers take the same attitude I take when speaking to a group of eighth graders. Sure, some of them could care less what I have to say, some of them will find it boring. But if one out of a group of 100 can be reached and made to think, "Hey, if this guy can, maybe I can," then it has been a great day for me. I always aim my presentation at that one student who might be listening and searching. Maybe I can fan the fire that is already burning inside them. Maybe with a little self-confidence and encouragement that student will have the nerve to write his or her own *The Watsons Go to Birmingham—1963.*

GENERAL COMMENTARY

Linnea Lannon

SOURCE: Knight-Ridder/Tribune News Service, December 27, 1995, p. 1227.

December [1995] has been a good month for Christopher Paul Curtis.

His first novel, the utterly delightful *The Watsons Go to Birmingham—1963,* was one of only eight notable children's books of 1995, according to the *New York Times Book Review.*

Valerie Lewis, a California bookseller who yearly touts a handful of the best children's books for "CBS This Morning," only had three young adult novels on her list Dec. 14; *The Watsons* was one.

It was one of five recommended books for 9- to 14-year-olds on the *Horn Book's* annual list of best books. *Publishers Weekly,* which first gave the novel a starred review when it came out in October and last month named it one of the Best Books of the Year, last week featured Curtis in an article about new children's authors to watch.

Just the week before Christmas, the German and French rights to the book were sold, and on the Internet Curtis has been mentioned, by readers who like to forecast these things, as a contender for the American Library Association's coveted Newbery Medal for young adult fiction, which will be awarded in January.

It only seems like he's an overnight success. In fact, success has been a long time coming.

Curtis, 42, who now lives in Windsor, Ontario, grew up in a family of five in Flint, Michigan, and much to his mother Leslie's dismay, followed his father to the Fisher Body Plant No. 1 when he graduated from high school in 1972. It was supposed to be only a summer job, but she worried that the money at the plant would distract Curtis from college—he'd been accepted at University of Michigan-Flint. Mom was at least partly right. Curtis spent 13 years on the assembly line—Sept. 15, 1972, to Sept. 25, 1985, to be exact—but he didn't forsake college.

He laughs that he's on the "30 and out" plan at U-M. He's one French class away from finishing an undergraduate degree at Flint, where he won Hopwood awards for his essays and an early draft of what became this book. He thinks that once he gets his bachelor's, he'll get a master's of fine arts at the Ann Arbor campus. If he does, he'll be one of the few creative writing students in the program who has already published a book.

The Watsons Go to Birmingham—1963 was written by hand in the children's section of the Windsor Public Library.

It does and doesn't resemble Curtis' life.

The first two-thirds of it introduces the reader to "the weird Watsons," as 10-year-old narrator Kenny believes the neighbors call his family. Weird? Maybe. Endearing? Definitely. Byron, 13, usually is harassing his younger brother and generally getting into mischief that seems harmless today but marked him as a troublemaker 30 years ago. Kenny, who has a wandering eye, is alternately impressed by and fearful of Byron. Younger sister Joetta is more mature than both boys combined.

Leslie Curtis, who now lives in Grand Rapids, Mich., was and is an avid reader—Christopher remembers stacks and stacks of books around the house when he was growing up. Mother Curtis laughed and cried at her son's first novel, although she admits when he sent her the manuscript in 1993, within a year of her husband Herman's death, she couldn't finish it.

"His dad was just a tremendous personality" whom she saw in her son's book. She has since read the novel and reports that some of it is familiar—including the family car, known in the novel as "the Brown Bomber."

Both she and her daughter Cydney mention the same scene as one that definitely happened: the scene in which Byron plays with matches one too many times. His mother threatens to burn his fingertips. That happened to Christopher.

"I had warned him and talked to him, and his father had talked to him," Leslie Curtis remembers. But their message was not getting through, and she decided something drastic was in order. Both women remember that Cydney, Christopher's younger sister, got hysterical and kept blowing out the matches her mother lit. "I was mad she was doing it, but glad," remembers Leslie Curtis of that day. Christopher escaped with his fingers unscathed and never played with matches again.

What is remarkable about that scene and so many others in Curtis' novel is not just that they are utterly believable—and so universally shared—but his ability to make you laugh at the same time you're thinking, "Uh-oh."

As the title suggests, the fictional family's life takes a serious turn on a journey south to visit their grandmother. (This part did not happen to the Curtis family.) It is a mark of Curtis' skill that he so easily makes the transition from humorous family vignettes to a life-threatening run-in with racism. Perhaps because Curtis didn't think the novel would be for children when he started it, there's nothing heavy-handed or preachy about the Watsons' brush with the civil rights movement.

"It's a wonderful teaching tool," says Wendy Lamb, Curtis' editor at Delacorte. She hopes the novel eventually will find its way into school curriculums. Lamb got Curtis' manuscript as one of about 400 submitted for the publisher's annual contest for a first young adult novel.

"I pulled it out because of its title," Lamb recalls. "I felt he was obviously trying to deal with something important."

That was in January 1994. In February she called him to say it wasn't going to win the contest—for reasons that had to do with Kenny's age and the novel's time period—but that she loved it and was sure Delacorte would want to publish it.

Not surprisingly, Lamb is impressed by Curtis' perseverance and the support he got from his family. His time off from work to write—more than a year around 1993—was engineered by his wife, Kaysandra, a nurse "who believed in my writing more than I did," says Curtis. Son Steven, unlike his dad, a whiz at typing, entered his father's daily writing into the family computer each night. Steven also was a good sounding board. "Lots of people can say they like it or they don't, but not many can say what exactly doesn't work. He can," boasts his dad. Helping set the mood on the cover are pictures of his parents and sister Cydney when she was 5 or 6.

The happy ending to this story would probably be that Curtis is now rich and famous. Not quite.

Delacorte's Lamb explains that young adult novels don't sell huge numbers unless they become classics. The initial printing of *The Watsons* was 5,000, not unusual but minuscule in comparison to such picture book phenomenons as Jon Scieszka and Lane Smith's *Math Curse,* which was published in October and, by the end of the holidays, was expected to top the 260,000 sales mark.

"What we want to do with children's books is keep them in print forever," says Lamb, who admits that pressures in the publishing business make this more difficult than it once was. "Eighty percent of our sales are to institutions—libraries, schools. Middle-grade and young adult novels don't sell that well in bookstores because people go in to buy picture books, and that's what the chains push."

And though *The Watsons* is doing unusually well for a first novel in terms of reviews and sales—it's in its third printing—"it takes teachers time to get a book like this into the curriculum. They have to read it and think about it and then decide if they can fit it in," Lamb says.

Still, *The Watsons Go to Birmingham—1963* has "its own momentum," observes Lamb.

So, it seems, does Curtis. He is going to take the first three months of 1996 off from his job in the warehouse of Allen Park's (Mich.) ADP-Automatic Data Processing to finish writing an adult novel he's been working on and is confident in. His wife expects him to continue to write in what for most would be an unusual office—the Windsor library's children's section.

"He'll talk to the children, help someone with homework, make faces. It's not a distraction for him," says Kay Curtis, who hopes her husband eventually makes enough money he can just write.

His family apparently expects no less.

"I've read a lot of Chris' writing over the years," says sister Cydney, who "knew by the fibs that he told that he could be" a great writer. "This is good," she says of *The Watsons,* "but I don't think it's his best. His best is yet to come."

Michael D. Schaffer

SOURCE: Knight-Ridder/Tribune News Service, January 26, 2000, p. K6367.

Nobody need tiptoe around Christopher Paul Curtis while he's writing.

Not when you consider that he taught himself to write fiction on an automobile assembly line.

And not when you know that he wrote his Newbery Award-winning novel, *Bud, Not Buddy,* in the children's section of the Windsor, Ontario, public library, with story-hour playing out in the background and curious children wandering by to ask him questions.

And not when you consider that this is an author whose technique is to imagine a character and let the character dictate the story to him while he—the author—takes it all down in long-hand with what he admits is "a sappy grin" on his face.

Last week, Curtis, 46, became the first African American since Mildred Taylor in 1976 (for *Roll of Thunder, Hear My Cry*) to win the American Library Association's Newbery medal, given to honor the best children's book of the previous year. Curtis also won the Coretta Scott King Award, given by the library association to recognize achievement by an African American children's author.

Curtis' first novel, *The Watsons Go to Birmingham—1963,* was a Newbery Honor Book, a runner-up for the prize, in 1996.

Not bad from someone who took up writing to keep the workplace from getting him down.

Both books feature a 10-year-old African American protagonist from Curtis' hometown, Flint, Michigan—in *The Watsons,* it's Kenny Watson, and in *Bud, Not Buddy,* it's Bud Caldwell. Both boys are tough and resourceful, but still share the sweetness, vulnerability and humor of childhood.

Bud, Not Buddy—a bittersweet, funny tale—is set in Michigan in the 1930s, against the gritty backdrop of the Great Depression and racism. Bud Caldwell is looking for his father. His mother (who told him never to let anyone call him Buddy because "Buddy is a dog's name or a name that someone's going to use on you if they're being false-friendly") has been dead for four years when the book opens. Bud, who has been living in an orphanage in Flint, flees an abusive family that has taken him in on temporary placement.

Bud is convinced that his father is the band leader Herman E. Calloway, who lives in Grand Rapids, 110 miles away. The resourceful Bud makes his way to Grand Rapids and tracks down Calloway—but what he finds is far different from what he expected.

Curtis has created a complex, marvelously crafted character in Bud, a child who believes you become an adult at six, because, "It's at six that grown folks don't think you're a cute little kid anymore. . . . It's around six that grown folks stop giving you little swats and taps and jump clean up to giving you slugs that'll knock you down and have you seeing stars in the middle of the day."

But that same child, who sleeps with his eyes barely closed and an open jackknife by his side for protection, believes in vampires and just wants to find a home.

"I think he's the product of his environment," Curtis said. " . . . He will do what's necessary." At the same time, Bud's mother, who loved him deeply, "made him a mannered child," the author adds.

While he has set *Bud, Not Buddy* in the Depression, Curtis said, his aim is to tell a story, not teach a history lesson. "I don't try to give a message," he said. "I really believe the story comes first. You get kids' attention first. . . . Then they can gain an idea of what was going on."

The book is aimed at readers nine and up, and some of Bud's adventures play well to that audience's innate affection for slapstick—as when Bud thinks a man who has stopped to help him on the road at night is a vampire because he has a box in his car with the label. "URGENT: CONTAINS HUMAN BLOOD!!!" Bud thinks it's a vampire snack; it's really a delivery to a local hospital.

Curtis says the key to his writing is finding his main character. "Once I get that lead character, the lead character tells me what's happening," Curtis said. He goes into what he describes as "a trance-like state" (his friends rib him about hearing voices) as he writes: "I get this stupid smile on my face, and I'm off." He writes where the character takes him, with no outline and no plan. "I don't know where it's going," he said.

Kenny Watson was a character who embodied parts of Curtis and his brother. Bud is "a wholly created character."

Curtis' success in creating a character like Bud is a tribute to tenacity. "Certainly, he has a great talent," said Debbi Chocolate, an African American author who has written 12 books for children and is currently working on a children's novel for Walker. " . . . If he's self-taught, he's done a great job of learning the craft."

Curtis had on-the-job training as a writer. For 13 years, from right after his high school graduation in 1972 until 1985, Curtis hung doors on the driver's side of Buicks as they inched by him on the assembly line at the Fisher Body Co. plant in Flint.

Thirteen long years.

The tedium, Curtis recalls, was "terrible." He wrote to relieve the boredom. Right there on the line, in half-hour bursts. He would do 30 doors, 30 minutes worth of work, then his partner on the line would do the next 30, freeing Curtis to practice his new craft.

He wasn't very good at it, he recalled in a telephone interview last week, but it did to take his mind off work. And by the time he was in his 40s-and several years out of the auto plant—the writing "started to work."

After he left the auto plant, he worked at several jobs and took a fling with politics, working for U.S. Sen. Donald W. Riegle Jr., D-Mich., in his Flint office and managing Riegle's 1988 campaign in Flint and Saginaw.

Finally, Curtis' wife, Kaysandra, a native of Trinidad and a registered nurse, urged him to take up writing full-time. He did, in 1993. (The two now live in Windsor, midway between Flint and Hamilton, Ontario, where Kaysandra had been living).

Curtis said his son, Steven, now 21, made helpful suggestions about *The Watsons.* His daughter, Cydney, 8, helped him with *Bud, Not Buddy* Cydney even wrote—and copyrighted—a song, "Mommy Says No," that a little girl in the book sings, Curtis said.

Bud, Not Buddy ran long in its original draft. "We had to cut a lot," Curtis said. But he and his editor, Wendy Lamb, belong to a mutual admiration society. He said he is "in awe" of her; she said he is "wonderful." This is fortunate because, as Curtis points out, he owes Random House (which owns Delacorte) three more books.

Curtis' success is good news for multiculturalism in children's literature, according to Chocolate. "The attention he's getting will bring attention all the way around" for writers of multicultural books for children, she said.

Publishers would like to see more African American authors, said Emily Easton, publisher of the Books for Young Readers department of Walker. But not that many new African American writers are coming into the children's field, Easton said.

The publishers' interest in diversity is not just a matter of marketing, according to Easton. Not all young readers are middle-class white children, she said. "We want (young readers) to be able to see themselves in children's books." And it is important for white readers to see children from other backgrounds, she added.

Curtis' success "will give his work a showcase, and that, in turn, validates (African American writers) in the general culture," Easton said.

But beyond that, she added, "it is wonderful that he has produced a book of that quality, that deserves that level of recognition."

TITLE COMMENTARY

📖 *THE WATSONS GO TO BIRMINGHAM— 1963* (1995)

Hazel Rochman

SOURCE: A review of *The Watsons Go to Birmingham—1963,* in *Booklist,* Vol. 91, No. 22, August, 1995, p. 1946.

Gr. 4-8. In a voice that's both smart and naive, strong and scared, fourth-grader Kenny Watson tells about his African American family in Flint, Michigan, in 1963. We get to know his strict, loving parents and his tough older brother, who gets into so much trouble his parents decide to take him back "home" to Birmingham, Alabama, where maybe his strong grandmother will teach him some sense. Several of the family stories are a bit self-conscious (we keep being told we're going to laugh as Dad puts on a show and acts the fool), but the relationships aren't idealized. Racism and the civil rights movement are like a soft rumble in the background, especially as the Watsons drive south. Then Kenny's cute little sister is in a Birmingham church when a bomb goes off. She escapes (Curtis doesn't exploit the horror), but we're with Kenny as he dreads that she's part of the rubble. in this compelling first novel, form and content are one: in the last few chapters, the affectionate situation comedy is suddenly transformed, and we see how racist terror can invade the shelter of home.

Publishers Weekly

SOURCE: A review of *The Watsons Go to Birmingham—1963,* in *Publishers Weekly* Vol. 242, No. 42, October 16, 1995, p. 62.

Evoking a full spectrum of emotions, this exceptional first novel is certain to reverberate within the reader's psyche. At first, the author concentrates his efforts on introducing the irrepressible, "weird" Watsons, an African American family living in Michigan during the early 1960s. Although the youngest member of the clan, Joetta, will play a key role in the drama, most of the action centers around the 10-year-old narrator, Kenny, and his older brother, Byron, whom Kenny alternately idolizes and fears. When Byron's antics—lighting tissue "parachutes" and flushing them down the toilet, dying his hair "Bozo clown" red—get to be more than his parents can handle, they decide to deliver him into the capable arms of stern Grandma Sands. The Watsons' trip to Grandma's house in Birmingham begins as an adventure in their spiffed-up "Brown Bomber" but ends as a horrific initiation to racism. After the Tom Sawyer-like hilarity of his opening passages, Curtis unabashedly draws his audience into one of the bleaker corners of American history, immersing them in the Watsons' shock and terror when the local church is bombed. Kenny, a witness to the bombing, relays his observations perceptively, painfully and memorably. An afterword enlarges the child's-eye view with an outline of the civil rights activism of the times and the violent reactions to it, reinforcing Kenny's seemingly unmediated account with grim truths about the struggle for racial equality. Ages 10-up.

Cindy Darling Codell

SOURCE: A review of *The Watsons Go to Birmingham—1963,* in *School Library Journal* Vol. 41, No. 10, October, 1995, p. 152.

Gr 6 Up—Kenny's family is known in Flint, Michigan, as the Weird Watsons, for lots of good reasons. Younger sister Joetta has been led to believe she has to be overdressed in the winter because Southern folks (their mother is from Alabama) freeze solid and have to be picked up by the city garbage trucks. Kenny, the narrator, does well in school and tries to meet his hard-working parents' expectations. After a string of misdeeds, Mr. and Mrs. Watson decide that tough guy, older brother Byron must be removed from the bad influences of the city and his gang. They feel that his maternal grandmother and a different way of life in Birmingham might make him appreciate what he has. Since the story is set in 1963, the family must make careful preparations for their trip, for they cannot count on food or housing being available on the road once they cross into the South. The slow, sultry pace of life has a beneficial effect on all of the children until the fateful day when a local church is bombed, and Kenny runs to look for his sister. Written in a full-throated, hearty voice, this is a perfectly described piece of past imperfect. Curtis's ability to switch from fun and funky to pinpoint-accurate psychological imagery works unusually well. Although the horrific Birmingham Sunday throws Kenny into temporary withdrawl, this story is really about the strength of family love and endurance. Ribald humor, sly sibling digs, and a totally believable child's view of the world will make this book an instant hit.

Kirkus Reviews

SOURCE: A review of *The Watsons Go to Birmingham—1963,* in *Kirkus Reviews,* Vol. 63, October 1, 1995, p. 1426.

Curtis debuts with a ten-year-old's lively account of his teenaged brother's ups and downs. Ken tries to make brother Byron out to be a real juvenile delinquent, but he comes across as more of a comic figure: getting stuck to the car when he kisses his image in a frozen side mirror, terrorized by his mother when she catches him playing with matches in the bathroom, earning a shaved head by coming home with a conk. In between, he defends Ken from a bully and buries a bird he kills by accident. Nonetheless, his parents decide that only a long stay with tough Grandma Sands will turn him around, so they all motor from Michigan to Alabama, arriving in time to witness the infamous September bombing of a Sunday school. Ken is funny and intelligent, but he gives readers a clearer sense of Byron's character than his own and seems strangely unaffected by his isolation and harassment (for his odd look—he has a lazy eye—and high reading level) at school. Curtis tries to shoehorn in more characters and subplots than the story will comfortably bear—as do many first novelists—but he creates a well-knit family and a narrator with a distinct, believable voice.

Heather Vogel Frederick

SOURCE: A review of *The Watsons Go to Birmingham—1963,* in *Publishers Weekly,* Vol. 242, No. 51, December 18, 1993, pp. 28-9.

Christopher Curtis's first novel (*The Watsons Go to Birmingham—1963,* published by Delacorte in Oct.) was almost called *The Watsons Go to Florida—1963.* In a conversation peppered with easy laughter and the kind of ready quips that make his novel so memorably humorous, Curtis relates the circuitous route his book traveled to publication.

The idea for his story of a middle-class African American family and their trip South during the height of the civil rights unrest germinated during a Curtis family road trip. The author had decided, unbeknownst to his wife, to drive straight through from his home in Ontario (just over the border from Detroit) to Florida. It was a dubious decision ("We drove through actual mountains, and I can't even remember them!" Curtis jokes), but while his family slept, Curtis started spinning a story in his head to help himself stay awake. After returning home, he wrote it down bit by bit. It took a while for the chapter vignettes to "congeal" into a novel, says Curtis, who originally had the Watson family, like his own, heading to Florida.

The only problem was, "When they got there, the story just died," Curtis recalls with chagrin. Stymied, he set the novel aside for a few months, until the day his then 14-year-old son came home from school with an assignment to read a poem about the civil rights era and the four girls murdered by a bomb in a Baptist church in Birmingham, Ala.

"A light went off," Curtis said. "That was it, and I tied the family in with the bombing."

In retrospect, he says, he's glad **The Watsons** evolved in such a roundabout way, as it prevented any foreshadowing in the chapters leading up to the shattering conclusion. "It might have taken away from the impact," Curtis explains.

Raised in a family of avid readers, Curtis, who counts Toni Morrison and Kurt Vonnegut as his favorite authors, always knew he wanted to be a writer, but it took a while—and a nudge from his wife, Kaysandra—to make the dream a reality. It was she who encouraged him to quit his factory job (Curtis had worked in an auto-body plant since leaving high school) and spend a year and a half finishing his novel. Finish it he did—and got a solid start on two other books to boot.

But if writing the novel was relatively easy, Curtis says, getting it published took some ingenuity. "Most publishers won't read unsolicited manuscripts, and most agents won't take on unpublished authors," he comments. So he decided to get around this potential catch-22 by entering his novel simultaneously in two contests—a multicultural children's fiction contest sponsored by Little, Brown, and Delacorte's annual young adult contemporary fiction contest ("which it didn't really qualify for, but sometimes you just have to take a shot").

Promptly rejected by Little, Brown ("I was crushed," he admits), Curtis says one of the best days of his life came when he returned home from work a couple of weeks later to find a message on his answering machine from Delacorte—letting him know that even though his novel didn't qualify for the contest (because it is not contemporary), they still wanted to publish it.

Curtis says he has tremendous admiration for editors—especially his own, Wendy Lamb. "To have that ability to read a book over and over and keep a fresh perspective is remarkable," he says. His own book went through two rewrites, which he says ultimately made it a better book, but he admits that he got to the point where "if they wanted to have the bomb destroy the whole family, I'd have said, 'Fine, just don't send it back to me again.'"

Although he didn't write *The Watsons* specifically as a children's book, Curtis is enjoying the "unexpected doors" that this categorization has opened for him. "I'm going into schools and getting a chance to meet librarians and teachers," says Curtis, who recently hosted a writing class at his son's school, something he calls "one of the most worthwhile things I've done."

He's also enjoying the attention his book has received—it has garnered across-the-board critical acclaim. The only downside to the praise, Curtis says, is that as he looks ahead to the books he hopes to finish up in '96, "it makes it scary for the next time!"

Somehow, readers suspect that he'll rise to the occasion.

Betsy Hearne

SOURCE: A review of *The Watsons Go to Birmingham—1963,* in *Bulletin of the Center for Children's Books,* Vol. 49, No. 5, January, 1996, pp. 157-58.

Despite its politically charged title and photodocumentary cover, this unexpectedly subtle fiction derives its power not from polemics but from patient development. A series of funny episodes delineates the Watson clan, an individualistic lot including smart ten-year-old Kenny (who recounts the tale with personality plus), his defiant older brother Byron, quirky little sister Joetta, affectionate Dad, and determined Momma. The center of attention—and trouble—is often Byron, whom Dad and Momma finally decide to take from their Flint, Michigan, home, where too

many temptations abound, to feisty Grandma's house in Birmingham, Alabama, in the hopes that his adolescence will pass into some sort of maturity. The scene-setting mischief ("Byron had gotten a conk! A process! A do! A butter!" . . . which his father promptly shaves off) and the drive south reach comic-epic proportions. After coasting from offhand humor ("Here that little egghead punk is") to deliberate—and kid-authentic—jokes ("A peon? Didn't you see *The Magnificent Seven?* Peons was them folks what was so poor that the rich folks would just as soon pee on them as anything else"), readers get used to the story's picaresque movement, only to find the ground suddenly shifting under them with an ominous rumble. It is the Birmingham church bomb that killed four children, one of whom Kenny believes for a while to be his sister. The poignancy of the ending lies in the protagonist's bright spirits darkening after this trauma, without the author's relinquishing control of a consistently fresh narrative voice. The contrast is startling, innovative, and effective in a strong first novel showing how—and why—the Civil Rights movement affected individual African Americans.

Martha V. Parravano

SOURCE: A review of *The Watsons Go to Birmingham—1963,* in *The Horn Book Magazine,* Vol. 72, No. 2, March-April, 1996, p. 195.

This impressive first novel begins as a lighthearted, episodic family story narrated by ten-year-old Kenny Watson. Most of Kenny's problems revolve around his older brother Byron, at thirteen "officially a teenage juvenile delinquent." Although he makes life miserable for Kenny, Byron is constantly in trouble: lighting fires, cutting school, and having his hair straightened into a "conk" against the express wishes of his parents. These early chapters are hilarious, especially the one in which the narcissistic Byron gets his lips frozen to the side-view mirror of the family car while giving himself a kiss. But the tone changes after the Watson parents decide that they've had enough of Byron's "latest fantastic adventures" and drive the family from Flint, Michigan, down to Birmingham, Alabama, where they plan to have strict Grandma Sands shape Byron up. There Kenny has his first encounter with the darker elements lurking under the surface of life. Although he has been warned away from one particular swimming hole because of whirlpools, Kenny disobeys and almost drowns, pulled under by the "Wool Pooh" (Winnie-the-Pooh's evil twin, a Byron fabrication intended to scare Kenny away from the dangerous swimming hole). As the book moves further from the comic to the tragic, the Wool Pooh makes another devastating appearance, this time at the bombing of the Sixteenth Avenue Baptist Church, where four little girls are killed. Kenny sinks into a deep depression, and—not so unexpectedly—it is Byron who pulls him out, with reassurances that his "baby bruh" is going to be all right, and with ruminations on the unfairness of life: "Kenny, things ain't ever going to be fair. How's it fair that two grown men could hate Negroes so much that they'd kill some kids just to stop them from going to school? . . . But you just gotta understand that that's the way it is and keep on steppin'." Curtis's control of his material is superb as he unconventionally shifts tone and mood, as he depicts the changing relationship between the two brothers, and as he incorporates a factual event into his fictional story. His use of the "Wool Pooh" as the personification of evil is effective and chilling. Curtis has created a wholly original novel in this warmly memorable evocation of an African-American family and their experiences both terrible and transcendent.

Jeanne Marcum Gerlach

SOURCE: A review of *The Watsons Go to Birmingham—1963,* in *The ALAN Review,* Vol. 23, No. 3, Spring, 1996, p. 210.

Curtis introduces the reader to ten-year-old Kenny and his family, the Watsons—Momma, Dad, Joetta, Kenny, and Byron—in his first, but unforgettable, novel. We meet the Watsons one super-cold Saturday in their home in Flint, Michigan. We immediately sense the family closeness through the comedic dialogue of the characters. However, we soon travel with the family from their somewhat calm life in the North to Birmingham, Alabama, where the Civil Rights movement was just beginning. Curtis introduces us to the South of the 1960s—a place where African Americans couldn't eat in restaurants, use public restrooms, or be seen on the streets after dark. The trip with Kenny and his family is realistic: I felt I was in the car with them. I saw the water fountains with the NO BLACKS signs. I saw the buses where African Americans stood near the rear. And I heard my African-American friends admit that they were afraid to travel in certain areas of our country. Traveling with the Watsons to Birmingham was like looking at a picture from the past. I trust that picture will keep changing for the better. I feel re-awakened. Thank you, Christopher Paul Curtis.

Felicity Wilkins

SOURCE: A review of *The Watsons Go to Birmingham—1963,* in *School Librarian,* Vol. 45, No. 4, November, 1997, p. 211.

This dull title hides a warm and lightly humorous story with underlying seriousness. It begins with the comical episode of Byron, the delinquent elder brother, getting his bottom lip stuck to the frozen wing mirror of the car when he goes out to scrape ice from the car in very cold Flint, Michigan. The other members of the 'weird' Watson family are Dad who likes to joke, Momma from down South, Kenny aged 10 who likes to read, and little sister Joetta. Byron gets into so much trouble that his parents decide to carry out their threat of sending him south to Grandma in Birmingham, Alabama to get him back on the straight and narrow in a new environment. The whole family heads south for a holiday to drop him off. They become caught up in an act of violence, part of the unrest caused by the Civil Rights Movement, which deeply affects the whole family. Byron and Kenny do a whole heap of growing up.

Competent readers of 10 upwards will enjoy this story; they will have to be competent to cope with the colloquial African Americanisms.

📖 *BUD, NOT BUDDY* (1999)

Publishers Weekly

SOURCE: A review of *Bud, Not Buddy,* in *Publishers Weekly,* Vol. 246, No. 32, September 1, 1999, p. 131.

As in his Newbery Honor-winning debut, ***The Watsons Go to Birmingham—1963,*** Curtis draws on a remarkable and disarming mix of comedy and pathos, this time to describe the travails and adventures of a 10-year-old African-American orphan in Depression-era Michigan. Bud is fed up with the cruel treatment he has received at various foster homes, and after being locked up for the night in a shed with a swarm of angry hornets, he decides to run away. His goal: to reach the man he—on the flimsiest of evidence—believes to be his father, jazz musician Herman F. Calloway. Relying on his own ingenuity and good luck, Bud makes it to Grand Rapids, where his "father" owns a club. Calloway, who is much older and grouchier than Bud imagined, is none too thrilled to meet a boy claiming to be his long-lost son. It is the other members of his band—

Steady Eddie, Mr. Jimmy, Doug the Thug, Doo-Doo Bug Cross, Dirty Deed Breed and motherly Miss Thomas—who make Bud feel like he has finally arrived home. While the grim conditions of the times and the harshness of Bud's circumstances are authentically depicted, Curtis shines on them an aura of hope and optimism. And even when he sets up a daunting scenario, he makes readers laugh—for example, mopping floors for the rejecting Calloway, Bud pretends the mop is "that underwater boat in the book Momma read to me, *Twenty Thousand Leaks Under the Sea*," Bud's journey, punctuated by Dickensian twists in plot and enlivened by a host of memorable personalities, will keep readers engrossed from first page to last. Ages 9-12.

Hazel Rochman

SOURCE: A review of *Bud, Not Buddy,* in *Booklist,* Vol. 96, No. 1, September 1, 1999, p. 131.

Gr. 4-6. Bud, 10, is on the run from the orphanage and from yet another mean foster family. His mother died when he was 6, and he wants to find his father. Set in Michigan during the Great Depression, this is an Oliver Twist kind of foundling story, but it's told with affectionate comedy, like the first part of Curtis' ***The Watsons Go to Birmingham*** (1995). On his journey, Bud finds danger and violence (most of it treated as farce), but more often, he finds kindness—in the food line, in the library, in the Hooverville squatter camp, on the road—until he discovers who he is and where he belongs. Told in the boy's naive, desperate voice, with lots of examples of his survival tactics ("Rules and Things for Having a Funner Life and Making a Better Liar out of Yourself"), this will make a great read-aloud. Curtis says in an afterword that some of the characters are based on real people, including his own grandfathers, so it's not surprising that the rich blend of tall tale, slapstick, sorrow, and sweetness has the wry, teasing warmth of family folklore.

Kathleen Isaacs

SOURCE: A review of *Bud, Not Buddy,* in *School Library Journal,* Vol. 45, No. 9, September, 1999, p. 221.

Gr 4-7-When 10-year-old Bud Caldwell runs away from his new foster home, he realizes he has nowhere to go but to search for the father he has never known: a legendary jazz musician advertised on some old posters his deceased mother had kept. A friendly

stranger picks him up on the road in the middle of the night and deposits him in Grand Rapids, MI, with Herman E. Calloway and his jazz band, but the man Bud was convinced was his father turns out to be old, cold, and cantankerous. Luckily, the band members are more welcoming; they take him in, put him to work, and begin to teach him to play an instrument. In a Victorian ending, Bud uses the rocks he has treasured from his childhood to prove his surprising relationship with Mr. Calloway. The lively humor contrasts with the grim details of the Depression-era setting and the particular difficulties faced by African Americans at that time. Bud is a plucky, engaging protagonist. Other characters are exaggerations: the good ones (the librarian and Pullman car porter who help him on his journey and the band members who embrace him) are totally open and supportive, while the villainous foster family finds particularly imaginative ways to torture their charge. However, readers will be so caught up in the adventure that they won't mind. Curtis has given a fresh, new look to a traditional orphan-finds-a-home story that would be a crackerjack read-aloud.

Roger Sutton

SOURCE: A review of *Bud, Not Buddy,* in *The Horn Book Magazine,* Vol. 75, No. 6, November, 1999, p. 737.

In a story that's as far-fetched as it is irresistible, and as classic as it is immediate, a deserving orphan boy finds a home. It's the Depression, and Bud (not Buddy) is ten and has been on his own since his mother died when he was six. In and out of the Flint, Michigan, children's home and foster homes ever since, Bud decides to take off and find his father after a particularly terrible, though riotously recounted, evening with his latest foster family. Helped only by a few clues his mother left him, and his own mental list of "Rules and Things for Having a Funner Life and Making a Better Liar Out of Yourself," Bud makes his way to a food pantry, then to the library to do some research (only to find that his beloved librarian, one Charlemae Rollins, has moved to Chicago), and finally to the local Hooverville where he just misses hopping a freight to Chicago. Undaunted, he decides to walk to Grand Rapids, where he hopes his father, the bandleader Herman E. Calloway, will be. Lefty Lewis, the kindly union man who gives Bud a lift, is not the first benevolent presence to help the boy on his way, nor will he be the last. There's a bit of the Little Rascals in Bud, and a bit more of Shirley Temple as his kind heart and ingenuous ways bring tears to the eyes of the crustiest of old men—not his father, but close enough. But Bud's fresh voice keeps the sentimentality to a reasonable simmer, and the story zips along in step with Bud's own panache.

Brian Bethune

SOURCE: A review of *Bud, Not Buddy,* in *Maclean's,* Vol. 112, No. 47, November 22, 1999, pp. 101-2.

Christopher Paul Curtis's first novel, *The Watsons Go to Birmingham—1963* was a marvellous evocation of a pivotal time in African-American history. His new book, *Bud, Not Buddy* (Random House), a poignant and very funny Depression-era story of a lonely black child, is easily as good. Ten-year-old Bud—who won't let anyone call him Buddy—has been in and out of a Flint, Mich., orphanage since his mother died four years earlier. Bud, disregarding hunger, fear and loneliness, runs away from a foster home to search for his father. His only clue is the posters his mother used to collect, advertising performances by Herman E. Calloway and his band, the wonderfully named Dusky Devastators of the Depression.

Curtis, who moved to Windsor from Flint in 1991, is an immensely skilled writer, capable of combining broad humour with subtle social commentary. Bud's many rules for 'Having a Funner Life' are amusingly expressed—No. 8, for example, warns children that when adults tell them to listen carefully, 'run as fast as you can because something real terrible is just around the corner.' In Curtis's hands the maxims come across quite clearly not as adult cynicism, but the hard-won wisdom of a hard-luck child. And in a neat reversal of a common stereotype, everyone described simply as a man or a woman or a child is black. It is the white folks, rare presences in Bud's world, who receive a colour identification in such phrases as 'me, a little white boy and a little girl.'.

Bud himself is one of the most appealing heroes in recent kids' books, a brave and resourceful child whose 'eyes don't cry no more.' Not, that is, until he realizes he has finally come among people who care for him. Then he shocks himself by dissolving into wracking sobs. It is one of the finest scenes in one of the year's best children's novels.

Andrea Sachs

SOURCE: A review of *Bud, Not Buddy,* in *Time* (New York), Vol. 155, No. 4, January 31, 2000, p. 68.

Chalk it up as yet another evil of stereotyping, but the term children's-book author does not summon to most minds the image of a 6-ft. 2-in., 240-lb. man with dreadlocks. Yet that description fits Christopher Paul Curtis, 46, and you can add "prizewinning" to the children's-book-author part. Last week Curtis' second book, ***Bud, Not Buddy,*** garnered an impressive twofer: the John Newbery Medal, awarded annually by the American Library Association to the best American children's book; and the Coretta Scott King Author Award for excellence by an African American writing for children and young adults.

Set in 1936, ***Bud, Not Buddy*** is narrated by Bud Caldwell, 10, who goes "on the lam" from an unpleasant foster home in Flint, Mich., in search of his father. Like his resourceful young hero, Curtis grew up in Flint. After graduating from high school, he joined the assembly line at Fisher Body Plant No. 1 and began writing during his breaks. He didn't set out to be a children's author. But, he says, "I felt I had a story to tell, and for some reason the voice came to me as a 10-year-old." Many years and several jobs later in 1995, his first book, *The Watsons Go to Birmingham—1963,* was published.

The father of two children, 21 and 8, Curtis credits his wife Kaysandra, a registered nurse, for encouraging him to write full time. The financial sacrifice has paid off: "As soon as this award was announced, my wife went from house hunting to mansion hunting."

Holly J. Morris

SOURCE: A review of *Bud, Not Buddy,* in *U.S. News & World Report,* Vol. 128, No. 4, January 31, 2000, p. 61.

Christopher Paul Curtis began his writing career on an auto assembly line. At 18, he worked at Fisher Body Plant No. 1 in Flint, Mich. Cars came down the line every other minute, so he and his partner would each do 30 in a row instead of alternating. Curtis wrote during his 30- minute breaks.

GM's loss was publishing's gain. Last week, the American Library Association announced that ***Bud, Not Buddy,*** Curtis's second novel for young readers, was the first to win both the Newbery Medal and the Coretta Scott King Author Award for African-American writers.

In the Depression-era take on the plucky orphan story, 10-year-old Bud Caldwell runs away from a foster home to find his dad, who he thinks may be a jazz musician. Grim historical details (a clash between hobos and Pinkerton guards) mesh with chilling scenes (nasty foster parents lock Bud in a shed full of hornets). Only Bud's sense of humor and weird slang keep the story light. He says "kiss my wrist" to sound tough—a phrase Curtis made up. "Little kids can't say kiss my butt," he explains.

Curtis, 46, researched the '30s for a book on the 1936-37 sit-down strike at the Fisher plant. But a story about his grandfather, a '30s band leader, took over, and Bud was born. Photos of his grandfathers appear in Bud's afterword: Herman F. Curtis, with his jazz band, the Dusky Devastators of the Depression!!!!!!, and Earl "Lefty" Lewis in his baseball uniform.

Some critics say the plot is tied up a little too neatly. "But Bud is such a wonderful character," says Janice Del Negro, editor of the *Bulletin of the Center for Children's Books,* "you really want him to have a happy ending."

Beth E. Andersen

SOURCE: A review of *Bud, Not Buddy,* in *Voice of Youth Advocates,* Vol. 22, No. 6, February, 2000, p. 245.

Curtis's magical touch in his debut novel, *The Watsons Go to Birmingham—1963* (Delacorte, 1995), is once again evident in all its powerful, funny glory in his latest lovely novel. Ten-year-old Bud Caldwell, wise beyond his years, is hit particularly hard by the Depression in 1936. Bud has been bounced back and forth between a Flint, Michigan, orphanage and foster care since his mother died when he was six. Fed up with beatings from those who take him in, Bud grabs his few meager treasures and sets out in search of his father. With determination and a cautious but curious spirit, Bud heads for Grand Rapids, home of Herman E. Calloway, legendary bass player and leader of a renowned jazz band. Convinced that Calloway is his long-lost father, Bud seeks a reunion. Bud's only guidebook is Bud Caldwell's Rules and Things for Having a Funner Life and Making a Better Liar out of Yourself, his own set of poignant, riotous tips for preserving sanity. In a scene of stunning hilarity, Bud is rescued by Lefty Lewis, who takes Bud to Grand Rapids, where the child learns yet again that life is not always what it seems. Curtis writes with a razor-sharp intelligence that grabs the reader by the heart and never lets go. His utterly believable depiction of the self-reliant charm and courage of *Bud, not Buddy,* puts this highly-recommended title at the top of the list of books to be read again and again.

Michael Cart

SOURCE: A review of *Bud, Not Buddy,* in *Booklist,* Vol. 96, No. 12, February 15, 2000, p. 1094.

The good news that Christopher Paul Curtis' second novel, *Bud, Not Buddy,* has won the Newbery Medal and the Coretta Scott King Award for fiction came as no surprise to fans of this gifted writer's first novel, *The Watson's Go to Birmingham—1963,* which I hailed in my 1996 Black History Month column as "a wonderfully auspicious debut." I was hardly alone in my appraisal. Curtis' comic and touching story about a Flint, Michigan, family that almost becomes the victim of a hate crime, was named both a Newbery and a Coretta Scott King Honor Book, was the winner of the Golden Kite Award from the Society of Children's Book Writers and Illustrators, was both a YALSA Best Book for Young Adults and a Top Ten Quick Pick, and . . . well, the list of its honors and awards fills an entire one-page flyer from the book's publisher. What a hard act Curtis crafted for himself to follow! Happily, it turns out there was no reason for apprehension, as readers of the award-winning *Bud, not Buddy* have already discovered. Once again, Curtis has written a laugh-out-loud book with serious underpinnings. This time it's not a church bombing in Alabama but, rather, the often-grim realities of life in the Great Depression, a time that, as Curtis notes in an afterword, was especially hard on African Americans.

Bud Caldwell, like Kenny Watson, is a 10-year-old from Flint who tells his story in his own voice. Bud, to put it mildly, has a lively imagination and a gift for exaggeration. "I'm not bragging," he tells us, "when I say that I'm one of the best liars in the world." And he punctuates his story with droll life lessons that he calls "Bud Caldwell's Rules and Things for Having a Funner Life and Making a Better Liar out of Yourself." Most to the point in this context is Rule Number 3: "If You Got To Tell a Lie, Make Sure It's Simple and Easy To Remember." But my personal favorite is Number 83: "If an Adult Tells You Not to Worry, and You Weren't Worried Before, You Better Hurry Up and Start 'Cause You're Already Running Late."

When we first meet him, Bud, orphaned by the death of his mother, is fleeing from an unhappy foster home, a place where "there wasn't anybody who cared what happened to me." Librarians will be delighted to know that the first place the fugitive goes for help is . . . well, let him tell it: "The only hope I had was the north side library. If I got there, maybe Miss Hill would be able to help me, maybe she'd understand and would be able to tell me what to do. And for now I could sneak into the library's basement to sleep."

To his sorrow, Bud discovers that the librarian, Miss Hill, has married and moved to Chicago, but, in a nod to the real world, history records that his loss was librarianship's gain, for Miss Hill, we learn, is none other than the legendary Charlemae Rollins.

With this avenue of help unavailable, though, Bud does what many kids during the Depression did: he hits the road. Determined to hop a freight west, Bud spends the night in a Hooverville, one of those crudely built cardboard camps that sprang up near railroad tracks all over the country and provided temporary shelters for the homeless, the impoverished, and the destitute victims of the Depression. There he discovers that adversity is colorblind. "There were more people than I first thought. They were all the colors you could think of, black, white, and brown, but the fire made everyone look like they were different shades of orange. There were dark orange folks sitting next to medium orange folks sitting next to light orange folks."

But even the Depression didn't eradicate unreasoning racial enmity and inequity. We will learn that laws in many localities prohibited African Americans from renting or holding title to land. But first there are more immediate dangers. Unable to catch the train, Bud decides to walk to Grand Rapids in the middle of the night. Fortunately, he is given a lift by a kind man named Lefty Lewis, who cautions, "Son, there just aren't too many places a young Negro boy should be traveling by himself; there're folks in this state that make your average Ku Kluxer look like John Brown. You were very lucky this time."

Like Miss Hill, the librarian, Lefty Lewis is based on a real person, Curtis' maternal grandfather, who, during the Depression, worked as a redcap at the train station in Grand Rapids and who, for many years, also pitched in the Negro baseball leagues. Curtis' other grandfather, Herman E. Curtis, who was a big bandleader during those same years, provides the inspiration for the man Bud believes to be his father: a

Grand Rapids-based musician named Herman E. Calloway, whose band, like Grandfather Curtis', is called "The Dusky Devastators of the Depression!!!!!!"

I have no way of knowing whether or not Curtis inherited his grandfather's musicianship, but I do know that he writes beautifully about the making of music. The scene in which Bud finally gets to hear the Devastators play is a tuneful tour de force, the next best thing to hearing the music itself, which is so gorgeous, an enchanted Bud tells us, "I could see now why this band got to have six exclamation points behind their name."

And enchanted is a good word to describe *Bud, not Buddy,* as well, in the dictionary sense of "to attract and delight." For surely Curtis' second novel will attract and delight countless readers with its genial good humor and its generosity of spirit.

As Lefty points out, Bud is lucky in his quest for a father. But there is more to it than that. His adventures—and occasional misadventures—have in common an orphan boy's necessary reliance upon the kindness of strangers. Precious few of them fail him. And in dramatizing Bud's experience, Curtis turns his novel into a celebration of the human capacity for simple goodness. Bud is, throughout, an altogether engaging character, and his search for a father—and the extended family that he finds instead—will warm readers' hearts and refresh their spirits.

Carol Otis Hurst

SOURCE: A review of *Bud, Not Buddy,* in *Teaching PreK-8,* Vol. 30, No. 7, April, 2000, p. 72, 74.

This year's Newbery Award book, *Bud, Not Buddy* by Christopher Paul Curtis is so perfect for classroom use that I'm going to devote the whole column to it this month. Add this book to your list of must-reads and your list for multiple copies and read-alouds if you work with kids from fourth grade up. As with the author's *The Watsons Go to Birmingham* (Bantam, 1997), we go from laughter to tears in the blink of an eye.

Quite a character. Once you meet Bud, you'll never forget him. His self-constructed set of rules for how to "Have a Funner Life and Make a Better Liar Out of Yourself" may remind some readers of Mouse's emergency rules in Betsy Byars' *The Eighteenth Emergency* (Viking, 1996), Bud belongs with Jerry Spinelli's *Maniac Magee* (Little Brown, 1990) and other authors' characters who enlighten the human experience and make us wish we could step into the action to help them find good homes.

The book is set in Michigan, in the 1930s. Bud's mother has been dead for four years when the novel opens, and Bud is in an orphanage. He holds the remnants of his once-loving home in a cardboard suitcase: flyers advertising Herman E. Calloway and various bands, a few mysteriously labeled rocks and his blanket.

The orphanage is repressive, but things go from bad to worse when he is put in a foster home where he's abused by the adults and the kids. After wreaking a funny, well-deserved, mild vengeance, Bud strikes out on his own, determined to walk from Flint, Michigan to Grand Rapids, the city listed in one of the flyers. Bud is convinced that his father must be Herman E. Calloway. Why else would his mother so carefully save those flyers?

Helpers and setbacks. There are, of course, many setbacks on the way to Grand Rapids, but also many people who lend a hand. At the mission where Bud is too late for the evening meal, a homeless family pretends that Bud is part of their family. A kind labor organizer finds Bud hiding near an intolerant village and takes Bud home to his own family before transporting him to his supposed father. Although Bud doesn't come face-to-face with racism, there are several allusions to it.

Bud reaches Grand Rapids, but his quest must continue. He's still in search of family because Calloway cannot possibly be his father.

A skillful story. Bud's irrepressible good nature, his innocence and his survival skills make him memorable. His literal interpretation of language and his belief system—which includes vampires, tokens and ritual behavior—allow us to see the world through the eyes of a delightful ten-year-old. The 1930s Great Depression setting and the hints of racism that the author weaves in skillfully make this book stand head and shoulders above the crowd.

There are many ways to use this book. Discussing the strengths exhibited by each character might be a good place to start. Others may want to discuss the likelihood of Bud finding distant family so easily.

Turning to Bud's survival list, it might be fun to make a class list for survival in the classroom. Would the list be different if we were living in the 1930s?

Read other books about runaways and survival in a city to compare with *Bud, Not Buddy* Many other books are set in the Depression and can be compared with this one. Try *Nothing to Fear* by Jackie French Koller (Harcourt Brace, 1993), Robert Newton Peck's *Arly's Run* (Walker, 1991), Ann Turner's *Dust for Dinner* (HarperCollins, 1995), Mildred Taylor's *Roll of Thunder, Hear My Cry* (Dial, 1976), and start research on the era with David F. Burg's *The Great Depression: An Eyewitness History* (Facts on File, 1996).

We learn a bit about the unionization of the railroad porters in *Bud Not Buddy.* A class list of the things you know from the reading and those you know from other sources can be constructed and checked for accuracy. Students may want to find out how many labor union members there are in their own extended families.

Any book for fourth grade and up that engages us with wonderful characters and leads us into lively social studies activities and discussions is a must. Run out and grab it.

Additional coverage of Curtis's life and works is contained in the following sources published by The Gale Group: *Black Writers,* Vol. 3; *Contemporary Authors,* Vol. 159; *Contemporary Authors New Revision Series,* Vol. 80; *Something about the Author,* Vol. 93.

Jackie French Koller
1948-

American novelist.

Major works include the *Dragonling* series (six volumes, 1990-1998), *Nothing to Fear* (1991), *The Primrose Way* (1992), *A Place to Call Home* (1995), *The Falcon* (1998).

INTRODUCTION

Best known for her young adult novels, Koller has written in a variety of genres for audiences ranging from toddlers to teens. Her works include fantasy, contemporary adventure, historical novels, and works that examine Native American culture at the dawn of U.S. history. Critics often remark favorably on the authenticity of language and characterization found in Koller's historical books, which reflect her comprehensive research. "I try to find as much original source material as possible—diaries, journals, letters," she told Diane Andreassi in an interview for *Authors and Artists for Young Adults (AAYA)*. "And then I also read extensively, including ethno-historical studies on the people and times." Koller has described herself as an advocate for children, noting in *Something about the Author* that as a society "we pay a lot of lip service to the importance of family values and education, but very little ever changes. Children should be our number one national priority—their health, their well being, their education."

BIOGRAPHICAL INFORMATION

Koller is a childhood storyteller-turned-author who tried for years to sell her first book. Both of her parents grew up in poverty; they met after World War II. Koller's grandparents endured the Great Depression, bouts of abusive alcoholism, and even jail time for Koller's grandfather, convicted of manslaughter in a hit-and-run accident. "Needless to say, my parents didn't have the best role models in the marriage or parenting department, . . . but they tried hard to give us children the best life they possibly could, and my memories of early childhood are good ones," Koller told *AAYA*. She points to her mother reading to her, to creating make-believe tales to amuse herself, and to developing a reading habit early on as important

aspects of her early literary development. A tall, studious tomboy, Koller went through an awkward childhood and adolescence, finding solace in books and in the peaceful surroundings of the Connecticut countryside. By the time she reached college, though, Koller began mixing more socially. She married George Koller in 1970. With the birth of their first child, Koller reflected on the joys of storytelling from her own youth and began to write. Following a picture book, *Impy for Always* (1989), Koller produced her first young adult novel, *Nothing to Fear*, the story of a poor Irish family during the Great Depression, which was inspired by the experiences of her mother. Over the next decade Koller produced several more volumes for readers of all ages. Koller lives with her husband, their youngest son and two Labrador retrievers on "ten quiet acres on a mountaintop in Western Massachusetts."

MAJOR WORKS

In creating period fiction for young adults, Koller sets out to demonstrate that the issues facing teenagers are universal and timeless. With *Nothing to Fear* (the title is derived from a famous depression-era quote from President Franklin D. Roosevelt, who declared that poverty-stricken Americans "have nothing to fear but fear itself") themes of personal responsibility and sacrifice color the tale of a New York City family during the Great Depression. The story focuses on Danny, the son of Irish immigrants who becomes head of the household after his father leaves town to find work. With much responsibility resting on his shoulders, Danny must learn survival skills and empathy for others. The latter comes when the family helps out a stranger whose hunger and poverty are even worse than their own. The novel was applauded by a *Kirkus Reviews* contributor, who saw in *Nothing to Fear* an "involving account of the Great Depression . . . conjuring an entire era from the heartaches and troubles of one struggling family."

In 1992 Koller published *The Primrose Way,* a well-received historical novel highlighting a young girl's cultural and personal awakening. In seventeenth-century Massachusetts, teenage Rebekah Hall lives with her father in a growing village. Rebekah's interests, however, lie beyond the town, with the local Native Americans. She befriends the tribal leader's niece, Qunnequawese, and gains insight into the native culture. Conflict arises when Rebekah begins to question her Puritan upbringing, and when she falls in love with the tribe's holy man, Mishannock. Several critics found *The Primrose Way* valuable not only as an engrossing coming-of-age tale but as a fresh interpretation of the story of America's early settlers. The novel "successfully de-romanticizes [the settlers'] struggles and avoids the absolutes (us-good, them-bad)," declared *Kirkus Reviews.* Themes of early Native American life also characterize Koller's 1999 children's book *Nickommoh! A Thanksgiving Celebration* (1999), which points out that the Narragansett tribe had a thanksgiving tradition predating the Pilgrims by many years.

Not all of Koller's novels are historically based. *A Place to Call Home,* which provides an examination of the foster care system in the United States, is set in contemporary times. When fifteen-year-old Anna returns from school and finds her home in shambles, she assumes her alcoholic mother has walked out on them again. The truth is more brutal: the mother has committed suicide by drowning. Striving against an unsympathetic system to keep her younger siblings with her, Anna finds herself committing her time, intelligence and energy in preserving "the greater good" of family unity.

Another modern-day novel, *The Falcon,* studies the tendency of teenagers to view themselves as invincible. The novel uses a journal-entry style to tell the story of Luke, a young boy struggling with an emotional disorder that leads to self-destructive behavior. When Luke's outbursts land him in a psychiatric hospital, he must overcome a deep emotional scar on his way to recovery. *School Library Journal* critic Alison Follos applauded Koller for creating an "incredibly well drawn" portrayal of a troubled teen.

For grade-school audiences, Koller has produced a number of books both whimsical and adventuresome. Her six-part *Dragonling* series, for example, unites humans and dragons in a quest to overcome evil tyrants. Koller's books for early readers, include *One Monkey Too Many* (1999), which combines reading and counting skills as monkey after monkey wreaks havoc on such activities as canoeing and bike riding. *Bouncing on the Bed* (1999), a picture book for pre-readers, presents joyful and soothing images of a toddler's happy day.

AWARDS

Koller's works have received a number of literary honors, including an American Library Association Best Books for Young Adults citation, an American Bookseller's Association Pick of the Lists award, a Bank Street College Annual Book Award, and a Junior Library Guild Honor Book citation.

AUTHOR COMMENTARY

Jackie French Koller

SOURCE: http://www.geocities.com/jackiekoller/bio.html

Well, I guess I've been a storyteller longer than I realized. In the sixth grade I remember spinning tales on the playground for the amusement of my friends. I even wrote my first novel that year. Chapter by chapter I would bring it in and pass it around and my friends would devour it like episodes of a soap opera. Sadly, I threw it away when I reached my teens, thinking it childish and embarrassing. Later, while in college, I worked summers on a factory assembly line. To relieve the boredom I made up stories on the spot. My co-workers would give me a character or situation and I'd be off and running.

In addition to loving stories, I've always loved children. I was the one grown-ups adored at family picnics—the one with my arms full of babies, and a little trail of toddlers everywhere I went. It wasn't until I had my first child, though, that my love of children and storytelling naturally flowed together and I began my first feeble attempts at writing stories for her. Two sons followed, and a lot more feeble attempts. Then, when my third child graduated from diapers, my husband gave me a brand new electric typewriter and I began to pursue in earnest my dream of being a children's book writer.

Three years later, in 1986, my first children's story was published in an anthology. It was a beginning, but it would be two more years of hard work before my first book would be accepted. That book, **Impy for Always,** came out in 1989. Dozens more have followed, and many, many others are in the works.

These days I live on ten quiet acres on a mountaintop in western Massachusetts with my husband, my youngest son and two Labrador retrievers.

TITLE COMMENTARY

IMPY FOR ALWAYS (1989)

Phillis Wilson

SOURCE: A review of *Impy for Always,* in *Booklist,* Vol. 85, No. 20, June 15, 1989, p. 1823.

Gr. 2-4. Eight-year-old Imogene, Impy for short, eagerly awaits a summer visit from her 12-year-old cousin, Teeny, whom she hasn't seen in two years. Impy's fond memories of their playing with dolls and enjoying a game of Marco Polo in the pool are clashed by the arrival of a mature Christina who isn't "into dolls anymore" and abhors getting wet. The inevitable breach escalates as Impy, unwilling to accept Christina's new interest in boys, retaliates and, in her misery, becomes a first-class pest. Hilarious, and to Christina, embarrassing escapades abound until, with compassionate good humor, she bridges the gap with a cookie-baking session. The visit will fly by for readers drawn into Koller's astute and sympathetic portrayal of each girl. The food for thought about accepting change is as delightfully digestible as the peanut-butter kisses they make together. Newsom's upbeat line drawings reflect the action of this warmly appealing story.

Roger Sutton

SOURCE: A review of *Impy for Always,* in *Bulletin of the Center for Children's Books,* Vol. 42, No. 11, July-August, 1989, p. 278.

Gr. 3-4. Cousin Teeny, twelve, has changed since her last visit two years before, and eight-year-old Imogene ("Impy") doesn't like the new *Christina* one bit: "She was right about not being teeny anymore. She was almost as tall as Imogene's mom, and she was getting all lumpy and curvy like Mom, too." Christina doesn't like to splash in the pool or play with dolls anymore, instead evincing an interest in obnoxious Michael Radnor, who once put cat droppings in Impy's doll's diaper. "'That's hysterical,' she shrieked. 'I *love it!* I have *got* to meet this guy.'" A convincing, if slight, acknowledgement of the puberty gap, this keeps things moving with plenty of clear-cut conflict, some slapstick mayhem, and realistic motivations from both sides. Although the ending (and the illustration) is sugary—"There's still lots of stuff we can do together, and no matter what, I'll always love you *Imogene*"—this is acceptable transitional reading for girls eager but not quite ready for Blume.

Ruth Semrau

SOURCE: A review of *Impy for Always,* in *School Library Journal,* Vol. 35, No. 13, September, 1989, p. 229.

Gr 2-4—Another title in the growing number of early chapter books. Koller looks at a familiar family conflict in a fresh and sympathetic way. Imogene (Impy), eight, is looking forward to a summer visit from her cousin Teeny, with whom she has enjoyed many games of swimming pool splash, mud pies, and doll fashion shows. Impy recoils in shock when the age difference of four years is underscored by Teeny's maturing body and her lack of interest in playing the old games. Impy takes her revenge on her cousin by reading her diary and allowing Michael, a neighbor, to see it. However, Teeny, now metamorphosed into Christina, has a mature spirit as well as body. After the requisite tears and recriminations, Christina talks Impy into a more understanding humor, and the two agree to be friends again on a slightly more grown-up footing. They part at visit's end with the protagonist hovering between being little-girl-Impy and big-girl-Imogene, while readers will hover between thinking, "How sweet" and "How unreal." Most 12-year-olds have less compassion and more "Drop dead, you little creep." Impy is lucky that her cousin isn't like the latter type. A book with potential appeal to children Impy's age.

📖 *THE DRAGONLING* (1990)

Carolyn Phelan

SOURCE: A review of *The Dragonling,* in *Booklist,* Vol. 87, No. 10, January 15, 1991, p. 1059.

Gr. 3-4. From the Springboard series, this beginning chapter book includes seven deftly drawn and shaded full-page pencil illustrations. The story concerns a boy who risks his life and the censure of his community to return a baby dragon to its home. Discovering that the dragons are herbivores, he tries to convince his people that they have nothing to fear from these supposed enemies. The book's feminist-pacifist message (the women of the village turn against their men and denounce the traditional dragon hunts at the novel's close) may be more than readers bargain for when they begin the short fantasy adventure. Still, libraries with a demand for fantasies at this reading level may find it a worthwhile choice.

Susan L. Rogers

SOURCE: A review of *The Dragonling,* in *School Library Journal,* Vol. 37, No. 2, February, 1991, p. 71.

Gr 2-4—Darek, nine, is envious of his older brother Clep's first dragonquest in spite of its inherent danger. When the hunters return to the village with their prize, the body of a Great Blue (one of the largest and fiercest of dragons), they also bring the body of Clep's best friend. Later that night, Darek discovers a whimpering young dragonling emerging from the dead beast's pouch. In spite of his lifelong conditioning to hate dragons, he finds himself befriending the orphan; in helping him find the Valley of the Dragons, he learns that the few dragons left in the valley have no natural enmity toward humans and need not be feared or hunted. In a final confrontation between creatures and villagers, Darek speaks up for harmony, and changes the future for them all. Simple and predictable stuff, indeed, but while this book lacks the depth or subtlety of Jane Yolen's or Anne McCaffrey's dragon books, it is entirely suitable for the intended beginning chapter-book audience. Full-page black-and-white drawings are scattered among the

brief chapters, depicting villagers in vaguely medieval dress and a thoroughly adorable dragonling. Darek and his new friend are sympathetic characters, at once brave and timid, charging forward while hanging back, like children everywhere. Young readers will identify with Darek, share his fondness for the dragon, and applaud their final success.

📖 *NOTHING TO FEAR* (1991)

Hazel Rochman

SOURCE: A review of *Nothing to Fear,* in *Booklist,* Vol. 87, No. 13, March 1, 1991, p. 1388.

Gr. 5-7. With the same soft glow that popular TV casts over the Depression, this long, warm family story told by plucky young Danny Garvey focuses on his growing up first-generation Irish Catholic American in a New York City tenement. It's the winter of 1933. Pa's unemployed, and he leaves his family to try to find a job on the road. Ma takes in washing, but when she falls ill and very nearly dies in childbirth, the burden falls on young Danny. There are lots of chuckles as well as lumps in the throat and mists in the eye and crotchety characters with hearts of gold. Readers will enjoy the combination of comedy, mischief, and melodrama, as the story switches from neighborly Sunday afternoons and Danny's awkward first date to his tearful parting with Pa in the rain. There is also a strong sense of the desperate times, usually distanced through the stories of friends and neighbors—evictions, Hoovervilles, the Dust Bowl, etc.—though Danny himself experiences the shame of begging. One bleak episode breaks the formula: Pa doesn't get home for Christmas, or for New Year's either, and Danny realizes that his own dream of going to find Pa is quest for escape, not manhood. Danny stays home and things slowly get better. Pair this with a girl's similiar experience of the Depression in Whitmore's *The Bread Winner.*

Ann Welton

SOURCE: A review of *Nothing to Fear,* in *School Library Journal,* Vol. 37, No. 5, May, 1991, pp. 93-4.

Gr 5-9—New York City youngster Daniel Garvey is around 11 when the Depression begins. At first he doesn't notice it much, but as the years go by, he sees the toll first in his neighborhood, as friends' families are evicted, and then in his own family. His father, out of work, takes to the road to find employment, and Daniel is left in charge of his expecting, ailing mother and his baby sister. Things go from bad to worse, until the family is rescued by someone who, at first blush, appears to be worse off than they. This differs from Pieter Van Raven's *A Time of Troubles* (Scribners, 1990) in that it deals with an eastern metropolitan population, not migrant workers. Less derivative than Van Raven's book, it also presents a view of the Depression that, if no less desperate, is less bleak. Daniel is an engaging protagonist who goes through numerous rites of passage familiar to young teens—first girlfriend, shaving, and the sudden realization that he is taller than his mother. He must also come to terms with his father's death and mother's remarriage. If it all works out a trifle too smoothly, the story still imparts the flavor of the time, and the strong plot line and numerous interesting supporting characters will hold readers' attention.

MOLE AND SHREW (1991)

Eunice Weech

SOURCE: A review of *Mole and Shrew,* in *School Library Journal,* Vol. 37, No. 10, October, 1991, p. 98.

K-Gr 2—The story of a developing friendship between a good-hearted but bumbling, nearsighted mole and a tidy, self-sufficient shrew. Mole accidently burrows his way into Shrew's bathroom cabinet after a horde of relatives crowd him out of his home. When he next shows up in Shrew's fireplace, she decides to help him find a new home before he destroys hers. They look at a number of available spots, but Mole finds none as suitable as Shrew's house. Late in the day, he discovers an empty chipmunk den next door to Shrew and moves in. Shrew's doubts about having Mole as a close neighbor grow as he comes to borrow various articles and stays for breakfast and lunch. She begins to change her mind when he returns the bucket filled with flowers and the hedge trimmers sharpened and invites her to join him for dinner at his house. Ormai's whimsical watercolors are rich in detail, bringing the animals to life in their cozy, country setting. This is a delightful read-aloud for younger *Wind in the Willows* fans, and the conversations between Shrew and Mole lend themselves to oral interpretation.

IF I HAD ONE WISH (1991)

Elaine Fort Weischedel

SOURCE: A review of *If I Had One Wish,* in *School Library Journal,* Vol. 37, No. 11, November, 1991, p. 120.

Gr 5-8—Alec Lansing, at 6'2", is the tallest boy in the eighth grade, but his athletic talent doesn't quite match his height. That's only one of his problems, however. A basically nice kid, he keeps getting himself into trouble. He resents the affection his parents show to his little brother, and gradually focuses on Stevie as the cause of all his difficulties. When the charm given him by a strange bag lady at the mall turns out to be real, Alec finds that his thoughtless wish that Stevie had never been born has become reality. This sets off a junior version of *It's a Wonderful Life.* Alec finds that his family, while materially much better off ("I'd traded my little brother in for a Porsche") has also changed in the affection for, and interest in, each other. Life without Stevie is definitely not better. Alec's attempt to locate the bag lady and undo his wish brings him into contact with the people at a shelter for the homeless and reinforces the lesson that kindness is a valuable commodity. Readers will readily identify with Alec's problems at home and school, and sympathize with his frustration with his little brother. Considering the way wealth changes his life, they will also accept his growing desire to have his brother, and his family, restored. Alec's confusion and panic as he realizes what has happened is nicely paced; the magic elements are underplayed and believable. In all, an interesting and thought-provoking story for those who have ever wished they didn't have to put up with younger siblings.

Publishers Weekly

SOURCE: A review of *If I Had One Wish,* in *Publishers Weekly,* Vol. 238, No. 50, November 15, 1991, p. 73.

Self-pitying Alec is struggling through eighth grade, plagued by six-year-old brother Stevie and unable to measure up to older sister Kelly. After being kind to an old woman, Alec is granted one wish; at the same time he gets grounded for not looking after Stevie. So Alec wishes his brother had never been born. He immediately regrets this, as he discovers not only that he misses Stevie, but that his wish has wider consequences. Alec's parents become less caring, more materialistic and more involved in their careers, and thus the wish is fulfilled by their decision to not have another child. The boy's mother, in particular, now a hustling lawyer, changes for the worse. Alec learns a lesson and manages to undo his wish. Readers will wish a potentially interesting look at sibling conflict had not been cut off by Koller's apparent desire to didactically champion traditional values and sex roles. The generic characters and simplistic handling of a complex problem will disappoint even those who share her views. Ages 9-13.

FISH FRY TONIGHT (1992)

Publishers Weekly

SOURCE: a review of *Fish Fry Tonight,* in *Publishers Weekly,* Vol. 239, No. 7, February 3, 1992, p. 79.

Intricate, sketchy watercolors draw the reader into a world of springtime flora and fauna as Mouse catches her biggest fish ever. She invites her friend Squirrel to a fish fry—"Bring a friend. Bring two or three!"—but as the invitation escalates the ensuing misunderstandings create hilarious havoc. Passing along Mouse's summons, each creature repeats her description of "a fish as B-I-G as me"; accordingly, the catch ends up bear-sized. When Mouse opens her door at the appointed hour, she is startled to discover" . . . friends by the dozen! / Friends by the scad! / More friends than Mouse / ever knew that she had." With a pinch of resourcefulness, she solves her social crisis in exemplary fashion. Though Koller's verse at times becomes ragged and doesn't scan, her characters' antics prove amusing and her word pictures occasionally charm—Mouse enjoys the brook's "ripples and dapples / that giggled and babbled." O'Neill's *(Mrs. Dunphy's Dog)* winsome cast and bucolic settings stylishly enhance the proceedings. Ages 4-8.

Elizabeth S. Watson

SOURCE: A review of *Fish Fry Tonight,* in *The Horn Book Magazine,* Vol. 68, No. 2, March/April, 1992, p. 192-93.

In a lilting, rhymed text Mouse's invitation to a fish fry is passed from one animal friend to another until "friends by the dozen! Friends by the scad! More friends than Mouse ever knew that she had" arrive,

to Mouse's surprised dismay. She recovers her aplomb and orders pizza for everyone, serving the one small fried fish as an hors d'oeuvre. The artist captures the animals' gleeful anticipation of a festive dinner party with humorous detail, although the illustrations are a bit soft; a bolder approach might have better suited the rambunctious text. A delightful tale that will charm any story-hour crowd—and if you happen to serve pizza, all the better.

Ilene Cooper

SOURCE: A review of *Fish Fry Tonight,* in *Booklist,* Vol. 88, No. 6, April 15, 1992, p. 1537.

Ages 4-7. Tired of housework, Mama Mouse goes fishing and, after a fierce struggle, lands a whopper. She invites her friend Rabbit over for dinner, telling him, "I caught a fish as B-I-G as me!" Rabbit runs into Badger and invites him along, repeating the "B-I-G as me" statement. As more and more guests get invited, the fish gets bigger and bigger until it's moose size rather than mouse size. Mouse almost faints when she spies the horde of animals outside her door. But Mouse is as inventive a hostess as she is able a fisherwoman. She orders a hundred pizzas and cuts the fish into hors d'oeuvres. Although it's common in kids' books to find some animals acting human while others are just animals, the juxtaposition here between the eaters and the eaten seems a little uncomfortable. That quibble aside, this fresh story has much going for it. Children will enjoy the repetition of the cumulative verse, giggling at the unwitting telling of a fish story. O'Neill's impressionistic watercolors surround the text and have a liveliness to them that their soft edges belie. A romp.

Marie Orlando

SOURCE: A review of *Fish Fry Tonight,* in *School Library Journal,* Vol. 38, No. 8, August, 1992, p. 138.

PreS-Gr 2—Delightfully rhythmic prose tells the story of Mouse, whose lazy-day fishing trip results in a grand catch "as B-I-G as me," prompting her to invite Squirrel and a few other friends to dinner. Carried away by Mouse's enthusiasm, Squirrel invites Rabbit; Rabbit, in turn, invites Badger; Badger invites Deer; and so on. With each invitation, the description of the fish's size grows; when an enormous crowd shows up at the door, Mouse quickly revises her menu, ordering pizzas and serving the fish as an hors d'oeuvre. Soft, sprightly drawings are highlighted with many whimsical touches (the back cover shows Mouse engrossed in *The Compleat Angler*); they perfectly complement a funny text that will be a joy to read aloud.

📖 *THE LAST VOYAGE OF THE MISTY DAY* (1992)

Carolyn Phelan

SOURCE: A review of *The Last Voyage of the Misty Day,* in *Booklist,* Vol. 88, No. 17, May 1, 1992, p. 1593.

Gr. 6-9. After her father's death, Denny moves with her mother from New York City to a cottage on the coast of Maine. Denny begins high school in Moose Hollow, where she feels out of place in every way. Battling the cold and the loneliness in addition to her grief, she befriends their mysterious neighbor, "Mr. Jones," an old man who spends his days repairing the battered wreck of a boat in which he lives. Koller's sensitive creation of the main characters will quickly draw readers into the story, which involves a mild love interest as well as Denny's relationships with her mother and their neighbor. However, when Mr. Jones' secret begins to unravel, the novel's center shifts from the characters themselves to ideas played out by the characters. Does Mr. Jones have the right to refuse medical treatment? In the final chapters, the story becomes more eventful, yet less involving. Still, this is a worthwhile choice for large collections.

Susan Knorr

SOURCE: A review of *The Last Voyage of the Misty Day,* in *School Library Journal,* Vol. 38, No. 6, June, 1992, pp. 116, 121.

Gr 5-8—Upon investigating a light on nearby Little Hog Island, Denny finds a secretive elderly man who is restoring an old boat and strikes up a friendship with him. The timing is opportune, as she had been at odds with her mother since their move to Maine after her father's death. Grudgingly, the old man allows her to help refurbish the boat and begins to serve as a reluctant grandfather figure to the teenager. When a robbery lands him in the hospital, and the daughter who has been searching for him is located, it's revealed that "Mr. Jones" is running away from cancer surgery and dreams of taking the *Misty Day* to a spot in the Bermuda Triangle. With a friend's

help, Denny sneaks him out of the hospital and he sails off to follow his dream. Koller's description of the work on the boat is nicely integrated into the story, but Denny's sudden outbursts and overblown emotional shifts, along with occasionally trite dialogue, may try readers' patience. And while the mystery of Mr. Jones's true identity will pull teens along, the fatal disease and escape from the hospital conclusion is an obvious one that has been done before.

📖 *THE PRIMROSE WAY* (1992)

Barbara Chatton

SOURCE: A review of *The Primrose Way,* in *School Library Journal*, Vol. 38, No. 9, September, 1992, p. 278.

Gr 8 Up—Puritan Rebekah Hall, 16, joins her father in the settlement of Agawam in the New World in 1633. There the independent girl befriends Qunnequawese, a Pawtucket girl. Rebekah develops a respect for her friend's way of life and spiritual values, falls in love with one of Qunnequawese's kinsmen, and must choose between two cultures. Koller is at her best when describing the dreary living conditions and the religious and social constraints of the Puritans, especially in relation to the glorious scenery and the simple lifestyle of the Native Americans. As in Speare's *The Witch of Blackbird Pond* (Houghton, 1958) and Farber's *Mercy Short* (Dutton, 1982; o.p.), these contrasts are made clear by the young narrator. Issues about separation of church and state, the scandalous idea of thinking for oneself, etc., are thoughtfully raised here and would provide provocative discussions in the social studies classroom. Koller's carefully researched book incorporates authentic language in a readable text. Glossaries, a pronunciation guide, bibliography, and an afterword are all helpful. The message about female freedom and the idealized image of Native American culture and beliefs are strikingly modern, but these are justified in the story. The seeds of the destruction of the Pawtucket are movingly conveyed. Readers may find the ending unrealistic, but highly satisfying. This novel, along with Speare's *The Sign of the Beaver* (Houghton, 1983), could be used for discussions of the historical clash of cultures in the U.S.

Ilene Cooper

SOURCE: A review of *The Primrose Way,* in *Booklist,* Vol. 89, No. 4, October 15, 1992, p. 272.

Gr. 7-10. Sixteen-year-old Rebekah Hall thinks she knows what awaits her in the New World, where she is joining her father in a Puritan settlement. She is in for a surprise. Her missionary father has moved to the wilderness, and though life is rough, Rebekah finds solace in what she believes will be her life's work—she will save the souls of the Pawtucket tribe. Two Indians become particularly important to her: Qunnequawese, a maiden who is learning English (and teaching Rebekah the Algonquin language in return), and Mishannock, a holy man, for whom Rebekah finds her feelings growing. Koller has a few awkward moments at first. Her characters' British syntax seems forced, and there are instances when she buys into the "noble savage" ideal, offering a group of Indians who are almost flawless. Her attitude toward Mishannock is positively reverential; he's wise, kind, good, and handsome. No wonder Rebekah runs off with him in the end, defying religion and family. Still, the story itself, both as history and as romance, is quite compelling, and Koller hits on a key issue as Rebekah must decide not only if her culture is the only "correct" one, but also what values of another group she can accept as her own. The source note at the back, the glossary of English and Algonquian words, and the bibliography show Koller's done her homework, and the research gives the book the ring of authenticity.

Publishers Weekly

SOURCE: A review of *The Primrose Way*, in *Publishers Weekly*, Vol. 239, No. 46, October 19, 1992, p. 80.

When the Puritans came to the New World hoping to discover a new Eden, they called themselves saints. At 16, however, Rebekah finds the primitive living conditions and ill treatment of the native peoples of Massachusetts a far cry from a godly paradise. The girl comes to question her faith and her society, and she finally resolves to run away with her Indian boyfriend, Mishannock. While Koller presents a vivid, fact-based portrait of New England in the mid-1600s, her characters lack a sense of immediacy. Rebekah emerges as a colorless heroine with an anachronistic understanding of the exploitation of the surrounding people and natural resources. Her love for Mishannock unfolds in cliches that make even the girl's happy ending seem flat. Fans of period romances might find the proceedings rather tame, but Koller's substantial bibliography and glossaries lend her book some historical value. Ages 12-up.

MOLE AND SHREW STEP OUT (1992)

Gary Young

SOURCE: A review of *Mole and Shrew Step Out*, in *Booklist*, Vol. 89, No. 2, September 15, 1992, p. 155.

Ages 4-8. "Everybody who is anybody." says Shrew, has been invited to the fancy ball at Mouse Manor. But Mole doesn't get an invitation and worries that he is nobody. When Shrew invites him to attend as her guest, he appears wearing all manner of tails with his black tie, much to his embarrassment when everyone just stares at him. Shrew, however, helps him out. Adults will think of *The Wind in the Willows*, of animals with good and bad human manners. Children will be absorbed by the full-color illustrations complementing a story that plays with words along the way but doesn't sacrifice sense to cleverness. The principal characters are well drawn in both text and artwork. The social conflict will be obvious, and the ending is both entertaining and instructive. The book would be good bedtime reading as well as the kind of book that children will want to read later by themselves. Further adventures wouldn't be a bad idea.

Karen James

SOURCE: A review of *Mole and Shrew Step Out*, in *School Library Journal*, Vol. 38, No. 12, December, 1992, p. 85.

K-Gr 2—If *"everybody* who is *anybody"* is invited to the ball at Mouse Manor, then Mole, who doesn't get a blue envelope with silver writing, determines he is nobody. Shrew asks him to escort her, instructing him to wear "black tie and tails" that he then goes about collecting from a lizard, a kite, etc. This makes him a laughingstock at the party, but supportive Shrew suggests they have a "Good Friends' Ball" and make sure nobody is left out. Ormai's watercolors create a *Wind in the Willows* world of well-dressed animals and cozy interiors, although the characters do not have the vivid personalities found in Grahame's story or Shepard's illustrations. The humor is not always successful, since many children will be as in the dark about black tie and tails as Mole, and will miss the full meaning of the situation even though his solution is obviously silly. That means the joke is on readers as well as on the hero. Still, the messages about friendship and the pain of not being accepted are clear without being overbearing, and the story leaves readers with warm, positive feelings.

📖 *A DRAGON IN THE FAMILY* (1993)

Tina Morrow Peak

SOURCE: A review of *A Dragon in the Family,* in *School Library Journal,* Vol. 40, No. 3, March, 1994, p. 200.

Gr 2-4—In this sequel to **The Dragonling** (Little, 1990), also set in the Middle Ages, Darek, a young boy, takes the dragon he has befriended to his village, where the people have always fought the creatures. Zantor's presence results in mistrust and the eventual arrest of the boy's father, who has allowed his son to keep the dragon. There's plenty of action as Darek and his friend save the man. The characters are believable, and their adventures, fears, and suspicions make for exciting reading for children moving into chapter books.

📖 *A PLACE TO CALL HOME* (1995)

Carolyn Noah

SOURCE: A review of *A Place to Call Home,* in *School Library Journal*, Vol. 41, No. 10, October, 1995, p. 155.

Gr 6-10—Mama's gone again, and it's hardly a surprise to 15-year-old Anna. The surprise comes later, when Mama doesn't come back, and Anna discovers her old yellow car submerged in the lake. Anna's desperate struggle to make a home for her two younger siblings leads her to Mississippi to trace her mother's escape route from her abused childhood and to seek her family and milieu. Anna, the black child of a white mother and unknown father, loves her two white siblings passionately, though she can't forget she's different. Poverty and sickness lead the young woman to abandon her fight to keep the household together and to turn to the social service agency that has scattered them before. This eloquent depiction of impoverishment and courage is set in the contemporary hills of Connecticut, where there are plenty of contrasts: destituion among wealth; grief hiding below apparent equanimity; bigotry within families; tenacity against all odds. Anna tells the story in the first person with warmth and immediacy. Among the cast of less credible characters are despicable Aunt Roe McCallum, who literally furnishes her home with foster children; and Nate Leon, Anna's white sweetheart and champion, who appears every time a rescue is needed. Nonetheless, *A Place to Call Home* is a fast-paced, compelling read, with a memorable and feisty heroine and satisfying social values. It will sit easily on the shelf next to Virginia Euwer Wolff's *Make Lemonade* (Holt, 1993).

Merri Monks

SOURCE: A review of *A Place to Call Home,* in *Booklist,* Vol. 92, No. 4, October 15, 1995, p. 396.

Gr. 7-10. Fifteen-year-old biracial Anna tries to care for her five-year-old sister and infant brother when her alcoholic mother disappears yet again. Anna discovers her mother's car in a nearby lake—evidence of her suicide. After hiding in a cabin in the woods and then being placed with an unloving foster family, Anna, in desperation, travels to her mother's hometown in Mississippi, hoping to find family and a home. Instead, she learns of the horrors of her mother's past and meets white grandparents who don't want her. In spite of the grimness and apparent hopelessness of Anna's situation, she finds help, love, friendship, and a home. Koller portrays a young woman of strength and character, whose search for love and roots is at the core of a sensitive and finely written novel that shows the tragic and all-too-common results of sexual abuse and rejection from one's family.

📖 *NO SUCH THING* (1996)

Publishers Weekly

SOURCE: A review of *No Such Thing,* in *Publishers Weekly,* Vol. 243, No. 52, December 30, 1996, p. 67.

Monsters, according to popular opinion, live under beds. Koller (the Mole and Shrew books), rather than deny these beasts' existence, questions their frightful intentions. In this mildly suspenseful tale, a boy named Howard tells his mother, "I heard [a monster] snurkling under my bed." Meanwhile, a young monster informs his mother that he hears a boy "sneezing on top of my bed." Left alone by their disbelieving parents, human and monster peek at each other and shriek in fear; only when their terror turns to tears do they dare a second, curious look. On the closing page, they trade places for a practical joke that's left to the reader's imagination: "'Oh, Mommy,' they both called together. 'mommy, come quick!'" Lewin (*Somebody Catch My Homework*) draws in loose, Quentin Blake-style gestures of pen and ink, and fills the negative space with watercolor washes of dusky blue and brown. She envisions Monster (who reads a scary comic titled *Boy*) as a warty green gargoyle with clawed toes, a boar's snout and tusks. Koller invents a monster vocabulary: Monster "whimples" when Howard whimpers, and "sniggles" when his friend giggles. The plot is predictable and even a bit shopworn, yet the energetic telling and agreeable illustrations could put some fears temporarily to rest. Ages 4-8.

Lauren Peterson

SOURCE: A review of *No Such Thing,* in *Booklist,* Vol. 93, No. 15, April 1, 1997, p. 1338.

Ages 5-8. Koller takes a familiar story and adds a humorous twist: from under the bed, a monster mother tells her frightened son, "There are no such things as boys." The story cuts back and forth, alternating typical night fright scenes between the boy and his mother with the monster version of the same scene taking place under the bed. In a clever final scene, boy and monster, having discovered each other, team up to trick the moms by switching places and giving one last call for help. Koller's timing is right on, and Lewin's illustrations, expressive watercolors accented with thick, loose black lines, have the same fast, humorous pace as the story. Librarians who think they don't need another monster-under-the-bed story might want to reconsider.

DRAGON QUEST (1997)

Carolyn Phelan

SOURCE: A review of *Dragon Quest,* in *Booklist,* Vol. 93, No. 13, March 1, 1997, p. 1164.

Gr. 3-5. Koller's illustrated chapter book continues the story begun in *The Dragonling* (1991) and *A Dragon in the Family* (1993). Jealous of the growing affection between his little dragon, Zantor, and the chief elder's daughter, Rowena, young Darek turns down the village leader's offer to buy Zantor as a gift for Rowena's birthday. Darek's refusal sets in motion a dragon hunt that will end in violence for the hunted, the hunters, or both. Written with regard for ethical concerns as well as headlong adventure, this full-of-action fantasy reads well. The delicately shaded pencil drawings sensitively depict the characters and underscore the drama. The ending is a bit of a cliff-hanger, but readers will look forward to the sequel that must be in the works.

THE FALCON (1998)

Roger Leslie

SOURCE: A review of *The Falcon,* in *Booklist,* Vol. 94, No. 16, April 15, 1998, p. 1436.

Gr. 7-12. Luke Carver resents his school journaling assignment until he discovers that writing is a non-threatening way to express his feelings—at least some of them. Those that are too painful he is only willing to begin exploring. And he is quick to abandon his explorations for tales of misadventures that always result in horrible consequences. When one such exploit lands him in a psychiatric ward, Luke must face an emotional demon that has haunted him for years. Instead of being a trite contrivance, the journaling serves as an integral stage of Luke's emotional evolution. Even better, Koller builds suspense through a series of incomplete thoughts (literally crossed out on the page) to transform an interesting character tale into a real page-turner. Luke's strong voice comes through quite believably. His family struggle is made more genuine by the fact that his parents' compassion is as much the catalyst for Luke's troubles as the strength that keeps Luke from taking his self-destruction to fatal extremes.

Alison Follos

SOURCE: A review of *The Falcon,* in *School Library Journal,* Vol. 44, No. 5, May, 1998, pp. 144-45.

Gr 9 Up—Luke's English teacher assigns the class a daily journal-writing project. So begins the day-to-day adventures of an athletic and socially active 17 year old. Luke's sarcastic tone colors his entries with teen "attitude." Despite his best efforts, persistent flashbacks hint at his past. Crossed-out entries on random pages intensify readers' interest in what he *isn't* saying. There are indications that something is wrong with his eyesight. He shares that he has had a number of slight car accidents and has spent some time recovering from surgery, but stifles the details. His parents' apprehension, particularly over his driving, spark his temper. Thrilled and stimulated by physical achievement, he increasingly pushes himself into more reckless and adventurous activities. Finally, a climb up a steep mountain results in an injury to his other eye. This accident, which may leave Luke totally blind, becomes the catalyst for the young man to confront his past. During his studied and cautious disclosure of events, the truth painfully emerges. Readers will be drawn in by the journal technique and empathize with Luke's personal battles. Koller's portrayal of a foolhardy teen who feels invincible and is naive about irreversible consequence is incredibly well drawn. The strength of this novel is Luke's appearance as an ordinary 17 year old, doing the usual high-energy teen stuff. His past seeps out surreptitiously, adding powerful impact to an already interesting life.

Publishers Weekly

SOURCE: A review of *The Falcon,* in *Publishers Weekly,* Vol. 245, No. 20, May 18, 1998, p. 80.

Luke Carver thinks that keeping a journal "sounds like a chick thing." Nonetheless, his English teacher wants him to write a little each day in preparation for the all important college essay he will have to compose next year. Once he gets going, the 17-year-old doesn't mind writing, and he's pretty good at it, too; a poem he wrote several years ago, "The Falcon," was published in a magazine. His entries initiate a compelling journey of self-discovery. Luke's descriptions of his recent "screw-ups"—blowing a couple of wrestling meets, wrecking the car several times and leaving the scene of an accident—seem to flow fast and furiously from his pen, but when his thoughts turn to a bigger crisis, losing his left eye, he stops short. Crossed-out, half-finished sentences provide a less-than-subtle trail of clues to the source of Luke's problems, including the guilt he feels for not living up to his parents' expectations. While Koller's (*A Place to Call Home*) foreshadowing feels clumsy and contrived, readers will feel the weight of the painful secret Luke has carried for four years, and they can't fail to miss his resemblance to the bird in his poem, who "sits / with his head sagging down / and his eyes staring up / a chain around his leg." Ages 12-up.

📖 *BOUNCING ON THE BED* (1999)

Hazel Rochman

SOURCE: A review of *Bouncing on the Bed,* in *Booklist,* Vol. 95, No. 11, February 1, 1999, p. 980.

Ages 1-4. With simple words and clear, light-filled watercolors, this picture book features a toddler who acts out an idyllic day, from bouncing on the bed at sunup to snuggling down at bedtime, "happy to be me." Each double-page spread shows a joyful activity—sliding down the stairs, wiggling, running, roll-

ing, splashing, dancing, hiding, playing, singing. Sometimes Mom and Dad are there: cooking ("She stirs the pot. I lick the spoon."), reading ("He says the words. I turn the page."), and a small dog is in every picture ("I throw a stick. He fetches it."). The sounds of the words with repetition and occasional rhyme are part of the sense ("Thump, thump, thumpety"), and, like Zita Newcome's *Toddlerobics* (1996), this will have young preschoolers joining in the playful movements and chanting along.

Marian Drabkin

SOURCE: A review of *Bouncing on the Bed,* in *School Library Journal,* Vol. 45, No. 4, May, 1999, p. 100-1.

PreS—An energetic preschooler bounces, slides, wiggles, runs, dances, hides, cooks, sings, and reads through the day, and finally snuggles in bed with a hug and a kiss from his parents. Lively, sun-drenched watercolor paintings on double-page spreads show an inviting summertime world. The outdoor scenes are filled with grass and flowers as the round-faced, blue-eyed child and his shaggy-haired dog splash through a brook and roll down a hill. The indoor scenes are more peaceful and cozy. Each phase of the day-waking, eating, playtime, bathing—is described in a short rhyme that uses the same verse form as "The Farmer in the Dell": "Bouncing on the bed, / I'm bouncing on the bed. / The sun is up. / The day is new. / I'm bouncing on the bed." (The text could be sung to the same tune, too.) With the large pictures and the familiar activities described, this book would be a good selection for toddler time, and the infectious rhythm of the verse will invite participation from preschool storytime participants.

📖 *ONE MONKEY TOO MANY* (1999)

Marilyn Bousquin

SOURCE: A review of *One Monkey Too Many,* in *The Horn Book Magazine,* Vol. 75, No. 2, March, 1999, p. 194.

Seven mischievous monkeys wreak havoc as "one monkey too many" climbs first onto a bike made for one, then into a golf cart for two, then into a canoe for three, and so on. The two monkeys on the bike crash into a ditch, the three monkeys in the golf cart splash into the lake, the four monkeys in the canoe drop over a waterfall. An infectious, rollercoaster rhythm sweeps us up ("'Yippee!' They all wiggled and giggled with glee. 'This cart made for two is fun-tastic for three!'") then lurches us forward so that even though we know what's coming ("'Oh no!' they exclaimed, as they jammed on the brake! One monkey too many splashed into the lake"), we're too caught up in the ride to want brakes of any kind. Pastel watercolors paint the monkeys in casual toddler clothes with innocent, nothin's-going-on-here facial expressions. But that's just the calm before the storm; Munsinger lets loose the mounting chaos with an unrestrained frenzy as she catapults monkeys, golf cart, canoe, oars, food, pillows, feathers and so much more across the page in full-blown hurricane fashion. Readers will appreciate the monkeys' undeterred nature: the rascals continually go back for more, hoodwinking the larger animals (adult-like lions and pigs) who dictate how many monkeys each scene can contain. Not even the author is spared a dose of monkey business when "one monkey too many" pulls a grand-finale gotcha that literally determines the uproarious fate of her book.

Stephanie Zvirin

SOURCE: A review of *One Monkey Too Many*, in *Booklist*, Vol. 95, No. 16, April 15, 1999, p. 1536.

Ages 4-7. "'One,' said the bikeman. / 'This bike is for one. / One monkey can ride it, / and one can have fun.'" But the moment the bikeman turns his back, out pops an extra monkey to share the fun—and suffer the raucous consequences. And so it goes—three monkeys cramming into a golf cart for two, five at a table for four—until Koller herself enters the picture and puts her foot down: "'Six,' said the author. / 'This book is for six. / The pages are full, / so no more of your tricks.'" The pictures, of course, make it plain that despite Koller's stern declaration, the monkeys have ideas of their own. The joke is delightful, and Munsinger's boisterous illustrations, with animal characters galore (including some hidden monkeys for children to spot), are full of expression, movement, and wacky comedy. Children with some previous knowledge of numbers will also have fun using the lively yarn for counting practice—up to seven.

Publishers Weekly

SOURCE: A review of *One Monkey Too Many,* in *Publishers Weekly,* Vol. 246, No. 16, April 19, 1999, p. 72.

This mischievous rhyming and counting book revels in excess. Just one more monkey always appears, to crash the bike built for one, to wreck the canoe just right for three and to turn a bed for five into a pillow fight for six. In the last spread, the monkeys jump off the page to deface the book itself: "One monkey too many came sneaking and . . . / . . . LOOK! / One monkey too many got into this book!" Munsinger's (*Hooway for Wodney Wat*) rambunctious, lively art is a joy: the monkeys are blithely bad, and the chaos into which every scenario devolves gives kids plenty of diversions to follow. In each new situation that arises, the artist shows the invading monkey hidden somewhere on the spread. Koller (*Mole and Shrew All Year Through*) turns the childhood impulse to join in the fun into a tale that will appeal to the imp in everyone. Ages 4-8.

Lauralyn Persson

SOURCE: A review of *One Monkey Too Many,* in *School Library Journal,* Vol. 45, No. 5, May, 1999, p. 92.

PreS-K This story begins as one deceptively calm monkey is presented with a bike: "'One,' said the bikeman. / 'This bike is for one. / One monkey can ride it, / and one can have fun.'" Another monkey is hiding behind the bikeman, though, and as soon as his back is turned, it joins the first on the bike, and before long they crash in a thoroughly satisfying way. Chaos builds throughout as the monkeys are offered a golf cart for two, a canoe for three, a table for four (in a fancy restaurant, of course), and a bed for five. The closing scene, in which Koller insists that the book is for six monkeys, is perfect for this funny story that's ideal for group sharing. The infectious rhythm of the text never falters, and Munsinger's illustrations, set against plenty of white space, revel in the gleeful monkey business. Spilling, breaking, dropping, and crashing have never been this much fun.

THE PROMISE (1999)

Ilene Cooper

SOURCE: A review of *The Promise*, in *Booklist*, Vol. 96, No. 1, September 1, 1999, p. 145.

Gr. 3-6. Here's a nineteenth-century story with a purposeful supernatural element. It is Matt's first Christmas without his mother. Trying to keep her traditions alive, he goes outside late at night to feed suet balls to the birds as she used to do. Suddenly, he and Sara, his Labrador retriever, are surprised by a bear. A chase ensues, and Sara is injured. Matt's mother always said that at midnight on Christmas Eve the animals can talk. Sara does "talk," communicating nonverbally with Matt, telling him he must go get help, but that she will survive; after some tense hours, she does. In some ways, this book seems like a made-for-TV movie, with most of the twists telegraphed ahead of time. But children will find the bear-versus-dog action exciting, and the book's compactness makes it a manageable piece of holiday fiction.

Eva Mitnick

SOURCE: A review of *The Promise,* in *School Library Journal,* Vol. 45, No. 10, October, 1999, p. 68.

Gr 3-5—It's Christmas Eve, the first since Ma died, and Matt, his little brother, Jamie, and their father are trying to keep their spirits up; they've decorated their cabin and given special treats to the farm animals. As Matt goes out with his dog, Sara, to leave suet balls in the trees for the birds, a bear looms up and chases them into the woods, where it wounds brave Sara and drives Matt up into a tree. The boy finally realizes that it's the suet balls that the animal is after and throws them as far away as possible. Now Matt is lost, Sara is near death, and a snowstorm has hit; in the Christmas miracle, Sara speaks to the boy briefly at midnight, directing him home. The time period and setting are unspecified but this story appears to take place sometime in the late 1800s or early 1900s. Matt narrates the tale in an easygoing, slightly folksy style that will appeal to kids. His adventure with the bear is scary and thrilling, and the references to Matt's deceased mother are moving. The short length, fast pace, and simple language make this a fine bridge for new chapter-book readers, at Christmas or anytime.

📖 *NICKOMMOH!: A THANKSGIVING CELEBRATION* (1999)

Publishers Weekly

SOURCE: A review of *Nickommoh!: A Thanksgiving Celebration,* in *Publishers Weekly,* Vol. 246, No. 39, September 27, 1999, p. 50.

If *Squanto* offers background to the Pilgrims' first Thanksgiving, Koller *(The Promise)* demonstrates that a celebratory gathering to commemorate the harvest, Nickommoh, had long been the custom on these shores. In prose with the cadence of a drumbeat, the author reveals the rhythms of Narragansett life, devoted to the Creator, Kautantawwitt, and punctuated by praise: "They come together, together to give thanks. Nickommoh!" In marked contrast to her usual style, Sewall's (*The Pilgrims of Plimoth*) scratchboard and gouache illustrations convey both simplicity and complexity. Even as she portrays individuals—men cutting poles for the great lodge, women covering the poles with bark, children playing tug-of-war—her compositions build a unity among the characters. Almost hypnotic in their power, art and text are infused with the communal spirit of Thanksgiving. Ages 6-9.

Margaret A. Chang

SOURCE: A review of *Nickommoh!: A Thanksgiving Celebration,* in *School Library Journal,* Vol. 45, No. 10, October, 1999, p. 140.

PreS-Gr 4—"It is *Taquountikeeswush,* the Moon of the Falling Leaves. . . . Time for the People to come together, together to give thanks. NICKOMMOH!" Koller's poetic narrative builds a sequence of activities: coming together, building a shelter, feasting, playing games, entering a sweat lodge, and dancing. Each double-page spread ends with the exclamation, "NICKOMMOH!," a word defined in the glossary as "a celebrational gathering." An author's note explains that "Long before the first Pilgrim set foot in the New World, Native Americans were celebrating rites of thanksgiving. . . . " Sewall's strongly composed, impressionistic illustrations have black outlines and rich earth tones to anchor and solidify the poetic text. Vivid descriptions draw readers into the life of the Narragansett Indian tribe who once lived in present-day Rhode Island. The writing is studded with words from the Narragansett language, which are all defined in an informative glossary. This engaging partnership of art and text will be a natural read-aloud in the weeks before Thanksgiving.

Karen Hutt

SOURCE: A review of *Nickommoh! A Thanksgiving Celebration,* in *Booklist,* Vol. 96, No. 6, November 15, 1999, p. 630.

Ages 5-8. Nickommoh was a harvest festival celebrated by the Narragansett tribe during Taquountikeeswush, the Moon of the Falling Leaves. Long before Europeans settled in North America, the Narragansett celebrated the harvest with three days of games, feasts, and contests of skill. Scratchboard and gouache illustrations in autumn colors spill across the pages, showing tribal members constructing sweat lodges, playing games, donning special garments, and dancing in great circles. Nickommoh, which means "give away," included a special dance for which people donated extra food, furs, and clothing. The sachem (leader) distributed the gifts to widows, orphans, and others in need. Unfortunately, there is no pronunciation guide for the many Narragansett words incorporated throughout the text, though definitions are appended. An excellent alternative to the many books about Thanksgiving.

Additional coverage of Koller's life and career is contained in the following sources published by The Gale Group: *Authors and Artists for Young Adults,* **Vol. 28;** *Contemporary Authors,* **Vol. 170;** *Something about the Author,* **Vols. 72, 109.**

Garth Nix
1963-

Australian novelist.

Major works include the *Very Clever Baby* series (1988-92), *The Ragwitch* (1990), *Sabriel* (1995), *Shade's Children* (1997), *Lirael: Daughter of the Clayr* (2000).

INTRODUCTION

Garth Nix has built a strong reputation on his fantasy novels, especially in his native Australia. Though he has written only a handful of books through the 1990s, Nix has received widespread appreciation for his work, with particular praise for his use of characterization in a genre that often pays more attention to action. Though he aims his novels to the young adult audience, Nix has said that he bases his writing on what he would want to read himself. While influenced by such authors as J. R. R. Tolkien and C. S. Lewis, Nix has succeeded in establishing his own voice. In all of his writing, Nix strives to avoid didacticism. "I never intentionally start with a theme or a message, or try to put one in," he told J. Sydney Jones in an interview for *Authors and Artists for Young Adults (AAYA)*. "I believe in stories, not didactic tracts." Still, there are recurring themes in Nix's fantasy books such as assuming responsibility "not only for yourself, but for others or even for whole societies."

BIOGRAPHICAL INFORMATION

A native of Melbourne, Australia, Garth Nix can argue that he was destined even before birth to become a fantasy author: "My mother was reading *The Lord of the Rings* when she was pregnant with me," Nix told *AAYA*. "So I absorbed this master work of fantasy *in utero,* as it were. Later on I became a great fan of Tolkien's stories." Raised in Australia's capital, Canberra, Nix enjoyed what he has called a "culture of reading" fostered by his parents. A self-described bookworm, the young boy spent much time at the local library, devouring the stories of Ursula Le Guin, Robert Louis Stevenson, and Robert Heinlein. He went on to earn a degree from the University of Canberra in 1986. Wanderlust often character-

ized the young man; his travels have included Eastern Europe, the Middle East, and Asia. In Australia Nix worked in publishing, eventually starting his own company, Gotley Nix Evans Pty Ltd. ("This career was forced upon him after every other writer took the lumberjack, prospector, deep sea diver and short-order cook jobs," as an *Ozemail.com* online biography puts it.) That step led to Nix's first published works, the satirical, adult-oriented *Very Clever Baby* series. In 1990 he produced his first fantasy novel, *The Ragwitch,* which pointed the way to most of his subsequent books. Following a brief stint in public relations, Nix took the step of becoming a full-time writer in 1998, and supplemented that career by becoming a part-time literary agent in 1999. With his partner, Anna, Nix lives in Coogee, Australia, "five minutes walk from the beach."

MAJOR WORKS

Seeking an entry into the fantasy realm, Nix published *The Ragwitch* in 1990 after working on the book for six years, the longest writing cycle to date for the author. The story follows siblings Paul and Julia who stumble upon a midden—literally a prehistoric garbage dump. There they find a nest containing a rag doll. No ordinary toy, the doll has the power to enslave others, and Julia is its first victim. Paul must enter a strange fantasy world to rescue his sister, in what *Australian Bookseller and Publisher* critic Ann Tolman calls "good adult mystic escapism with considerable imaginative experiences for the reader."

However, it was Nix's next novel, *Sabriel,* that would earn him awards and plaudits as a rising star in the fantasy genre. The inspiration for this young adult tale came from the author's journey from London to Pakistan; the exotic locales come into play as the book's heroine, young Sabriel, is trained by her necromancer father to follow in his footsteps. While accepting her destiny as one who can raise the dead (albeit for good purposes only), Sabriel must embark on a classic quest to save her father, protector of the magical Old Kingdom. Critical reaction to *Sabriel* focused on the effectiveness of a young girl as protagonist: in a genre dominated by male characters, more than one reviewer cited the strong, sensible, and sensitive Sabriel as providing a good role model for young readers of both genders.

Nix follows *Sabriel* with a "near sequel," *Lirael: Daughter of the Clayr.* The action returns to the Old Kingdom twenty-two years later, where Sameth, son of Sabriel, continues in the family tradition of magic. Nix has called *Lirael* more complex than its predecessor, "told for a large part from two different viewpoints" and bringing in "more of the underlying story of the world," as he points out in AAYA.

Shade's Children, another quest tale set in the distant future, centers on a young psychic, Gold-Eye, who runs away from the cruel Overlords who harvest children's brains to transplant into their evil minions. In this book Nix challenges young readers to face more difficult themes of betrayal and sacrifice. "Grim" is the word some critics used to describe the author's vision of a post-apocalyptic future, though Donna L. Scanlon, in *Voice of Youth Advocates,* also sees in the havoc a glimmer of hope. "And it is this hope that sustains the reader through the nail-biting plot to the satisfying conclusion."

Nix's satiric side can be seen in a trio of books called the Very Clever Baby series. These are parodies of easy-readers aimed at expectant parents and are meant as gag gifts and icebreakers.

AWARDS

Nix's debut fantasy novel earned him his first literary award when *The Ragwitch* was cited as a Notable Book by the Children's Book Council. Later, *Sabriel* earned several honors: Notable Book citation and Best Book for Young Adults citation, American Library Association (ALA); Best Fantasy Novel and Best Young Adult Novel; Aurealis Award for excellence in Australian Speculative Fiction; and an "Outstanding Title" citation from *Voice of Youth Advocates.* *Shade's Children* also was named an "Outstanding Title" and an ALA Best Books winner.

AUTHOR COMMENTARY

Garth Nix

SOURCE: "How I Write: The Process of Creating a Book," retrieved from http://www.ozemail.com.au/garthnix/writing.html

This is a brief overview of how I go about writing a book, which may well be quite different from many other writers and different to how you like to work yourself. However, in amongst the cries of 'how could he work like that!' there may be some useful pieces of information to help with your own writing.

To me, there are really four stages to writing a book, though they do overlap each other, swap places at times or even take over for far longer than they should. These stages are: thinking, planning, writing and revising.

THINKING

Most of my books seem to stem from a single image or thought that lodges in my brain and slowly grows into something that needs to be expressed. That thought may be a 'what if?' or perhaps just an image. *Sabriel* largely began from a photograph I saw of Hadrian's Wall, which had a green lawn in front of it and snow on the hills behind it. Many other thoughts, conscious or otherwise, grew out, upon and over that single image, both before and during the writing of the book.

Typically I seem to think about a book for a year or so before I actually start writing. In this thinking stage, I often write a few key points in my 'ideas' notebook. . . . At this stage, I merely put down bullet points or mnemonics that will remind me of what I was thinking. This can be very useful later on, particularly if the gestation period for a book is several years.

PLANNING

For all my longer works (i.e. the novels) I write chapter outlines so I can have the pleasure of departing from them later on. Actually, while I always do depart from them, writing a chapter outline is a great discipline for thinking out the story and it also provides a road map or central skeleton you can come back to if you get lost. I often write the prologue or initial chapter first to get the impetus for the story going and then write the outline. Usually, I have to write a revised chapter outline two or three times in the course of writing the whole book, but once again it does focus the mind on where the story is going and where you want it to go. . . .

WRITING

Short stories, articles and items on my web site I type straight into the computer (mostly a Macintosh, though I also use a PC) in Microsoft Word. However, I write the novels longhand first. Nowadays I use a Waterman fountain pen (for **Shade's Children** and **Lirael**), though I used felt-tips earlier.

The advantages of writing longhand are several, at least for me. First of all, I write in relatively small handbound notebooks which are much more transportable than any sort of computer, particularly since you can take them away for several weeks without having to consider power supplies, batteries or printing out. Parts of **Sabriel,** for example, were written on a trip through the Middle East. Parts of **Shade's Children** and **Sabriel** were written at the beach.

The other major advantage is that when I type up a chapter from my notebook, I rewrite as I type, so the first print-out is actually a second draft. Sometimes I change it quite a lot, sometimes not so much, but it gives me a distinctive and separate stage where I can revise. . . .

REVISING

As I said, when I type the handwritten words, I am also carrying out my first major stage of revision. However, I usually have to go through at least two revision stages after that. The first of these is when I first print out the typed chapter. I go through it and make changes in pen, which I will take in later. The second stage (and sometimes a third time as well) occurs when the entire manuscript is finished for the first time. I leave that big, beautiful pile of print-out on the shelf for a few weeks, then sit down and read the whole thing, making corrections as I go.

Finally, I bundle the MS. off to my Australian and US publishers and wait for their reaction(s), which generally will include some suggestions for revision and occasionally a request for rewriting. Sometimes these will be good, worthwhile changes and I take them in. Sometimes they are not, and I argue about them and—unless I can be convinced otherwise— refuse to alter the text. Basically, I try and keep an open mind, since there is nearly always room for improvement.

KEEPING MOTIVATED

I'm often asked by would-be writers how I can write a full-length novel which takes a year or more to get done. My stock answer is that I never sit down and think 'I have to write a novel today'. I sit down and think 'I have to write a chapter', or 'revise a chapter' or 'finish the chapter'. That way, it's only ever 2,500-5,000 words that are the immediate goal.

As a further motivational gimmick, I always use the word count utility when I've finished typing a chapter, and write that down, with a running total of words and the date in the front of my first notebook for the current work (each novel takes between five and six of those red and black numbers).

I also write down the music I've been listening to as I write and anything else that might be interesting to look back upon. Like the fact that I uploaded my first home page on 19 April 1996! . . .

The word count is a relatively small thing, but it has an amazing psychological effect, particularly as more and more chapters appear and the word total grows. I find it very encouraging, particularly in the first third of the book, which always seems to take me half the time.

SUMMARY

Here are several one liners which sum up my writing philosophy. Some I've made up and some are probably paraphrases of other people's sayings, only I can't remember who said them.

'You can't write if you don't read.'

'Just write one chapter at a time and one day you'll be surprised by your own finished novel.'

'Writing anything is better than not writing something perfect.'

'Read, write, revise, submit, repeat.'

'Never believe the first twenty publishers who reject your work. For the twenty-first, submit something new.'

'A goatee and a garret are all very well, but you have to actually write to be a writer.'

Garth Nix with Claire E. White

SOURCE: "A Conversation with Garth Nix," downloaded from http://www.writerswrite.com/journal July-August, 2000.

Award-winning Young Adult and Children's author Garth Nix was born in 1963. He grew up in Canberra, the federal capital of Australia. After working briefly for the Australian Government, Garth took a long holiday in Europe, returning in 1983 to study for a B.A. in Professional Writing from the University of Canberra. Around this time, he also put in four years as a part-time soldier (or "weekend warrior") with the Australian Army Reserve. After taking his degree in 1986, he worked in a bookshop for some time, then moved to Sydney, where he had various jobs in the publishing industry, from sales rep to publicist, until in 1991 he became a senior editor with a major multinational publisher. Leaving to travel in Eastern Europe, the Middle East and Asia in 1993, Garth returned to Sydney in 1994 to work as a PR consultant. In 1996, he started a new company, Gotley Nix Evans Pty Ltd., with two partners. He notes that this career was forced upon him after every other writer took the lumberjack, prospector, deep sea diver and short order cook jobs. Garth stopped working actively at Gotley Nix Evans in January 1998, and was a full-time writer till May 1999 when he joined Curtis Brown, Australia's largest literary agency, as a part-time agent.

His first published book was *The Ragwitch,* a young adult fantasy published by Forge in 1995, which was followed by *Sabriel* and *Shade's Children* (HarperCollins). *Shade's Children* was short listed for the 1997 Aurealis Awards, is an ALA Best Book for Young Adults, an ABA Pick of the Lists, a CBCA Notable Book, and has been shortlisted for the Heartland Prize (U.S.), the 2000 Pacific Northwest Reader's Choice Awards (U.S.), the South Carolina Reader's Choice Awards, the Evergreen YA Award and the Garden State Young Reader's Awards. *Sabriel* won both the Best Fantasy Novel and Best Young Adult Novel in the 1995 Aurealis Awards. It is also an American Library Association (ALA) Notable Book, an ALA Best Book for Young Adults, a CBCA No-

table Book, a LOCUS magazine Recommended Fantasy novel, listed in 1997 Books for the Teenage (New York Public Library), listed in Best Science Fiction, Fantasy and Horror (VOYA) and it was short listed for six U.S. State awards.

Garth has also written theatre restaurant shows (in collaboration with several friends), short stories and the three Very Clever Baby Books (now being republished by Text Publishing). Garth is also the author of a novelization of the X-Files episode "The Calusari," which was published in June 1997 by HarperTrophy. He has completed the book *Lirael,* which is set in the same world as Sabriel, but 20 years later. It is the first half of a story that will be continued in *Abhorsen. Lirael* is scheduled to be published by Allen & Unwin in Australia and HarperCollins in the U.S.A. in March, 2001. His books are known for their humor, wit, depth of character and imagination.

Garth's newest project is writing an exciting six-book fantasy series for Scholastic and LucasFilm called *The Seventh Tower.* Book One, *The Fall,* has just been released to stellar reviews, and Scholastic has created a major web site for the series, which features sophisticated animation and music. *The Seventh Tower* is a children's fantasy which follows the adventures of young Tal, in his search for the Sunstones that he must have in order to save his family—and his future. The world in which the series is set is totally dark; the sun only shines above the mysterious Veil, which sits high in the atmosphere above the Seven Towers where Tal's people live.

Garth now lives in Coogee, Australia, five minutes walk from the beach, with his partner Anna, a book editor. His recreational interests include fishing, body-surfing, collecting books of all kinds, reading, films, writing and lunch. He also maintains a popular web site which gives more information about his books.

Garth talked to us about *The Fall,* the first in his new Seventh Tower series, how he got his start as an author, and how he approaches the craft of writing.

What kinds of books did you like to read when you were a boy?

I've always read very widely, a habit that started very early. One of my favorite books as an eight or nine year old was a 1930s encyclopedia called *Arthur Mee's Children's Encyclopaedia.* I used to read entire volumes of that over several weeks, paying equal attention to science, history, literature and so on. But my favorite part of it was the color section on heraldry and the list of old English coins, like how many groats equaled a penny and so on. This was probably indicative of the sort of writer I would become. Later on, I read a lot of science fiction, fantasy and history (both novels and non-fiction). Many of the books I read then I have included in my list of favorites on my web site.

When did the writing bug hit you?

I probably always had it without really being conscious of it. I have always liked making up stories. I wrote quite a few stories through my school years and would contribute articles to the school magazine and so on. I didn't actively realize that I really wanted to make writing my main life's work until I was 19. I was traveling through England and Europe, re-reading lots of my favorite books in the places that inspired them. On that trip I wrote a large part of very bad and forever to be unpublished fantasy novel and several short stories. When I got back to Australia, a telegram came for me (this was in 1984 when they still had telegrams) accepting a short story and offering quite substantial payment. The arrival of that telegram probably crystallized my ambition to be a writer. Fortunately I had enough common sense to realize that I would have to do other things to make a living while I wrote. Since I didn't sell another story for years this was just as well.

What led up to your first book being published?

I knew I wanted to be a writer, but I also knew that I probably should go and get a university degree to help my employment prospects.

Fortunately I was able to combine the two ambitions by studying for a Bachelor of Arts in Professional Writing at what is now the University of Canberra. While I majored in scriptwriting and theatre, I was also able to write half a novel as part of my course. I then wrote the other half while I was taking the first steps on my other career, in book publishing. By the time I finished that book, **The Ragwitch,** I was an editor working for an academic publishing house. It had taken me five years to write it, very off and on, and it shows all the ambition and flaws of a typical first novel. The third publisher I sent it to decided to give it a try. Later, it was published in the U.S.A. by the sixteenth publisher I sent the Australian edition to, in the days before I had a New York agent.

Let's talk about **The Seventh Tower.** *How did this series come into being?*

At the very basic level, it came from the success of my novel **Sabriel.** An editor at Scholastic, who liked that book, had emailed me to say so and to say that

he'd love to work with me on something. I said I'd love to work with him and Scholastic. This was all very general, nice stuff for authors and editors to say to each other, but a few months later I got an e-mail saying that Scholastic was working with LucasFilm to create a new fantasy series. Would I be interested? I replied that I might be, but not if was just novelizing existing material as I found that sort of work (which I had done once with an X-Files episode for HarperCollins) really did not suit me. So we talked back and forth, totally via email, and my agent got involved and over several months the nature of exactly what I would do became clear.

How much freedom did you have in terms of characters and plot? I understand that you got a few "seed ideas" or suggestions for the series from LucasFilm and Scholastic.

As I mentioned, I didn't want to do something where I was just novelizing existing work. Fortunately, Scholastic and LucasFilm were very flexible. They had a list of "ideas and influences" for the sort of thing they were after, but it was general enough for me to feel there was room to create the sort of unique and interesting story I wanted to at least try and tell. The list included points like "a castle where everything outside is dark," "a closed society similar to feudal Japan" or "the architecture of Gaudi." I got this list and was then free to go away and develop the world, the overall story and the characters. I wrote two documents for Scholastic and LucasFilm, a "Backgrounder" on the world and setting and a "Story Outline" for the whole series of six books. Both of these were then further developed by me in consultation with my Scholastic editor and editors at LucasFilm. I admit I was concerned that I might be getting into the sort of working arrangement screenwriters often suffer from, of the "it's great but we need a campfire scene here" variety, but that hasn't occurred and I've enjoyed as much creative freedom as I've had with any other book, coupled with lots of valuable editorial input.

What is the most challenging aspect of writing **The Seventh Tower** *series?*

I've had to write these books fairly quickly, faster than I normally would. I'm basically writing a book every two months or so, and then revisiting it a month later to look at the editorial feedback and revise, expand or contract. This is quite do-able, but I am a naturally lazy person who likes to have lots of daydreaming "fallow" time to let stories develop in my unconscious. Mind you, I'm not sure that if I had more time this would show in the books. I probably would write them in exactly the same time just spread out over more weeks. The other challenge is that there is an immediate story (of Tal and Milla and their adventures), a bigger story (which is gradually revealed) and a complex past (which influences both the immediate and the big story). While the immediate story is the main narrative, I have to keep in mind the big story and the past and let parts of both trickle into what is happening right now. Since I am also working out many of the details of the big story and the past as I go, this is a bit like juggling lots of different things of varying shapes and sizes, any one of which will ruin the book if it gets dropped.

Tal is an interesting and complex protagonist. He's a good person—but his first instincts aren't always selfless, although he usually makes the right choice in the end, especially when it involves protecting his family. Were there any characteristics you were specifically trying to avoid with Tal?

I tend to only have a very basic idea of what one of my characters is like at the beginning, and then they develop through the action. Often I look back at a book and I wonder how they ended up the way they did. With Tal, I knew he was rather naive, deeply committed to his family, and that he had more courage than he knew. He's also a thirteen something boy.

Tal's shadowguard is a wonderful creation. What was your inspiration for the shadowguards of the children and the Spiritshadows, which the adults receive on the Day of Ascension?

In the original LucasFilm/Scholastic notes, they wanted the characters to have magical companions of some sort. I toyed with a number of possible companions and reasons for their existence. Shadows were fairly obvious from the start, because we all have them. As the nature of the Dark World developed and so did the importance of light, it was a fairly easy step to think of shadows that are not simply shadows . . .

How do you approach the creation of the magical system in a new fantasy world? What are some of the elements that you consider?

I think there is some danger even in the words "magic system". It implies a magic like a technology, where everything is worked out and there is no mystery. I tend to think only of the very basics, like what the magic looks like and how it is cast, and then let it develop through the course of the story. The magic

has to be consistent to maintain the reader's suspension of disbelief, but not so worked out and described that it becomes mundane and no more interesting than an electric stove or a rifle.

I must admit I am quite fond of Great-Uncle Ebbitt. Will we be seeing more of him in future tales?

Yes, you will. I'm fond of him, too. Great-Uncle Ebbitt is a bit like an erratic comet that careers across the sky every now and then. Bright, fascinating and completely unpredictable.

I'd like to talk a bit about **Shade's Children.** *What was your inspiration for the novel?*

It's always difficult to pin down exact inspirations for books. With *Shade's Children,* I think that the seed of the idea came from when I was living in a house in a leafy inner suburb of Sydney. One day there was a strange rumble under the ground, and it turned out that the house was built directly over a largely unused railway line. I'd lived there a year without a train going underneath. I looked the railway line up on the map and discovered where it came out, which was near a park. I went and had a look. As I stood looking in the mouth of the tunnel, there was a rare moment in a big city when I couldn't hear any noise: no cars, no planes, no people. That made me think, what would happen if everyone disappeared? Of course, there were lots of other inspirations for *Shade's Children* to, but the railway tunnel and those moments of silence are an inspiration I can identify.

One of the criticisms of the Harry Potter books and some other children's literature is that the adults are not portrayed in a positive light (which theory seems to ignore the fact of life that many adults are not positive role models!) In **Shade's Children,** *for example, the only real nurturing adult is the mysterious Shade. How should adults be portrayed in children's literature? Do you feel children's authors have a duty to keep any certain values or ideals in mind when writing for children (such as good eventually overcoming evil?)*

I subscribe to the belief that "if you want to send a message, use Western Union." In other words, if the values or moral messages are too overt, the story will suffer and no one will read it (which paradoxically means they won't get the message either). Children don't like to be preached to any more than adults do. On the other hand, while I always try and tell a good story, I can't help but infuse my moral and ethical views into any book I write, consciously or not. I don't agree that adults are portrayed in a negative light in Harry Potter. There are both good and bad adults, the good being most of the staff of Hogwarts, the Weasley parents etc. In *Shade's Children,* Shade is both a good and bad adult. Adults should be portrayed as is required by the story: good, bad or a mixture of the two. Sometimes a book may only have bad adults, but another may only have good ones. The nature of the story and the context in which the adult characters appear is much more important than any hard and fast rules about always having "good" or "bad" characters of any kind.

It is important to bear in mind the age group a book is for. Children are not a homogenous mass, and neither are children's books. There is a big difference between picture books, junior novels, the classic children's novel for the 9-12 market, and young adult novels. How an author addresses (or doesn't) ethical and moral issues depends greatly on the intended audience. Issues that can only be attacked allegorically in a 9-12 age group novel can be the major, overt subject of a Young Adult novel. Parents, librarians and booksellers have an important role to play here, too, making sure that children are emotionally and intellectually capable of tackling particular books. Some readers read well above their age, others do not.

I don't believe authors need to keep any specific values or ideas in mind while they are writing for children, but I do think authors need to be aware of their audience, and of the effect their work may have. So if they want to address particularly sensitive topics or taboos, they have to do so consciously and carefully. This is very different to toeing a particular moral line or leaving things out.

Certainly I don't think good always has to triumph over evil; it depends on the story and the aims of the book. For example, I could envisage telling a story where the inaction of people leads to the triumph of evil. But I would include the hope that this would lead to the people involved doing better next time. Is that story then really about the triumph of evil, or is it about the awakening of opposition to evil?

I understand there are two sequels to **Sabriel** *in the works. Can you tell us a bit about them?*

I originally wrote the two books as one, long single volume that I have since cut in two and substantially revised. The first book is called *Lirael: Daughter of the Clayr,* the second is *Abhorsen.*

Lirael begins 14 years after the events of *Sabriel.* Lirael is a young girl growing up in the Clayr's Glacier, among the almost totally female Clayr, who can

see the future in ice. But Lirael, alone of all the Clayr, does not have the Sight. She does have other gifts though, and a destiny and inheritance that no one could suspect. With her one friend, the Disreputable Dog, she has to leave the Glacier to discover the truth about her past and the nature of a threat to the entire future of the Kingdom.

Abhorsen continues this story. Fans of *Sabriel* will be pleased to hear that Sabriel, Touchstone, Mogget and others all return in the new books and numerous questions that I get in e-mails will be answered, like "do Sabriel and Touchstone get married?", "what is Touchstone's real name?", "What is Mogget?" etc.

Unfortunately, *Lirael: Daughter of the Clayr* won't be out till March, 2001. It was slated for October, 2000, but has been delayed. This is almost completely the publisher's fault this time, though I have to admit it was my fault it got delayed in the first place from March, 2000 to October, 2000.

Tell us about **The Very Clever Baby Books.**

They're little books that I first made back in 1988 as presents for some friends expecting babies, on the basis that all parents think their babies are geniuses. Each one is only 12 pages long and about the same size as a greeting card. Basically, they feature a character called Freddy the Fish and are supposed to be for "Very Clever Babies Aged 3-6 Months". Since no babies that age can read and the books have very big words like 'Ichthyologist' and 'Tetradontidae' it is surprising that some people don't get the joke. There are three at present, *Very Clever Baby's First Reader, Very Clever Baby's Ben*Hur* and *Very Clever Baby's First Christmas.* They are only published in Australia, by Text Publishing, but I hope to find an American publisher with a suitable sense of humor one of these days.

I'd like to talk about the creative process. You have said that there are four stages that you go through when writing a book: thinking, planning, writing and revising. Would you describe the planning element for us?

This is a complex question. But the shorter answer is as follows: There are four stages to writing a book, though they overlap, swap places at times or even take over for far longer than they should. These stages are: thinking, planning, writing and revising.

THINKING

Most of my books seem to stem from a single image or thought that lodges in my brain and slowly grows into something that needs to be expressed. That thought may be a "what if?" or perhaps just an image. Typically I seem to think about a book for a year or so before I actually start writing. In this thinking stage, I often write a few key points in my "ideas" notebook, usually just bullet points or mnemonics that will remind me of what I was thinking. This can be very useful later on, particularly if the gestation period for a book is several years.

PLANNING

For all my longer works (i.e. the novels) I write chapter outlines. Writing a chapter outline is a great discipline for thinking out the story and it also provides a road map or central skeleton you can come back to if you get lost. I often write the prologue or initial chapter first to get the impetus for the story going and then write the outline. Because no story ever follows an outline exactly, I often have to write a revised chapter outline two or three or four times in the course of writing the whole book, but each time it gives an opportunity to focus the mind on where the story is going and where you want it to go.

WRITING

Short stories, articles and items on my web site I type straight into the computer. However, I write the novels longhand first. The advantages of writing longhand are several, at least for me. First of all, I write in relatively small handbound notebooks which are much more transportable than any sort of computer, particularly since you can take them away for several weeks without having to consider power supplies, batteries or printing out. The other major advantage is that when I type up a chapter from my notebook, I rewrite as I type, so the first print-out is actually a second draft.

REVISING

When I type the handwritten words, I am also carrying out my first major stage of revision. However, I usually have to go through at least two revision stages after that. The first of these is when I first print out the typed chapter. I go through it and make changes in pen, which I will take in later. The second stage (and sometimes a third time as well) occurs when the entire manuscript is finished for the first time. I leave the print-out on the shelf for a few weeks, then sit down and read the whole thing, making corresctions as I go. Finally, I bundle the manuscript off to my Australian and U.S. publishers and wait for their reaction(s), which generally will include some suggestions for revision and occasionally a request for

rewriting. Sometimes these will be good, worthwhile changes and I take them in. Sometimes they are not, and I argue about them and—unless I can be convinced otherwise—refuse to alter the text. Basically, I try and keep an open mind, since there is nearly always room for improvement.

What did you learn from your work as both and editor and as a literary agent? How have those experiences affected your writing?

Working as an editor on a very wide range of fiction and non-fiction has, I think, given me a good feel for narrative structure. I always had an instinct for it, but my years as an editor helped me hone my skills, to work out how and where stories are flawed or why non-fiction work doesn't achieve what it sets out to do. Unfortunately, this doesn't always carry over to my own work. I was always a hopeless copy editor and this still applies. I am not good at line editing. Give me the big picture any time! Working as a literary agent, which I still do part-time, is useful for staying connected to the industry and well-informed. But mainly I work as an agent because I find full-time writing too solitary. I enjoy going to the office and talking to my clients and finding great books and selling them to publishers . . . but only if I have at least half the week to write!

What do you enjoy most about writing young adult and children's fiction? Do you feel it gives you more freedom as a writer than writing strictly for adults? (Of course, many adults enjoy your books, as well.)

To be honest, most of the time I don't think about the fact that I am writing for children or young adults. I simply enjoy telling the story and the way I naturally write seems to work well for both young and older audiences. I also don't really think about freedom. Because my natural writing voice seems to inhabit the Young Adult realm (which is accepted as being for children who are becoming adults and adults who haven't forgotten being younger), I haven't had to change it, which is when I would start thinking about freedom or the lack of it.

The Seventh Tower *is your first series book. How are you enjoying writing a series, as opposed to writing a stand-alone, such as* **Shade's Children?**

I'm enjoying it a lot, for a variety of reasons. The six books of **The Seventh Tower** are really one big story told in self-contained episodes. So it's a bit like a serial novel, in the tradition of Dickens (or more recently Stephen King). That's fun, writing only one or two books ahead of the one being published. I'm also enjoying the resources of LucasFilm and Scholastic that has put behind the books. It's fun to be involved in something where lots of people are enhancing the basic work. Of course, the other side of that is a loss of control and ownership, but as I entered into the series very open-eyed about what each party would get out of it, that's OK.

Shade's Children and Sabriel are Young Adult crossovers—that is, they are read by both teens and the adult fantasy audience. How did you approach writing The Seventh Tower series, which is aimed at younger readers? Did you consciously simplify any elements of your writing?

Yes, I have pared down my writing style to some degree. Obviously the books are considerably shorter and that impacts upon how I tell the story. There is also a greater focus on the exterior action, rather than the character's interior thoughts and emotions. Though the latter are still there!

What are your pet peeves in life?

Heavy traffic. Cupboards that won't stay shut. Narrow-minded, backwards-looking politicians like the current Australian Prime Minister.

Rumor has it that you cook a mean breakfast. What would you prepare for a special brunch for favorite friends?

Usually I like to try and be a short-order cook, so I give them a choice of eggs (scrambled, fried, poached), grilled tomato, fried bacon, fried potato, grilled sausage, fried mushrooms, toast, coffee, tea, fruit juice, fruit. The art is in serving everybody everything they want at the same time, with everything cooked exactly right. To really enjoy a breakfast like this, it should be preceded by rising before dawn and fishing for several hours (and if successful, grilled fish can be added to the menu).

What is your advice to aspiring writers?

Read a lot, and read widely (not just in one genre or area). Write as often as you can, even if it's only a few paragraphs at a time. Submit a lot, even if you only get rejections (all writers get rejections). Most of all, don't give up.

TITLE COMMENTARY

SABRIEL (1996)

Sally Estes

SOURCE: A review of *Sabriel,* in *Booklist,* Vol. 93, No. 3, October 1, 1996, p. 350.

Gr. 7-12. The mage Abhorsen is an "uncommon necromancer," who, rather than raising the dead like others of the art, lays the dead back to rest or binds those that will not rest. Sabriel, his daughter, has been sent for her safety to boarding school outside the Old Kingdom, where she is in her last year when she receives her father's sword and necromancy tools, which means that Abhorsen is either dead or trapped in the realm of Death. Determined to find her father, Sabriel enters the Old Kingdom, which is under attack from the minions of Kerrigor, an evil being who once was human. There, with the aid of Mogget, a Free Magic elemental who is bound in feline form to be the servant of Abhorsen, and Touchstone, a young man whose past harbors a terrible secret, Sabriel goes up against Dead spirits, Shadow Hands, gore crows, and the like, in a desperate quest to find her father's body and fetch his spirit back from Death. Nix has created an ingenious, icy world in the throes of chaos as Kerrigor works to destroy the Charter that binds all things for the good of the land and its inhabitants. The action charges along at a gallop, imbued with an encompassing sense of looming disaster. Sabriel, who entered the Old Kingdom lacking much of the knowledge she needs, proves to be a stalwart heroine, who, in the end, finds and accepts her destiny. A page-turner for sure, this intricate tale compares favorably with Philip Pullman's *The Golden Compass* and will surely appeal to the same [audience].

Publishers Weekly

SOURCE: A review of *Sabriel,* in *Publishers Weekly,* Vol. 243, No. 43, October 21, 1996, p. 84

Sabriel is in her last year at Wyverley College, a private school in Ancelstierre, where Magic does not work, but near the Border with the Old Kingdom, where it does. She and her father are also highly skilled necromancers, who fight the dead who seek to return to Life. But when her father is somehow trapped in Death, she must journey into the Old Kingdom to find him. She does not know that it is wracked by struggle (like that in Ursula LeGuin's *The Far-*

thest Shore)—a magician has brought chaos by refusing to die and hopes to use Sabriel and her father to further consolidate his power. Sabriel goes on a long journey throughout a densely imagined world, learning as she goes, and meeting such strange characters as Mogget, a raging natural force contained in the shape of a cat. She also develops a relationship with Touchstone, a young man who turns out to be as crucially involved as she is. Although Sabriel is possessed of much heavy knowledge ("A year ago, I turned the final page of *The Book of the Dead*. I don't feel young any more"), she is still a teenager and vulnerable where her father and love for Touchstone are concerned, making her a sympathetic heroine. Rich, complex, involving, hard to put down, this first novel, an Australian import, is excellent high fantasy. The suitably climactic ending leaves no loose ends, but readers will hope for a sequel. Ages 12-up.

Ann A. Flowers

SOURCE: A review of *Sabriel,* in *The Horn Book Magazine,* Vol. 73, No. 1, January-February, 1997, p. 64.

A compelling fantasy has for a heroine Sabriel, the daughter of the Abhorsen, the necromancer whose duty is to protect the Old Kingdom: unlike other mages, he has the power to bind the dead as well as to bring the dead back to life. Sabriel has been brought up outside the Old Kingdom in a boarding school in a neighboring country. When her father's sword and the seven silver bells he uses to control the spirits of the dead are delivered to her, she realizes that he is in great jeopardy and sets out for the Old Kingdom to save him. She gains companions—tart and mocking Mogget, an undead spirit held captive in the form of a cat; and Touchstone, a handsome soldier rescued from the dead. Sabriel comes to the realization she herself is now the Abhorsen and that saving the Old Kingdom from the most powerful of undead spirits depends on her. The final battle is gripping, and the bloody cost of combat is forcefully presented. The story is remarkable for the level of originality of the fantastic elements—the bells; the Paperwing, a glider of sorts; Sabriel's position, a combination of warrior maiden and necromancer—and for the subtle presentation, which leaves readers to explore for themselves the complex structure and significance of the magic elements.

M. Jean Greenlaw

SOURCE: A review of *Sabriel,* in *The ALAN Review,* Vol. 24, No. 3, Spring, 1997.

The juxtaposition of a prologue that sets the scene in a fantasy world where Sabriel is born dead and brought back to life by her necromancer father and the first chapter, set in an obviously modern world, gains the reader's immediate attention. Sabriel comes from the Old Kingdom and is drawn back into it when her father dies. Her quest is to rescue him from the river of death, as he is a special necromancer, the Abhorsen, whose task is to lay the undead back to rest. Sabriel and two companions struggle with the legions of evil until it becomes obvious what her fate is: She is the new Abhorsen and her companion Touchstone is the last of the royal line. The story is rife with the trappings of fantasy, including magical bells and swords, and cats and other creatures that are more than they seem. Nix is a new and welcome voice in the fold of those who write high fantasy. He creates a believable setting and peoples it with characters who are fascinating and about whom one cares. The adventure is dramatic enough to make a reader lose a night's sleep, because the book cannot be put down.

SHADE'S CHILDREN (1997)

Publishers Weekly

SOURCE: A review of *Shade's Children,* in *Publishers Weekly,* Vol. 244, No. 24, June 16, 1997, p. 60.

Plunge directly into a nightmare—a scrawny boy flees monstrous trackers in an urban wasteland. Gradually the reader learns that Earth has been taken over by the terrible Overlords, the laws of physical reality warped, all adults killed, the brains and body parts of children raw material for endless war games. Led by an all-too-human artificial intelligence known as Shade, a forlorn resistance battles on, with hope only because the misfit warriors have special talents that came with the Change. Throughout the struggle, hints that Shade's sympathies are not irrevocably human add additional suspense. Although the trappings here are science fiction, Nix tells essentially the same story as he did in *Sabriel:* a desperate quest by a talented few, aided by a potentially treacherous Other, to destroy the source of the power of an evil force that has poisoned the world. As in the author's previous book, the alternate world he creates is amply imagined and the twists and turns of the action-filled plot compelling, though the flat banality of the Overlords' evil is disappointing, as is the sketchy characterization of the four major protagonists. But while the book lacks some of the emotional depth of Nix's first work, it will draw (and keep) fans of the genre. Ages 12-up.

Kirkus Reviews

SOURCE: A review of *Shade's Children*, in *Kirkus Reviews*, Vol. 65, August 15, 1997, p. 1309.

This novel from Nix (**Sabriel**, 1995) combines plenty of comic-book action in a sci-fi setting to produce an exciting read. Through a projector that can bend dimensions, the alien Overlords freeze time and make anyone over 14 vanish off the face of the Earth. What is left is a world of terrified children who are herded into dormitories, where their brains are eventually harvested and wired into the circuitry of the Overlord's willing beasts. Over the years, a handful of teens have found a home in the secret submarine base of Shade, a computer generated holographic program and the only nurturing adult sensibility on the planet. The narrative follows the escape of Gold-Eye, a boy with precognizance, and his subsequent recruitment and training with Ella, Drum, and Ninde, who comprise one of Shade's crackerjack squads. Predictably, the group is involved in a mission to take out the Overlord's projector; Nix deftly weaves in a few surprising plot twists, and the teens must grapple not only with betrayal, but the loss of half their team in battle. The author pulls off a happy ending without straining credibility largely through the characters' sacrifice—a satisfying end to an action-adventure with uncommon appeal outside the genre.

Ann A. Flowers

SOURCE: A review of *Shade's Children*, in *The Horn Book Magazine*, Vol. 73, No. 5, September-October, 1997, p. 576.

A slick, dark, engrossing science fiction novel establishes a world ruled by the Overlords. All adults have disappeared, and children's bodies and minds are harvested at the age of fourteen for the raw material used to create monsters who fight endless battles for their masters. Children escape from time to time, but most are caught and killed by the various monsters—Myrmidons, Trackers, Ferrets, Wingers, and Scream-ers. One escapee, Gold-Eye, has the good fortune to be found by a party of young guerrilla fighters who are directed by Shade. Their headquarters is in an old submarine, and Shade, a scientist who no longer has a human form and exists as a computer construct, is dedicated to the overthrow of the Overlords. Gold-Eye is added to the team of Drum, huge and powerful but chemically castrated; Ella, the wily and clever leader; and Ninde, a pretty girl with special talents for foreseeing the future. Shade sends them on perilous expeditions to recover information and, finally, into the headquarters of one of the Overlords. As their expeditions continue, leading to a riveting climax, the reader becomes uneasily aware that something is not quite right; too many teams have been killed, and some of Shade's children are deserting. This unsettled feeling is intensified by the sometimes obscure printouts of scientific data, archival interviews, discussions, and lists inserted between each chapter. Each of the team of young people is brilliantly and sympathetically characterized (Ella, in particular), and their devotion to each other is affecting. The author leaves the reader to draw many conclusions from scattered evidence, hence capturing and holding the audience's attention all the way to the bittersweet ending. Grim, unusual, and fascinating.

Sally Estes

SOURCE: A review of *Shade's Children* in *Booklist*, Vol. 94, No. 3, p. 320.

Gr. 7-12. The author of the well-received fantasy **Sabriel** (1996) turns to science fiction in this dynamic page-turner. The story is set in a future when everyone older than 16 has vanished from earth, which is now ruled by seven mysterious Overlords, who raise children in Dorms until they reach age 16 and are stashed in the Meat Factory, where they are kept unconscious until their body parts are fused into hideous creatures used not only in brutal war games but also in tracking down and capturing any young people who escape the Dorms. The main character is escapee Gold-Eye, who joins a team working for Shade, the computer-generated person of a former research scientist. This team of four ESP-gifted individuals is involved in making sorties in search of information and materiel to reverse the Change enacted by the Overlords.

Characterizations, the loathsome constructs, the fast-paced action, and the intensity of the entire situation make for exciting reading, but on reflection, the scientific underpinnings of good sf just aren't there; there are too many loose ends, the setup is unsatisfactory, and the ending is too abrupt and weak; nevertheless, readers will relish the immediacy of the adventure.

Janice M. Del Negro

SOURCE: A review of *Shade's Children,* in *Bulletin of the Center for Children's Books,* Vol. 51, No. 3, November, 1997, p. 94.

It is a near-future earth inhabited only by those humans under the age of fourteen, a future ruled by Overlords from a parallel universe engaged in a violent, sadistic game of "hunt the children." Only Shade stands between the children and certain death; only Shade can return the world to the way it was before the coming of the Overlords. Shade is a computer hologram, the mind, psyche, and personality of the only adult remaining on earth. Shade trains those that have escaped from the Overlords to survive in this strange new world, and interspersed throughout the narrative chapters are interviews with Shade's trainees, telling how they escaped the Overlords and came to Shade, what they know about the world before the Overlords, and what they've learned since. This is, for all its sci-fi trappings, a survival story in which four disparate individuals become a team so closely aligned that three risk their lives for one. The plot has a little of everything—a post-apocalyptic setting, the perfect YA cast (no adults except the bad guys), and short bursts of chapters that hint at horrors, violence, and betrayal. The mechanism of the arrival and departure of the Overlords is simplistic, characterization is slim, and the conclusion is precipitous. No consequences are seen from the rule of the Overlords; they simply go back where they came from and the world returns to the way it was before they arrived. Even with these apparent anomalies, the action-packed plot has enough momentum to keep sci-fi enthusiasts reading until the happy if illogical conclusion.

Additional coverage of Nix's life and works is contained in the following sources published by The Gale Group: *Authors and Artists for Young Adults,* Vol. 27; *Contemporary Authors,* Vol. 164; *Something about the Author,* Vol. 97.

Animal Farm

George Orwell

(Pseudonym of Eric Arthur Blair) English novelist, essayist, critic, and journalist.

Major works include *Down and Out in Paris and London* (1933), *Burmese Days* (1934), *The Road to Wigan Pier* (1937), *Homage to Catalonia* (1938), *Coming Up for Air* (1939), *Animal Farm* (1945), *Nineteen Eighty-Four* (1949).

Major works about the author include *George Orwell* (Laurence Brander, 1954), *Orwell and the Left* (Alex Zwerdling, 1974), *George Orwell: A Life* (Bernard Crick, 1980), *The Crystal Spirit: A Study of George Orwell,* enlarged edition (George Woodcock, 1984), *The Politics of Literary Reputation: The Making and Claiming of "St. George" Orwell,* (John Rodden, 1989).

The following entry presents criticism of Orwell's novel *Animal Farm* (1945).

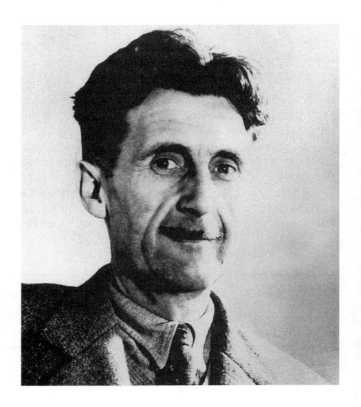

INTRODUCTION

Orwell is significant for his unwavering commitment, both as an individual and as an artist to personal freedom and social justice, and *Animal Farm* is the first and arguably the finest example of the fusion of artistic and political purpose in his writing. This deceptively simple animal fable about a barnyard revolt satirizes the consequences of the Russian Revolution, while also suggesting reasons for the universal failure of most revolutionary ideals. Orwell's skill in creating a narrative that functions on several levels is almost unanimously applauded, and most negative assessments of the novel, both upon its first publication in 1945 and in the decades since, have criticized Orwell's political opinions and not his crafting of the narrative, which is generally regarded as a masterpiece of English prose. Orwell's ability to perceive the social effects of political theories inspired Irving Howe to call him "the greatest moral force in English letters during the past several decades."

BIOGRAPHICAL INFORMATION

Orwell was born into a lower-middle-class family that struggled to provide him with an education. His mother managed to find him a place in a preparatory school where, despite his intellectual accomplishments, he felt demeaned because of his low social standing. In his essay "Such, Such Were the Joys" Orwell explained the guilt and shame he felt throughout his school years and how those experiences fostered his extreme sensitivity to social victimization. After attending Eton College on a scholarship, Orwell enlisted in the Indian Imperial Police. Stationed in Burma, he encountered the harsh realities of colonial rule: his reactions are vividly evoked in the essays "Shooting an Elephant" and "A Hanging," and in the novel *Burmese Days*. Although *Burmese Days* has often been criticized for its awkward attempts at descriptive writing, it has also been called an excellent study of the guilt, hypocrisy, and loneliness that infects the rulers of a subject population.

Orwell left the police after five years, determined to become a writer. His first novel, *Down and Out in Paris and London*, which was based on a year he spent in self-imposed poverty, sympathetically examines the life of the poor. While writing this book Orwell discovered that the lower classes of society are exploited much like colonial subjects. His indignation over this fact is reflected throughout his subsequent work. Orwell's other novels written during the 1930s deal with victimization: his protagonists are confused individuals, preyed upon by society and their own weaknesses, who attempt to rebel against their lot and fail. During this period Orwell also wrote two books of autobiography and social criticism. In *The Road to Wigan Pier* (1937), commissioned by the socialist Left Book Club, Orwell described the life of English coal miners, but he enraged his sponsors by examining at length the failure of socialists to address the needs of England's poor. In December 1936 Orwell traveled to Barcelona to investigate and write about the causes and progress of the Spanish Civil War. He joined a militia unit and fought with the Republicans. After being wounded, Orwell returned to England and wrote *Homage to Catalonia,* an account that depicts the absurdities of warfare, the duplicity of every political ideology, and the essential decency of ordinary people caught up in events beyond their control.

Orwell's first major critical and popular success as an author came with the publication of *Animal Farm* in 1945. The search for a publisher for *Animal Farm* had taken eighteen months, for the novel was rejected by numerous publishing firms on the grounds that it was too harsh a criticism of the Soviet Union, then a British ally. One publisher said that it was too negative in its outlook, failing to affirm any point of view, while an American publisher turned it down because "animal stories" were not popular in the United States. Once the novel appeared, however, it was an immediate success, garnering enthusiastic reviews and selling out its first edition in a matter of months. In his 1946 essay "Why I Write," Orwell stated that "every line of serious work that I have written since 1936 has been written, directly or indirectly, against totalitarianism and for democratic Socialism, as I understand it." He went on to say that *"Animal Farm* was the first book in which I tried, with full consciousness of what I was doing, to fuse political purpose and artistic purpose into one whole."

His income from the book's sales, though not great, enabled him in the spring of 1947 to rent a house on the Scottish island of Jura, where he began work on a new novel. In December of 1947 Orwell was hospitalized for treatment of the tuberculosis from which he had suffered since his mid-thirties. He spent the first half of 1948 in Hairmyres Hospital in Glasgow, and on his release returned to Jura to complete the novel, tentatively entitled *The Last Man in Europe*

but ultimately called *Nineteen Eighty-Four.* Although very ill and under a doctor's orders to work no more than an hour each day, Orwell was unable to find a typist willing to come to the isolated island, so he prepared the final manuscript of *Nineteen Eighty-Four* himself. He collapsed almost immediately upon completing the task and was bedridden for the remaining two years of his life.

PLOT AND MAJOR CHARACTERS

In *Animal Farm* Orwell revived a project that may date back to his time in Spain, in which he hoped to explain his fears for society through a simple story. In particular, at a time when Soviet dictator Josef Stalin was widely praised for battling Nazi Germany, he wished to separate socialist ideals from Stalin's self-serving distortions of them. "One day," Orwell later recalled, "I saw a little boy . . . driving a huge cart-horse along a narrow path, whipping it whenever it tried to turn. It struck me that if only such animals became aware of their strength we should have no power over them, and that men exploit animals in much the same way as the rich exploit the proletariat." His fantasy became *Animal Farm,* the tale of a barnyard revolt against human masters that parallels the rise and decline of socialism in the Soviet Union.

The story opens as animals expel Mr. Jones from his farm and create an "animalist" republic. Most animals have simple dreams of justice, but the pigs are greedy and cunning, and in the end they use "animalist" rhetoric to justify their own tyranny. *Animal Farm* is considered an amazingly successful blend of political satire and childlike fable. Snowball and Napoleon, the pigs who formulate the animals' revolutionary principles and who govern the farm following the overthrow of the human masters, represent Leon Trotsky and Josef Stalin, even to Snowball's eventual ouster by Napoleon, who subsequently rewrites the history of the revolution to make Snowball appear to be a villain collaborating with the humans who are constantly scheming to retake the farm. The pig Squealer represents the official Soviet news agency Pravda; his persuasive oratory convinces the animals that with pigs in charge conditions are better than ever, when in fact they are worse. The simple and hardworking cart-horses and the anonymous sheep stand for whole classes of people whose uncomprehending complicity aids the tyrants who pervert revolutionary ideals of equality to establish themselves as the new ruling elite.

CRITICAL RECEPTION

Nothing in Orwell's career indicated that his desire to write politically committed literature that was "also an aesthetic experience" would find expression in a skillfully executed animal fable. *Animal Farm* has been described by J. R. Hammond, for example, as "totally different in style and conception from anything Orwell had previously written," and by Laurence Brander as "a sport, out of [Orwell's] usual way; and yet more effective in the crusade to which he was dedicated than anything else he wrote." *Animal Farm* does represent a radical departure from the documentaries, essays, and novels that Orwell wrote in the 1930s; however, many commentators have noted that Orwell was undoubtedly aware that the genre of the beast fable was uniquely suited to his own purposes of social and political satire. Traditionally in such fables, each animal represents not only itself—and in the finest examples of the genre the animal characters are always recognizable as animals—but also a single aspect of human nature which the author has fixed upon for comment, thus avoiding the psychological complications inherent in presenting fully developed human characters. As George Woodcock has noted, "A fable drives home its satiric intent by presenting a simplification of complex happenings of life." The conventions of the animal fable enabled Orwell to examine simply and directly the multifarious moral decisions made within a political system. According to Rama Rani Lall: "In *Animal Farm* the animals are consistently animals, and Orwell keeps the reader conscious simultaneously of the human traits satirized and of the animals as animals. He has successfully played upon the two levels of perception, making us feel that his animals are really animals and are yet as human as ourselves. Though he has couched his criticism in the simplest of terms, it is convincing because of the realistic pictures of animal life."

Although Orwell intended *Animal Farm* to depict the inevitable course of all revolutions, the Soviet Union was the primary target of the novel's pointed allegory. Critics have demonstrated many parallels between Orwell's narrative and the history of the U.S.S.R. from the time of the Revolution through World War II. Commentators hostile to Orwell's political position have endeavored to demonstrate that the novel is an inadequate treatment of extremely complicated issues, or that *Animal Farm* does not contain exact parallels to the historical events being satirized and is therefore invalid. Others maintain that Orwell's negative opinions about human nature and the development of political revolutions rendered *Animal Farm* primarily an expression of his own pessimism and thus without relevance to social or political reality. Nevertheless, most critics concur that the basic plot of the novel closely parallels events in the Soviet Union.

In addition to its critique of Soviet politics, the novel was also intended as an illustration of the inherent dangers of all totalitarian systems. One of the novel's primary themes is the inevitable failure of the egalitarian ideals that first encourage revolt against an established order. According to Orwell, the violence necessary to overthrow one system and establish another carries over into the new regime and leads to abuses of power on the part of the new leaders, who seek to retain their hold. Cyril Connolly writes that "the commandments of the Animal Revolution, such as 'no animal shall kill another animal' or 'all animals are equal' can perhaps never be achieved by a revolutionary seizure of power, but only by the spiritual operation of reason or moral philosophy in the animal heart." Many critics maintain that long after historical awareness of the Russian Revolution as the main target of Orwell's satire fades, the novel will retain its powerful appeal because of its universally applicable message about the dangers of totalitarian rule.

AUTHOR COMMENTARY

George Orwell

SOURCE: "Preface to the Ukrainian Edition of *Animal Farm*," in *The Collected Essays, Journalism and Letters of George Orwell: As I Please, 1943-1945,* Vol. III, edited by Sonia Orwell and Ian Angus, Harcourt Brace Jovanovich, 1968, pp. 402-06.

On my return from Spain I thought of exposing the Soviet myth in a story that could be easily understood by almost anyone and which could be easily translated into other languages. However the actual details of the story did not come to me for some time until one day (I was then living in a small village) I saw a little boy, perhaps ten years old, driving a huge cart-horse along a narrow path, whipping it whenever it tried to turn. It struck me that if only such animals became aware of their strength we should have no power over them, and that men exploit animals in much the same way as the rich exploit the proletariat.

I proceeded to analyse Marx's theory from the animals' point of view. To them it was clear that the concept of a class struggle between humans were pure illusion, since whenever it was necessary to exploit animals, all humans united against them: the true struggle is between animals and humans. From this point of departure, it was not difficult to elaborate the story. I did not write it out till 1943, for I was always engaged on other work which gave me no time; and in the end, I included some events, for example the Teheran Conference, which were taking place while I was writing. Thus the main outlines of the story were in my mind over a period of six years before it was actually written.

I do not wish to comment on the work; if it does not speak for itself it is a failure. But I should like to emphasise two points: first, that although the various episodes are taken from the actual history of the Russian Revolution, they are dealt with schematically and their chronological order is changed; this was necessary for the symmetry of the story. The second point has been missed by most critics, possibly because I did not emphasise it sufficiently. A number of readers may finish the book with the impression that it ends in the complete reconciliation of the pigs and the humans. That was not my intention; on the contrary I meant it to end on a loud note of discord, for I wrote it immediately after the Teheran Conference which everybody thought had established the best possible relations between the USSR and the West. I personally did not believe that such good relations would last long; and, as events have shown, I wasn't far wrong. . . .

TITLE COMMENTARY

📖 *ANIMAL FARM* (1945)

Cyril Connolly

SOURCE: A review of *Animal Farm,* in *Horizon,* London, Vol. XII, No. 69, September, 1945, pp. 215-16.

Mr. Orwell is a revolutionary who is in love with 1910. This ambivalence constitutes his strength and his weakness. Never before has a progressive political thinker been so handicapped by nostalgia for the Edwardian shabby-genteel or the underdog. It is this political sentimentality which from the literary point of view is his most valid emotion. *Animal Farm* proves it, for it truly is a fairy story told by a great lover of liberty and a great lover of animals. The

farm is real, the animals are moving. At the same time it is a devastating attack on Stalin and his "betrayal" of the Russian revolution, as seen by another revolutionary. The allegory between the animals and the fate of their revolution (they drive out the human beings and plan a Utopia entrusted to the leadership of the pigs—Napoleon-Stalin, Snowball-Trotsky—with the dogs as police, the sheep as yes-men, the two cart-horses, Boxer and Clover, as the noble hardworking proletariat), and the Russian experiment is beautifully worked out, perhaps the most felicitous moment being when the animal "saboteurs" are executed for some of the very crimes of the Russian trials, such as the sheep who confessed to having "urinated in the drinking pool" or the goose which kept back six ears of corn and ate them in the night. The fairy tale ends with the complete victory of Napoleon and the pigs, who rule Animal Farm, with a worse tyranny and a far greater efficiency than its late human owner, the dissolute Mr. Jones.

Politically one might make to Mr. Orwell the same objections as to Mr. Koestler for his essay on Russia in *The Yogi and the Commissar*—both allow their personal bitterness about the betrayed revolution to prejudice their attitude to the facts. But it is arguable that every revolution is "betrayed" because the violence necessary to achieve it is bound to generate an admiration for violence, which leads to the abuse of power. A revolution is the forcible removal of an obsolete and inefficient ruling-class by a vigorous and efficient one which replaces it for as long as its vitality will allow. The commandments of the Animal Revolution, such as "no animal shall kill any other animal" or "all animals are equal" can perhaps never be achieved by a revolutionary seizure of power but only by the spiritual operation of reason or moral philosophy in the animal heart. If we look at Russia without the particular bitterness of the disappointed revolutionary we see that it is an immensely powerful managerial despotism—far more powerful than its Czarist predecessor—where, on the whole, despite a police system which we should find intolerable, the masses are happy, and where great strides in material progress have been made (i.e. independence of women, equality of sexes, autonomy of racial and cultural minorities, utilization of science to improve the standard of living, religious toleration, etc.). If Stalin and his regime were not loved as well as feared the Animal Farm which comprises the greatest landmass of the world would not have united to roll back the most efficient invading army which the world has ever known—and if in truth Stalin is loved then he and his regime cannot be quite what they appear to Mr. Orwell (indeed Napoleon's final brutality to

Boxer—if Boxer symbolises the proletariat—is not paralleled by any incident in Stalin's career, unless the Scorched Earth policy is indicated). But it is unfair to harp on these considerations. *Animal Farm* is one of the most enjoyable books since the war, it is deliciously written, with something of the feeling, the penetration and the verbal economy of Orwell's master, Swift. It deserves a wide sale and a lengthy discussion. Apart from the pleasure it has given me to read, I welcome it for three reasons, because it breaks down some of the artificial reserve with which Russia is written about, or not written about, . . . because it restores the allegorical pamphlet to its rightful place as a literary force, and lastly because it proves that Mr. Orwell has not been entirely seduced away by the opinion-airing attractions of weekly journalism from his true vocation, which is to write books.

George Soule

SOURCE: "Orwell's Fables," in *The New Republic,* Vol. 115, No. 9, September 2, 1946, pp. 266-67.

George Orwell in his critical writings shows imagination and taste; his wit is both edged and human. Few writers of any period have been able to use the English language so simply and accurately to say what they mean, and at the same time to mean something. The news that he had written a satirical allegory, telling the story of a revolution by farm animals against their cruel and dissolute master, and of their subsequent fortunes, was like the smell of a roast from a kitchen ruled by a good cook, near the end of a hungry morning. The further news that this book had been chosen and was being pushed by the Book of the Month Club, though it occasioned surprise, was pleasant because it seemed to herald one of those instances when unusual talent of the sort rarely popular receives recognition and a great tangible reward.

There are times when a reviewer is happy to report that a book is bad because it fulfills his hope that the author will expose himself in a way that permits a long deserved castigation. This is not one of them. I was expecting that Orwell would again give pleasure and that his satire of the sort of thing which democrats deplore in the Soviet Union would be keen and cleansing. Instead, the book puzzled and saddened me. It seemed on the whole dull. The allegory turned out to be a creaking machine for saying in a clumsy way things have been said better directly. And many of the things said are not instantly recognized as the essence of truth, but are of the sort which start endless and boring controversy.

Orwell does know his farm animals and gives them vivid personalities. Many will recognize Benjamin, the donkey who never commits himself, never hurries and thinks that in the end nothing much matters. Mollie the saddle horse, who wanders from the puritanical path of the revolution to seek ribbons for her mane, the cat who never does any work, the hens who sabotage by laying their eggs in the rafters, Clover and Boxer, the powerful, trusting and honest draught horses, are all real enough. But these spontaneous creatures seem in action like circus animals performing mechanically to the crack of the storyteller's whip.

Part of the trouble lies in the fact that the story is too close to recent historical events without being close enough. Major, the aged pig who on his deathbed tells the animals of their oppression and prophesies revolution, must be Karl Marx. His two followers who lead the revolution, Napoleon and Snowball, are then readily identified as Lenin and Trotsky. This identification turns out to be correct in the case of Snowball, but the reader soon begins to puzzle over the fact that Napoleon disapproves the project of building a windmill—an obvious symbol for electrification and industrialization—whereas this was Lenin's program. The puzzlement is increased when Napoleon chases out Snowball as a traitor; it was Stalin who did this.

And so it goes through incident after incident. The young dogs are alone selected for schooling; later they appear as the secret police. Is this a picture of Soviet education? The pigs not only keep the best food for themselves, but also become drunkards, taking over the pasture reserved for retirement of the superannuated in order to raise the necessary barley. Of course prohibition was abolished early in the revolution, but have the leaders drunk too much and has social insurance been abolished? There is a pathetic incident when Boxer, the sturdy and loyal old work horse, is sent off to be slaughtered and turned into dog food and bone meal, under the pretext that he is being hospitalized. Just what part of Soviet history corresponds to this?

Nobody would suppose that good allegory is literally accurate, but when the reader is continually led to wonder who is who and what aspect of reality is being satirized, he is prevented either from enjoying the story as a story or from valuing it as a comment. Masters like Swift and Anatole France, with whom Orwell is compared in the blurbs, were not guilty of this fault. They told good stories, the interest of which did not lie wholly in their caricature. And their satire, however barbed, was not dependent on identification of historical personages or specific events.

The thoughtful reader must be further disturbed by the lack of clarity in the main intention of the author. Obviously he is convinced that the animals had just cause for revolt and that for a time their condition was improved under the new regime. But they are betrayed by their scoundrelly, piggish leaders. In the end, the pigs become indistinguishable from the men who run the other nearby farms; they walk on two legs, have double and triple chins, wear clothes and carry whips. Animal Farm reverts to the old Manor Farm in both name and reality.

No doubt this is what George Orwell thinks has happened in Russia. But if he wants to tell us why it happened, he has failed. Does he mean to say that not these pigs, but Snowball, should have been on top? Or that all the animals should have been merged in a common primitive communism without leaders or organization? Or that it was a mistake to try to industrialize, because pastoral simplicity is the condition of equality and cooperation? Or that, as in the old saw criticizing socialism, the possibility of a better society is a pipe-dream, because if property were distributed equally, the more clever and selfish would soon get a larger share and things would go on as of old? Though I am sure he did not intend this moral, the chances are that a sample poll of the book-club readers in the United States would indicate that a large majority think so and will heartily approve the book on that account.

There is no question that Orwell hates tyranny, sycophancy, deceitful propaganda, sheeplike acceptance of empty political formulas. His exposures of these detestable vices constitutes the best passages in the book. There have been plenty of such abuses in Russia. They also crop up in other places. It is difficult to believe that they determined the whole issue of the Russian revolution, or that Russia is now just like every other nation. No doubt in some respects she is worse than most; in other respects she may be better.

It seems to me that the failure of this book (commercially it is already assured of tremendous success) arises from the fact that the satire deals not with something the author has experienced, but rather with stereotyped ideas about a country which he probably does not know very well. The plan for the allegory, which must have seemed a good one when he first thought of it, became mechanical in execu-

tion. It almost appears as if he had lost his zest before he got very far with the writing. He should try again, and this time on something nearer home.

Adam de Hegedus

SOURCE: A review of *Animal Farm,* in *The Commonweal,* Vol. XLIV, No. 22, September 13, 1946, pp. 528-30.

It was not a far-fetched comparison which at the time [*Animal Farm*] was published in England, likened it to *Gulliver's Travels* or rather to its chapter which is devoted to the country of the Houyhnhnms and deals with Gulliver's adventures in the realm of the horses.

On the other hand, many readers of this book would be unable to get away from *Animal Farm*'s great relevance to contemporary Russia and might think it is nothing beyond a very brilliant and very cruel satire on the communist experiment.

The temptations to regard it purely and simply as a short and brilliant *roman à clef* are very great indeed. The reader experiences a little thrill in discovering famous characters in cruel disguises. The old boar who tells the animals at Manor Farm of his dream of a happy future world in which they will not be exploited and slaughtered by Man is surely Lenin. Boxer, the strong, kind, slow-witted horse, who is heroic in an emergency, easy to mislead and fundamentally decent is obviously the Common Man who is getting more and more frightened of the century which Mr. Henry Wallace dedicated to him. In Napoleon the Machiavellian pig it is very difficult not to see Stalin, whereas Snowball the dreamer pig, who is expelled from Animal Farm and provides an excellent scapegoat for the future failures of the experiment is Trotsky. And who can be the rest of the pigs, who had helped to transform Manor Farm into "Animal Farm" under the war-cry, "Two legs bad, four legs good" and who enjoy special privileges for their leadership? They are surely members of the Communist Party.

In any case the revolution succeeds in the name of *all animals are equal,* but soon enough there are quarrels between the two pig-leaders: Snowball the dreamer and Napoleon the realist. Snowball is driven out.

Now, Snowball during the revolution had been awarded the decoration of "Animal Hero First Class" and his expulsion causes great surprise, though the sheep and the hens quickly learn that Snowball was a traitor and the decoration had been awarded by mistake. And so the story continues, about as one would expect. Finally "Animal Farm" adopts a new slogan: *all animals are equal but some animals are more equal than the rest.*

Animal Farm, however, is deeper and larger than this, in the same way as Swift's Gulliver is of a more permanent significance than just being an attack on the Tory Party in eighteenth century England. It has implications—and they are many—which are older and more universal than the past and present of the Union of Soviet Socialist Republics. It gives a splendid illumination of Acton's immortal thesis according to which power corrupts and absolute power corrupts absolutely. It also supplies a very simple, very clear and to my mind a very adequate statement on man's craving for the absolute, which is the most powerful basis of nationalism: the most important, most real and most threatening political problem of our time, which an orthodox Marxist can never see in its true proportion. He still maintains that the economic problem is more important than the political problem and that the two—the twin problems of our century—cannot be separated from each other. Orwell knows that this is not the case and that the economic problem is the lesser of the two, though being "nearer the camera" it most of the time appears to be out of correct proportion. He also knows that a man who loves his country unreasonably in as many words issues an invitation to any ruling oligarchy to be exploited and trampled upon.

> The revolution goes wrong at Animal Farm, the old doctrines, the shining words of the Constitution which were painted on the barn door are perverted, yet the animals never gave up hope.
>
> More, they never lost, even for an instant, their sense of honor and privilege in being members of Animal Farm. They were still the only farm in the whole country—in all England!—owned and operated by animals. Not one of them, not even the youngest, not even the newcomers who had been brought from farms ten or twenty miles away, ever ceased to marvel at that. And when they heard the gun booming and saw the green flag fluttering at the masthead, their hearts swelled with imperishable pride, and the talk turned always towards the old heroic days, the expulsion of Jones, the writing of the Seven Commandments, the great battles in which the human invaders had been defeated. None of the old dreams had been abandoned. The Republic of the Animals which Major had foretold, when the green fields of England should be untrodden by human feet, was still believed in. Some day it was com-

> ing: it might not be soon, it might not be within the lifetime of any animal now living, but still it was coming. . . .

Passages like these seem to contain a good deal of survival value for *Animal Farm.* Because it is a parable, it escapes the great pitfall of reportage and documentary writing which by their very natures leave their material without significance. Orwell, however, is an artist, who knows precisely how effective it can be not to say explicitly what he means, and this little tale of a hundred and twenty odd pages has more explosive energy and actuality than a five hundred page carefully documented report on Russia. More than that: it is poetry, which is the type of journalism "that stays news."

Orwell is not angry with Russia, or with any other country, because that country "turned Socialist." On the contrary he is angry with Russia because Russia does not believe in a classless and democratic society. His anger and frustration are those of the man who—like himself—in spite of his social origin and upbringing, had for months been dishwasher and a Down and Out In Paris And London and who—like himself—went to fight for democratic Spain in an anti-Stalin loyalist battalion. In short, Orwell is angry with Russia because Russia is *not* socialist.

Laurence Brander

SOURCE: *George Orwell,* Longmans, Green and Co., 1954, pp. 171-82.

Animal Farm is one of those apparently chance pieces a prose writer throws off, which immediately becomes more popular than his more ambitious writings. A sport, out of his usual way; and yet more effective in the crusade to which he was dedicated than anything else he wrote.

For once, the gaiety in his nature had completely taken charge. He was writing about animals, whom he loved. He had had a rest of nearly three years from serious writing. He wrote with zest, and although humour rarely travels across national boundaries, his enjoyment has been shared everywhere. Humour travels most easily in peasant portraiture, as in *The Good Soldier Schweik* and *Don Camillo*; and in animal stories. Not many books have been translated into so many languages so successfully and so quickly as *Animal Farm.*

It was conceived and "sweated over" between November 1943 and February 1944. The worst of the war was over and its outcome assured; it was possible to write again. Orwell never stampeded with the herd, so while everyone around him was praising Russian victories, he wrote a little story to remind people what Stalinism was really like. It was his most effective sermon; many preachers are most successful with the adults during the children's sermon.

The theme is closely connected, therefore, with *Homage to Catalonia* and *1984,* and no doubt the moment of its conception decided its form. It was no time to preach overtly against Russian political methods. It was not the moment for a didactic novel. But a slip of a story, gay and droll in the tradition of animal stories, was just the thing. The story goes along so gaily, and yet the stark satire is always there like a skull behind an innocent smiling face. The animal characters fit cunningly to their human counterparts. There is a mocking similarity between what the pigs say and what politicians say. And there is such stupidity and perfidiousness in all the humans do; as if, judged by decent animal standards, we are very poor creatures indeed. It is the Houyhnhnm theme of Swift repeated. *Animal Farm* has the Swiftian indictment of the offending race of humankind.

The style, like the form, is unique in Orwell's work. He had been a master of the descriptive way of writing from the beginning, from the opening words of *Down and Out,* but he had never before achieved pure narrative. In *Animal Farm,* from the start, we feel the special power of the storyteller. The animals expel the farmer and his men and take over the farm. The farmer tries to come back but is driven away. The other farmers do not interfere because they look forward to taking the farm over cheaply when the animals have ruined it. The animals, led by the pigs, do not make a mess of it, and the farm is well enough run for the authorities to leave it alone. Eventually, the pigs turn out to be harder slave-drivers than men, so in the end the neighbouring farmers make friends with the pigs and admit that they have much to learn from the labour conditions on Animal Farm.

There is no looseness anywhere in the structure. The story is rounded, the end joining the beginning. The opening speech of the old boar, Major, is answered at the end in the words of Mr. Pilkington and Napoleon. The various levels of satire are similarly rounded, so that the story and all its implications form circles each in its own plane.

The convention of writing animal stories is as old as AEsop in European literature and has been used in England from Chaucer's time. Every animal corresponds to a human type, and though there were many animals in the Ark, there are still human types to place against them. Orwell restates the convention right at the beginning, in the meeting of the animals:

> At one end of the big barn, on a sort of raised platform, Major was already ensconced on his bed of straw, under a lantern which hung from a beam. He was twelve years old and had lately grown rather stout, but he was still a majestic-looking pig, with a wise and benevolent appearance in spite of the fact that his tushes had never been cut. Before long the other animals began to arrive and make themselves comfortable after their different fashions. First came the three dogs, Bluebell, Jessie, and Pitcher, and then the pigs who settled down in the straw immediately in front of the platform. The hens perched themselves on the window-sills, the pigeons fluttered up to the rafters, the sheep and cows lay down behind the pigs and began to chew the cud. The two cart-horses, Boxer and Clover, came in together, walking very slowly and setting down their vast hairy hoofs with great care lest there should be some small animal concealed in the straw. . . .

> The two horses had just laid down when a brood of ducklings, which had lost their mother, filed into the barn, cheeping feebly and wandering from side to side to find some place where they would not be trodden on. Clover made a sort of wall round them with her great foreleg, and the ducklings nestled down inside it and promptly fell asleep. . . . Last of all came the cat, who looked round, as usual, for the warmest place, and finally squeezed herself in between Boxer and Clover; there she purred contentedly throughout Major's speech without listening to a word of what he was saying.

It is an enchanting description. There is the bustle and excitement of assembly, just as in Chaucer's *Parlement of Foules*:

> And that so huge a noyse gan they make
> That erthe, and eyr, and tre, and every lake
> So full was, that unethe was there space
> For me to stonde, so full was all the place.

There is the pleasure of watching each animal comporting itself according to its nature. The animal kingdom at once becomes a reflection of human society.

The scene is a parody of a successful meeting of the political opposition. Get the people together with some bait. Turn on the orator to bemuse them, and send them away feeling happy and satisfied, but with the seeds of revolt planted where you want them. The best thing in the parody is the mockery of the egotistical gravity of political rabble-rousers:

I feel it my duty to pass on to you such political wisdom as I have acquired. I have had a long life. I have had much time for thought as I lay alone in my stall, and I think I may say that I understand the nature of life on this earth as well as any animal now living.

Three days later, Major dies and the spotlight falls upon two younger boars, Napoleon and Snowball, the Stalin and Trotsky of the story. Napoleon was "not much of a talker" but had "a reputation for getting his own way." Snowball was intellectually quicker, but "was not considered to have the same depth of character." (Part of the fun of the animal story is the enormous gravity of the author's approach to his characters.) Snowball obviously has much more brains than Napoleon. It is Snowball who paints the seven commandments against the end wall of the barn, and when it comes to the battle for Manor Farm, and Jones the farmer tries to recover his property, it is Snowball who has prepared and drilled the animals for the expected attack. It is Snowball who leads them and Snowball who is wounded. In the whole episode, Napoleon is never mentioned.

As the community develops, it is observed that Snowball inspired the "Animal Committees," while Napoleon took no interest in such things. Snowball "formed the Egg Production Committee for the hens, the Clean Tails League for the Cows . . . the Whiter Wool Movement for the sheep. . . . " This is the sort of exuberant invention of absurd trivialities that Swift enjoyed in Gulliver. Napoleon, meanwhile, said that "the education of the young was more important than anything that could be done for those who were already grown up." Snowball had altruism, the essential social virtue; Napoleon had a lust for power, and intended to get it by making the animals "less conscious," and that was all he meant by educating the young. Eventually Napoleon wins by his education of a litter of young hounds, who attack Snowball after his eloquent exposition of the windmill scheme, and chase him out of the farm. At his best moment, just when his altruistic plans for giving warmth, food and comfort to all the animals are completed and ready to be carried out, Snowball's brutal rival strikes. It is the same sort of dramatic timing that we shall find in *1984,* an ironic twist to the satire.

After that, the Snowball theme is the denigration of the fallen hero. The animals are all greatly upset by the incident, and Napoleon's young lieutenant, Squealer, works hard to make them less conscious of what has happened:

"He fought bravely at the Battle of the Cowshed," said somebody.

"Bravery is not enough," said Squealer. "Loyalty and obedience are more important. And as to the Battle of the Cowshed, I believe the time will come when we shall find that Snowball's part in it was much exaggerated. Discipline, comrades, iron discipline! That is the watchword for today. One false step, and our enemies would be upon us. Surely, comrades, you do not want Jones back?"

"Discipline!" the invariable cry of the political gangsters who are destroying freedom and truth. That is the first step in the legend that Snowball is the source of evil. The legend grows step by step with the building up of Napoleon as the leader who thought of everything and is the father of the farm. The windmill was of course really Napoleon's own idea, and Snowball had stolen the plans from among Napoleon's papers. When the windmill falls down at the first puff with wind, Napoleon himself comes forth and snuffs around till he smells Snowball. "'Comrades,' he said quietly, 'do you know who is responsible for this? Do you know the enemy who has come in the night and overthrown our windmill? SNOWBALL!' he suddenly roared in a voice of thunder."

Next spring, it was discovered that Snowball "stole the corn, he upset the milk-pails, he broke the eggs, he trampled the seed-beds, he gnawed the bark off the fruit-trees." A typical touch of hypnosis is supplied when "the cows declared unanimously that Snowball crept into their stalls and milked them in their sleep." Napoleon orders a full investigation, and Squealer is able to tell the animals that "'Snowball was in league with Jones from the very start! He was Jones's secret agent all the time. It has all been proved in documents which he left behind him and which we have only just discovered.'" The authentic note this, and it is heard again when Boxer argues that Snowball was once a good comrade: "'Our leader, Comrade Napoleon,' announced Squealer, speaking very slowly, and firmly, 'has stated categorically—categorically, comrade—that Snowball was Jones's agent from the very beginning.'"

Boxer was too simple to be safe. So the dogs are set on him, but he kicks them aside and releases the one he traps under his vast hoof only on Napoleon's orders. At the trial, the confessions of the animals are invariably of complicity with Snowball. Later it is discovered that far from being the hero of the Battle of the Cowshed, Snowball was censured for showing cowardice. At all these stages the simple animals are very much perplexed. Eventually it is shown (by the discovery of further documents) that Snowball fought on Jones's side at the Battle of the Cowshed. The animals are perplexed at each stage of this long denigration, but they are tired, overworked and underfed and do not remember clearly and the lies are so persuasively put across that at every stage they believe.

This parable of human perplexity in the face of contemporary propaganda methods is told with great skill. It is one of Orwell's most effective treatments of the problem which had focused his attention since his experiences in Spain.

Squealer is the modern propagandist, the P.R.O. [public relations officer] who explains away the worst with the best of spurious reasons. He is a familiar type, with: "very round cheeks, twinkling eyes, nimble movements, and a shrill voice. He was a brilliant talker, and when he was arguing some difficult point he had a way of skipping from side to side and whisking his tail which was somehow very persuasive. The others said of Squealer that he could turn black into white."

He was the mouthpiece of the pigs, the new class who were elbowing their way into power by the methods Orwell marks in an essay on James Burnham: "All talk about democracy, liberty, equality, fraternity, all revolutionary movements, all visions of Utopia, or 'the classless society,' or 'the Kingdom of Heaven on Earth,' are humbug (not necessarily conscious humbug) covering the ambitions of some new class which is elbowing its way into power."

In contrast to Squealer is Moses, the tame raven, who specialized in the kingdom of heaven, but not on earth. Moses disappeared completely for years when the animals took over. It was only when the pigs were in complete control and had turned themselves into an aristocracy at the expense of the lean and hungry animals that Moses returns. His tales of Sugar Candy Mountain, where "it was Sunday seven days a week, clover was in season all the year round, and lump sugar and linseed oil grew on the hedges," are useful again, and in no way threaten the power of the pigs.

Moses has his allowance of a gill of beer a day from the pigs and he does no work. Squealer works hard all the time. He represents the organized lying practised in totalitarian states, which, Orwell says in **"The Prevention of Literature"**: "is not, as is sometimes claimed, a temporary expedient of the same nature as military deception. It is something integral to totalitarianism, something that would still continue even if concentration camps and secret police forces had ceased to be necessary."

Squealer comes into his own when Snowball is expelled, after making his name on the milk-and-apple question. All supplies had been reserved for the pigs, and there is some grumbling: "Many of us actually dislike milk and apples. I dislike them myself. Our sole object in taking these things is to preserve our health." Needless to say, for the purpose of keeping Jones away.

At the moment of Snowball's expulsion, when Napoleon takes over the leadership, Squealer is at his best: "'Comrades,' he said, 'I trust that every animal here appreciates the sacrifice that Comrade Napoleon has made in taking this extra labour upon himself. Do not imagine, comrades, that leadership is a pleasure!'"

When there is any fighting, Squealer is unaccountably absent. His time comes afterwards, when the victory has to be celebrated.

> "What victory?" said Boxer. . . .
>
> "Have we not driven the enemy off our soil? . . . .".
>
> "Then we have won back what we had before," said Boxer.
>
> "That is our victory," said Squealer.

A few mornings after that conversation, all the pigs are suffering from a dreadful hangover. It is the drollest incident in the book, and like everything else has its satirical implications.

> It was nearly nine o'clock when Squealer made his appearance walking slowly and dejectedly, his eyes dull, his tail hanging limply behind him, and with every appearance of being seriously ill. He called the animals together and told them that he had a terrible piece of news to impart. Comrade Napoleon was dying!
>
> A cry of lamentation went up. Straw was laid down outside the doors of the farmhouse, and the animals walked on tiptoe.

The next bulletin was that Comrade Napoleon had pronounced a solemn decree as his last act on earth: "the drinking of alcohol was to be punished by death." Within a couple of days the pigs are busily studying books on brewing and distilling.

Squealer is central. He keeps the animals quiet. He puts their minds at rest. He has the air of a beneficent being, sent to make animals happy. He is the agency by which they become "less conscious."

Napoleon develops in personality. He takes on the character of the legendary Leader more and more. He becomes progressively remote. From the beginning he is quite different from Snowball and Squealer. He has none of their mercurial qualities; he is no talker. In the range of porcine character—which would seem to be as great as the human range—he is at the other extreme: a saturnine, cunning pig. A deep pig, with a persistent way of getting what he wants. He is by far the strongest character on the farm. Just as Benjamin, the donkey, has the clearest idea of things, and Boxer, the cart-horse, is the strongest physically.

Boxer's simplicity of character is sentimental comedy of the purest kind. It is the story of the great big good-natured person who thinks harm of nobody, believes all is for the best, so everybody should work as hard as possible and then a little harder still. He is so simple that he does not see his questions are dangerous, and when the pigs make an effort to eliminate him—which is quite hopeless because of his great strength—he never understands what has happened. In the tiny Orwell gallery of pleasant characters, Boxer is the favourite. He is the expression of Orwell's liberal belief in the people: "one sees only the struggle of the gradually awakening common people against the lords of property and their hired liars . . . ". He is the great big gentle peasant, the finest flower of the good earth; and he has the usual reward. When at last he collapses from overwork, the pigs pretend to send him to hospital, and sell him to the knacker. It is the only time that Benjamin, the donkey, forsakes cynicism for action. He attempts a rescue, but too late. With the money they get from the knacker, the pigs buy another case of whisky and hold a Boxer memorial dinner.

Squealer is able to give a complete narrative of Boxer's last moments in hospital and is able to quote his last words: "Long live Animal Farm! Long live Comrade Napoleon! Napoleon is always right." Fortunately, too, he is able to refute the ridiculous rumour that Boxer was sent to the knacker. "The animals were enormously relieved to hear this."

The last stage of the story comes with the legend on the end of the barn which has replaced the seven commandments. None of the animals ever detected that only four of them were commandments and the others were statements of belief. None, except probably Benjamin, who gave no sign, ever quite realized how they were modified. One by one they had been broken down and now they had all disappeared and in their place stood the legend: "All animals are equal but some are more equal than others." The significance of this expunging of the law is explained in Orwell's essay on *Gulliver's Travels,* where he says:

In a Society in which there is no law, and in theory no compulsion, the only arbiter of behaviour is public opinion. But public opinion, because of the tremendous urge to conformity in gregarious animals, is less tolerant than any system of law.

Squealer arranged public opinion. The pigs were now walking on two legs and wearing clothing. Soon they were indistinguishable from the other farmers, except only in their superior discipline over their workers. Mr Pilkington, proposing the toast of "Animal Farm" at the dinner which the pigs gave to their neighbours, put it very well: " . . . a discipline and an orderliness which should be an example to all farmers everywhere. He believed that he was right in saying that the lower animals on Animal Farm did more work and received less food than any animals in the county."

Was it wonderful that when the poor animals gazed in they "looked from pig to man, and from man to pig, and from pig to man again; but already it was impossible to say which was which"?

The question one poses at the end of this fairy story is whether Orwell had given up hope that mankind would ever find decent government. It is very difficult here, as in *1984,* to decide. He had said in his essay on Swift that: "Of course, no honest person claims that happiness is *now* a normal condition among adult human beings; but perhaps it *could* be made normal, and it is upon this question that all serious political controversy really turns."

Essentially, *Animal Farm* is an anatomy of the development of the totalitarian State: "In each great revolutionary struggle the masses are led on by vague dreams of human brotherhood, and then, when the new ruling class is well established in power, they are thrust back into servitude." *(Second Thoughts on James Burnham.)*

It is a comment on all revolution: "History consists of a series of swindles, in which the masses are first lured into revolt by the promise of Utopia, and then, when they have done their job, enslaved over again by new masters." (Same essay.)

Nothing is more obvious than where Orwell's sympathies lay. But whether he hoped that the common man could learn to find rulers is not clear. In *Animal Farm* he is an artist, posing great questions imaginatively; not a preacher, proclaiming a revelation.

Christopher Hollis

SOURCE: *A Study of George Orwell: The Man and His Works,* Henry Regnery Company, 1956, pp. 150-53.

The story of **Animal Farm** is so familiar that it hardly needs detailed recapitulation. An old boar, of the name of Major, on the brink of death summons to the barn all the animals on the farm of a broken-down drunkard, called Jones, and gives to them his farewell message—the result of his long meditation on life. It is that the enemy of all animals is Man. Man lives by exploiting his animals. The animals produce their food of one sort or another, but they are not allowed to draw for themselves any benefit from their increased production. Man seizes it all for his own need, allows to the animals only sufficient to keep them alive and able to work, cynically and ruthlessly exploits them in their lives and as cynically and ruthlessly destroys them as soon as their days of work are done. Let the animals rise up, expel the enemy Man and run the farm as a co-operative farm of animals in the animals' own interest.

Three days later Major dies, but he has left behind him his message of revolt. The animals are, it is true, not as yet clear how to carry into practice this gospel of revolt. They meet and sing together their new hymn "Beasts of England." An unpremeditated accident eventually brings on the revolt. One midsummer eve Jones gets drunk in the neighbouring village of Wilmington. The hired men milk the cows, and then go off for a day's rabbiting, leaving the animals unfed. In the afternoon, when the animals can stand their hunger no longer, one of the cows breaks in the door of the store-shed with her horn and all the animals rush in and start helping themselves from the bin. Jones wakes up from his drunken slumber. He and the men rush out with whips in their hands and start laying about them. Though there had been no plan of resistance, the animals turn on Jones and the men, attack them and, before they know where they are, have driven them helter-skelter from the farm.

Thus the animals established themselves with unexpected ease as the masters of the farm. It is Orwell's humour to show no great difficulty in the task in which they had expected their main difficulty—in the seizure of power—but enormous and finally fatal difficulty—in the task which they had hardly expected to present a problem at all—in the exercise of power when seized. With the death of Major the leadership of the animals falls into the hands of the two leading pigs, Snowball and Napoleon—for Orwell throughout represents the pigs as far more intelligent than any of the other animals. Of these he explains with delicious mock solemnity that Napoleon was "not much of a talker" but had "a reputation for getting his own way." Snowball was quicker, but "was not considered to have the same depth of character." There is a full and vivid portrait gallery of other animals of which the most notable are Boxer, the good, stupid, unsuspicious horse, of immense physical strength, to whose unquestioning mind the remedy for all problems was to work harder—Squealer, another pig, who was, as it were, the P.R.O. [public relations officer] to Napoleon—Benjamin, the donkey, the only cynic among the animals, who knows that life has always been hard, believes that it always will be hard and is sceptical of all promises of improvement, and Moses, the raven, who does no work but continually tells to the other animals his tale of the Sugar Candy Mountains above the sky where "it was Sunday seven days a week, clover was in season all the year round and lump-sugar and linseed oil grew on the hedges."

In the early days of Animal Farm the animals have to prepare themselves for the inevitable counter-attack when Jones and his fellow men will attempt to recapture the farm. The rivalry between Snowball and Napoleon is becoming increasingly evident and they differ and quarrel on every point of policy, but in face of the threat of Man's attack they do not dare to let things come to an open breach. Then in October Jones attacks and, owing to the heroism and strategy of Snowball, he is driven off in rout at the Battle of the Cowshed.

After the defeat of Jones there is no longer any reason why Snowball and Napoleon should preserve even an appearance of amity. The fundamental difference between them is that Snowball thinks that the animals should "send out more pigeons and stir up rebellion among the animals on other farms," while Napoleon thinks that "what the animals must do was to produce firearms and train themselves to the use of them." They also differ over Snowball's ambition to build a windmill to which Napoleon is opposed.

Napoleon bides his time. He has made himself the master of a litter of young puppies which he is secretly training up as his gendarmerie. Then when the day comes, he suddenly introduces these dogs, as they have by then become, into the assembly and lets them loose on Snowball, whom they chase from the farm. It is then that the pace of the degradation increases. More and more Napoleon and the pigs who are faithful to him seize for themselves almost all the food of the farm. The other animals are forced down to a standard of living lower than that which they had in Jones's time. They have to work harder. Whenever anything goes wrong on the farm, the fault is ascribed to Snowball, who is supposed to be lurking in a near-by farm and making nocturnal raids into Animal Farm. He was, the animals are told, in league with Jones from the first. Documents had proved it. The history of Animal Farm is unblushingly falsified. The animals are told, first, that Snowball's part in the Battle of the Cowshed was greatly exaggerated, then that he had in fact fought in it on Jones's side. The windmill is built, but the animals are now told that it was Napoleon who was in favour of it all along and Snowball who was against it. To all complaints that the animals may make at their hard lot the invariable and crushing reply is, "Do you want Jones back?" They must put up with all hardships as the only alternative to this more awful fate.

In the original constitution the animals had sworn to have no dealings with Man, but the next summer Napoleon announces the new policy by which the Farm is to trade with neighbouring men in order to obtain certain essential materials of life. The trade is of course to be kept entirely in Napoleon's own hands. No other animals than he are to have any contact with the surrounding men. Then he moves into Jones's house and establishes it as his palace. He lives a life increasingly remote from the other animals by whom he is rarely seen. In the autumn a storm blows down the windmill, but of course it is explained that its destruction is not at all due to defects in building but to the sabotage of Snowball. The winter is a hard one and there is a situation bordering on rebellion—particularly among the hens who object to the seizure of their eggs for the purpose of trade with men. Napoleon deals with it in characteristically unhesitating and terrible fashion.

> The four pigs waited, trembling, with guilt written on every line of their countenances. Napoleon now called upon them to confess their crimes. They were the same four pigs as had protested when Napoleon abolished the Sunday Meetings. Without any further prompting they confessed that they had been secretly in touch with Snowball ever since his expulsion, that they had collaborated with him in destroying the windmill and that they had entered into an agreement with him to hand over Animal Farm to Mr. Frederick. They added that Snowball had privately admitted to them that he had been Jones' secret agent for years past. When they had finished their confession, the dogs promptly tore their throats out, and in a terrible voice Napoleon demanded whether any other animal had anything to confess.

> The three hens who had been the ringleaders in the attempted rebellion over the eggs now came forward and stated that Snowball had appeared to them in a dream and incited them to disobey Napoleon's orders. They, too, were slaughtered. Then a goose came forward and confessed to having secreted six ears of corn during the last year's harvest and eaten them in the night. Then a sheep confessed to having urinated in the drinking pool, urged to do this, so she said, by Snowball—and two other sheep confessed to having murdered an old ram, an especially devoted follower of Napoleon, by chasing him round and round a bonfire when he was suffering from a cough. They were all slain on the spot. And so the tale of confessions and executions went on, until there was a pile of corpses lying before Napoleon's feet and the air was heavy with the smell of blood, which had been unknown there since the expulsion of Jones.

After that the old song "Beasts of England" is suppressed, and there is substituted for it Minimus's new song,

> Animal Farm, Animal Farm,
> Never through me shalt thou come to harm.

One after another the commandments on which Animal Farm was built are found to have been secretly altered. For "No animal shall kill another animal," the animals now find the commandment to read, "No animal shall kill another animal without cause." "No animal shall sleep in a bed" is now "No animal shall sleep in a bed with sheets." It had been Napoleon's plan to sell a load of timber to their neighbouring human farmer, Frederick, with the money for which he will buy machinery for the windmill. The timber is delivered and five-pound notes are paid to the animals in exchange. It is only when through their agent the animals attempt to use the five-pound notes for purchases that they find that Frederick has cheated them and that the notes are forgeries. Napoleon attempts to enlist the alliance of the animals' other neighbour, Pilkington, against Frederick, but Pilkington is unsympathetic. "Serves you right," he says. The humans determine on a second attack on Animal Farm. They come this time armed with guns. They destroy the windmill but are driven off in a second defeat.

It is a few days later that the pigs discover a case of whiskey in Jones's cellar, and it is, naturally enough, at the same time that the commandment "No animal shall drink alcohol" is found now to read "No animal shall drink alcohol to excess."

All comes to a climax when the faithful Boxer one day falls down between the shafts and is no longer strong enough to work. Under the pretence that they are sending him to the vet to be cured, the pigs sell him to a knacker, tell the other animals that he has died at the vet's, in spite of having received every attention, and that his last words were "Forward, Comrades!! Forward in the name of Rebellion! Long live Animal Farm! Long live Comrade Napoleon! Napoleon is always right!" With the money that they have received from Boxer's carcass the pigs buy a case of whiskey and hold a banquet in Jones's house.

The great mark of Animal Farm had been its hostility to everything that went on two legs. "Four legs good, two legs bad" had been the continual bleat of the sheep and four legs had been the great mark of animalism, of animal solidarity. But now the pigs set themselves to learning how to walk on two legs. The motto of the Farm is changed into "All animals are equal, but some animals are more equal than others," and one day the pigs emerge from Jones's house walking on two legs and with whips in their hands. They take out subscriptions to *John Bull, Tit-Bits* and the *Daily Mirror.* The obedient sheep, trained in secret by Squealer, change their bleat of "Four legs good, two legs bad" into "Four legs good, two legs better."

After their second defeat in the Battle of the Windmill the neighbouring men had given up all hope of defeating and destroying the animals, nor indeed once the pigs had shown themselves as ready to impose discipline on their animals as was any human farmer, was there any longer any need, from their point of view, for them to do so. A policy of peaceful coexistence in every way suited them better. Parties of men used to come on visits to the farm and were taken round on conducted tours. At last there comes the night of the great banquet of alliance between the human Pilkington and Napoleon. The animals, looking in through the windows, see pigs and men sitting together and hear the exchange of congratulatory speeches. Mr. Pilkington "believed that he was right in saying that the lower animals on Animal Farm did more work and received less food than any animals in the county. . . . If you have your lower animals to contend with, we have our lower classes." As the celebrations proceed, the pigs, the animals notice, come to look more and more like men and the men more and more like pigs. "The creatures outside looked from pig to man and from man to pig, and from pig to man again, but already it was impossible to say which was which." But assimilation cannot bring harmony. They fall to playing cards, and the banquet breaks up into chaos as Mr. Pilkington and Napoleon each play the ace of spades simultaneously.

The interpretation of the fable is plain enough. Major, Napoleon, Snowball—Lenin, Stalin and Trotsky—Pilkington and Frederick, the two groups of non-Communist powers—the Marxian thesis, as expounded by Major, that society is divided into exploiters and exploited and that all the exploited need to do is to rise up, to expel the exploiters and seize the "surplus value" which the exploiters have previously annexed to themselves—the Actonian thesis that power corrupts and the Burnhamian thesis that the leaders of the exploited, having used the rhetoric of equality to get rid of the old exploiters, established in their place not a classless society but themselves as a new governing class—the greed and unprincipled opportunism of the non-Communist states, which are ready enough to overthrow the Communists by force so long as they imagine that their overthrow will be easy but begin to talk of peace when they find the task difficult and when they think that they can use the Communists to satisfy their greed—the dishonour among total thugs, as a result of which, though greed may make original ideology irrelevant, turning pigs into men and men into pigs, the thugs fall out among themselves, as the Nazis and the Communists fell out, not through difference of ideology but because in a society of utter baseness and insincerity there is no motive of confidence. The interpretation is so plain that no serious critic can dispute it. Those Russian critics who have professed to see in it merely a general satire on bureaucracy without any special reference to any particular country can hardly be taken seriously.

Yet even a total acceptance of Orwell's political opinions would not in itself make *Animal Farm* a great work of art. The world is full of animal fables in which this or that country is symbolized by this or that animal, and very tedious affairs the greater number of them are—and that, irrespective of whether we agree or disagree with their opinions. To be a great book, a book of animal fables requires literary greatness as well as a good cause. Such greatness *Animal Farm* surely possesses. As Orwell fairly claimed, *Animal Farm* "was the first book in which I tried, with full consciousness of what I was doing, to fuse political purpose and artistic purpose into one whole"—and he succeeded.

The problems that are set by this peculiar form of art, which makes animals behave like human beings, are clear. The writer must throughout be successful in preserving a delicate and whimsical balance. As Johnson truly says in his criticism of Dryden's *Hind and the Panther,* there is an initial absurdity in making animals discuss complicated intellectual problems—the nature of the Church's authority in Dryden's case, the communist ideology in Orwell's. The absurdity can only be saved from ridicule if the author is able to couch his argument in very simple terms and to draw his illustrations from the facts of animal life. In this Orwell is as successful as he could be—a great deal more successful incidentally than Dryden, who in the excitement of the argument often forgets that it is animals who are supposed to be putting it forward. The practical difficulties of the conceit must either be ignored or apparently solved in some simple and striking—if possible, amusing—fashion. Since obviously they could not in reality be solved at all, the author merely makes himself ridiculous if he allows himself to get bogged down in tedious and detailed explanations which at the end of all cannot in the nature of things explain anything. Thus Orwell is quite right merely to ignore the difficulties of language, to assume that the animals can communicate with one another by speech—or to assume that the new ordinance which forbids any animal to take another animal's life could be applied with only the comparatively mild consequence of gradual increase in animal population. He is justified in telling us the stories of the two attacks by men for the recapture of the Farm but in refusing to spoil his story by allowing the men to take the full measures which obviously men would take if they found themselves in such an impossible situation. The means by which the animals rout the men are inevitably signally unconvincing if we are to consider them seriously at all. It would as obviously be ridiculous to delay for pages to describe how animals build windmills or how they write up commandments on a wall. It heightens the comedy to give a passing sentence of description to their hauling the stone up a hill so that it may be broken into manageable fractions when it falls over the precipice, or to Squealer, climbing a ladder to paint up his message.

The animal fable, if it is to succeed at all, ought clearly to carry with it a gay and light-hearted message. It must be full of comedy and laughter. The form is too far removed from reality to tolerate sustained bitterness. Both Chaucer and La Fontaine discovered this in their times, and the trouble with Orwell was that the lesson which he wished to teach was not ultimately a gay lesson. It was not the lesson that mankind had its foibles and its follies but that all would be well in the end. It was more nearly a lesson of despair—the lesson that anarchy was intolerable, that mankind could not be ruled without entrusting power somewhere or other and, to whomsoever power was entrusted, it was almost certain to be abused. For power was itself corrupting. But it was Orwell's twisted triumph that in the relief of the

months immediately after the war mankind was probably not prepared to take such dark medicine if it had been offered to it undiluted. It accepted it because it came in this gay and coloured and fanciful form.

The film version gives to *Animal Farm* a happy ending. The animals all the world over, hearing how Napoleon has betrayed the animal cause, rise up against him at the end and in a second revolution expel him. After this second revolution, we are left to believe, a rule of freedom and equality is established and survives. But of course this ending makes nonsense of the whole thesis. It was the Orwellian thesis, right or wrong, that power inevitably corrupts and that revolutions therefore inevitably fail of their purpose. The new masters are necessarily corrupted by their new power. The second revolution would necessarily have failed of its purpose just as the first had failed. It would merely have set up a second vicious circle.

Animal Farm possesses two essential qualities of a successful animal fable. On the one hand the author of such a fable must have the Swift-like capacity of ascribing with solemn face to the animals idiotic but easily recognized human qualities, decking them out in aptly changed phraseology to suit the animal life—ascribe the quality and then pass quickly on before the reader has begun to find the point overlaboured. This Orwell has to perfection. Thus:

> Snowball also busied himself with organizing the other animals into what he called Animal Committees. He was indefatigable at this. He formed the Egg Production Committee for the hens, the Clean Tails League for the cows, the Wild Comrades' Re-education Committee (the object of which was to tame the cats and rabbits), the Whiter Wool Movement for the sheep, and various others, besides instituting classes in reading and writing. On the whole these projects were a failure. The attempt to tame the wild creatures, for instance, broke down almost immediately. They continued to behave very much as before and, when treated with generosity, simply took advantage of it. The cat joined the Re-education Committee and was very active in it for some days. She was seen one day sitting on a roof talking to some sparrows who were just out of reach. She was telling them that all animals were now comrades and that any sparrow who chose could come and perch on her paw; but the sparrows kept their distance. . . .

But what is also essential—and this is often overlooked—is that the writer should have himself a genuine love of animals—should be able to create here and there, in the midst of all his absurdity, scenes of animal life, in themselves realistic and lovable. In that Chaucer, the first and greatest of Orwell's masters in this form of art, pre-eminently excelled. It was in that that Orwell himself excelled. He had always been himself a lover of animals, intimate with their ways. "Most of the good memories of my childhood, and up to the age of about twenty," he wrote in **"Such, Such Were the Joys,"** "are in some way connected with animals," and it was the work with animals which attracted him in maturer years to agricultural life. There is a real poetic quality, mixed whimsically in with absurdity, in his picture of the first meeting of the animals in the barn with which the book opens. . . .

As I say, there is no difficulty in interpreting the symbolism of the story. But it is not quite so certain what is the total moral that we are supposed to draw from it. Is it that there is some special evil and fraud in Communism which makes it inevitable that all communist movements will turn only into a new and worse tyranny? or is it rather that power is in itself, to whatever ideology it may nominally be allied, inevitably corrupting? that all promises of equality and liberty will prove inevitably to be deceptions? and that history does not, and cannot, consist of anything other than the overthrow of old tyrants in order that new tyrants may be put in their place? It is obvious that the second alternative was much more natural to Orwell's mind than the first and that Conservatives who hailed *Animal Farm* as an attack simply on Communism interpreted it too narrowly and too much to suit their own convenience. Orwell's whole record from Spanish days onwards shows his impartial hatred of all tyrannies and of all totalitarian claims, and as a matter of history, it was against what he thought of as a fascist tyranny that he first enlisted to fight. In *Animal Farm* itself we must not be diverted by the satire on the animals from noticing how utterly worthless are without exception the parts played by men, who represent the conservative principle. He complained of Mr. Rayner Heppenstall's radio version of it for "casting a sop to those stinking Catholics." There is no hint of a suggestion that Jones, a drunken brute, who was letting the farm down, did not deserve all that he got. The parts that he displayed both when he had the farm and after he lost it were alike discreditable. His men were no better. When Jones was away drunk they took advantage of his absence not to feed the animals. The two neighbouring farmers—Pilkington, "an easygoing gentleman farmer who spent most of his time in fishing, or hunting according to the season"—and Frederick "a tough, shrewd man, perpetually involved in lawsuits

and with a name for driving hard bargains"—are equally worthless. Their sole motive is greed. They are willing to destroy the animals, if possible, and, if it is not possible, to make out of them what they can, and they are incapable of honouring their bargains. The lesson of *Animal Farm* is clearly not merely the corrupting effect of power when exercised by Communists, but the corrupting effect of power when exercised by anybody. As for the Communists being worse than other people—clearly, rightly or wrongly, Orwell did not think that Communists were worse than Fascists. By Fascists he really meant Nazis, for he never bothered much about Mussolini one way or the other and, although in Catalonia he called the followers of Franco Fascists, he specifically recognized that they were something different. But Fascists, if Fascists means Nazis, he thought to be worse than Communists. It was of no great moment what were the nominal creeds either of the one party or the other, for absolute power tends to corrupt absolutely, and the totalitarian is in practice, whatever he may profess, solely concerned with maintaining and extending his power. It is power politics and nothing but power politics.

But was there then no remedy and no hope? There was certainly no hope in anything like the modern circumstances of life that we should see anything of the nature of free and equal society. From time to time Orwell expresses a hope that we may be moving "eventually" to such a consummation, but with no great confidence and for no very clear reason. "Of course no honest person claims that happiness is *now* a normal condition among adult human beings," he writes, "but perhaps it *could* be made normal, and it is upon this question that all serious political controversy really turns." All the evidence is, he admits, that we are moving away from it. All that we can really say is that time has a certain mollifying influence and that, though all governments are tyrannies, old tyrannies are less ruthless than new. The rule of law is a great deal better than the rule of public opinion or of an arbitrary tyrant. "In a society in which there is no law, and in theory no compulsion, the only arbiter of behaviour is public opinion. But public opinion, because of the tremendous urge to conformity in gregarious animals, is less tolerant than any system of law." Therefore it might appear that the conclusion that ought to follow is that no régime would be very good but that the least bad would be a moderate conservative régime—a régime which preserved the traditional structure of society and at the same time preserved the liberal principles so that those parts of it that in the development of events showed signs of collapse might be at necessity modified—indeed something of the nature of what we in the West call free institutions. The clean choice of Socialist theory between production for profit and production for social use, which Orwell had himself to some extent offered in **"England, Your England,"** belongs to the lecture room rather than to real life. In the real world of the years after 1945, with the Socialists leaving so many industries under private enterprise and the Conservatives leaving so many industries nationalized, nationalization was clearly a matter of the balance of advantage and disadvantage in each particular case rather than of absolute good and evil. It was not a stark choice of one sort of society against another sort. The policy which Orwell believed that Dickens recommended to the nineteenth century should, it would seem on this argument, be the sort of policy which he should recommend to the twentieth century.

I should myself be prepared to argue that this was the conclusion which Orwell ought to have drawn from his own writings in general and from *Animal Farm* in particular. But it must be admitted that it was not a conclusion which Orwell ever did explicitly draw. As a reporter of fact Mr. Brander is substantially accurate when he writes, "Orwell wrote very little about the Church in his criticism of society. He classed it with Conservatism as no longer serious enough to be considered." Orwell's complaint was not so much against an ideal philosophy of Conservatism, for which, when he found it, he had a reasonable respect, as against those who called themselves Conservatives and had captured the Conservative machine. His complaint against them was that they were at once too arrogant and too compromising. They were too arrogant in so far as they tended to claim their privileges as something which they had deserved and to arrogate to themselves the airs of superior people. These very claims obscured the true case for Conservatism which was that society had to be arranged, that there was little reason to think that it would ever be arranged ideally well, that it was fatally easy for men to fritter away all their energies in agitation and scheming for its rearrangement and that therefore there was always something to be said, within limits, for accepting society broadly as it is and getting on with the business of living. It may very well turn out that there would be more liberty that way than down a more revolutionary, more ideally perfectionist, road—and liberty was what really mattered. Even in his most revolutionary moods—as in **"England, Your England"**—he was, if we analyse his argument, primarily concerned with the proclamation of a libertarian and egalitarian purpose. Once the purpose was proclaimed he was quite

content in practice to let things move forward at a slow and conservative pace. Willing to impose drastic sufferings upon himself, he never, save in moments of special exaltation, imagined that it would be possible to impose such drastic sufferings on society at large and to preserve freedom.

But a more important complaint against the Conservatives was that they were too compromising. While the case for Conservatism was that it stood for traditional ways and ancient liberties against the menace of the new philosophies, the Conservatives in practice, he complained, had shown themselves always only too ready to do a deal with the new philosophies and "the stream-lined men," as Pilkington did his deal with Napoleon, as soon as the "stream-lined men" had shown themselves to be in the least tough and strong. They did a deal with the Fascists before the war and with the Communists in the Anglo-Russian alliance during the war. Orwell despaired of the Conservatives because the Conservatives despaired of Conservatism. They were without principle.

A. E. Dyson

SOURCE: "Orwell: Irony as Prophecy," in *The Crazy Fabric: Essays in Irony,* Macmillan and Co. Ltd., 1965, pp. 197-219.

[A] few words about *Animal Farm.* Though based on the Russian Revolution and its aftermath, this grim little parable is by no means about Russia alone. Orwell is concerned to show how revolutionary ideals of justice, equality and fraternity always shatter in the event. The ironic reversals in *Animal Farm* could be fairly closely related to real events since the work was written (this is not the least of their effectiveness) as well as to the events on which they were based.

The charting of disillusionment is not new to our political scene. Shakespeare in *Julius Caesar,* Hobbes in *Leviathan,* Milton and the Romantic Poets, have all had their say. What *is* new about our modern disillusionment is its scale. More insistently than ever before, revolutionaries have proclaimed the liberation of the common man; more ironically than ever before, the common man has had to pay for revolution with his liberty, his happiness and sometimes his life.

But Orwell was never himself committed to revolutionary hopes, as the left-wing poets of the '30s were, and his charting of disenchantment was to this degree less extreme. He fought in Spain, but with grave doubts about his own side, which events did everything to confirm. His critique of revolution is basically simple, and embodies the same doubts about human nature which made benevolent paternalism more realistic for him, perhaps, than the ideal of a People's Republic. *Animal Farm* offers insights which were later spelt out, more abstractly, in the Black Book of *1984.* There always have been three classes of society, and there always will be. These are the high, the middle and the low. The war between the classes is necessary, and in normal circumstances could never have an end. The basic political reality is a struggle for power, and the basic reality of power is the ambition and self-aggrandisement of the few at the expense of the many. In this battle, ideals of justice, liberty and brotherhood are so many counters, which the various parties at different times find useful. The middle class is especially adroit in its use of them when it needs to enlist the superior numbers of the lower class in what is essentially its private cause. These ideals are emotionally explosive for two main reasons. The first is that they receive lip-service from most of us, so that politicians are enabled to manipulate the worst in us by way of what we are accustomed to regard as the best. The second is that a handful of idealists really do believe them, and those who do (such as Boxer in *Animal Farm,* or Shakespeare's Brutus) become enormously helpful by reason of their prestige. The politicians who use such slogans are, however, motivated by conscious cynicism of the deepest kind. It is a cynicism more realistic, if less amiable, than the hopes of the men whom they dupe.

In this broad approach to his theme, Orwell agrees with Bertrand Russell in taking the lowest possible view of politicians. He sees them not as ordinary men caught up in events too big for them, and forced against their will into evil moulds, but as depraved men, who have been drawn to politics in the first place by the corrupting search for power. "Sensible men do not have power," he once wrote, and the obverse of this is that the men who do have power are evil, since "sensible" in this context is a moral term. It is interesting to notice that Orwell agrees with most revolutionaries in his estimate of the men who are actually ruling us, but differs sharply in his assessment of what will happen when they are swept away. The new masters will not be saviours, restoring to us a primitive freedom. On the contrary, they will be oppressors in their turn, resembling their predecessors in ambition and cruelty, and differing only in the extremes to which these motives will lead them when stability and tradition have been removed.

Orwell's heart is with the political idealists, but his head gives its verdict the other way. In *Animal Farm*

the rise of the pigs to power is presented as inevitable. Our sense of inevitability is mediated through the pervasive irony, which uses a tone of almost bedtime cosiness to unfold the horrors of the tale. We observe the pigs coming into the ascendancy almost at once, as they persuade their fellow animals through a characteristic interplay of idealism and fear. When the machinery of naked power passes into their hands, idealism is totally replaced by fear. We are shown the ensuing power struggle among the pigs at the top, with the emergence of the more evil of the two to supreme power. Events continue to unfold with something of the unassailable logic of a dream. The defeated pig is transformed into an enemy, who can both canalise hatred and justify oppression. The ruling pig is apotheosised into human semblance, and ends in alliance with the hated humans who were originally deposed. These events are intensified by our sense that human nature itself is on trial. If we detect some inevitability in the progress of events, Orwell relies on no dialectic of history to sustain this, but only on his profoundly depressing assessment of political power. The whole range of contributory causes unfolds as we watch—the cruel intelligence of the pigs, the brutality (so easily harnessed) of the dogs, the casual selfishness of the cat, the vanity of the donkey, the heroic stupidity of Boxer, the moronic stupidity of the numerically preponderating sheep. Even when writing *The Road to Wigan Pier,* Orwell had been sufficiently sickened by his experience of imperialism to record: "At that time failure seemed to me the only virtue." In *Animal Farm,* the only virtue is Boxer's failure: yet can a man at once so decent and dynamic as Orwell rest in perceptions such as these?

Stephen Greenblatt

SOURCE: "George Orwell," in *Three Modern Satirists: Waugh, Orwell, and Huxley,* Yale University Press, 1965, pp. 35-74.

Throughout Orwell's early novels, journals, and essays, democratic socialism existed as a sustaining vision that kept the author from total despair of the human condition, but Orwell's bitter experience in the Spanish Civil War and the shock of the Nazi-Soviet pact signaled the breakdown of this last hope and the beginning of the mental and emotional state out of which grew *Animal Farm* and *1984.* The political disappointments of the late '30s and '40s did not in themselves, however, disillusion Orwell—they simply brought to the surface themes and tensions present in his work from the beginning. . . . [The] socialism Orwell believed in was not a hardheaded, "realistic" approach to society and politics but a rather sentimental, utopian vision of the world as a "raft sailing through space, with, potentially, plenty of provisions for everybody," provided men, who, after all, are basically decent, would simply use common sense and not be greedy. Such naïve beliefs could only survive while Orwell was preoccupied with his attacks on the British Raj, the artist in society, or the capitalist system. The moment events compelled him to turn his critical eye on the myth of socialism and the "dictatorship of the proletariat," he discerned fundamental lies and corruption. Orwell, in his last years, was a man who experienced daily the disintegration of the beliefs of a lifetime, who watched in horror while his entire life work was robbed of meaning.

The first of his great cries of despair was *Animal Farm,* a satirical beast fable which, curiously enough, has been heralded as Orwell's lightest, gayest work. Laurence Brander, in his biography of Orwell paints a charming but wholly inaccurate picture of *Animal Farm,* presenting it as "one of those apparently chance pieces a prose writer throws off . . . a sport out of his usual way," supposedly written by Orwell in a state where "the gaiety in his nature had completely taken charge . . . writing about animals, whom he loved." The surface gaiety, the seeming good humor and casualness, the light, bantering tone are, of course, part of the convention of beast fables, and *Animal Farm* would be a very bad tale indeed if it did not employ these devices. But it is a remarkable achievement precisely because Orwell uses the apparently frivolous form of the animal tale to convey with immense power his profoundly bitter message. Critics like Laurence Brander and Tom Hopkinson who marvel at Orwell's "admirable good humour and detachment" miss, I think, the whole point of the piece they praise. *Animal Farm* does indeed contain much gaiety and humor, but even in the most comic moments there is a disturbing element of cruelty or fear that taints the reader's hearty laughter. While Snowball, one of the leaders of the revolution of farm animals against their master, is organizing "the Egg Production Committee for the hens, the Clean Tails League for the cows, the Wild Comrades' Re-education Committee . . . , the Whiter Wool Movement for the sheep," Napoleon, the sinister pig tyrant, is carefully educating the dogs for his own evil purposes. Similarly, the "confessions" forced from the animals in Napoleon's great purges are very funny, but when the dogs tear the throats out of the "guilty" parties and leave a pile of corpses at the ty-

rant's feet, the scene ceases to amuse. Orwell's technique is similar to [a device used by Evelyn] Waugh, who relates ghastly events in a comic setting.

Another critical mistake in appraising *Animal Farm* is made, I believe, by critics like Christopher Hollis who talk of the overriding importance of the author's love of animals and fail to understand that Orwell in *Animal Farm* loves animals only as much or as little as he loves human beings. To claim that he hates the pigs because they represent human tyrants and sympathizes with the horses because they are dumb animals is absurd. Nor is it necessary, as Hollis believes, that the truly successful animal fable carry with it "a gay and light-hearted message." Indeed, the very idea of representing human traits in animals is rather pessimistic. What is essential to the success of the satirical beast fable, as Ellen Douglass Leyburn observes, is the author's "power to keep his reader conscious simultaneously of the human traits satirized and of the animals as animals." The storyteller must never allow the animals to be simply beasts, in which case the piece becomes a nonsatirical children's story, or to be merely transparent symbols, in which case the piece becomes a dull sermon. Orwell proved, in *Animal Farm,* his remarkable ability to maintain this delicate, satiric balance.

The beast fable, an ancient satiric technique in which the characteristic poses of human vice and folly are embodied in animals, is, as Kernan points out, "an unrealistic, expressionistic device" [Alvin Kernan, *Modern Satire,* 1962] which stands in bold contrast with Orwell's previous realistic manner. But the seeds for *Animal Farm* are present in the earlier works, not only in the metaphors likening men to beasts but, more important, in Orwell's whole attitude toward society, which he sees as an aggregation of certain classes or types. The types change somewhat in appearance according to the setting—from the snobbish pukka sahibs, corrupt officials, and miserable natives of *Burmese Days* to the obnoxious nouveaux riches, greedy restaurateurs, and overworked plongeurs of *Down and Out in Paris and London,* but there remains the basic notion that men naturally divide themselves into a limited number of groups, which can be isolated and characterized by the astute observer. This notion is given dramatic reality in *Animal Farm,* where societal types are presented in the various kinds of farm animals—pigs for exploiters, horses for laborers, dogs for police, sheep for blind followers, etc. The beast fable need not convey an optimistic moral, but it cannot portray complex individuals, and thus it can never sustain the burden of tragedy. The characters of a satirical animal story may be sly, vicious, cynical, pathetic, lovable, or intelligent, but they can only be seen as members of large social groups and not as individuals.

Animal Farm has been interpreted most frequently as a clever satire on the betrayal of the Russian Revolution and the rise of Stalin. Richard Rees comments that "the struggle of the farm animals, having driven out their human exploiter, to create a free and equal community takes the form of a most ingeniously worked-out recapitulation of the history of Soviet Russia from 1917 up to the Teheran Conference. And indeed, despite Soviet critics who claim to see only a general satire on bureaucracy in *Animal Farm,* the political allegory is inevitable. Inspired by the prophetic deathbed vision of Old Major, a prize Middle White boar, the maltreated animals of Manor Farm successfully revolt against Mr. Jones, their bad farmer, and found their own utopian community, Animal Farm. The control of the revolution falls naturally upon the pigs, particularly upon Napoleon, "a large, rather fierce-looking Berkshire boar, not much of a talker, but with a reputation for getting his own way," and on Snowball, "a more vivacious pig than Napoleon, quicker in speech and more inventive, but . . . not considered to have the same depth of character." Under their clever leadership and with the help of the indefatigable cart horses Boxer and Clover, the animals manage to repulse the attacks of their rapacious human neighbors, Mr. Pilkington and Mr. Frederick. With the farm secured from invasion and the Seven Commandments of Animalism painted on the end wall of the big barn, the revolution seems complete; but as the community develops, it is plain that there are graver dangers than invasion. The pigs at once decide that milk and apples are essential to their well being. Squealer, Napoleon's lieutenant and the ablest talker, explains the appropriation:

> "Comrades!" he cried. "You do not imagine, I hope, that we pigs are doing this in a spirit of selfishness and privilege? Many of us actually dislike milk and apples. . . . Our sole object in taking these things is to preserve our health. Milk and apples (this has been proven by Science, comrades) contain substances absolutely necessary to the well-being of a pig. . . . We pigs are brainworkers. . . . Day and night we are watching over your welfare. It is for *your* sake that we drink that milk and eat those apples. Do you know what would happen if we pigs failed in our duty? Jones would come back!"

A growing rivalry between Snowball and Napoleon is decisively decided by Napoleon's vicious hounds, who drive Snowball off the farm. Laurence Brander sees Snowball as a symbol of "altruism, the essential social virtue" and his expulsion as the defeat of "his

altruistic laws for giving warmth, food and comfort to all the animals." This is very touching, but unfortunately there is no indication that Snowball is any less corrupt or power-mad than Napoleon. Indeed, it is remarked, concerning the appropriation of the milk and apples, that "All the pigs were in full agreement on this point, even Snowball and Napoleon." The remainder of *Animal Farm* is a chronicle of the consolidation of Napoleon's power through clever politics, propaganda, and terror. Dissenters are ruthlessly murdered, and when Boxer can no longer work, he is sold to the knacker. One by one, the Commandments of Animalism are perverted or eliminated, until all that is left is:

ALL ANIMALS ARE EQUAL BUT SOME ANIMALS ARE MORE EQUAL THAN OTHERS.

After that, it does not seem strange when the pigs live in Jones' house, walk on two legs, carry whips, wear human clothes, take out subscriptions to *John Bull, Tit-Bits,* and the *Daily Mirror,* and invite their human neighbors over for a friendly game of cards. The game ends in a violent argument when Napoleon and Pilkington play an ace of spades simultaneously, but for the animals there is no real quarrel. "The creatures outside looked from pig to man, and from man to pig, and from pig to man again; but already it was impossible to say which was which."

The interpretation of *Animal Farm* in terms of Soviet history (Major, Napoleon, Snowball represent Lenin, Stalin, Trotsky) has been made many times and shall not be pursued further here. It is amusing, however, that many of the Western critics who astutely observe the barbs aimed at Russia fail completely to grasp Orwell's judgment of the West. After all, the pigs do not turn into alien monsters; they come to resemble those bitter rivals Mr. Pilkington and Mr. Frederick, who represent the Nazis and the Capitalists. All three major "powers" are despicable tyrannies, and the failure of the revolution is not seen in terms of ideology at all, but as a realization of Lord Acton's thesis, "Power tends to corrupt; absolute power corrupts absolutely." The initial spark of a revolution, the original intention of a constitution may have been an ideal of the good life, but the result is always the same—tyranny. Communism is no more or less evil than Fascism or Capitalism—they are all illusions which are inevitably used by the pigs as a means of satisfying their greed and their lust for power. Religion, too, is merely a toy of the oppressors and a device to divert the minds of the sufferers. Moses, the tame raven who is always croaking about the sweet, eternal life in Sugarcandy Mountain, flies after the deposed Farmer Jones, only to return when Napoleon has established his tyranny.

Animal Farm remains powerful satire even as the specific historical events it mocked recede into the past, because the book's major concern is not with these incidents but with the essential horror of the human condition. There have been, are, and always will be pigs in every society, Orwell states, and they will always grab power. Even more cruel is the conclusion that *everyone* in the society, wittingly or unwittingly, contributes to the pigs' tyranny. Boxer, the noblest (though not the wisest) animal on the farm, devotes his unceasing labor to the pigs, who, as has been noted, send him to the knacker when he has outlived his usefulness. There is real pathos as the sound of Boxer's hoofs drumming weakly on the back of the horse slaughterer's van grows fainter and dies away, and the reader senses that in that dying sound is the dying hope of humanity. But Orwell does not allow the mood of oppressive sadness to overwhelm the satire, and Squealer, "lifting his trotter and wiping away a tear," hastens to announce that, after receiving every attention a horse could have, Boxer died in his hospital bed, with the words "Napoleon is always right" on his withered lips. Frederick R. Karl, in *The Contemporary English Novel,* believes that *Animal Farm* fails as successful satire "by virtue of its predictability," but this terrifying predictability of the fate of all revolutions is just the point Orwell is trying to make. The grotesque end of the fable is not meant to shock the reader—indeed, chance and surprise are banished entirely from Orwell's world. The horror of both *Animal Farm* and the later *1984* is precisely the cold, orderly, predictable process by which decency, happiness, and hope are systematically and ruthlessly crushed.

George Woodcock

SOURCE: *The Crystal Spirit: A Study of George Orwell,* Little, Brown and Company, 1966, pp. 190-98.

For more than six years, from the end of 1938 to early 1945, Orwell published neither fiction nor any important autobiographical writing, and even in terms of actual work there was a gap of more than four years between the termination of *Coming Up for Air* early in 1939 and the commencement of *Animal Farm* some time in 1943. Yet these were not wasted years for him, even as a writer. Nearly half the pieces in his *Collected Essays* were first published between 1939 and 1943, and almost all the others in this rather massive volume appeared between 1944 and 1947. To these eight busy years, in other words, belongs virtually all the critical writing Orwell considered important enough to preserve, plus a great many po-

litical essays and three polemical pamphlets (*The Lion and the Unicorn* in 1941, *James Burnham and the Managerial Revolution* in 1946, and *The English People* in 1947), plus the scores of uncollected articles and reviews which appeared in the *Tribune, Partisan Review, Observer, Manchester Evening News* (for which he did a weekly book column for two or three years) and a dozen small journals and little magazines. All this he did, it must be remembered, while he was still working either at the BBC or editorially at the *Tribune* and while he was allowing at least part of his spare time to be consumed by a series of "causes" from the Home Guard to the Freedom Defense Committee. His life was also expanding in other ways, for it was during this period that he ceased to be a real solitary, and though he never became a truly gregarious man, at least he now felt himself accepted on his own terms and built up that extraordinary variety of friendships which mellowed his final years. All these forms of action seemed to stimulate each other, and doubtless they were all stimulated by the atmosphere of the time, for the war years and the period immediately after peace, up to about the time when Orwell left for the Hebrides, were much more lively from a literary and a political point of view than the period from 1948 or 1949 down to the present.

In the case of Orwell it was not merely that he worked with immense energy and produced a great quantity of writings of various kinds. There was an extraordinary change in quality, which had been foreshadowed by *Homage to Catalonia,* also the product of a period of life in a peculiarly stimulating atmosphere. Orwell's expository writing became steadily clearer and more flexible, and his critical powers, first demonstrated impressively in the long 1939 essay on Charles Dickens, were inspired and informed by an awareness which he would call political, but which—seen in the perspective of the years—seems rather to have been moral in essence. Orwell was always a moralist, even at Eton if one is to accept Cyril Connolly's account of him in *Enemies of Promise,* and when he acquired political opinions they merely channeled his moralism, but by no means tamed it. The test always came when political expediency or party interests clashed with his ideas of what might be true or decent; most often—and always in his later years—it was party interest that he let go in favor of decency.

The influence of this moral-political awareness can be seen not merely in an increased sensitivity to the social and ethical dimensions of a book or a situation he might be discussing, but also in the directness of writing it began to foster, even when he turned back again near the end of the war from essays to fiction. He tried to write, as he put it, "less picturesquely and more exactly." And he gave a more definitely political character than before to the theme of caste and alienation which re-emerges, in varying forms, in all his late works, beginning with *Animal Farm.*

"Animal Farm," said Orwell in 1947, "was the first book in which I tried, with full consciousness of what I was doing, to fuse political purpose and artistic purpose in one whole." He succeeded admirably, and produced a book so clear in intent and writing that the critic is usually rather nonplussed as to what he should say about it; all is so magnificently there, and the only thing that really needs to be done is to place this crystalline little book into its proper setting.

Conciseness of form and simplicity of language are the qualities which immediately strike one on opening *Animal Farm* after having read Orwell's earlier works of fiction. The fable is about a third the length of *Keep the Aspidistra Flying,* though the events of which it tells are much more complicated, and it is written in a bare English, uncluttered by metaphor, which contrasts strongly with both the elaborately literary diction of *Burmese Days* and the racy but sometimes over-rich narrative style of *Coming Up for Air.*

> Mr. Jones, of the Manor Farm, had locked the henhouses for the night, but was too drunk to remember to shut the popholes. With the ring of light from his lantern dancing from side to side, he lurched across the yard, kicked off his boots at the back door, drew himself a last glass of beer from the barrel in the scullery, and made his way up to bed, where Mrs. Jones was already snoring.

So it begins, and so it continues to the end, direct, exact and sharply concrete, letting events make their own impacts and stimulating the creation of mental pictures, so that one remembers the book as a series of lively visual images held together by a membrane of almost transparent prose.

There was no doubt in Orwell's mind about his intention in writing *Animal Farm.* He felt that the English in 1943 were allowing their admiration for the military heroism of the Russians to blind them to the faults of the Communist regime, and he also believed that the Communists were using their position as unofficial representatives of Russia in England to prevent the truth from being known, as they had done in Spain. *Animal Farm* was meant to set his compatriots thinking again.

At that time Orwell was fascinated by the craft of pamphleteering, which had something of a wartime vogue among British writers, so that not only likely people, such as Orwell, Read and Spender, produced pamphlets, but even unlikely people such as Forster, Eliot and Henry Miller. Besides the three unimpressive and not very successful pamphlets which he himself wrote in the 1940's, Orwell edited with Reginald Reynolds an anthology of classic pamphlets from the past, entitled *British Pamphleteers;* he believed that a revival of pamphleteering was possible and desirable. In a pamphlet one could state a case simply and concisely, and it would stand on its own feet as no article in a periodical could ever do. But pamphleteering in fact never took on that new lease of life in the postwar years which Orwell had anticipated; this was due partly to lack of interest among the booksellers and partly to the devitalization of British politics after 1945.

Yet *Animal Farm,* which was really a pamphlet in fictional form, did succeed, because it created within the dimension of a fable a perfect and self-consistent microcosm. There was nothing very original about the basic idea of a community of animals acting like men, which had been used about fifteen hundred years before by the anonymous Indian author of that extraordinary collection of political fables, the *Panchatantra.* But, like the author of the *Panchatantra,* Orwell gave his work freshness by inducing that peculiar blend of humor, incongruity and apparent candor which creates in the reader a willingness to suspend disbelief and to transfer himself in mind into the changed dimensions of a world where the pursuits of men can be seen dispassionately because it is animals which are following them.

Orwell liked animals, though he detested the sentimental British animal cult. In his world picture animals, children, oppressed people stood on one side, and the oppressors, whether they were farmers, schoolteachers, sahibs or party bosses, on the other. In *Burmese Days* . . . the relationship of Asians to animals is quite clear, and later on in *Nineteen Eighty-Four* there were to be several identifications of proles with animals. "Proles and animals are free," runs one of the Party slogans, and O'Brien, Winston Smith's tormentor, voices the dogma of the Inner Party when he says that "the proletarians . . . are helpless, like the animals. Humanity is the Party. The others are outside—irrelevant." On the other hand, for Winston in his rebellion, an inestimable power seems to lie in "the animal instinct . . . that was the force that would tear the Party to pieces."

In *Animal Farm* it is the outsiders, the helpless ones, who rise in rebellion and destroy the power of the oppressors, personified in the drunken Mr. Jones. The idea of class division which in earlier books comes very near to the conception of two nations, rich and poor, is here modified to suggest two kinds—men and animals. "All men are enemies. All animals are comrades," says the prophetic old boar Major in his great oration shortly before the uprising.

The original division between man and animal corresponds to the old social division between hereditary upper and lower castes or classes which Orwell represented in his earlier works. But his experiences in Spain had led him to delve into the history of the development of power structures during revolutions, and on this subject he was now as knowledgeable as anyone outside the ranks of specialist historians. He had learned that social caste could be replaced by political caste, and *Animal Farm* is a study in fable form of this process at work in a minuscule world which we can observe as closely as a community of ants under the glass lid of a formicarium.

The history of the revolution betrayed in the animal world is based, therefore, partly on what Orwell had seen of the Communist usurpation of power in Spain and partly on what he had read of the Russian Revolution and its abortion by the Bolsheviks. But his anticommunism does not mean that he is on the side of the traditional ruling class, represented by men. On the contrary, when the animals originally rise in revolt against the tyrannical Farmer Jones, he wins our sympathies for them, and we remain on their side throughout their subsequent struggles with humanity, accepting the fact that no matter what the pigs may do, no animal wants to be ruled again by Farmer Jones or his kind.

Yet from the very first day of insurrection it is evident that a new elite is replacing the vanished human rulers—the elite of the pigs, who are the equivalent of the Party. Immediately they arrogate privileges to themselves—first a monopoly of milk, then of apples. They become supervisors, while the other animals, with the sole exception of that arch anticollectivist, the cat, do the work. The pigs, it should be noted, are united when it is a question of defending their rights as an elite against the other animals. Orwell had no intention of making *Animal Farm* an apology for Trotskyism, as he makes quite clear in a conversation which Julian Symons recorded:

> And just in case I had any illusions about his attitude, he pointed out that Trotsky-Snowball was potentially as big a villain as Stalin-Napoleon, although he was Napoleon's victim. The first note of corruption was struck, he said, when the pigs

secretly had the cows' milk added to their own mash, and Snowball consented to this first act of inequality.

The struggle between Snowball and Napoleon is in fact a struggle within the party elite whose final result, whichever had won, would have been the increased consolidation and centralization of power in the hands of the pigs. This is what happens when Napoleon outmaneuvers Snowball and immediately after his expulsion initiates the career of purges, atrocities and deepening tyranny that reproduces in minuscule the history of the Russian Revolution from 1917 to the 1940's.

At no point in *Animal Farm* does Orwell shift his side. Though it is a third-person story, as all fables are, the point of view of the reader is always nearest to that of the unprivileged animals, and perhaps nearest of all to that of Benjamin, the sad and cynical old donkey who sides with no factions and always says that "life would go on as it had always gone on—that is, badly." Yet despite his exposure of the mounting iniquities committed by the pig elite, Orwell never falls into the error of suggesting that the farmers are any better. On the contrary, there is really nothing to choose, and the book ends in that fantastic scene in which the pigs entertain the neighboring farmers in a social gathering, and the other animals, looking in, see a quarrel break out over cheating at cards.

> Twelve voices were shouting in anger, and they were all alike. No question, now, what had happened to the faces of the pigs. The creatures outside looked from pig to man, and from man to pig, and from pig to man again; but already it was impossible to say which was which.

In other words, old and new tyrannies belong to the same family; authoritarian governments, whether they are based on the codes of old social castes or on the rules of new political elites, are basically similar and present similar dangers to human welfare and to liberty. For the interests of oppressors are identical; as Mr. Pilkington jests at a more peaceful stage in the banquet, "If you have your lower animals to contend with, we have our lower classes!"

By transferring the problems of caste division outside a human setting, Orwell was able in *Animal Farm* to avoid the psychological complications inevitable in a novel, and thus to present his theme as a clear and simple political truth. In the process he left out one element which occurs in all his other works of fiction, the individual rebel caught in the machinery of the caste system. Not until he wrote *Nineteen Eighty-Four* did he elaborate the rebel's role in an *Animal Farm* carried to its monstrously logical conclusion.

Keith Alldritt

SOURCE: *The Making of George Orwell: An Essay in Literary History,* Edward Arnold, 1969, pp. 147-50.

Orwell became famous with the publication of *Animal Farm* in 1945. Upon this book, together with *Nineteen Eighty-Four* and the essays, his reputation continues chiefly to rest. Today it is very difficult to share the admiration with which *Animal Farm* was received when it first appeared. All the comparisons with *Gulliver's Travels* and *Candide* that are to be found in the contemporary reviews must now seem, twenty years on, extremely damaging to Orwell's book. And only when we recall that its publication coincided with the beginning of the Cold War does its instant success become understandable. Certainly as a mocking allegory of the first thirty years or so of the Russian revolution it is a work of considerable poise, a poise that derives from Orwell's long nurtured cynicism about communism, which had resisted the indulgent attitude to Russia born of the war-time alliance as much as it had resisted the fashionable communism of literary and intellectual circles during the thirties. But for the reader of today it is this very poise which makes the book trivial. The allegory is too pat, the confidence of the narrator (the confidence of one telling a nursery tale) too secure. Orwell's "fairy story" is only a clever form for expressing a set of opinions that have been held so long that they no longer admit the complexity of the experience they claim to explain.

The story of the humanised beasts of *Animal Farm* treats of events that are in many ways similar to those in which Orwell himself had participated in Spain. As in *Homage to Catalonia,* we have an account of a revolution created by a community undergoing persecution and deprivation. But idealism and communal energy and purpose do not long endure, we are told again, and the selfish and the unscrupulous take over the revolution and recreate the same sort of class system and exploitation which the revolution had overthrown. It is a measure of the poverty of *Animal Farm* that it does little more than rehearse these "points." In *Homage to Catalonia* such conclusions were merely one part of an intense and movingly evoked experience. But in *Animal Farm* they form the totality of what the book has to offer us. We

may perhaps derive some pleasure from elucidating the allegory. We may identify old Major, the aged porker who has the dream and who provides the ideological impulse to the revolution, as Karl Marx, and we may recognise the quarrel between Napoleon and Snowball as representing the rift between Stalin and Trotsky. And we may like to find the allegorical counterparts of the treason trials, the emergence of the Soviet secret police, the drive for technological achievement, the perversion of the ideals of the revolution and the misuse of propaganda. Nevertheless, if there is any pleasure in making such discoveries, it is hardly a literary pleasure. Indeed, in specifically literary terms, there is only one aspect of the book that continues to interest us and that is its form, and the particular tone of voice which this form enjoins upon the author. And the form is noteworthy not because of any particular distinction which it involves for the book, but rather because it is Orwell's first renewed effort to solve the problem of form in prose fiction which had been abandoned since the writing of *Coming Up For Air.*

Animal Farm is subtitled "A Fairy Story." Since the book does not tell of fairies, nor yet of the magical, this description seems hardly appropriate. Still it does suggest one intention of the book, which is to tell a story directly and simply. In this respect Orwell's purpose is a characteristic one, namely the vigorous sweeping aside of jargon, cant and hypocrisy and the presenting of issues clearly and intelligibly. But this sort of intention always has its attendant dangers and in the telling of his fairy story Orwell has succumbed to them. His account of revolution is greatly oversimplified; it is too obvious, too facile, too easy. For whatever we may think of the Russian revolution or, for that matter of any revolution, we cannot but be aware that the crises of a society are much more complex than Orwell is here able to suggest. And the feelings about revolution which the book elicits are as unsophisticated as the narrative itself. Take, for instance, the emotional climax of the book which comes when Boxer, the loyal and hard-working but unintelligent work horse, emblematic of "the common people," is sold to the knackers by the pig-commissars when he becomes too ill to work any more. The feelings of simple compassion and absolutely righteous indignation which this incident is calculated to evoke may be tolerable in a nursery tale that has no pretentions to being anything other than a nursery tale. But in one which lays claim to offer the adult intelligence some feeling for the realities of modern social and political life, they cannot, because of their crudity and sentimentality, merit serious attention. At the cost of this sort of oversimplification the sustained poise of the narrative is purchased. Clearly Orwell enjoys the easy confidence to which the position of a teller of nursery tales entitles him. The avuncular security and the poker-faced humour bestowed by the conventions of the form solve completely the difficult problem of the author-reader relationship which in the past had proved so troublesome. But in order to enjoy writing in this way, Orwell has made himself oblivious of the complexity of the experience with which his story purports to deal. He has here found a form which is easy and pleasing to him, but which is a means for turning away from the disturbing complexities of experience rather than for confronting them. It allows only of simple ideas, easy responses and obvious conclusions.

This particular form of the nursery story has been borrowed from that cosy world prior to the first World War upon which . . . Orwell was so ready to dwell. *Animal Farm* especially reminds us of Kipling's stories for children. The laws of the revolution that are painted on the wall of the cowshed and chanted by the animals clearly owe something to "The Law of the Jungle" in Kipling's *Second Jungle Book.* Indeed the central device of *Animal Farm,* the convention of humanised animals, may also derive most immediately from Kipling's *Jungle Book.* And Orwell's narrative tone is obviously modelled on that of the *Just So Stories.* And of course there is the Dickensian element, that traditional element which endures beneath the experimentalism in every one of Orwell's novels and shows the strength of the premodern and the unmodern in his literary sensibility. The humour of the book, when it is not "just so" humour, is Dickensian, achieved by the use of "the unnecessary detail" which Orwell in his critical essay had identified and given examples of and relished as "the unmistakable mark of Dickens's writing." For instance, an important stage in Comrade Napoleon's gradual abandonment of the principles of animalism occurs when he sits down at table to eat. But in relating this, Orwell tells just a little bit more; he "always ate," he tells us, "from the crown Derby dinner service which had been in the glass cupboard in the drawing room." This comic surface of the prose is the major effect of *Animal Farm.* The book is, in fact, a piece of literary self-indulgence. As a writer Orwell has here taken refuge in a simple, comfortable Edwardian form which allows him a perspective upon the modern world and a relationship with his reader which, however relaxed they may be, are neither engaging nor illuminating.

Robert A. Lee

SOURCE: *Orwell's Fiction,* University of Notre Dame Press, 1969, pp. 118-27.

In **"Why I Write"** (1947), Orwell remarked that "*Animal Farm* was the first book in which I tried, with full consciousness of what I was doing, to fuse political purpose and artistic purpose into one whole." Orwell's political purposes, though varied, had been consistently present to that point in his career; however, their infusion into his novels had been the obstacle he had to overcome to achieve fully realized and coherent art. The polemicist and essayist, concerned with political problems, causes, and effects, found the form of art difficult. And the struggle for appropriate form had become more crucial following Spain, as *Coming Up For Air* witnesses. For Orwell, politics had been a *sine qua non*; the common constituents of imaginative writing—character, image, narrative—were for him obstructions rather than guideposts. He is thinking of *Burmese Days,* for example, when he says that it is "invariably where I lacked a *political* purpose that I wrote lifeless books and was betrayed into purple passages, sentences without meaning, decorative adjectives and humbug generally." Yet we also know that Orwell's impulses were toward "artistic purpose." Furthermore, his intention in the last years of his life was purportedly "to make a complete break from his former polemical, propagandist, way of writing and to concentrate on the treatment of human relationships" [Tom Hopkinson, *George Orwell,* 1962]. Despite Hopkinson's notion of a "complete break"—obviously, given *Animal Farm* and *1984,* Orwell never denied politics completely—some purposes of the essayist never left him. But Orwell had come to realize that the stance of the polemicist, never long hidden even in his self-termed "naturalistic" novels, must be abandoned. And no form suited the abandonment of this role better than the beast fable: Not only was the narrator, the potential polemicist, gone, but the demands of the appropriate conventions provided an impersonality and distance which created art, not journalism.

That the beast fable was a natural choice for Orwell is borne out by John Wain [in his *Essays on Literature and Ideas,* 1963]. *Animal Farm* is

> . . . so remarkably similar in its tone, and in the balanced fairness of its judgments, to the critical essays as to be, almost, seen as one of them. It is, after all, a fable, and a fable is closer to criticism than to fiction in the full imaginative sense.

Yet this is surely not the whole truth. Imagination must be given a more important role than Wain is willing to ascribe to it; and the underlying requirements of this form seem to me to run exactly contrary to "balanced fairness," indeed one of the consistent aspects in Orwell's essays. The essential characteristic of the beast fable is irony: The form provides for the writer "the power to keep his reader conscious simultaneously of the human traits satirized and of the animals as animals" [Ellen Douglass Leyburn]. It demands of the reader a constant awareness of the double vision: Animal allegory prescribes two levels of perception which interact to purvey the irony in comparisons and contrasts. Orwell's essays are ironic only when they verge on fiction, as in the near-tales **"A Hanging"** and **"Shooting an Elephant."** In the kind of essays Wain has in mind, Orwell is honest and straightforward; the tone is that of the open, forthright speaker.

The use of this form provided an approach to art that Orwell clearly needed, one that differed from the conventional socially oriented novels he had been writing where he had fallen into pitfalls he now was recognizing. The need Orwell felt to criticize and attack social evils could now be subsumed into an artistic mode which by its very nature provided contrast and hence criticism. Paradoxically, the loss of a putative narrator and the gain of impersonalness that Orwell found in this form allow for a more intense criticism of social injustice and inequity than he had managed in his novels. The beast fable is in many ways the ideal form in which to articulate attack. The presence of beasts provides a ready-made vehicle for the tenor of the hatred in this essentially metaphorical mode. The correlation of a man, or a class of men, as swine or sheep allows savage hatred on the subnarrative level and concurrently provides the coolness of impersonalness in the facade of the narrative. As I. A. Richards says of the properly functioning metaphor [in *The Philosophy of Rhetoric* (1936)], the vehicle should not be "a mere embellishment of a tenor which is otherwise unchanged but the vehicle and tenor in co-operation give a meaning of more varied powers than can be ascribed to either."

Whatever Orwell gained artistically with *Animal Farm* was matched by the popular success the book enjoyed. It was the first of his books to achieve substantial commercial success, was a Book-of-the-Month Club selection in the United States, had a large sale, and was translated into many languages. Perhaps for the first time in his life, Orwell was moderately well off. The economic prosperity the book brought him was paralleled by critical accolades, and to this day *Animal Farm* is of all his works the most consistently praised. A judgment such as that of Frederick Karl, who finds the book a failure because of the "predictability" of the satire, is rare. The consensus of approval is represented by a spectrum of praise that ranges from Tom Hopkinson's pronouncements that not only is it "by far Orwell's finest book," but it is one of only two present-day books so good that before it "the critic abdicates," to Sir Richard Rees's only slightly less enthusiastic encomium that the book is a "little masterpiece" in form and style.

Because *Animal Farm* is so different from anything else that Orwell wrote, it is difficult to assess it in relation to his other works. It deserves much praise simply for succeeding despite the problems that this form and Orwell's particular use of it contain. I am thinking of the dangers of allegory in general and of the specific political allegory that informs *Animal Farm*. The principal danger of allegory in fiction is artificiality: The secondary level may demand such precise equivalents that it comes to dominate the tale, with the result that the primary narrative loses its pretense of reality and spontaneity. I think it is clear that this does not happen in *Animal Farm*. The allegory of the Russian Revolution and subsequent events is probably only noticeable to the eye which has been made aware of it.

Briefly, the narrative sets up equivalents with the history of political action in Russia from roughly 1917 to the Second World War. Major and Snowball are Lenin and Trotsky; Napoleon is Stalin; and the warring farms and farmers around Manor Farm naturally come to stand for Germany (Frederick) and the Allies (Pilkington). Certain events in the story are said to represent events of history: The timber deal, in which Frederick later reneges on the animals, is of course the short-lived Russo-German alliance of 1939; the card game at the end of the book is supposed to represent the Teheran Conference following the war. The correlations are more elaborate than this, and while there are some inconsistencies in the precise political allegory it is notable that one need pay little heed to this to understand the book in its full political significance. Instead of being just an allegory of twentieth-century Russian politics, *Animal Farm* is more meaningfully an anatomy of all political revolutions. As A. E. Dyson says, *Animal Farm* "is by no means about Russia alone. Orwell is concerned to show how revolutionary ideals of justice, equality and fraternity always shatter in the event." I would submit that the implications of this little book are wider yet: It is not merely that revolutions are self-destructive—Orwell also is painting a grim picture of the human condition in the political twentieth century, a time which he has come to believe marks the end of the very concepts of human freedom.

Nevertheless, the book starts with a relatively light tone. Mr. Jones—the commonplace name serves to diminish the importance of the human being in the story, yet gives a universal, "Everyman" quality—remembers to lock the henhouses for the night, but he is "too drunk to remember to shut the popholes." The picture of the drunken farmer, drinking his last glass of beer for the night and lurching up to bed while the animals come alive in the barn, reminds us of the cartoons (and Orwell's interest in the popular arts is surely at play here) and is primarily low keyed; at the same time, however, we note the irresponsibility of the farmer, neglecting—and endangering—those in his care. Later Jones will neglect to milk the cows, biologically a more serious omission; later yet, the pigs will also forget the milking, an ironic parallel that reveals the subsequent corruption of the revolution at the same time as it makes the pigs like humans—at that stage of the revolution a heinous sin. Nonetheless, the meeting of the animals while the humans sleep, though latently serious, forms a picture which is primarily whimsical. The description of the animals gathering for the meeting reveals the essential technique of the beast fable: Our concurrent awareness of both human and animal qualities and the several ironies which this perspective creates.

> The two cart-horses, Boxer and Clover, came in together, walking very slowly and setting down their vast hairy hoofs with great care lest there should be some small animal concealed in the straw. Clover was a stout motherly mare approaching middle life, who had never quite got her figure back after her fourth foal. Boxer was an enormous beast, nearly eighteen hands high, and as strong as any two ordinary horses put together. A white stripe down his nose gave him a somewhat stupid appearance, and in fact he was not of first-rate intelligence, but he was universally respected for his steadiness of character and tremendous powers of work.

The contrast beween the strength of the horses and the fragility of the smaller, hidden animals places the scene unmistakably in the beast world; at the same time, the description of Clover's failure to get back her figure, a phrase Orwell surely chose for its commonplace, cliche quality, is representative of radical human nature. The menagerie, in fact, demonstrates a spectrum of human qualities and types, from the pigs, who take up the front seats in the audience, to Benjamin the donkey, the cynic of the farm, and to Mollie, the white mare, vain and foolish. These introductory descriptions are woven into the structure of the plot: For her vanity, Mollie will ultimately be excluded from the farm; in his cynicism, Benjamin will come to see but be incapable of changing the reality of the revolution; and the pigs will come to occupy not only the front but the total of the farm.

The awareness of simultaneous levels of animal and human existence is nicely maintained by Orwell in all the story's aspects. Major's speech, describing his dream in which man has disappeared from the earth and is replaced by animals, is at once a logical demonstration of wish fulfillment in the dream at a bestial level and a gospel of economic revolution easily understandable at the human level. ("Man is the only creature that consumes without producing" is, of course, an ironic variation of Marxian anticapitalism.) Orwell reinforces this irony by having Major's speech full of biological analogies: "The life of an animal is misery and slavery: that is the plain truth. But is this simply part of the order of nature? Is it because this land of ours is so poor that it cannot afford a decent life to those who dwell upon it?" We slide back and forth between reading this as Marxian dogma, excoriating capitalism and calling for a proletarian revolution, and reading it in terms of the mistreated animals—and we are reminded of the irresponsibility of Farmer Jones.

Moreover, there is the possibility of a fourth kind of irony: In his reading of *1984* [in *Politics and the Novel* (1957)] Irving Howe remarks that Emmanuel Goldstein's book, *The Theory and Practice of Oligarchical Collectivism,* imitates Trotsky's style in "his fondness for using scientific references in nonscientific contexts." Although there is a slightly different usage here, the employment of biological language in a political context is obviously related. We begin to be aware of the complexity of this seemingly simple little book. It is not simple political allegory, but neither is it merely classical satire built on multiple or "receding planes." The various levels interact thematically: Animals are like humans; humans are, pejoratively, only like animals; human politics are really no more profound than natural biology.

The book is also constructed on a circular basis. Major's speech builds to the rhetorical climax of "All animals are comrades," which apothegm is immediately punctuated by the dogs' pursuit of some rats that they see. A vote is taken and the rats become "comrades," followed by the animals banding together against their common enemy, man, under the aegis of the motto, "All animals are equal." The remainder of the book will be a series of dramatic repudiations of these mottoes, a return to the tyranny and irresponsibility of the beginning. The only change will be in the identity of the masters, and, ironically, even that will be only partially changed.

At the opening of the second chapter Major dies, the prophet who articulated the revolutionary ideals and in whose name they will be carried out—and perverted. Snowball and Napoleon, two pigs, assume the leadership of the rebellion, aided by their public-relations man, Squealer. And these three codify the ideals of Major into Animalism, "a complete system of thought." But Animalism, obviously analogous to communism, is significantly instituted without any plan. The rebellion occurs spontaneously: Once again Jones neglects to feed the animals, who break into the barn for food when "they could stand it no longer." Jones and his hired man come in and the animals, "with one accord, though nothing of the kind had been planned beforehand," attack the men and chase them off the farm. "And so almost before they knew what was happening, the Rebellion had been successfully carried through: Jones was expelled, and the Manor Farm was theirs." Orwell stresses the spontaneity of the Rebellion to make clear that the social revolution *per se* is not the object of his satire. He emphasizes that no matter how bad things become for the animals later—and they do become bad—the animals "were far better off than they had been in the days of Jones." Though this fact will itself have to be qualified, there is a justness in the statement. Not only does the revolution's spontaneity diminish the importance of Napoleon and Snowball's plotting—and thus provide a dramatic irony about their supposed accomplishments—but the motive, hunger, justifies the revolution more basically and irrefutably than the soundest of political theories. The revolution sprung, not from theory, but from real, natural need. No matter how corrupt the ideals of the revolution become, Orwell never questions the validity of the uprising: The target here is not social—and socialistic—revolution, contrary to the many who simply want to see the book as a satire of communism, but rather the target is the inability of humans to live within a community of ideals.

The inevitable corruption of the revolution is presaged immediately. The animals have driven out their former masters.

> For the first few minutes the animals could hardly believe in their good fortune. Their first act was to gallop in a body right round the boundaries of the farm, as though to make quite sure that no human being was hiding anywhere upon it; then they raced back to the farm buildings to wipe out the last traces of Jones's hated reign. The harness-room at the end of the stables was broken open; the bits, the nose-rings, the dog-chains, the cruel knives with which Mr. Jones had been used to castrate the pigs and lambs, were all flung down the well. The reins, the halters, the blinkers, the degrading nosebags, were thrown on to the rub-

bish fire which was burning in the yard. So were the whips. All the animals capered with joy when they saw the whips going up in flames.

The reaction is understandable; but the description of the inevitable and immediate violence that seems to follow all revolutions foreshadows that this revolution will suffer the common fate of its genre: reactionary cruelty, the search for the scapegoat, the perversion of the ideals of the revolution, and the counter-revolution. Thus, the good intentions of the animals are immediately endangered when it is learned that the pigs "had taught themselves to read and write from an old spelling book which had belonged to Mr. Jones's children" [the critic adds in a footnote that "it is noteworthy that these children never appear in the book: They obviously would enjoy a natural sympathy that would be contrary to the antipathy the humans receive in the fable"]. The pigs' reading ability is a valuable skill for the animals, one which is necessary to run a farm, even for animals. But it is also patently a human attribute, and one which already violates one of Major's cardinal tenets: "Remember also that in fighting against Man, we must not come to resemble him."

If seeds of destruction are immediately present, the positive aspects of the rebellion achieve their high peak with the codification of the "unalterable law by which all the animals on Animal Farm must live for ever after," the Seven Commandments.

> 1. Whatever goes upon two legs is an enemy.
> 2. Whatever goes upon four legs, or has wings, is a friend.
> 3. No animal shall wear clothes.
> 4. No animal shall sleep in a bed.
> 5. No animal shall drink alcohol.
> 6. No animal shall kill any other animal.
> 7. All animals are equal.

This "unalterable law" provides the major structural basis for the rest of the fable. From this point on the plot reveals a gradual alteration of these commandments, ending in the well-known contradiction that epitomizes the new nature of the farm at the end of the book. But here, Orwell's technique is of immediate irony: The animals are watching the commandments being painted on the barn when the cows begin to low, needing to be milked. They are milked, and the milk is placed in front of the animals, at which many "looked with considerable interest." But Napoleon, "placing himself in front of the buckets," will not even mix it with the hens' mash, as "Jones used sometimes to," and it disappears, eventually into Napoleon's own mash. Selfishness is the note on which the chapter concludes, following the spontaneous and successful take-over of the farm and the articulation of unselfish ideals by which all the animals are to live.

The next concern on Animal Farm is to get the hay in, and we see further spoiling of the revolution's ideals as the pigs supervise rather than work. From the beginning, all animals are *not* equal. But one must be careful. In light of what is to happen, it is easy to see that the pigs' managerial role is further foreshadowing of the ultimate perversion of the seventh commandment, but this does not mean that the revolution is therefore wrong, or that Orwell thinks that all revolutions are inevitably self-corrupting. Both farms and revolutions need leaders, managers; and, for all their evil, the pigs are the most capable animals on the farm. Orwell may be suggesting—and this would be far more profound—that capable people are inevitably evil; or, conversely, that evil people are inevitably the most capable.

The capability of the pigs, and their management, is reflected in the success of the farm: There is no wastage, no stealing. It is the biggest harvest in the farm's history; in addition, though the animals work hard, there is no leisure. Each animal works "according to his capacity." The Marxian slogan at the base of the success of the farm seems to me to prove conclusively that Orwell does not question socialistic ideology. He does question the failure of ideology to accommodate human variety, implicit in the missing half of the quotation. At this point, Orwell specifically avoids mention of what goes *to* each animal: The irony of "need" is already apparent in what the pigs have taken and will be reinforced by the future miniscule gains of the other animals.

Orwell further stresses the human variability which undermines the best—or the worst—of systems in the character of Mollie, the vain mare more interested in ribbons than in harvests, and in the description of the cat, who disappears when there is work to be done. It is important that these animals are portrayed kindly and humorously: The cat, for example, "always made such excellent excuses, and purred so affectionately, that it was impossible not to believe in her good intentions." We soon learn the real nature of these "good intentions." The cat is spied one day talking to some sparrows who were "just out of her reach. She was telling them that all animals were now comrades and that any sparrow who chose could come and perch on her paw; but the sparrows kept their distance." We are reminded again of the natural, biological basis of the revolution—and remembering this we cannot blame the cat. If this attempt by the

cat is at one level an ironic mirror of the pigs' later, horrifying "education" of the puppies into vicious trained killers, it is simultaneously natural—which the pigs' deed is not. Orwell reminds us of natural instinct and its inevitable conflict with political absolutism. It is to the point that Mollie soon leaves the farm. She is seen one day being stroked by a human on the outskirts of the farm; Clover finds sugar and several ribbons hidden under the straw in her stall. And so Mollie disappears, to be seen pulling a cart, her coat "newly clipped and she wore a scarlet ribbon around her forelock. She appeared to be enjoying herself, so the pigeons said." In political terms, she is, of course, a heretic, and her selfish behavior is inconsistent with selfless social ideals. But there is no intention on Orwell's part to criticize her. He rather suggests that too strict attention to the harsh, social demands of life obscures the love of beauty in the world. Any criticism seems rather to be directed at a political norm which makes the esthete the apostate.

For political and social demands do dominate life at Manor Farm; and the demands become more complex. Pilkington and Frederick spread stories about horrible conditions on the farm, stories which are contradicted by rumors among their animals about the wonderful paradise that exists on Animal Farm. Neither set of rumors is true, of course, and Orwell develops the consequences of such misrepresentation. The Farmers' animals begin to revolt in varying degrees—"bulls which had always been tractable suddenly turned savage, sheep broke down hedges and devoured the clover . . . ," while the humans, hearing in the song of Animal Farm "a prophecy of their future doom," invade the farm. It is not the social situations or conflicting ideologies that Orwell concerns himself with, but the misrepresentations, the falsification and distortion of fact, which he indicates leads ineluctably to disaster and misery. Falsification is at the heart of the main internal struggle on the farm, and the way fact is distorted and misrepresented is graphically pictured in the rivalry between Snowball and Napoleon over the construction of the windmill.

Snowball (who is a brilliant orator, compared with Napoleon, who was "better at canvassing support for himself in between times") conceives of a plan for a windmill, which Napoleon graphically disdains (he urinates on the plans). At the meeting in which the final vote for approval is to be taken, nine enormous dogs, "as ferocious as wolves," suddenly appear and chase Snowball off the farm; the dogs return and sit by Napoleon, wagging their tails, "as the other dogs had been used to do with Mr. Jones." And it is just a short time until Squealer appears to announce blandly that Napoleon, "who had advocated it from the beginning," himself proposes the building of the windmill. More is suggested here than the simple power struggle attendant on all revolutions, or the more specific over-throw of Trotsky, the party theoretician and planner, by calculating Stalin. The symbol of the windmill suggests much about Orwell's complex attitudes toward the political concepts within the story well beyond the primary irony of the pigs' manipulation of the hopes of *Animal Farm's* animals. The windmill has Quixotic overtones: Orwell suggests that the way the animals focus all their efforts on building it is a false and deluded if heroic struggle. The windmill becomes the means by which Napoleon controls deviation; he uses it to direct the animals' attention away from the growing shortages and inadequacies on the farm, and the animals ignorantly concentrate all their efforts on building the windmill—but its symbolic nature suggests an empty concentration, a meaningless, unheroic effort, for the idea is literally misguided.

At the same time the symbol works in other directions. The windmill is analogous in the political allegory to the New Economic Policy. As such, it functions in much the same way as do other symbols of secular paradise in twentieth-century writing. Dams and bridges replace churches as representations of man's hopes for eternity; the windmill becomes a symbol of "secular heaven," placed in the future, but now in a temporal sense. . . .

The construction of the windmill, its subsequent destruction in a storm (during which the hens hear a gun go off in the background; the allusion is probably to World War I), and its rebuilding provide the linear movement of the plot in the rest of the book. The thematic development is centered on the progressive alteration of the Seven Commandments. Two monstrous indignities are suffered by the animals, but even these are thematically secondary. There is a bitter winter on the farm and rations become scarce: "starvation seemed to stare them in the face." A scapegoat is needed, and Snowball is conveniently used by Napoleon—who blatantly tells the other animals that not only is Snowball responsible for all the mysterious destruction that suddenly begins to occur on the farm, but that his brave actions in fighting the humans at the Battle of the Cowshed, *which all the animals witnessed,* had never happened. This is, of course, a direct prevision of the rewriting of history in *1984.* "Four days later," after being warned by Napoleon that Snowball's secret agents are still among them, the animals are ordered to assemble in the yard. Suddenly the dogs attack four of the other pigs and Boxer; but Boxer easily fights them off.

Presently the tumult died down. The four pigs waited, trembling, with guilt written on every line of their countenances. Napoleon now called upon them to confess their crimes. They were the same four pigs as had protested when Napoleon abolished the Sunday Meetings. Without any further prompting they confessed that they had been secretly in touch with Snowball ever since his expulsion, that they had collaborated with him in destroying the windmill, and that they had entered into an agreement with him to hand over Animal Farm to Mr. Frederick. They added that Snowball had privately admitted to them that he had been Jones's secret agent for years past. When they had finished their confession, the dogs promptly tore their throats out, and in a terrible voice Napoleon demanded whether any other animal had anything to confess.

In an obvious parallel to the purge trials of the 1930's, three hens come forward and admit to having heard Snowball speak to them "in a dream"; they are slaughtered. A goose confesses to pilfering six ears of corn, followed by a sheep who, "urged to do this" by Snowball, had urinated in the drinking pool, in turn followed by two more sheep who had murdered a ram. "And so the tale of confessions and executions went on, until there was a pile of corpses lying before Napoleon's feet and the air was heavy with the smell of blood, which had been unknown there since the expulsion of Jones."

Orwell has managed to dramatize, in two short, terror-laden pages, the very essence of this strange psycho-political phenomenon of our times: the ritualistic, honestly believed but obviously spurious confession. The ramifications of the motif in contemporary literature are many: One is reminded of a parallel such as Rubashov in *Darkness at Noon* and that, in a political age which denies individual selfhood, the only way of asserting one's self may be through pain or its extension, death. Ontologically and eschatologically, it may be preferable to die horribly and perhaps anonymously than to live as a cipher. However, I wish to consider the relative *insignificance* of the horrors that have passed, as physical terror becomes thematically subsidiary to the falsification of history and the denial of objective reality. Following this scene, the animals leave, led by Boxer and Clover. Boxer, unable to understand, thinks it "must be due to some fault in ourselves. The solution, as I see it, is to work harder." And so he trots up to the windmill to resume dragging loads of stone to it. The other animals huddle about Clover on the hillside.

It was a clear spring evening. The grass and the bursting hedges were gilded by the level rays of the sun. Never had the farm—and with a kind of surprise they remembered that it was their own farm, every inch of it their own property—appeared to the animals so desirable a place.

Clover, looking down on this scene, remembers the promise and the hope of the revolution on the night she heard Major's speech, and her thoughts sum up the earlier images of the strong mare protecting the ducklings and recall the maxim at the base of the society, "Each working according to his capacity, the strong protecting the weak." Even here, she has "no thought of rebellion or disobedience," for the fundamental value of the revolution is reasserted: "Even as things were, they were far better off than they had been in the days of Jones." But the phrase "even as things were" implies too much, and so Clover, trying to somehow reestablish her continuity with that now quickly changing past, "feeling this to be in some way a substitute for the words she was unable to find," begins to sing the song, *Beasts of England,* which epitomized the egalitarian ideals Major expounded. The animals are singing the song when Squealer appears to announce that "by a special decree of Comrade Napoleon, *Beasts of England* had been abolished." Squealer tells the astonished animals that the reason is that "in *Beasts of England* we expressed our longing for a better society in days to come. But that society has now been established. Clearly this song had no longer any purpose."

The irony is of course the claim for a "better society," as the animals sit in the shadow of the heap of freshly slaughtered corpses. But the implications are more profound. Terror, bestiality, senseless death are all dreadful and shattering experiences; but they are at least comprehensible and do not radically alter the conceptualized values of the survivors. Far more terrifying is the overt alteration of consciousness which follows the slaughter, the blatant misrepresentation of the past, *which goes unchallenged.* The animals can only "sense" that the new song ("Animal Farm, Animal Farm / Never through me shalt thou come to harm") is different from *Beasts of England.* Squealer's pronouncement that the "better society" has now been established is uncontroverted. The commandments, which have begun to be altered recently, are now more rapidly and unquestioningly changed—and change pervades Animal Farm. A proposed timber deal vacillates between Pilkington and Frederick until the animals are forced to admit "a certain bewilderment, but Squealer was soon able to convince them that their memories had been at fault." Ironically, one of Major's prescriptions had been not to indulge in trade with the humans. Here the animals are not even sure whom the trade is with, much less can they remember past dogma.

The animals can no longer recognize reality, but they somehow manage to finish the windmill, concurrent with Napoleon's double-dealing with Pilkington and Frederick. We see the simultaneous strength and weakness, the goodness and corruption, that has evolved from the original rebellion. Despite all, the animals finish the windmill—they can accomplish a nearly impossible task—but at the same time, Napoleon, cheating and being cheated in his dealing, precipitates an attack upon the farm by Frederick and his followers (World War II, in the allegory). Though the animals win the battle, many are grievously injured and the windmill is destroyed. But Squealer declares that they have a "victory," "we have won back what we had before." And so the animals celebrate—each is given an apple, two ounces of corn for each bird, and three biscuits for each dog—while Napoleon gets drunk. The mere inequity, the surface irony is compounded by the inevitable falsification of fact. The next morning the animals discover that the fifth commandment did not read, as they had thought, "No animal shall drink alcohol," but instead "No animal shall drink alcohol *to excess.*"

It is not the threat of violence, even the radically inexplicable self-violence which the deracinated individual must, ironically, bring upon himself for his own secular salvation in a wholly political world, nor the war, nor the social injustice that man is suffering that is the cancer of our times, but the loss of "objective truth." Choices vanish in a society which has no bases for choice.

The most darkly pessimistic aspect of *Animal Farm* is that the animals are unable even to recognize their new oppression, much less combat it. The difference is that the pigs control language; Mr. Jones controlled only action—not thought. Orwell portrays at least three animals as being potentially able to stand up to the state (in an admittedly limited yet meaningful way), yet each is inadequate in a vital respect. Boxer has probably enough power and strength to overthrow Napoleon's regime. When Napoleon's vicious dogs attack him, Boxer simply "put out his great hoof, caught a dog in midair, and pinned him to the ground. The dog shrieked for mercy and the other two fled with their tails between their legs." But Boxer is stupid; he cannot comprehend the present, much less conceptualize the past. He ingenuously looks to Napoleon to see whether or not he should let the dog go; when the slaughter is over, he retreats to work, thinking the fault must lie within the animals. Thus, his fate is not as pathetic, as some critics read the scene in which he is taken away, kicking in the truck, as it is the inevitable fate of utter stupidity. The most complex thought that Boxer can express is "if Comrade Napoleon says it, it must be right," in the face of blatant, gross falsification. Boxer's basic goodness, social self-sacrifice, and impressive strength are simply inadequately used; the stupidity which wastes them suggests interesting qualifications about Orwell's reputed love of the common man, qualifications which become even stronger when considered in light of the descriptions of the proles in *1984.*

Clover is more intelligent and perceptive than is Boxer, but she has a corresponding lack of strength. Her "character" is primarily a function of her sex: Her instincts are maternal and pacifistic. She works hard, along with the other animals, but there is no picture of any special strength, as there is with Boxer. And even with a greater intelligence, her insights are partial. Things may indeed be better than they "had been in the days of Jones," but, in the context of the slaughter of the animals, "it was not for this that she and all the other animals had hoped and toiled." Both perceptions are right, but both are incomplete. In both cases, Clover senses that there is something further to be understood, but just as Boxer uncomprehendingly moves to toil, so does Clover wistfully retreat to song—only to have this articulation of the past's ideals suddenly changed, without her dissent. A paradigm appears: Boxer is marked by great strength and great stupidity; Clover has less physical power but has a corresponding increase in awareness; the equation is completed with Benjamin, who sees and knows most—perhaps all—but is physically ineffectual and socially irresponsible.

Benjamin, the donkey, "was the oldest animal on the farm, and the worst tempered. He seldom talked, but when he did, it was usually to make some cynical remark. . . . " As archetypal cynic, Benjamin remains aloof and distant, refusing to meddle in the farm's affairs, but seeing all. He expresses no opinion about the rebellion; he works on Animal Farm "in the same slow, obstinate way" that he did on Manor Farm; he only remarks enigmatically that "Donkeys live a long time." Beneath the surface cynicism, he is, almost predictably, blessed with a heart of gold: He is devoted to Boxer, and it is he who discovers the plot to deliver Boxer to the glue-maker. But Benjamin is essentially selfish, representing a view of human nature that is apolitical, and thus he can hardly be the voice of Orwell within the book, as some readers hold. To Benjamin, the social and political situation is irrelevant: Human nature suffers and prospers in the same degree, no matter who is the master. He believes "that things never had been, nor ever could be much better or much worse—hunger, hardship, and disappointment being, so he said, the unalterable law of life." We know too much about Orwell's social beliefs from other contexts to assume that Benjamin speaks for Orwell here. Yet it is only fair to note that Benjamin sees most, knows most, is obviously the most intelligent and perceptive of all the animals on the farm, including the pigs. To a certain extent, he represents intelligence without the effectuating and necessary strength; perhaps more profoundly, he demonstrates the Orwellian heinous sin of irresponsible intelligence. The posture of assuming that only the very worst is inevitable in life, that change for the better is a delusion, and that the only alternative is a retreat into a social self-pity is exactly the posture from which Orwell presumptively jerks Gordon Comstock in *Keep the Aspidistra Flying.*

With the means of opposition to Napoleon's totalitarian rule so portrayed, there is little suspense in the outcome of the situation the novel describes. Years pass. Jones dies in an inebriate's home; Boxer and Snowball are forgotten by nearly all, for a new generation of animals has grown up. The situation on the farm is unchanged for most of the animals. The farm is more prosperous now, but the fruits of prosperity never pass beyond Napoleon and his comrades. And the attempt to judge whether the present situation is better or worse than it had been under Jones is fruitless.

> Sometimes the older ones among them racked their dim memories and tried to determine whether in the early days of the Rebellion, when Jones's expulsion was still recent, things had been better or worse than now. They could not remember. There was nothing with which they could compare their present lives: they had nothing to go upon except Squealer's lists of figures, which invariably demonstrated that everything was getting better and better.

Again, the condition itself is not as depressing as the loss of the rational criteria which allow evaluation. The denial of memory enables control of the present, and hence of the future.

"And yet the animals never gave up hope." For they do retain one ineradicable achievement: equality. "If they went hungry, it was not from feeding tyrannical human beings; if they worked hard, at least they worked for themselves. No creature among them went on two legs. No creature called any other 'master.' All animals were equal." The social and economic hopes of the revolution may have become lost in the actualities of history, but the primary political gain of the revolution remains valid for the animals. Orwell articulates this one, final achievement of the animals. But within a page Squealer and Napoleon appear, walking on their hind legs. Yet even this sight is not the final violation of hope. Clover and Benjamin walk around to the barn to read the seventh commandment:

ALL ANIMALS ARE EQUAL BUT SOME ANIMALS ARE MORE EQUAL THAN OTHERS

After this, "it did not seem strange" that the pigs take the humans' newspapers, that the pigs dress like humans, invite neighboring humans in to feast and drink, that the name of the farm is changed back to Manor Farm, and that, in the final image of the book, the pigs become indistinguishable from the humans. The book has come full circle, and things are back as they were. If this is so, Benjamin's judgment becomes valid: Things do remain the same, never much worse, never much better; "hunger, hardship, and disappointment" are indeed the "unalterable law of life."

Power inevitably corrupts the best of intentions, apparently no matter who possesses the power: At the end, all the representatives of the various ideologies are indistinguishable—they are all pigs, all pigs are humans. Communism is no better and no worse than capitalism or fascism; the ideals of socialism were long ago lost in Clover's uncomprehending gaze over the farm. Religion is merely a toy for the corrupters, neither offensive nor helpful to master or slave. But perhaps more distressing yet is the realization that everyone, the good and the bad, the deserving and the wicked, are not only contributors to the tyranny, are not only powerless before it, but are unable to understand it. Boxer thinks that whatever Napoleon says is right; Clover can only vaguely feel, and cannot communicate, that things are not exactly right; Benjamin thinks that it is in the nature of the world that things go wrong. The potential hope of the book is finally expressed only in terms of ignorance (Boxer), wistful inarticulateness (Clover), or the tired, cynical belief that things never change (Benjamin). The inhabitants of this world seem to deserve their fate.

One must finally ask, however, with all this despair and bleakness what are the actual bases for the tyranny of Animal Farm. Is the terrorism of the dogs the most crucial aspect? Is it this that rules the animals? Boxer's power is seen as superior to this violence and force. Is the basis of the tonal despair the pessimistic belief in the helplessness of the mass of the animals? Orwell elsewhere states again and again his faith in the common people. It seems to me that the basis of this society's evil is the inability of its

inhabitants to ascertain truth and that this is demonstrated through the theme of the corruption of language. So long as the animals cannot remember the past, because it is continually altered, they have no control over the present and hence over the future. A society which cannot control its language is, says Orwell, doomed to be oppressed in terms which deny it the very most elemental aspects of humanity: To live in a world which allows the revised form of the seventh commandment of Animal Farm is not merely to renounce the belief in the possibility of human equality, but in the blatant perversion of language, the very concept of objective reality is lost.

The mode by which the recognition of reality is denied is the corruption of language. When a society no longer maintains its language as a common basis by which value, idea, and fact are to be exchanged, those who control the means of communication have the most awful of powers—they literally can create the truth they choose. *Animal Farm,* then, seems to be in one respect only an extension of *Burmese Days*— the common problem is the failure of communication and its corollary, community. But if in *Burmese Days* their failure was contingent, in *Animal Farm* it is brought about by willful manipulation. The next logical step is seen in *1984,* where the consequences press to the premonition of apocalypse.

Alex Zwerdling

SOURCE: *Orwell and the Left,* Yale University Press, 1974, pp. 88-96.

Much of Trotsky's book *[The Revolution Betrayed]* expounds a theory of the inevitable *stages* of revolution, a subject that haunted Orwell's imagination and was finally to produce *Animal Farm.* Trotsky constantly compares the Russian and French revolutions, and finds many similarities in their development. Nor is he averse to generalization: "It is sufficiently well known that every revolution up to this time has been followed by a reaction, or even a counter-revolution. This, to be sure, has never thrown the nation all the way back to its starting-point, but it has always taken from the people the lion's share of their conquests. The victims of the first reactionary wave have been, as a general rule, those pioneers, initiators, and instigators who stood at the head of the masses in the period of the revolutionary offensive." A pessimistic observer might modify Marx's theory that revolutions are the engines of history by commenting that some of the trains seemed to shuttle back and forth between two fixed points. But Trotsky insists that even in the inevitable counter-revolution, the nation is never brought *all* the way back to its starting point.

In Orwell's speculations about revolution as a method for achieving socialist goals, this was one of the major points at issue. He became far less confident than Trotsky that real progress was achieved through revolution, and his own view at times approaches Lord Acton's gloomy conviction that every revolution "makes a wise and just reform impossible." As early as 1938, the central idea of *Animal Farm* was running through Orwell's mind: "It would seem that what you get over and over again is a movement of the proletariat which is promptly canalised and betrayed by astute people at the top, and then the growth of a new governing class. The one thing that never arrives is equality. The mass of the people never get the chance to bring their innate decency into the control of affairs, so that one is almost driven to the cynical thought that men are only decent when they are powerless." Clearly Orwell still hesitates to accept this idea: he says he is "almost driven" to it. It remained an unresolved issue in his mind for years, and one can see why. His socialist faith made him need to deny it; his temperamental pessimism must have found it congenial. He could neither resolve the question nor forget it—perhaps the ideal condition for the creation of a vital literary work.

Orwell's uncertainty about revolution eventually produced *Animal Farm* and was responsible for the considerable ambiguity of the book. An ironic allegory is bound to mystify many of its readers, no matter how easy it is to identify the historical parallels on which it is based. We know that Orwell had a great deal of difficulty getting *Animal Farm* into print, and it is generally assumed that publishers rejected it because they did not want to publish an anti-Soviet satire in the middle of the war. Yet T. S. Eliot's letter of rejection from Faber makes it clear this was not the only problem the book raised. Eliot complains that "the effect is simply one of negation. It ought to excite some sympathy with what the author wants, as well as sympathy with his objections to something: and the positive point of view, which I take to be generally Trotskyite, is not convincing." He goes on to suggest that Orwell "splits his vote" by refusing to confirm any of the standard Western attitudes toward the Soviet Union.

Eliot's argument suggests a thoroughly confused sense of Orwell's purpose. If *Animal Farm* can be said to have a "positive point of view" at all, it is certainly not Trotskyite: Snowball is hardly its tragic hero. The difficulties of understanding *Animal Farm* largely stem from its interpretation as an exclusive attack on the Soviet Union. Orwell's purpose, however, is more general: he is interested in tracing the inevitable stages of any revolution, and he shapes his

fable accordingly. This is not to deny that the literal level of the story is almost exclusively based on Soviet history. But although Russia is his immediate target, Orwell says the book "is intended as a satire on dictatorship in general." He was faithful to the details of Soviet history, yet he did not hesitate to transform some of its most important elements.

The most striking of these is the omission of Lenin from the drama. Major (the idealist visionary who dies before the revolution takes place) is clearly meant to represent Marx, while Napoleon and Snowball act out the conflict in the postrevolutionary state between Stalin and Trotsky. Lenin is left out, it seems to me, because Orwell wants to emphasize the enormous disparity between the ideals of the revolution and the reality of the society it actually achieves. Lenin was the missing link in this process, both visionary and architect of the new state, but from Orwell's longer historical perspective, his brief period of power must have seemed like an irrelevant interlude in the stark drama that was unfolding. The heirs of Lenin had in fact begun to transform him into a myth even before he was dead; they legitimized their power by worshipping at his shrine. In order to demythify the Russian Revolution and present the Bolshevik leaders as they really were, Orwell must have felt compelled to eliminate the mythical hero altogether.

Such radical departures from history are of course Orwell's prerogative in constructing a story intended to have more general significance. He says in a preface to *Animal Farm* that "although the various episodes are taken from the actual history of the Russian Revolution, they are dealt with schematically and their chronological order is changed; this was necessary for the symmetry of the story." One might add that it was also necessary in order to achieve Orwell's purpose in writing it. This raises the question of how the topical and generic levels of satire in the book are related, and one might clarify the issue by citing the case of Swift, who was in some sense Orwell's model.

When *Gulliver's Travels* was first published, many read the book as an essentially partisan political document, a propaganda piece for the opposition party. Yet Swift himself wrote to his French translator that, if *Gulliver's Travels* could only be understood in England, it was a failure, for "the same vices and the same follies reign everywhere . . . and the author who writes only for a city, a province, a kingdom, or even an age, deserves so little to be translated, that he does not even deserve to be read." In the same way, *Animal Farm* is concerned both with the Russian Revolution and, by extension, with the general pattern of revolution itself. As the Stalinist period recedes into the distant past, Orwell's book (if it survives as a literary work) will more and more be appreciated as generic rather than topical satire, just as *Gulliver's Travels* has come to be.

Orwell chose to write his book in the form of a fable partly to give the pattern of historical events permanent mythic life, to emphasize that he was dealing with typical, not fortuitous, events. He is interested in constructing a paradigmatic social revolution, and the pattern that emerges is meant to apply to the Spanish Civil War and to the French Revolution (the main character, after all, is named Napoleon) as well as to the Russian one. Orwell's story suggests that revolutions inevitably go through several predictable stages. They begin with great idealistic fervor and popular support, energized by millennial expectations of justice and equality. The period immediately following a successful revolution is the Eden stage. There is a sense of triumphant achievement; idealistic vision is translated into immediate reality; the spirit of community and equality are everywhere apparent. Old law and institutions are broken and replaced by an inner, yet reliable, concern for the common good. The state has, for the moment, withered away.

Slowly the feeling of freedom gives way to the sense of necessity and bondage, "we" becomes "I-they," spirit turns into law, improvised organization is replaced by rigid institutions, equality modulates to privilege. The next stage is the creation of a new elite which, because of its superior skill and its lust for power, assumes command and re-creates the class structure. Its power is first universally granted but gradually must be upheld against opposition by terror and threat. As time goes on, the past is forgotten or expunged; the new elite takes on all the characteristics of the old, prerevolutionary leadership, while the rest of the society returns to the condition of servitude. The transition is too gradual to be dramatic, although it has its dramatic moments, and it is constantly presented in the guise of historical inevitability or as a necessary response to conspiracy or external danger. A scapegoat is found to explain the disparity between ideal and actual. The exploited class remains exploited basically because of its doggedness and stupidity but also because, having no taste for power, it is inevitably victimized by the power-hungry. In every new society—even if it consists exclusively of those without previous experience of power—some will rise above their fellows and assume the available positions of authority. When their power and privileges are consolidated, they will fight to keep them. The only surviving vestiges of revolution will be its rhetoric and its (conveniently altered) history. The reality of "equality" and "justice" will have withered away, to be replaced by the state.

"The effect," Eliot had said, "is simply one of negation." His objection raises the question of whether *Animal Farm* should be considered in moral terms at all. At this point in his career Orwell's mind had begun to work in an increasingly analytic way. He was interested in understanding the structure of revolution rather than in proposing a better way to achieve social goals. Eliot complains that the book fails to "excite some sympathy with what the author wants." Yet great satire has often been written out of the despairing sense that "what the author wants" may be unattainable. Orwell's socialism is not an act of faith. If he has a "positive point of view" at all in writing *Animal Farm,* it is the hope that socialists will be able to face the hard truths he presents rather than continue to accept the various consoling illusions their movement has generated to account for its disappointments.

And yet realism is not his only goal; he is also finally a moralist. In the essay on Dickens, Orwell makes an important distinction between the moralist and the revolutionary, which I take to be crucial for an understanding of his purpose in *Animal Farm.* Dickens, he says, is a moralist: "It is hopeless to try and pin him down to any definite remedy, still more to any political doctrine. . . . Useless to change institutions without a 'change of heart'—that, essentially, is what he is always saying." Orwell realized that the need for a "change of heart" has been used as "*the alibi of people who do not wish to endanger the status quo,*" but he insists, that this does not make Dickens a reactionary apologist. The paradox can only be explained by understanding the writer's relation to the moment in which he writes:

> I said earlier that Dickens is not *in the accepted sense* a revolutionary writer. But it is not at all certain that a merely moral criticism of society may not be just as "revolutionary"—and revolution, after all, means turning things upside down—as the politico-economic criticism which is fashionable at this moment. Blake was not a politician, but there is more understanding of the nature of capitalist society in a poem like "I wander through each charter'd street" than in three-quarters of Socialist literature. Progress is not an illusion, it happens, but it is slow and invariably disappointing. There is always a new tyrant waiting to take over from the old—generally not quite so bad, but still a tyrant. Consequently two viewpoints are always tenable. The one, how can you

improve human nature until you have changed the system? The other, what is the use of changing the system before you have improved human nature? They appeal to different individuals, and they probably show a tendency to alternate in point of time.

The passage is remarkable for the sense it gives of Orwell's long historical perspective and his ability to see a particular artistic choice (Dickens's and, at this point, his own) as being in perpetual conflict with its equally legitimate opposite. The attitude could be described as dialectical, except that Orwell does not stress the synthesis which grows out of each clash. Rather, he sees the conflict as eternal: the point of view is far from the ultimate optimism of Hegel and Marx. At a particular moment in time, then, the moralist who voices his outrage at what is accepted, even though he has no idea how things might be changed, is more of a revolutionary than the "revolutionary" writer who endorses the most advanced form of social engineering. Most revolutionaries, as Orwell also points out in the Dickens essay, "are potential Tories, because they imagine that everything can be put right by altering the *shape* of society; once that change is effected, as it sometimes is, they see no need for any other."

It is at this moment—when a given revolution has more to preserve than to transform—that it is ripe for the moralist's exposé. Orwell felt that Soviet society had reached this stage, although most of the socialist camp still saw in it only its earlier, triumphant achievement. In performing this task, he hoped he might also make his audience aware that the illusion they cherished was only a particular example of a temptation they would meet again—the habit of substituting wish for reality.

It is, finally, impossible to talk about the political or moral purpose of *Animal Farm* without considering its tone. If the book is an exposé, it is certainly a remarkably unindignant one. Critics have praised its detachment, economy, and tight formal control; yet in a work with a serious political purpose, these qualities may not be as desirable as they are in purely aesthetic terms. There is truth in Mark Schorer's objection that *Animal Farm* "undid its potential gravity and the very real gravity of its subject, through its comic devices." From the first page, Orwell's fable is marked by a sense of acceptance and composure. The satire is benevolent, the ridicule affectionate, the ingenuity and sophistication very far from impassioned preaching. It is as though the story of *The Revolution Betrayed* were retold a century later by a specialist in the ironies of history. Far more than

Nineteen Eighty-Four, Animal Farm is written for posterity. The surprising thing is that it should have been the earlier book.

To describe the tone of *Animal Farm* in a few phrases is to suggest that it is consistent. Yet there are important moments in the book when Orwell's comic perspective is quite clearly abandoned. For example: "Napoleon stood sternly surveying his audience; then he uttered a high-pitched whimper. Immediately the dogs bounded forward, seized four of the pigs by the ear and dragged them, squealing with pain and terror, to Napoleon's feet. The pigs' ears were bleeding, the dogs had tasted blood, and for a few moments they appeared to go quite mad." The passage stands at the beginning of the scene meant to parallel the Stalinist purge trials, and it is typical of the tone of gravity Orwell employs to describe the reign of terror that now begins at Animal Farm. The purge trials are the first events in Soviet history that Orwell considers tragically. Although terror was not, of course, invented by Stalin, there is something about the Moscow Trials which Orwell cannot treat as a predictable part of his paradigmatic revolution, something new in human history. It is, perhaps, the triumph of the big lie in Napoleon's justification for this slaughter of the innocents, the false confessions and abandonment of objective truth it involves. Here was something Orwell could not treat with composure and ironic detachment.

Orwell's tone in both *Animal Farm* and *Nineteen Eighty-Four* is determined by his sense of the uniqueness or typicality of the events he records. As long as he describes what he considers an inevitable stage of revolution, he can allow himself the long, detached historical perspective and the ironic tone that is its aesthetic correlative. When, on the other hand, he senses that some new, unexpected, and therefore perhaps avoidable form of tyranny has appeared, his response is very different: he permits himself the indignation of first discovery. *Nineteen Eighty-Four* . . . is different in tone from *Animal Farm* primarily because it is a reaction to certain terrifying events in modern history that could not have been foreseen in the first years of the century in which they occurred.

Richard I. Smyer

SOURCE: *Primal Dream and Primal Crime: Orwell's Development as a Psychological Novelist,* University of Missouri Press, 1979, pp. 104-10.

As a number of critics have noted, the basic assumption of *Animal Farm* is that revolutions are bound to fail, merely replacing one group of oppressors with another. The ideals of equality and justice cannot be actualized because the existence of the liberated farm demands a continuous interaction with the surrounding world of humanity, which, in terms of the allegory, stands for oppression and exploitation. Paradoxically, the need to maintain an economically and politically viable society, a need that can be met only by reinstituting a hierarchical order and by trafficking with human beings, inevitably leads to the subversion of the beasts' utopian aims.

The action of *Animal Farm* takes place between two poles: at one extreme is the condition of animality, representing loyalty, decency, and a mode of existence untouched by the evil associated with the wielding of political power. At the other end is the immoral behavior of the animals' human masters, whose ways Old Major warns them against adopting. The tale records the unavoidable deterioration of the farm as the utopian dream transforms itself into the ugly reality of another tyranny.

However, we should remember that if this political fable has a tragic quality, it also has a comic dimension. This becomes clearer if we bear in mind that the basic design of the work is the innocence-guilt polarity. The problem implied by this tension has to do with morality rather than political practicality: the central concern is the preservation of innocence, not the success or failure of revolutionary activity. The essential action is a movement either toward or away from one pole or the other. The comic aspect of *Animal Farm* derives from the fact that for some of the animals the movement toward immoral humanity is no sooner begun than it is reversed, and their innocence is left intact.

A key factor in this pattern is that of intellectual superiority. "Generally recognised as being the cleverest of the animals," the pigs "naturally" become the teachers and organizers in the farm community. Because the pigs are the only animals able to substitute long-range planning for mere impulse, they are destined to lead the revolution, a role that unavoidably exposes them to moral corruption. The outward signs of their lost innocence start to appear during the second revolutionary stage (after the forcible ouster of Farmer Jones) when, as a result of their expanded awareness, they develop a historical consciousness. It is the descendants of Old Major who transform, and in effect pervert, his simple teachings into a "complete system of thought." As leaders the pigs must articulate goals and implement them by means of specific programs entailing institutionalized duties and restraints. In so doing, they are led to embrace the

world of men with its brutality and double-dealing. The pigs, whose increased self-consciousness quickly turns to selfishness, are the first to betray communal solidarity by their cunning theft of milk intended for all the animals. And Napoleon's slaughter of animals that are guilty of petty offenses represents the appearance in their midst of cruelty, heretofore a uniquely human quality. Thus the development of political cunning, the end result of the pigs' innate intellectual capacity, involves an exodus from the innocence and stasis of the old farm and a wandering in the spiritual wilderness of political activism, in the unregenerate world of history.

Remembering Orwell's disinclination to attribute revolutionary power hunger to the lower classes, we need not be surprised that for the humbler beasts the failure of the revolution is closely linked to the fact that their garden has not been lost. Before they can be defiled by the taint of humanity, the humbler beasts are saved by a series of fragmentations. The physical movement of the pigs toward the farmhouse, where they take up residence, outwardly expresses the unbridgeable moral gulf that Orwell needs to place between rulers and ruled. And not only must the guilty be segregated from the innocent but also guilt-provoking knowledge must be fragmented from consciousness. The humanoid animals must be shown wholly cut off from the other beasts, and the minds of the latter must remain inviolate from even the awareness of evil. Because their violent overthrow of Farmer Jones springs from impulse and not from ideological formulations—"with one accord, though nothing of the kind had been planned beforehand, [the animals] flung themselves upon their tormentors"—their innocence is not imperiled by power hunger and the moral ambiguities associated with the assumption of a politico-historical identity. The humbler beasts are not guilty, indeed, cannot be guilty, of the premeditation of the political ideologist: " . . . almost before they knew what was happening, the Rebellion had been successfully carried through."

Sheer mental incapacity preserves the animals' minds and spirits from the consciousness of evil. Because their memories are short, the humbler animals are not sure whether or not they earlier had passed a resolution against trade. Consequently Napoleon's proposal to begin commercial relations with the outside world gives them only a vague discomfort. For the same reason, the animals need feel no uneasiness about the breakdown of their social experiment after the pigs selfishly alter the wording of the commandment against sleeping in Jones's bed; and the rulers' slight rewording of the prohibition against killing sets the minds of the naive beasts at rest over the execution of supposedly disloyal comrades.

Since revolution implies change, the revolutionary identity is rejected when change is denied. While Napoleon physically reorganizes the old farm and Snowball puffs an electrification program to produce a technologically sophisticated utopia, something entirely new in animal experience, their ignorant subjects feel that life is no better now than before. The humbler beasts prefer the song "Beasts of England," which expresses their longing for a utopia vaguely situated in the future, to the recently adopted hymn celebrating the existence of a new order in the present. It is a sign of the animals' relatively untainted consciousness that they finally forget Snowball's vision of luxury, and even the rebellion itself becomes "only a dim tradition."

If the general action of *Animal Farm* is so structured as to express Orwell's need to see the common people uncorrupted by revolutionary ambitiousness, the career of Boxer exemplifies the ruinous effects of upward leveling. Boxer is an emblem of the old-style working class, and throughout most of the fable he is one of the least human members of the community. By nature he is a beast of burden, and it is his basically worker-animal role of tireless drudge that earns him the admiration of his comrades. In fact, it is just this predilection for mindless toil that, in making him ignorant of the leaders' wickedness, renders his spirit immune (at least in the beginning) from the revolutionary urges triggering the pigs' latent viciousness: "His two slogans, 'I will work harder' and 'Napoleon is always right,' seemed to him a sufficient answer to all problems."

At first Boxer's innocence and goodness are not affected by the rebellion. Jones's stable boy, whom Boxer fears he has slain during the fighting, suddenly comes to life; and later the horse, as though disclaiming any impious desire to benefit personally from the installation of an electricity-generating windmill, wishes only that it may be "well under way" before his retirement.

In time, however, we see signs of an ominous change in Boxer. During the fray that is almost fatal for the stable boy, the ordinarily gentle Boxer, as though mimicking his human oppressors, becomes bipedal, a gesture releasing a savagery alien to his normal behavior: " . . . the most terrifying spectacle of all was Boxer, rearing up on his hind legs and striking out with his great iron-shod hoofs." Significantly Boxer's

eventual doom is described in terms of an inner pollution, symbolized by the ingestion of medicine taken from Jones's bathroom and administered by the pigs. With this potion, this "human" element, inside him, Boxer shows the first signs of consciously giving up his identity as a worker and moving toward an upper-class (porcine-humanoid) status: he begins to look forward to retirement when he will have the "leisure to study and improve his mind" by learning the alphabet. It is consistent with Orwell's apprehensions that Boxer, thinking that his entry into the world of humanity will bring him renewed vitality (he is supposedly being taken to a veterinary surgeon), is actually being shipped off to a horse slaughterer.

If Boxer's fate indicates his creator's alarm at those forces eating away the class identity of the common people, the final state of the pigs expresses Orwell's certainty that political ambition has a morally destructive effect on the leadership. The two aces of spades that the porcine and human card players simultaneously throw down at the end of the fable symbolize both the pigs' ethical decay and, given the deadly significance of the ace of spades, the passing away of their working-class identities.

In the world of *Animal Farm,* revolution becomes a matter of good lost and evil got. Because it involves a development in the direction of "humanity," of evil, revolutionary activity is the greatest threat to the animals' spirit. But as I have already indicated, the farm is a split world: one region in which the knowledge of evil and change cannot thrive and another in which baseness and mutability cannot be denied. In the end, the humble and ignorant beasts are still victims. Yet as the story of Boxer reveals, this is the necessary condition for the preservation of their innocence, their group identity. If they are still oppressed, they are also still untainted, still the communal embodiment of the socialist ideals of brotherhood and equality.

Animal Farm is, in effect, a fairy tale, a mixture of fantasy and harshness, of mysterious dangers happily overcome by some characters and terrible punishments falling on the heads of others. The subject animals exist in a comic world, their goodness and simplicity magically protected from the witch's brew of politics and revolution. But their leaders are captives in a world of fearful transformations—where the Circe of awareness turns pigs into men.

There is another transformation that bears on Ben's second reading aloud. During the narrative appear signs that Boxer and Ben are doubles, and as such they dramatically express the conflict in the mind of their creator, Orwell the writer-intellectual trapped in an age of political madness. Like Orwell, suffering from a lung ailment, Boxer is the enthusiastic true believer who becomes involved heart and soul in the revolution, working year after year to turn the old farm into a brave new utopia. If Boxer is sheer energy and commitment, Ben, the friend and constant companion with whom Boxer hopes to share his retirement, is the horse's prudential self, his knowing half. It is a mark of his freedom from dangerous ambition that in contrast to Boxer, who marvels at the windmill, Ben remains unenthusiastic. Because he rejects progress, he feels confident of being immune to the fearful changes occurring on the farm: "Donkeys live a long time," he asserts. "None of you has ever seen a dead donkey."

Yet there is something disturbingly ambiguous about Ben, who occupies an indefinite position between the porcine state of cunning, immorality, and historical awareness, and the ahistorical animal world of impulse, ignorance, and innocence. His class identity is uncomfortably vague. Lacking the selfishly humanoid wiliness of the pigs, he is not a leader; however, his mental capacity—he can "read as well as any pig"—keeps him from being wholly within the realm of the humbler animals. We might regard him as a representation of the disillusioned intellectual of the 1940s who, unlike his less perceptive compatriots, is cursed with the dispiriting awareness of the inevitable degeneration of revolutionary idealism into power worship. Figuratively as well as literally he can read the handwriting on the wall.

To repeat my earlier observation, twice, not once (as Orwell erroneously states), Ben has read, has broken his rule. That is, more than once, and more than the narrator cares to admit, Ben has revealed an affinity with the porcine condition of intelligence, and therefore, evil. To add to the ominous significance of this second transgression, the exercise of this humanoid skill involves the pronunciation of words that themselves represent the breaking of a rule, the subversion of the seven commandments established to keep the animals free from the corrupting effects of humanization.

Ben's fate is rather curious. Soon after reading aloud a second time, the donkey simply drops out of the narrative, even though he is one of the more important and more fully developed characters. One explanation for this abrupt and puzzling disappearance is that Orwell—too intimately acquainted with the intellectual's inner complexity to leave Ben in the

thoughtlessly innocent realm of the humbler animals, yet morally repelled by the other alternative—allows the donkey to vanish into a limbo apart from either polarity. This turn of events underscores Orwell's view regarding the moral vulnerability of the intellectual unprotected by the mental limitations that make the lower animals, the common folk, resistant to inner contamination. The intellectual cannot combine escape with self-preservation. It is through a blind, instinctive assertion of their original collective identity that the animals remain inviolate. The intellectual's only refuge entails a self-negating loss of identity.

Because Ben's dilemma is so close to that of Orwell, the latter has failed to treat this character with the same artistic objectivity as he has done with the others. This need not, however, be the last word on the matter, for Ben's vanishing act calls attention to some interesting technical and thematic developments in *Animal Farm.* For one thing, since Ben is defined in terms of an inner tension between the desire to participate in the innocence of the humbler beasts and an effort to suppress the humanoid-porcine qualities that prevent this, he is a more complex and, therefore, more realistic character than the others, even Boxer, who unself-consciously play out their two-dimensional allegorical roles of goodness and villainy, naive enthusiasm and single-minded cunning.

In **"Inside the Whale,"** Orwell predicts that the "autonomous individual is going to be stamped out of existence" with the advent of totalitarianism, a warning reiterated several years later in "Literature and Totalitarianism." A few months after the publication of *Animal Farm,* he explained why under a tyranny the idea of personal autonomy was illusory. To be autonomous one had to be "free *inside,*" but in a totalitarian society even one's thoughts were controlled by the state. In fact, with the loss of free expression the mind itself becomes torpid, for it is "almost impossible to think without talking."

Ben is the autonomous individual caught in a double bind. The refusal to voice an opinion about the animals' utopian experiment is supposed to insure his moral survival as well as his physical safety, yet his reluctance to speak out makes him in effect a silent partner to the pigs' conspiracy and gradually erodes his autonomy. His disappearance from the narrative suggests that he has been "stamped out of existence."

There may be an emblematic connection between the disappearance of this relatively complex character and Zwerdling's observation [in *Orwell and the Left,*

1974] that during the forties Orwell was consciously attempting to abandon the conventions of the realistic novel, which, because of its documentary specificity and thematic obliqueness, was not flexible enough to satisfy Orwell's artistic needs or to deliver a direct message within the context of an enlarged historical perspective. By employing the fable, Orwell could invest *Animal Farm* with "permanent mythic life" and set forth the basic pattern of social revolution.

The transparency of the fable, its ability to convey meaning directly and with a minimum of authorial intrusion, makes the withdrawal of Ben appropriate, since he lacks the allegorical simplicity of the other figures. In *Coming Up for Air,* Tubby Bowling, the passive common man, fades away into a state of potentially self-destructive apathy; whereas the other Bowling, Bowling the author's mouthpiece, has, as the observer and recorder of his alter ego's decline into quietism, the last word. This, however, is not the case in *Animal Farm,* where Ben, as much the judgmental Orwellian persona in his silences as in his speech, is not allowed to outlast the narrative. This circumstance hints at Orwell's willingness to draw back from the events, to let the story (the final half dozen pages, at least) tell itself. The impression we are left with is that in the world of the forties there are no safe heights from atop which an author or his persona can calmly survey the violence below and formulate grand generalizations.

The withdrawal of the authorial commentator from the dramatized narrative action may also indicate a change in Orwell's relationship to the modernist tradition. The Orwell of the thirties often was making a forced march to join ranks with the moderns. Partly to achieve his childhood goal of literary fame, partly to expand his intellectual and imaginative horizons, Orwell chose as models those writers generally considered most sensitive to the moral and psychological ambiguities of contemporary man. From *Burmese Days* to *Coming Up for Air,* the Orwellian voice is noticeably derivative, and at times we feel that Orwell's admiration for such writers as Eliot and Joyce has outstripped his ability to adapt their imaginative worlds to his own creative aims. . . . [During] the forties Orwell turned his attention to other literary models better suited to the atmosphere of the age, with its technologically sophisticated barbarism, its tyrants able to mesmerize whole populations, and its rejection of the idea of individual freedom.

Finally, it is worth noting that in exposing the savagery concealed behind the official ideology of revolutionary activism, Orwell has chosen a relatively primitive literary form, the animal tale. Whether or not [Orwell's childhood friend] Jacintha Buddicom is correct in claiming that the original source of *Animal Farm* is Beatrix Potter's *The Tale of Pigling Bland* (which the young Blair read to her), the decision to examine social conflict "from the animals' point of view" suggests Orwell's willingness to experiment with a view of reality normally associated with a child's perspective and attitudes, his and ours. Although such an approach is obviously useful in creating ironic and satiric effects, we should be aware of the dangerous game Orwell the fabulist is engaged in when he blurs the distinction between man and animal to reveal the viciousness of the former. For the adult, the animal is something to be used as physical or literary beast of burden, as a source of amusement, as prey, or as object of scientific examination. But for the child—and this includes the child within the adult—the animal is a marvel, a source of wonder, perhaps even a magical being. In exploiting this creature for adult ends (for example, sociopolitical commentary), the writer has risked violating the sacred grove of his own childhood world. What remains of the child's primal response to life may wither away if yoked to the adult's moralistic or political obsessions.

David Wykes

SOURCE: "The Great Fictions: *Animal Farm* and *1984,*" *A Preface to Orwell,* Longman, 1987, pp. 125-33.

ANIMAL FARM: ARTISTRY

Animal Farm appears on many syllabuses, and teachers can often tell of readers whose first experience of the book has left them quite unaware of meanings other than those of the story itself. The allegorical dimension has not appeared; the historical application is unmade. Such readers have failed with the book, but quite pardonably, for so self-contained and self-sustaining is Orwell's tale that it never insists on its applications. A skilled reader, absolutely ignorant of all twentieth-century history, could be expected to detect that *Animal Farm* is, at very least, a fable, but the skilled reader would understand the conventions of fable. But if one knows nothing about literary convention, the fact that animals don't talk except in art is not enough.

The self-sustaining and self-contained story of *Animal Farm* is enormously deft, and before turning to the meanings that surround the central narrative, we should acknowledge the artistry that Orwell commands there.

Most impressive of all his achievements is the atmosphere of genuine tragedy which gradually envelops the unfolding story. Orwell seems to have handicapped himself drastically for the attaining of such a mood. The beast fable simplifies radically, especially in the depiction of character, and normally its effects are comic, at most pathetic. The book is a short one, often printed in less than a hundred pages, which does not seem to give time for the cumulative effects of tragic feeling. And a pervasive, hilarious, though bitter irony runs through the whole thing.

Orwell meets each of these limiting factors head-on. Like Swift in *A Modest Proposal,* he rigorously controls his own presence in the story while everywhere the force, even violence, of his own feelings comes through. The success of the animals' revolution, for example, is really euphoric because Orwell invests the event with his own passionate detestation of tyranny.

> They had never seen animals behave like this before, and this sudden uprising of creatures whom they were used to thrashing and maltreating just as they chose, frightened them almost out of their wits.

The animal revolution is a real 'objective correlative' for all the deep emotion Orwell feels for the greatest and most necessary human action, the strike back against tyranny, the action which—in numerous forms—pervades all his writing. When the animals gallop in ecstasy round the farm from which Jones has fled, their joy is Orwell's pleasure in the attainment of freedom. Never, in any way, does he later imply that the revolution was a mistake, that a return to Manor Farm would be best. Benjamin the donkey is in many ways a sympathetic character, but his passive conservatism—'things never had been, nor ever could be much better or much worse'—is not Orwell's. The whole satiric point of his book is that Manor Farm *is* re-established, by the failure of the revolution. The whip in the trotter of the bi-pedal Napoleon is a sardonic irony, but a measure too of tragic loss. Late in the book, after the first 'purge', the animals—the 'lower animals'—gather again on the knoll from which they had first gazed on the liberated farm. On the day after the revolution 'they could hardly believe that it was all their own'. Now, 'with a kind of surprise they remembered that it was their own farm'. In the unarticulated thoughts of Clover, Orwell puts into words the tragedy of their loss.

> These scenes of terror and slaughter were not what they had looked forward to on that night when old Major first stirred them to rebellion. If she herself had had any picture of the future, it had been of a society of animals set free from hunger and the whip, all equal, each working according to his capacity, the strong protecting the weak. . . . Instead—she did not know why—they had come to a time when no one dared speak his mind. . . . (VII)

Clover's only expression of these feelings is to begin to sing *Beasts of England.* 'The other animals sitting round her took it up, and they sang it three times over—very tunefully, but slowly and mournfully, in a way they had never sung it before.' Orwell follows this brilliantly conceived lamentation with a fine stroke of bitter irony. Squealer announces the abolition of their anthem. 'In *Beasts of England* we expressed our longing for a better society in days to come. But that society has now been established. Clearly this song has no longer any purpose.' Such reasoning of the need, and the progress of tyranny by tiny steps, each inscrutable yet glossed with rationalization, is a method that is not absurd to compare to that of *King Lear.* And Orwell manages his simplified characters and the brevity of his narrative so as to strengthen the tragic impression.

The movement of history in the realistic novel—*War and Peace, The Quiet Don, Dr Zhivago,* or *August, 1914*—seems to demand great length of narrative and complex multiplicity of character. Something similar is found in those tragedies of Shakespeare where individuals' lives are most clearly projected against the background of public life: *Lear, Hamlet, Antony and Cleopatra, Coriolanus.* History is Orwell's subject in **Animal Farm,** and although individuals dramatize the story, the tragedy is not an individual's tragedy. The simplified individuality of the beast fable allows the story of history to be the tragedy, and allows that story to be told with great narrative economy. The convention of the beast fable will allow the animals to be individuals only as long as their representative nature is felt. The animals are convincingly a whole people, a nation. Thus the tragic 'emotion of multitude' which Yeats found in the paralleling of plots in *King Lear* is present in the simplicity, both of characterization and of narrative, in **Animal Farm.** The passage of time does not need the turning of many pages. We know the characters completely very quickly; the changes in their existence are the movement of history itself. And the bitter irony of the book is that of an inevitability that mocks the inevitability of revolution. Once the 'new class' of Napoleon, Snowball, and the pigs begins to emerge, it is inevitable that all of the Seven Commandments of Animalism will be broken and hence rewritten. Indeed, in 'but some are more equal than others' Orwell found the perfect climax for the ironical advance of the narrative. When the last commandment is rewritten (and its rewriting becomes inevitable with the incident of the milk, at the end of Chapter II), the book's perfection of form and statement is complete.

ANIMAL FARM: PROPAGANDA

> As an instrument of destructive propaganda it has no equal anywhere; its effect upon succeeding generations is unparalleled outside religious history; had its author written nothing else, it would have ensured his lasting fame.
>
> Isaiah Berlin, of *The Communist Manifesto*

Animal Farm is a weapon Orwell designed for the campaign he fought after the Spanish War in order to save Western Socialism from the 'Soviet myth'. He wanted it to be 'a story that could be easily understood by almost anyone and which could be easily translated into other languages' (3/110). The form of fable he chose and the brevity of the text are means to the essential end of universal access and unmistakability. Orwell is unrelentingly didactic, so firmly so, indeed, that the 'aesthetic' success of *Animal Farm* involves the book in some ideological tangles (see below).

The particular purpose of Orwell's fable brings to mind his interest in another form of writing, the pamphlet (he collected pamphlets and began publishing an anthology of them). The 'greatest of all socialist pamphlets', as Isaiah Berlin has called *The Communist Manifesto,* provides the ideas in Major's speech to the animals (I), but it also governs the basic form and strategy—the shape—of *Animal Farm. The Communist Manifesto* is simple and powerful; its rhetoric is sweeping, a bold picture—or poster—in primary colours; its irony is heavy but effective. In Marx's German and in translation, it is one of the most widely read books of all time. *Animal Farm* is planned to reproduce every one of these features, and does. Orwell was not only providing an alternative reading of Marxist history but also a formal alternative to the most influential Marxist book. *Animal Farm* is a spiritual parody of *The Communist Manifesto.*

ALLEGORICAL INGENUITY

At the Moscow Book Fair some years ago, a copy of *1984* was allowed to remain on display at the stand of a Western publisher. A copy of *Animal Farm,* however was resolutely excluded by the authorities. When one studies the allegorical details of the book,

it is not hard to see why. The events of *Animal Farm* are transformations of the events of the Russian Revolution, and the wit Orwell displays in finding farmyard parallels for the events of history is amazing, undeniably one of the great pleasures of reading it. This should be emphasized for, as in other aspects of the book, this success too poses ideological problems.

Orwell said that, in basing the book on the actual history of the Russian Revolution, he dealt with the episodes schematically and changed their chronological order: 'this was necessary for the symmetry of the story.' (3/110) Changes include the omission of a Lenin figure. Major is Marx, Napoleon Stalin, and Snowball Trotsky. Lenin, the combination of idealist and prototypical totalitarian, is a complex personality with a complex rôle. Since Orwell wished to emphasize idealism's collapse into tyranny, a figure combining both elements, rather than embodying one or the other, would demand the novel's resources of complexity and not the fable's simplifications. The omission greatly helps 'the symmetry of the story'.

On every page, in tiny details as well as in large elements, Orwell's ingenuity is manifest. Jones the Farmer, who represents the Czarist régime, has 'fallen on evil days. He had become much disheartened after losing money in a lawsuit, and had taken to drinking more than was good for him.' The demoralization and social collapse of Russia after the reverses of the First World War are embodied in perfectly natural details. The Nazi-Soviet non-aggression pact of 1939 is figured in Napoleon's sale of timber to Frederick (Frederick the Great as 'ancestor' of Hitler). The discovery that Frederick's banknotes are forgeries is followed by Frederick-Hitler's invasion (VIII). Jeffrey Meyers, who has made the most detailed list of Orwell's parallels, includes a spectacular item from the Great Purge trial of Bukharin in 1938.

> Gorky's secretary Kryuchkov confessed, 'I arranged long walks for Alexei Maximovich, I was always arranging bonfires. The smoke of the bonfire naturally affected Gorky's weak lungs.' During the purge in *Animal Farm,* 'Two other sheep confessed to having murdered an old ram, an especially devoted follower of Napoleon, by chasing him round and round a bonfire when he was suffering from a cough.'

Wonderful comedy, dripping blood.

Writing to one of his publishers, Orwell suggested a small change.

> In Chapter VIII . . . when the windmill is blown up, I wrote 'all the animals including Napoleon flung themselves on their faces'. I would like to

alter it to 'all the animals except Napoleon' . . . I just thought the alteration would be fair to J. S. [Joseph Stalin], as he did stay in Moscow during the German advance. (3/98)

Both the desire to be fair and the attention to detail are typical.

Orwell's wit in transforming details in his allegory is perhaps excelled by his reproduction in new terms of the states of mind necessary for totalitarianism. He wonderfully conveys, for instance, the incessant re-writing of the past and the ever-abundant rationalizations necessary to adjust theory to reality.

> You have heard then, comrades . . . that we pigs now sleep in the beds of the farmhouse? And why not? You did not suppose, surely, that there was ever a ruling against *beds*? A bed merely means a place to sleep in. A pile of straw in a stall is a bed, properly regarded. The rule was against *sheets,* which are a human invention. (VI)

The satire of Squealer, however, differs in an impor-tant way from the other details cited above. Those details refer specifically to Russian events, but Squealer, although the Soviet experience provides ample justification for his existence, represents a wider, general tendency. He might as easily be a Je-suit as a party-line Communist. A pair of hard ques-tions about *Animal Farm* concern the extent to which it addresses general questions about the process of revolution in history, and the extent to which it is bound to the specific instance of the Russian Revolu-tion. In a letter of 1947, Orwell said the book was 'intended as a satire on dictatorship in general', but it is reasonable to feel some doubt about the book's presentation of that intention. Does the book address general questions about the process of revolution in history, or is it too tightly bound to the specific in-stance of the Russian Revolution? Does Orwell's in-genuity in finding parallels for Russian events draw the eye away from wider applications? Is the general lesson of the book that all revolutions fail?

HARD QUESTIONS

When he wrote *Animal Farm,* Orwell had several worrying questions about Socialism on his mind. His main objective, or at least the objective he started with, was—as we have seen—to separate democratic Socialism from what had happened in Russia: 'the destruction of the Soviet myth was essential if we wanted a revival of the Socialist movement.' But more fundamental questioning occurred too. Looking back at the history of revolutions, Orwell had to com-bat the doubt of their efficacy. Had revolutions really advanced the cause of liberty? Had they really brought Socialism closer? And—a still graver doubt—did the experience of Socialist revolutions, particularly the Russian one, indicate that Socialism, or the ambition for Socialism, leads inevitably to to-talitarianism? Was the lust for power so ingrained in human nature that it would always thwart the ideal of liberty, equality, and fraternity?

These were not rhetorical questions for Orwell. He genuinely debated them, and voiced the debate in his journalism. In *Animal Farm,* however, decisions of literary form combine to endorse one point of view, with the result that the book is a brilliant rhetorical success while advancing an ideological position that was in fact gloomier and more certain than the one at which Orwell himself had arrived. Orwell was think-ing through real doubts about Socialism, but the book he had written seems to confirm those doubts. He had made it easy for conservatives to use his book to attack democratic Socialism itself, to make up his mind for him.

The choice of beast fable was brilliant for the reduc-tive simplicities of satire, but as a weapon it has two edges. Beast fable is a conservative aesthetic, pre-senting conservative estimates of human nature. It links outward shape unbreakably to predominating traits of character: sheep are silly, easily led, without individuality; donkeys are individualistically anarchic and stubborn; pigs are gross, greedy, and selfish. Or-well, it is true, modifies conventional links of this kind for his own purposes. The pigs have to be intel-ligent, for example, which does not seem to conform to farmyard experience. (Orwell kept a pig on Jura, and loathed it: 'disgusting brutes . . . we are all long-ing for the day when he goes to the butcher.' (4/126) But once established the characteristic is permanent. Seen through the lens of beast fable, human nature is split into separate components and is governed by a presumption of permanence.

Now the permanence, the unmodifiability, of human nature is an issue that separates conservatives from those who pointedly call themselves 'progressives'. When he was writing *Animal Farm,* Orwell was de-bating this issue for himself. The book alone, how-ever, because it is a beast fable, seems to indicate that Orwell had come down on the conservative side.

Why, for instance, do the pigs become the new class? Why, at the end, are they indistinguishable from hu-mans in the eyes of the 'lower' animals? In the story, the only possible explanation is that they behave that way because of their 'nature'. They justify themselves by pointing to the facts of the animals' revolution, but such justifications all follow the form of Squealer's definition of a bed. The real motive is selfishness.

Trotsky, to explain the corruption of the Soviet Revolution, had written *The Revolution Betrayed,* which, as Alex Zwerdling shows, had greatly helped Orwell's thinking. Trotsky rejects all psychological, spiritual, or 'human nature' explanations for the re-establishment of class privilege in the Soviet Union. His reasons for it are historically, geographically, and economically specific to the case of the Russian Revolution. And he believes that the stage Russia has reached will lead to a further revolution which will realize the original goals. 'All indications agree that the further course of development must inevitably lead to a clash between the culturally developed forces of the people and bureaucratic oligarchy'.

Orwell was neither so optimistic nor so willing to rely solely on historical and case-specific explanations. It is true that at the end of *Animal Farm* the re-establishment of tyranny means that a second revolution will be needed to free the animals again, but the story gives no hint of optimism that such a revolution will come or be more successful than the first if it did come. A second revolution, moreover, would presumably have to get by without the pigs, who, having proved themselves naturally corrupt, could not be trusted with leadership. Their intelligence, however, would also be lost to the revolution. When one tries to translate this into human and social terms, awful complexities appear. The pigs of beast fable are one factor in the human mind and in human society. How can one such strand, no longer conveniently isolated within porcine form, be identified, never mind suppressed? The shape and conventions of Orwell's story combine to support the view that revolutions fail because of what a theologian would call original sin. Human nature is corrupt and cannot, in earthly existence, be perfected. The revolution in Orwell's fable can neither exist without its pigs (old Major, too, is a pig) nor triumph as long as they exist.

When Orwell debated these issues outside *Animal Farm,* his positions were more tentative and less pessimistic. Six months after finishing the book, he wrote an article about Arthur Koestler (3/68) which is fascinating, particularly as a commentary on *Animal Farm.* Orwell identifies the Moscow trials as the central subject of Koestler's work. 'His main theme is the decadence of revolutions owing to the corrupting effects of power, but the special nature of the

Stalin dictatorship has driven him back into a position not far removed from pessimistic Conservatism.' Orwell reads Koestler's novel about Spartacus, *The Gladiators,* as an allegorical discussion of modern proletarian revolution. 'Revolutions always go wrong—that is the main theme', but on the question of *why,* Koestler falters. The freed slaves in his novel fail because of their hedonism, the expectation of being able to live in a post-revolutionary paradise. 'If Spartacus is the prototype of the modern revolutionary', says Orwell, 'he *should* have gone astray because of *the impossibility of combining power with righteousness.*' [my italics] Orwell does not immediately elaborate on this statement. Taken as an axiom, it seems to be as pessimistically conservative as any position found in Koestler; it indicts the lust for power as the fatal enemy of righteousness, and the lust for power seems to be a constant in human nature.

Yet as he discusses Koestler's writings, Orwell is clearly far from totally accepting the pessimism he finds there. Koestler 'comes near to claiming that revolutions are of their nature bad. . . . Revolution, Koestler seems to say, is a corrupting process.' Orwell is stating this view without identifying himself with it, and when he comes to summarize Koestler's situation, he reveals a train of thought that significantly modifies the conclusion one draws from *Animal Farm.* Koestler has retained a belief in what Orwell calls 'hedonism'; this 'leads him to think of the Earthly Paradise as desirable'.

> Perhaps, however, whether desirable or not, it isn't possible. Perhaps some degree of suffering is ineradicable from human life, perhaps the choice before man is always a choice of evils, perhaps even the aim of Socialism is not to make the world perfect, but to make it better. All revolutions are failures, but they are not all the same failure.

Orwell has thought beyond *Animal Farm.* Major's speech at the beginning of that book offers a vision, in the words of *Beasts of England,* 'Of the golden future time'. The glad day will bring 'Riches more than mind can picture, / Wheat and barley, oats and hay', but this hedonistic image is more than balanced, in Major's speech and in the song, by the more important vision of freedom: 'Rings shall vanish from our noses, / And the harness from our back.' In his thoughts on Koestler, Orwell downplays hedonism still further. He seems prepared to accept lowered expectations, but not to align himself with pessimistic conservatism. The defeat of tyranny will not produce an earthly paradise, but it is still the purpose of revolution. To reshape his conclusion somewhat: all revolutions are failures, but some are less failures than others. Orwell continued to believe that the revolution was betrayed, yet *Animal Farm* shows failure as inherent in revolution.

In *Animal Farm* time is circular, another pessimistic and conservative image. From tyranny to revolution to tyranny is a figure of no progress, of cycles going nowhere. Yet outside his book, Orwell would not draw that conclusion. On the more difficult problem of combining power with righteousness, *Animal Farm* is again negative, but the problem continued to haunt Orwell, and is investigated at length in his last book and second great fiction, *1984.*

Alok Rai

SOURCE: "The Roads to Airstrip One," in *Orwell and the Politics of Despair,* Cambridge University Press, 1990, pp. 113-16.

The matter of *Animal Farm,* both text and context, is rich in ironies—not all of them, be it said, intentional. *Animal Farm* is, as every schoolboy knows, a brilliant farmyard cartoon of the tragic course of the Russian Revolution. The dreamt-of revolution of the beasts is systematically, cynically, betrayed by operators and tyrants who mouth the rhetoric of equality and liberation. The taciturn Napoleon-Stalin outmanoeuvres the vivacious Snowball-Trotsky and drives him into exile. The 'revolution' passes through the familiar processes of distortion and cruelty, episodes of hunger and hardship, frame-ups, confessions, liquidations, ending up in the most famous thesis of the betrayed revolution: 'All animals are equal, but some animals are more equal than others.' The historical referents of this fabulous account have been identified often enough—and, at this level, there is little further to be said. The transposition of real historical events, the cruel ironies of a familiar history, into farmyard terms is little short of scintillating. It is also, by the same token, drastically reductive.

Its subsequent and durable popularity has obscured the fact that Orwell's *Animal Farm* was a calculated outrage, a deliberately provocative affront to the contemporary admiration for the Soviet Union, whose armies were fighting with epic heroism against Hitler's dread war machine. This background is crucial to a correct understanding of Orwell's brilliantly serious jest. The wartime popularity of the Soviet Union was an oft-repeated theme in Orwell's BBC broadcasts. Commenting on German anti-Bolshevik propaganda, Orwell went so far as to say that it 'was foredoomed to failure because the anti-Russian sentiment on which the Axis propagandists seem to be playing is almost non-existent in the Anglo-Saxon countries'. However, he thought, such propaganda might find sympathetic listeners 'among the wealthier classes all over Europe'. In his broadcast of 13 June 1942, Orwell welcomed the recently signed Anglo-Russian Treaty about wartime coordination and post-war collaboration: 'the two regimes are now in far greater political and economic agreement than would have been possible or even thinkable five years ago. It means, in fact, that the ancient ghost of Bolshevism and "bloody revolution" has been laid for ever.' This new-found respectability of the Soviet Union—as also the popularity—could support several different conclusions. It might, for instance, be seen as an index or factor of the processes that conduced towards the Labour victory of 1945. Orwell however had for several years been of the opinion that the interests of the Soviet Union were antithetical to those of socialism, and the endorsement of the Soviet regime by His Majesty's Government was hardly likely to make him change his mind. He was, thus, surprised by the 'Upper Crust' delight at the dissolution of the Comintern in 1943: 'a fact which I record but cannot readily explain', because, of course, in Orwell's eyes, 'the Comintern has been one of the worst enemies the working class has had' (II:46). From his somewhat eccentric location, therefore, raising the 'ancient ghost of Bolshevism' once again, albeit in a left-wing version, could well appear to be a sacred and lonely *socialist* duty.

When first offered for publication in early 1944, *Animal Farm* was so far out of line with prevalent opinion, and official policy, that it nearly ended up not being published at all. Or published, in despair, as a broadsheet by Orwell's impecunious friend, the poet Paul Potts—which might have been very nearly the same thing. The story of the rejections of the *Animal Farm* ms is well known. Cape rejected it on advice from the Ministry of Information, and relayed, in its rejection letter, the 'imbecile' (III, 207) advice that the ms might become more acceptable if the *Animal Farm* elite were depicted not as pigs but as other, less offensive beasts. T. S. Eliot rejected it on behalf of Faber, and Orwell reports an American publisher turning it down on the grounds that 'animal stories did not sell well in the U.S.A.' Stung by the rejections, Orwell wrote an angry 'preface' to the projected broadsheet which, in the event, was not used because Warburg, finally, decided to publish the unwanted ms. The rest is history. *Animal Farm* became one of the publishing sensations of our time, and Orwell's 'provocation' achieved apotheosis as a universal school text. 'If liberty means anything at all', Orwell wrote in the 'lost' preface, 'The freedom of the press', in early 1944 when the popularity of the Soviet Union was at its height, 'it means the right to tell people what they do not want to hear.' Ironically enough, it was written in defence of a fable that people never seem to tire of.

However, Orwell's achievement in *Animal Farm* is ironic not only in respect of the disjunction between its anticipated unpopularity and its popular success, it is ironic also in respect of the gap between what Orwell had first intended to write, and the fable he actually wrote. Explaining the genesis of *Animal Farm* in the 'Author's preface to the Ukrainian edition of *Animal Farm*' (III:110), Orwell said:

> if only animals became aware of their strength we should have no power over them . . . I proceeded to analyse Marx's theory from the animals' point of view. To them it was clear that the concept of a class struggle between humans was pure illusion . . . the true struggle is between animals and humans. From this point of departure, it was not difficult to elaborate the story.

It is evident from this that *Animal Farm* had been intended as an allegory of the common people, awaking to a realisation of their strength and overthrowing their oppressors—a sort of farmyard version of *The Lion and the Unicorn*. In working out the fable, however, in the winter of 1943-4, the euphoria has collapsed. In 1954 a critic suggested that *Animal Farm* was not really about the Russian Revolution but rather about the English 'revolution' which had seemed imminent in *The Lion and the Unicorn*. At a superficial level, this is clearly wrong. The tragic course of the Russian Revolution was very much in Orwell's mind in *Animal Farm*, to the extent that he made a correction, at proof stage, in recognition of Stalin's bravery, in the face of the German advance on Moscow: when the windmill was blown up, 'all the animals except Napoleon', he insisted, 'flung themselves on their faces' (III, 359). In an unpublished letter to his agent, now in the Berg collection in New York, Orwell wrote: 'If they question you again, please say that *Animal Farm* is intended as a satire on dictatorship in general but *of course* the Russian Revolution is the chief target. It is humbug to pretend anything else.' However, at a deeper level, it is still possible to see that the disappointment of his wartime hopes—his feeling that 'the political advance we seemed to make in 1940 has been gradually filched away from us' (111, 226)—lent its specific accent of anguish and despair to Orwell's

critique of the Russian Revolution. In this mood, the grotesque transformation of the Russian Revolution, of which Orwell had been openly critical for some time, became a paradigmatic instance of *all* attempts at revolutionary social transformation.

Valerie Meyers

SOURCE: "*Animal Farm*: An Allegory of Revolution," in *Modern Novelists: George Orwell*, St. Martin's Press, 1991, pp. 101-13.

In spite of Orwell's well-known opposition to continued British rule in India (where **Burmese Days** was banned) he was hired in August 1941 to produce programmes for the Indian section of the BBC's Eastern Service, to counter Japanese and German radio propaganda. Two million Indian volunteer troops were fighting on the British side, and the BBC's task was to maintain Indian support. For more than two years Orwell prepared weekly news bulletins, commissioned cultural talks and discussions, adapted stories, wrote dialogues and reviews. Because paper was in short supply, newspapers and magazines, the outlets for Orwell's work, were very restricted. Broadcasting allowed him to keep up his political comment and literary journalism. W. J. West has convincingly suggested that Orwell's experience in radio adaptation and in condensing, simplifying and arranging information for propaganda purposes largely accounts for the success of *Animal Farm*—its speed of composition (Orwell completed it in three months, after leaving the BBC in November 1943), its clarity and conciseness, its universality of appeal, its radically different form from any of Orwell's previous work.

'*Animal Farm*', Orwell wrote, 'was the first book in which I tried, with full consciousness of what I was doing, to fuse political purpose and artistic purpose into one whole'. In his preface to the Ukrainian edition, published in 1947, Orwell said that he wanted to write the book in a simple language because he wanted to tell ordinary English people, who had enjoyed a tradition of justice and liberty for centuries, what a totalitarian system was like. His experience in Spain had shown him 'how easily totalitarian propaganda can control the opinion of enlightened people in democratic countries' and he wrote the book to destroy the 'Soviet myth' that Russia was a truly socialist society.

In the 1930s European intellectuals idealised the Soviet Union. Even E. M. Forster, a relatively non-political writer, commented in an essay of 1934, 'no political creed except communism offers an intelligent man any hope'. Throughout the 1930s Orwell had been sceptical about the Soviet version of current events in Russia; in Spain he saw Spanish Communists, directed by Moscow, betray their allies. In the late 1930s news reached the West of the infamous Purge Trials, which took the lives of three million people and sent countless others to forced labour camps in order to make Stalin's power absolute. In 1939 Stalin signed a non-aggression pact with Hitler, which allowed the Germans to overrun Poland and Czechoslovakia. Orwell's indignant reaction to these events provoked him to write this powerful pamphlet.

THE GENRE OF *ANIMAL FARM*

Orwell particularly valued the vigorous, colourful and concrete style of pamphlets and wanted to revive the genre. **Animal Farm** was his contribution to the English tradition of Utopian pamphlets, which originated in Thomas More's *Utopia* (1516). Like *Utopia*, **Animal Farm** is brief, light and witty, but has a serious purpose. More's pamphlet attacked the monarch's excessive power and the cruel dispossession of tenant-farmers by the lords who enclosed lands for sheep-grazing; Orwell's attacks the injustice of the Soviet regime and seeks to correct Western misconceptions about Soviet Communism.

More invented the device of satirising contemporary society by contrasting it with a traveller's account of a distant country. His narrator talks to Raphael Hythloday, who has just returned from Utopia (a name derived from the Greek, meaning 'no place' or 'nowhere'—). In contrast to the majority of Englishmen, who suffer poverty and constant war, the Utopians are rational and kind, own everything in common and share everything equally. War, envy, greed and pursuit of personal riches or power are unknown.

More's narrator remarks sceptically that he 'cannot conceive of authority among men that are equal to one another in all things'. He cannot imagine a world where no one has greater status or wealth than anyone else. More raised the fundamental question, which Orwell took up centuries later, of whether it is possible for men to live together fairly, justly and equally. More's answer is ethical: that there is no point in changing our social system unless we change our morality; his pamphlet urges us to take responsibility for improving our society. While More's Utopia is totally imaginary, Orwell's Animal Farm is based on the first thirty years of the Soviet Union, a real society pursuing the ideal of equality. His book argues that this kind of society hasn't worked, and couldn't.

Orwell said that Jonathan Swift's *Gulliver's Travels* (1726) 'has meant more to me than any other book ever written'. Far longer and more complex than *Utopia*, it uses the same device of a traveller's tales to attack contemporary society, but the various places Gulliver visits are satiric renderings of aspects of English society. Orwell's Animal Farm, like Swift's Lilliput and Blefuscu, is a coded satiric portrait of a real society, an anti-utopia which, by castigating real evils, suggests what society ought to be like.

Orwell probably took a hint from the final part of *Gulliver's Travels*, Book IV, where Gulliver encounters a society formed by a superior species of horse, the Houyhnhnms, who are able to talk and conduct their lives rationally (in contrast to the savage Yahoos nearby, who, to his horror, turn out to be apelike humans). This comparison between men and animals, in which animals are superior, may have suggested the form of Orwell's pamphlet. Orwell was also familiar with Wells's *Island of Dr Moreau*, a science-fiction novel about a doctor who turns animals into men. But this novel uses the natural goodness of animals as a contrast to the evil of modern scientific man. Unlike Swift and Wells, Orwell uses animals to symbolise human characters.

THE POLITICAL ALLEGORY

Orwell's critique of Soviet Communism is a beast-fable, a satiric form in which animals are used to represent human vice and folly. Chaucer's 'Nun's Priest's Tale', one of the *Canterbury Tales*, is an early example in English. On the level Chaucer's tale is a comic farmyard tale of a proud cock, Chanticleer, who falls prey to the fox and manages to escape; on another it is a witty and learned essay on the significance of dreams; on another, and more serious, level it is an allegory of the Fall of Man, in which Chanticleer represents Adam being tempted by the Devil. **Animal Farm,** a brief, concentrated satire, subtitled 'A Fairy Story', can also be read on the simple level of plot and character. It is an entertaining, witty tale of a farm whose oppressed animals, capable of speech and reason, overcome a cruel master and set up a revolutionary government. They are betrayed by the evil power-hungry pigs, especially by their leader, Napoleon, and forced to return to their former servitude. Only the leadership has changed. On another, more serious level, of course, it is a political allegory, a symbolic tale where all the events and characters represent events and characters in Russian history since 1917, in which 'the interplay between surface action and inner meaning is everything'. Orwell's deeper purpose is to teach a political lesson.

As he noted in his Ukrainian preface, Orwell used actual historical events to construct his story, but rearranged them to fit his plot. Manor Farm is Russia, Mr Jones the Tsar, the pigs the Bolsheviks who led the revolution. The humans represent the ruling class, the animals the workers and peasants. Old Major, the white boar who inspires the rebellion in the first chapter, stands for a combination of Marx, the chief theorist, and Lenin, the actual leader. Orwell makes Old Major a character whose motives are pure and idealistic, to emphasise the positive goals of the revolution, and makes him die before the rebellion itself. In actuality Lenin died in 1924, well after the revolution. Lenin himself set up the machinery of political terror which Stalin took over. The power struggle between Stalin and Trotsky (which Orwell satirises in chapter 5) happened after Lenin's death, not immediately after the revolution, as Orwell's account suggests.

The *Communist Manifesto* (1848) of Karl Marx and Friedrich Engels provided a theoretical basis for the revolutionary movements springing up in Europe in the latter part of the nineteenth century. Marx interpreted all history as the history of class struggle, arguing that the capitalist classes, or bourgeoisie, the owners of the means of production, are inevitably opposed to the interests of the wage-earning labourers, or proletariat, whom they exploit. This eternal conflict can only be resolved by revolution, when workers take over the means of production, share the fruits of their labours equally, and set up 'the dictatorship of the proletariat'. Marx's ideal was an international brotherhood of workers (for he believed that the interests of the working classes of all nations would unite them, causing them to cross barriers of race and culture, against the common enemy) and a future classless society. Old Major's speech in the first chapter parodies the ideas of the *Communist Manifesto*. He says: 'Only get rid of Man, and the produce of our labour would be our own.' Their goal should be the 'overthrow of the human race': in the coming struggle 'All men are enemies. All animals are comrades.' In chapter 3 'everyone worked according to his capacity', an echo of the Marxist slogan, 'From each according to his abilities, to each according to his needs.'

Each animal stands for a precise figure or representative type. The pigs, who can read and write and organise, are the Bolshevik intellectuals who came to dominate the vast Soviet bureaucracy. Napoleon is Stalin, the select group around him the Politburo, Snowball is Trotsky, and Squealer represents the propagandists of the regime. The pigs enjoy the privileges of belonging to the new ruling class (special food, shorter working hours), but also suffer the consequences of questioning Napoleon's policies.

The other animals represent various types of common people. Boxer the carthorse (whose name suggests the Boxer Rebellion of 1900, when revolutionaries tried to expel foreigners from China), is the decent working man, fired by enthusiasm for the egalitarian ideal, working overtime in the factories or on the land, willing to die to defend his country; Clover is the eternal, motherly working woman of the people. Molly, the unreliable, frivolous mare, represents the White Russians who opposed the revolution and fled the country; the dogs are the vast army of secret police who maintain Stalin in power; the sheep are the ignorant public who repeat the latest propaganda without thinking and who can be made to turn up to 'spontaneous demonstrations' in support of Napoleon's plans. Moses, the raven, represents the opportunist Church. He flies off after Mr Jones, but returns later, and continues to preach about the Sugarcandy Mountain (or heaven), but the pigs' propaganda obliterates any lingering belief. Benjamin the donkey, the cynical but powerless average man, never believes in the glorious future to come, and is always alert to every betrayal.

Orwell's allegory is comic in its detailed parallels: the hoof and horn is clearly the hammer and sickle, the Communist party emblem; 'Beasts of England' is a parody of the 'Internationale', the party song; the Order of the Green Banner is the Order of Lenin, and the other first- and second-class awards spoof the fondness of Soviet Russia for awarding medals, for everything from exceeding one's quota on the assembly line or in the harvest to bearing a great many children. The poem in praise of Napoleon imitates the sycophantic verses and the mass of paintings and sculptures turned out to glorify Stalin. In chapter 8, Squealer's presentation of impressive figures to show that food production had gone up, and the thin layer of grain sprinkled over the sacks to deceive Whymper, the agent, correspond to the well-known practice in totalitarian regimes of falsifying figures to project a positive image abroad.

Each event of the story has a historical parallel. The Rebellion in chapter 2 is the October 1917 Revolution, the Battle of the Cowshed in chapter 4 the subsequent Civil War. Mr Jones and the farmers represent the loyalist Russians and foreign forces who tried, but failed, to dislodge the Bolsheviks. The hens' revolt in chapter 7 stands for the brutally suppressed 1921 mutiny of the sailors at Kronstadt, which challenged the new regime to release political prisoners and grant freedoms of speech and the press. Napoleon's deal with Whymper, who trades the farm's produce at Willingdon market, represents Russia's 1922 Treaty of Rapallo with Germany. Orwell emphasises Napoleon's decision to trade because it breaks the First Commandment, that 'whatever goes upon two legs is an enemy'. Official Soviet policy was hostile to Germany, a militaristic, capitalist nation, but the Treaty revealed that the Communist regime had been trading arms and heavy machinery, and would continue to do so.

Mr Frederick of 'Pinchfield', renowned for his cruelty to animals and for appropriating others' land, represents Hitler, though his name also suggests the despotic eighteenth-century Prussian king Frederick the Great. Mr Pilkington of 'Foxwood' stands for Churchill and England, a country dominated by the fox-hunting upper classes. The Windmill stands for the first Five-Year Plan of 1928, which called for rapid industrialisation and collectivisation of agriculture. Its destruction in a storm in chapter 6 symbolises the grim failure of this policy. Chapter 7 describes in symbolic terms the famine and starvation which followed. The hens' revolt stands for the peasants' bitter resistance to collective farming, when they burned their crops and slaughtered their animals. The animals' false confessions in chapter 7 are the Purge Trials of the late 1930s. The false banknotes given by Frederick for the corn represent Hitler's betrayal of the Nazi-Soviet Pact of 1939, and the second destruction of the Windmill, by Frederick's men, is the Nazi invasion of Russia in 1941. The last chapter brings Orwell up to the date of the book's composition. He ends with a satiric portrait of the Teheran Conference of 1943, the meeting of Churchill, Roosevelt and Stalin, who are now allies. The quarrel over cheating at cards predicts the falling-out of the superpowers as soon as the war ended.

Animal Farm's apparent simplicity disguises Orwell's ingenuity in fitting all these complex historical events into a simple and persuasive plot. Like the three wishes of a fairy tale, the Seven Commandments are an effective structural device. Their stage-by-stage alteration charts the pigs' progressive rise to power and lends the narrative a tragic inevitability. This change also symbolises a key theme of the book: the totalitarian falsification of history. The pigs' gradual acquisition of privileges—apples, milk, house, whisky, beer, clothes—leads to the final identification of pig and human, Communist and capitalist.

The plot's circular movement, which returns the animals to conditions very like those in the beginning,

provides occasions for vivid irony. In the first chapter they lament their forced labour and poor food, but by chapter 6 they are starving, and are forced to work once more. In chapter 1 Old Major predicts that one day Jones will send Boxer to the knacker, and in chapter 9 Napoleon fulfils the prophecy by sending him to the slaughterhouse. In chapter 7, when various animals falsely confess their crimes and are summarily executed by the dogs, 'the air was heavy with the smell of blood, which had been unknown there since the expulsion of Jones'. These ironies all emphasise the tragic failure of the revolution, and support Benjamin's view that 'life would go on as it had always gone on—that is, badly' (ch. 5).

Though all the characters are types, Orwell differentiates the two most important figures, Napoleon and Snowball, so that they resemble their real-life counterparts both in the broad lines of their characterisation and in their two major disagreements. Like Stalin, Napoleon 'has a reputation for getting his own way' (ch. 2), takes charge of indoctrinating the young, sets up an elaborate propaganda machine, cultivates an image of omnipotent, charismatic power (a 'personality cult'—), surrounding himself with bodyguards and fawning attendants. Like Trotsky, Snowball is an intellectual, who quickly researches a topic and formulates plans; he is a persuasive orator, but fails to wrest the leadership from Napoleon.

Napoleon and Snowball's quarrel over the Windmill represents their dispute over what should take priority in developing the Soviet Union. Stalin wanted to collectivise agriculture, Trotsky was for developing industry. Ultimately Stalin adopted both programmes in his first Five-Year Plan, just as Napoleon derides Snowball's plans, then uses them as his own. Their most fundamental disagreement was whether to try to spread the revolution to other countries, as classical Marxism dictated, or confine themselves to making a socialist state in Russia. Napoleon argues for the latter, saying that the animals must arm themselves to protect their new leadership, Snowball that they must send more pigeons into neighbouring farms to spread the news about the revolution. Just as Stalin abandoned the idea of world revolution, so at the end Napoleon assures the farmers that he will not spread rebellion among their animals.

Expelled from the Politburo in 1925, Trotsky went into exile in 1929 and was considered a heretic. His historical role was altered, his face cut out of group photographs of the leaders of the revolution; in Russia he was denounced as a traitor and conspirator and in 1940 he was assassinated in Mexico City by a

Stalinist agent. Similarly, Snowball is blamed for everything that goes wrong in Animal Farm, and the animals are persuaded that he was a traitor from the beginning. Orwell did not share the view (of Isaac Deutscher and followers of Trotsky) that the revolution would have turned out differently had Trotsky, and not Stalin, become the leader after Lenin's death. Orwell makes Snowball equally bloodthirsty and immoral. In chapter 4, as Boxer grieves over the apparent death of the stableboy whom he has kicked in the battle, Snowball urges him not to be sentimental, because 'the only good human being is a dead one'. Trotsky defended the killing of the Tsar's children, on the grounds that the murderers acted on behalf of the proletariat.

It has been said that the very act of reducing human characters to animals implies a pessimistic view of man, and that in *Animal Farm* the satiric vision is close to the tragic. Orwell turns elements of comedy into scenes of tragic horror. In chapter 5, for example, Napoleon comically lifts his leg to urinate on Snowball's plans. But shortly afterwards he summons the dogs and orders them to rip out the throats of those who confess their disloyalty. In one instance Napoleon's contempt is amusing, in the next horrifying. Boxer's characteristics are similarly double-edged. In chapter 3 his earnest dimwittedness contrasts amusingly with the pigs' sharpness: while he is labouring to master the alphabet, and can't get past D, Snowball is engaging in parody-dialectic, explaining that birds can be included in the rule that 'Four legs good, two legs bad', since 'A bird's wing . . . is an organ of propulsion and not of manipulation.' But Boxer's trusting simplicity also leads to his death, in one of the most moving scenes in the book.

The beast-fable is not only a device that allows Orwell's serious message to be intelligible on two levels; the use of animal to represent man is basic to his whole theme. We can readily grasp that animals are oppressed and feel it is wrong to exploit them and betray their trust. Orwell counts on our common assumptions about particular species to suggest his meaning. The sheep and their bleating are perfect metaphors for a gullible public, ever ready to accept policies and repeat rumours as truth. We commonly believe pigs are greedy and savage, even to the point of devouring their young. Orwell also uses the natural animosity of cats to sparrows, dogs to rats, to suggest the social and ethnic conflicts which belie Marx's dictum that workers' common interests outweigh differences of race and nationhood. And, most central to his theme, their 'short animal lives' suggests the book's tragic vision: that the passivity and ignorance of ordinary people allows an evil leadership to stay in power.

Orwell wanted his central figure to typify the modern dictator, whose lust for power is pathological and inhuman. Napoleon's swift, secret cruelty makes the other animals seem all too human in comparison. In a review of Hitler's *Mein Kampf,* Orwell described Napoleon, Hitler and Stalin as the quintessential modern dictators, who stayed in power for similar reasons: 'All three of the great dictators have enhanced their power by imposing intolerable burdens on their peoples'. To create Napoleon, Orwell combines aspects of both Stalin and Hitler (just as the totalitarian society in *Nineteen Eighty-Four* shares characteristics of both Stalinist Russia and Nazi Germany). The animals make enormous sacrifices to complete the Windmill, only to find that it is used to grind corn (for trade), not to make their lives easier, as Snowball had promised. Napoleon 'denounced such ideas as contrary to the spirit of Animalism. The truest happiness, he said, lay in working hard and living frugally' (ch. 10). This maxim sounds an ironic echo of the Nazi slogan 'Arbeit macht frei' ('Work liberates'—), which decorated the entrance to Auschwitz. The knacker's van which carries Boxer off to the slaughterhouse, and the deception used to induce him to enter it, recall the deportations of Jews to the death-camps, and the mobile extermination vans used to round up and murder small groups of villagers. By making Napoleon a boar Orwell also drew on the literary and historical associations of Shakespeare's *Richard III,* the literary archetype of the ugly, charismatic, absolutist schemer, whose heraldic emblem was the boar.

The beast-fable form not only allowed Orwell to convey a complex message in simple terms, but was also admirably suited to his habits as a writer: his tendency to reduce characters to type, to see society as groups of competing economic interests; his narrator's detachment from the characters; his preference for grammatically simple sentences and unpretentious vocabulary. The prose succeeds brilliantly at balancing entertainment and argument because Orwell blends homely, even clichéd, language with sophisticated diction. In chapter 3, for example, 'the work of the farm went like clockwork' when the animals were in charge; into this simple fabric Orwell inserts a word with Marxist overtones: 'with the worthless *parasitical* human beings gone there was more for everyone to eat.' The context makes the word perfectly comprehensible to someone who does not know its meaning, yet if we know the word we can appreciate an additional layer of meaning—the suggestion that the animals have been indoctrinated with the Marxist view of capitalists as parasites, who own the means of production but do no work. The pleasure of reading **Animal Farm** lies in recognising the double meanings, the political and historical parallels, in the story.

In a book where distortion of language is an important theme, every word counts. Orwell's simple language points out the absurd contradictions between public political statements and private perceptions of their meaning. In chapter 6 all extra work is voluntary, but animals who refuse to do it lose half their rations; in chapter 9 Squealer announces a 'readjustment' of rations, instead of the more accurate 'reduction'. This double-talk culminates in the last chapter, when the Commandments are reduced to one: 'All animals are equal' now has added to it 'but some are more equal than others'. The comic effect of these verbal distinctions does not diminish the tragedy of the revolution betrayed.

ORWELL'S CRITIQUE OF MARX

Marx's most revolutionary idea is that no social form is unalterable. Since all monarchies, class systems, governments are made by man, they can be destroyed and replaced by a better, fairer system, in which men would no longer be exploited. Marx thought it historically inevitable that workers would revolt, seize the means of production, and set up a centralised government, which he termed, paradoxically, a 'dictatorship of the proletariat'. The government of the Soviet Union, however, was ruled by a new élite, a collective oligarchy, some of whom were derived from the proletariat. Orwell described such governments as 'a sham covering a new form of class-privilege'.

Orwell had always been fascinated by the corrupting effects of power and the relative weakness of good and decent people in the face of evil intelligence. In **Animal Farm** Orwell argues that, however desirable the ideal, man's instinct for power makes the classless society impossible. In his allegory, a Marxist revolution is doomed to fail, because it grants power, once again, to a select few. Major's speech 'had given to *the more intelligent animals* . . . a completely different outlook on life'.

To oppose Marx, Orwell turned to a classic seventeenth-century work of political philosophy, Thomas Hobbes's *Leviathan* (1651). A fiercely anti-revolutionary writer, Hobbes presents views of man and politics diametrically opposed to those of Marx. According to Hobbes, the life of man is 'solitary, poor, nasty, brutish and short', and all human beings are inclined to 'a perpetual and restless desire after power, which ceaseth only in death' (*Leviathan,* Book 1, ch. 11). Far from seeing men as capable of creating a new society to ensure their equality, Hobbes thought that only fear of death made men control their lust for power sufficiently to band together to form a commonwealth, an artificial machine to protect them from their enemies. For Hobbes, the one requirement of government, of whatever kind, was that it be strong enough to hold warring factions in check. He considered it inevitable that society be divided into social classes.

There are several important echoes of Hobbes in **Animal Farm.** Ironically, Marx-Major paraphrases Hobbes in the first chapter, when he says, 'our lives are miserable, laborious, and short'. In the last chapter, when the animals can no longer remember the promises of the revolution, Benjamin expresses the Hobbesian opinion that 'hunger, hardship and disappointment . . . [are] the unalterable law of life'. Alone of all the animals, Benjamin refuses either to hope or be disappointed, and his commentary often suggests a Swiftian cynicism, such as when he refuses to read, on the ground that there is nothing worth reading. This choice turns out to be the wise one, when we consider how the written word has been manipulated by the pigs.

But we should not assume that Benjamin's voice represents Orwell's. Orwell did not agree with Hobbes's political philosophy, nor did he, like Swift, find mankind ultimately disgusting. He simply believed that the rise of Russian totalitarianism could best be explained by Hobbes's theory, rather than by Marx's. Orwell summed up his attitude to revolution in the preface to a collection of British pamphlets:

> The most encouraging fact about revolutionary activity is that, although it always fails, it always continues. The vision of a world of free and equal human beings, living together in a state of brotherhood—in one age it is called the Kingdom of Heaven, in another the classless society—never materialises, but the belief in it never seems to die out.

Orwell had great difficulty publishing **Animal Farm,** which he completed in February 1943, for Russia had become an ally in the war against Germany, and was suffering heavy losses. Though he praised the style and compared it to Swift, T. S. Eliot, a director of Faber, spoke for most publishers when he rejected it because 'we have no conviction that this is the right point of view from which to criticise the political situation at the present time'. He told Orwell that he found the ending unsatisfactory because 'your pigs are far more intellectual than the other animals, and therefore the best qualified to run the farm', and that clearly all that was needed was 'more public-spirited pigs', though, as Orwell's book shows, revolutionary leaders are rarely public-spirited. Finally published in August 1945, *Animal Farm* was given the highest praise by Graham Greene and by Edmund Wilson, but some critics refused to accept the validity of Orwell's attack on Soviet Communism. Cyril Connolly defended Russia, asserting that 'despite a police system which we should find intolerable, the masses are happy, and . . . great strides in material progress have been made'. Northrop Frye considered the allegory superficial, and sneered at the ending, asserting that the moral of the book is 'the reactionary bromide' that 'you can't change human nature'. But Orwell's book does not pretend to be a probing analysis of Russian Communism. His purpose was to expose the totalitarian nature of the Russian government in as simple and effective a form as possible, and in this he succeeded. It is a cautionary tale, but what it suggests about power and revolution is not reducible to a formula.

As for the criticism that Orwell's satire is exaggerated, the book's continued popularity (in illegal editions) in Eastern Europe shows that his satire is as accurate as it is enduring. As recently as September 1987, customs officials at the Moscow International Book Fair cleared the British exhibitors' shelves of *Animal Farm*. There can be no better certification of its truth.

V. C. Letemendia

SOURCE: "Revolution on *Animal Farm*: Orwell's Neglected Commentary," in *Journal of Modern Language,* Vol. XVIII, No. 1, Winter, 1992, pp. 127-37.

In the last scene of George Orwell's "fairy tale," *Animal Farm,* the humbler animals peer through a window of the farmhouse to observe a horrible sight: the pigs who rule over them have grown indistinguishable from their temporary allies, the human farmers, whom they originally fought to overthrow. The animals' fate seems to mirror rather closely that of the common people as Orwell envisaged it some six years before commencing *Animal Farm*: "what you get over and over again is a movement of the proletariat which is promptly canalized and betrayed by astute people at the top, and then the growth of a new governing class. The one thing that never arrives

is equality. The mass of the people never get the chance to bring their innate decency into the control of affairs, so that one is almost driven to the cynical thought that men are only decent when they are powerless." Obviously *Animal Farm* was designed to parody the betrayal of Socialist ideals by the Soviet regime. Yet it has also been interpreted by various readers as expressing Orwell's own disillusion with any form of revolutionary political change and, by others, as unfolding such a meaning even without its author's conscious intention. It is time now to challenge both of these views.

Orwell himself commented of *Animal Farm* that "if it does not speak for itself, it is a failure." The text does indeed stand alone to reveal Orwell's consistent belief not only in democratic Socialism, but in the possibility of a democratic Socialist revolution, but there is also a considerable body of evidence outside *Animal Farm* that can be shown to corroborate this interpretation. The series of events surrounding its publication, and Orwell's own consistent attitude towards his book provide evidence of its political meaning. Meanwhile, of the two extant prefaces written by Orwell, the one designed for the Ukrainian edition, composed in 1947, is of particular political interest. Orwell's correspondence with his friends and acquaintances on the subject of *Animal Farm* provides a further source of information. Some of these letters are well known to Orwell scholars, but his correspondence with Dwight Macdonald, with whom he became friends when he was writing for the American journal, *Partisan Review,* does not appear to have been fully investigated. Macdonald himself raised a direct question about the political intent of *Animal Farm* and was given a specific answer by Orwell, yet this fascinating evidence has apparently been neglected, in spite of the generous access now available to his correspondence in the Orwell Archive.

Commentators on Orwell find it easy to conclude from *Animal Farm* the utter despair and pessimism either of its author, or of the tale itself. It must be remembered, however, that through his allegory Orwell plays a two-sided game with his reader. In some ways, he clearly emphasizes the similarities between the beasts on Animal Farm and the humans whom they are designed to represent; at other times, he demonstrates with both humor and pathos the profound differences separating animal from man—differences which in the end serve to limit the former. In doing so, he forces his reader to draw a distinction between the personalities and conduct of the beasts and those of the human world. Of course, the animals are designed to represent working people in their initial social, economic, and political position in the society not just of Animal Farm but of England in general. The basic antagonism between working class and capitalist is also strongly emphasized by the metaphor: pig and man quarrel fiercely at the end of the story. The diversity of the animal class, like the working class, is equally stressed by the differing personalities of the creatures. Just because all have been subjected to human rule, this does not mean that they will act as a united body once they take over the farm. The qualities which, for Orwell, clearly unite the majority of the animals with their human counterparts, the common working people, are a concern for freedom and equality in society and a form of "innate decency" which prevents them from desiring power for any personal gain. While this decency hinders the worker animals from discovering the true nature of the pigs until the final scene, it also provides them with an instinctive feeling for what a fair society might actually look like. Yet Orwell was obviously aware, in using this metaphor, that the animals differ fundamentally from their human counterparts. Unlike men, the majority of the beasts are limited naturally by their brief lifespan and the consequent shortness of their memory. Moreover, their differentiated physical types deny them the versatility of humans. Their class structure is fixed by their immutable functions on the farm: a horse can never fill the role of a hen. The class structure of human society, in contrast, is free from such biological demarcations. These two profoundly limiting aspects of the animal condition, in which men share no part, finally contribute to the creatures' passivity in the face of the pig dictatorship. The metaphor, then, cannot be reduced to a simple equivalence, in the way that the pigs reduce the seven Commandments of Animal Farm to one.

Evidently the animals lack education and self-confidence in spite of the active role which most of them played in the first rebellion and, in the case of some, are naturally stupid. Orwell is not implying by this the hopelessness of a proletarian revolution: he rather points to the need for education and self-confidence in any working class movement if it is to remain democratic in character. Both of these attributes, he appears further to suggest, must come from within the movement itself. The crude proletarian spirit of the common animals necessarily provides the essential ingredient for a revolution towards a free and equal society, but it needs careful honing and polishing if it is not to fall victim to its own inherent decency and modesty. If this simple, instinctive decency is to be preserved in the transition from revolution—which is all too easy—to the construction of a new society—which is not—other kinds of virtue are also necessary and must at all costs be developed by the working class if it is not to be betrayed again. The text itself, however, hints at disaster for the rule of the pigs. Their single tenet asserting that some animals are more equal than others is in the end a meaningless absurdity. In spite of their great intellectual gifts, the pigs are ultimately the most absurd of all the farm animals, for they are attempting to assume a human identity which cannot belong to them. It is left to the reader to ponder the potential for political change, given the evident weakness and vanity at the core of the pig dictatorship. The final scene of the book, moreover, reveals the disillusionment of the working beasts with their porcine leaders, an essential step in the process of creating a new revolution.

Evidence external to the text of *Animal Farm* is not required to establish the political meaning within its pages. Yet an examination of Orwell's attitude towards the book during the difficult period in which he tried to have it published only strengthens the conclusions drawn here. Even before *Animal Farm* was finished, Orwell was quite aware that it would cause controversy because of its untimely anti-Stalinist message, and he predicted difficulties in publishing it. He was, of course, correct: the manuscript was refused by Gollancz, Andre Deutsch, and Jonathan Cape—in the latter case on the advice of the Ministry of Information. Meanwhile, Orwell declined an offer to publish the book in serial form in Lady Rhondda's *Time and Tide,* explaining that the politics of the journal were too right-wing for his tale, only to be turned down by T. S. Eliot at Faber and Faber, his next choice of publisher. The end of the story is well known to Orwell scholars: Orwell went finally to Frederick Warburg, who accepted the manuscript, and upon its publication in August 1945, it was well received and soon selected by the Book-of-the-Month Club. Orwell's interest in the major publishing houses, as well as his reluctance to approach Frederick Warburg as a first choice and his willingness at one desperate point to pay himself to have the work reproduced in pamphlet form show that he wanted it to reach the public at all costs and to address as wide an audience as possible from as unprejudiced a political context as he could find. Naturally, Lady Rhondda's journal would not have been suitable: his purpose was not to congratulate conservatives or even liberals on the failure of the Russian Revolution, however scathing his criticism of the Stalinist regime within the allegory. Furthermore, Orwell stood firmly against any suggested alterations to the text, particularly in the instance of his representation of the Bolsheviks as pigs. He made no excuses for *Animal Farm*—as he would in the case of *Nineteen Eighty-Four*—and must have considered its message to be fairly clear, for he offered no press releases to correct misinterpretations of the book from either right- or left-wing political camps. On the contrary, it rather seems that he was proud of the quality, as much as the political timeliness, of the book and expected it to require no external defence or explanation; this opinion did not appear to change.

Some further indication of Orwell's own view of *Animal Farm* may be found in the two prefaces he wrote for it. Of the two, only the Ukrainian preface was actually published. Its original English version, written early in 1947, has never been found, and only a translation from the Ukrainian is available to Orwell scholars. This presents the possibility that various errors or subtle alterations of meaning might have remained uncorrected by the author when it was first translated from English to Ukrainian. Written two years after the English preface, the Ukrainian piece obviously betrays a purpose very different from that of its predecessor, as a result supplying the reader with far more direct commentary on the text. Orwell makes it clear here that he "became pro-Socialist more out of disgust with the way the poorer section of the industrial workers were oppressed and neglected than out of any theoretical admiration for a planned society." His experiences in Spain, he states, gave him first-hand evidence of the ease with which "totalitarian propaganda can control the opinion of enlightened people in democratic countries." Not only were the accusations against Trotskyists in Spain the same as those made at the Moscow trials in the USSR; Orwell considers that he "had every reason to believe that [they] were false," as far as Spain was concerned. Upon his return to England, he discovered "the numerous sensible and well-informed observers believing the most fantastic accounts of conspiracy, treachery and sabotage which the press reported from the Moscow trials." What upset him most was not the "barbaric and undemocratic methods" of Stalin and his associates, since, he argues, "It is quite possible that even with the best intentions, they could not have acted otherwise under the conditions prevailing there." The real problem, in his view, was that Western Europeans could not see the truth about the Soviet regime, still considering it a Socialist country when, in fact, it was being transformed "into a hierarchical society, in which the rulers have no more reason to give up their power than any other ruling class." Both workers and the intelligentsia had to be disabused of this illusion which they held partly out of wilful misunderstanding and partly because of

an inability to comprehend totalitarianism, "being accustomed to comparative freedom and moderation in public life." To make possible, then, a "revival of the Socialist movement" by exposing the Soviet myth, Orwell writes that he tried to think of "a story that could be easily understood by almost everyone and which could be easily translated into other languages."

He claims that although the idea came to him upon his return from Spain in 1937, the details of the story were not worked out until the day he "saw a little boy, perhaps ten years old, driving a huge cart-horse along a narrow path, whipping it whenever it tried to turn." If the horse could only become aware of its own strength, the boy would obviously have no control over it. Orwell found in this a parallel with the way in which "the rich exploit the proletariat," and he proceeded from this recognition "to analyse Marx's argument from the animals' point of view." For them, he argues, the idea of class struggle between humans was illusory; the real tension was between animals and men, "since whenever it was necessary to exploit animals, all humans united against them." The story was not hard to elaborate from this, Orwell continues, although he did not actually write it all out until 1943, some six years after the main ideas had been conceived of. Orwell declines to comment on the work in his preface, for "if it does not speak for itself, it is a failure." Yet he ends with two points about details in the story: first, that it required some chronological rearrangement of the events of the Russian Revolution, and, second, that he did not mean pigs and men to appear reconciled completely at the end of the book. On the contrary, "I meant it to end on a loud note of discord, for I wrote it immediately after the Teheran Conference [parodied by the final scene in *Animal Farm*] which everybody thought had established the best possible relations between the USSR and the West. I personally did not believe that such good relations would last long. . . . "

It seems, then, that as much as Orwell wanted to explain how he had arrived at Socialism and at his understanding of totalitarianism, he sought to indicate in this preface to Ukrainian readers how workers and intelligentsia in Western Europe, but especially in England, misperceived the difference between the Soviet Union of 1917 and that of twenty and thirty years later. *Animal Farm* was, according to its author, an attempt to strip away the mythical veil shrouding the Stalinist regime; simultaneously, however, he was trying to renew what had been lost through this deception and to revive the original spirit of the Socialist movement. It seems possible to conclude that Orwell is suggesting the presence of just such a double intention within the allegory. One point in the preface, however, requires clarification. Orwell's reference to the animals' view that the real class struggle lay between animals and humans suggests, in the context of the allegory, the absence of any significant class struggle between members of the ruling class—or humans—since they will readily forget their differences and unite to oppress animals. This appears confusing when applied to Marx's theory, which Orwell claims as the theoretical basis of this insight, and furthermore it does not capture the thrust of the story itself, in which the divisions between animals are exposed in detail, rather than those between humans, or even between humans and animals. But Orwell makes it quite clear here that he refers to an animal perspective in defining the class struggle as one between humans and beasts. Certainly the point of departure was, in both the Russian situation and in this particular allegory, the identification and removal of the most evident class of oppressors. In this initial movement, the oppressed class was not mistaken politically; what came afterwards in both instances, though, demonstrated that the first movement of revolutionary consciousness had not been sustained in its purity, since the goals of the revolution gradually began to be violated. Orwell's remark in the preface that "[f]rom this point of departure [the animals' view of the class struggle], it was not difficult to elaborate the rest of the story" cannot be taken as an admission that the animals' perspective was perfectly correct. Of course, the book debunks such a simplistic interpretation of the class struggle, in spite of its initial accuracy.

By revealing the divisions within the animal ranks, Orwell is cautioning his reader to question the animal view of the class struggle, for the crucial problem that even the wise Old Major does not predict in his identification of the real enemy is the power-hunger of the pigs. By allegorical implication, this points rather interestingly to Orwell's identification of a flaw in the Marxian theory of revolution itself. Although its starting point is clearly the animals' partially accurate but insufficient analysis of the class struggle, the allegory in its course reveals more and more drastically the inadequacy of such a view as a basis for post-revolutionary society. Part of Old Major's vision is indeed debunked, while the truth of the initial insight about class struggle is never denied, and the story, as has been seen, ends on a note of hope. Orwell's final point in the preface constitutes the only correction and very mild apology that he would make about the text, even though he had had roughly two years to assess the critical response—and hence the variety of misinterpreta-tions—circulating about *Animal Farm.* Here he is warning his reader about the subtlety of his allegory: pigs and humans may come to look the same at the end, but they are still essentially enemies and share only a greed for power. For it is indeed the dispute between farmers and pigs which completes the transformation of pig to man and of man to pig.

If the Ukrainian preface was written for an unknown audience, the English preface was designed for readers with whom Orwell was much more familiar. Written in 1945, when he was still bitterly upset over the difficulties of printing unpopular political commentary in wartime Britain, the English preface is concerned not with the content of the story but with the question of whether he would be free to publish it at all because of current political alliances, intellectual prejudices, and general apathy over the need to defend basic democratic liberties. Attacking as he does here the political toadying of the Left intelligentsia in Britain to the Stalinist regime, Orwell presents *Animal Farm* as a lesson for the well-educated as much as the uneducated. Meanwhile, the fact that he makes no reference in this preface to the details of the book indicates his strong confidence in its political clarity for English readers, although his bitter tone shows, as Crick suggests, Orwell's acute sense that he was being "persecuted for plain speaking" before *Animal Farm* was published. Since the English preface does not actually offer an interpretation of *Animal Farm* explaining Orwell's political intention, it is necessary to look for this information in his more private communications on the subject.

Orwell commented explicitly on his book to his friends Geoffrey Gorer and Dwight Macdonald. Crick states that Orwell gave a copy of *Animal Farm* to Gorer having marked in it the passage in which Squealer defends the pigs' theft of the milk and apples. He told Gorer that this "was the key passage." This emphasis of Orwell's is reiterated and explained more fully in a letter to Dwight Macdonald written shortly after *Animal Farm* first appeared in the United States, in 1946. Macdonald was one of a group of American intellectuals who had broken with Soviet Communism as early as 1936 and had gone to work with Philip Rahv and William Phillips on *Partisan Review.* From January 1941 to the summer of 1946, Orwell had sent regular "letters" to the review and had had cause to correspond with Macdonald fairly frequently. Macdonald was later to move to the editorship of *Politics,* described by Orwell in a letter to T. S. Eliot as "a sort of dissident offshoot" of *Partisan Review,* and had already championed a review written by Orwell that had been rejected for political reasons by the *Manchester Evening News.* This shared political understanding soon developed into a literary friendship which lasted until Orwell's death in 1950.

In September 1944, Orwell had already written to Macdonald expressing his views about the Soviet Union. Given that only a few months separated the completion of *Animal Farm* from this letter, it seems safe to assume that the views expressed in both might be similar. To Macdonald, Orwell stated, "I think the USSR is the dynamo of world Socialism, so long as people believe in it. I think that if the USSR were to be conquered by some foreign country the working class everywhere would lose heart, for the time being at least, and the ordinary stupid capitalists who never lost their suspicion of Russia would be encouraged." Furthermore, "the fact that the Germans have failed to conquer Russia has given prestige to the idea of Socialism. For that reason I wouldn't want to see the USSR destroyed and think it ought to be defended if necessary." There is a caution, however: "[b]ut I want people to become disillusioned about it and to realise that they must build their own Socialist movement without Russian interference, and I want the existence of democratic Socialism in the West to exert a regenerative influence upon Russia." He concludes that "if the working class everywhere had been taught to be as anti-Russian as the Germans have been made, the USSR would simply have collapsed in 1941 or 1942, and God knows what things would then have come out from under their stones. After that Spanish business I hate the Stalin regime perhaps worse than you do, but I think one must defend it against people like Franco, Laval etc."

In spite of its repressive features and its betrayal of basic human freedoms, then, Orwell still considered the Soviet regime to be vital as an example to the working class everywhere. The real danger lay in the idea that it defined Socialism. What was most needed was a new form of democratic Socialism created and maintained by the people. He offers meanwhile the possibility that such democratic forms of Socialism elsewhere might actually have a benign effect on the Russian regime. In the allegorical context of Animal Farm, Napoleon's dictatorship would still seem to be a step forward from that of the human farmers—according to Orwell's letter, the rule of "the ordinary stupid capitalists." For animals outside the farm, it would provide a beacon of hope—so long as the truth about the betrayal taking place within was made plain to them. For it would now become their task to build their own movement in a democratic spirit which might, in Orwell's words, "exert a regenerative influence" on the corruption of the pigs' realm.

When *Animal Farm* finally appeared in the United States in 1946, Macdonald wrote again to Orwell, this time to discuss the book: "most of the anti-Stalinist intellectuals I know . . . don't seem to share my enthusiasm for *Animal Farm.* They claim that your parable means that revolution always ends badly for the underdog, hence to hell with it and hail the status quo. My own reading of the book is that it is meant to apply to Russia without making any larger statement about the philosophy of revolution. None of the objectors have so far satisfied me when I raised this point; they admit explicitly that is all you profess to do, but still insist that implicit is the broader point. . . . Which view would you say comes closer to your intentions?"

Orwell's reply deserves quoting in full: "Of course I intended it primarily as a satire on the Russian revolution. But I did mean it to have a wider application in so much that I meant that that kind of revolution (violent conspiratorial revolution, led by unconsciously power-hungry people) can only lead to a change of masters. I meant the moral to be that revolutions only effect a radical improvement when the masses are alert and know how to chuck out their leaders as soon as the latter have done their job. The turning point of the story was supposed to be when the pigs kept the milk and apples for themselves (Kronstadt.) If the other animals had had the sense to put their foot down then, it would have been all right. If people think I am defending the status quo, that is, I think, because they have grown pessimistic and assume there is no alternative except dictatorship or laissez-faire capitalism. In the case of the Trotskyists, there is the added complication that they feel responsible for events in the USSR up to about 1926 and have to assume that a sudden degeneration took place about that date, whereas I think the whole process was foreseeable—and was foreseen by a few people, e.g. Bertrand Russell—from the very nature of the Bolshevik party. What I was trying to say was, 'You can't have a revolution unless you make it for yourself; there is no such thing as a benevolent dictatorship.'"

Yes, *Animal Farm* was intended to have a wider application than a satire upon the Russian regime alone. Yes, it did indeed imply that the rule of the pigs was only "a change of masters." Yet it did not condemn to the same fate all revolutions, nor for a moment suggest that Farmer Jones should be reinstated as a more benevolent dictator than Napoleon. According to Orwell's letter, the problem examined by *Animal Farm* concerns the nature of revolution itself. Unless everyone makes the revolution for him or herself without surrendering power to an elite, there will be little hope for freedom or equality. A revolution in which violence and conspiracy become the tools most resorted to, one which is led by a consciously or unconsciously power-hungry group, will inevitably betray its own principles. Failing to protest when the pigs kept the milk and apples for themselves, the other animals surrendered what power they might have had to pig leadership. Had they been "alert and [known] how to chuck out their leaders" once the latter had fulfilled their task, the original spirit of Animal Farm might have been salvaged. The book itself, Orwell makes clear in his letter, was calling not for the end of revolutionary hopes, but for the beginning of a new kind of personal responsibility on the part of revolutionaries. The most important barrier in the way of such a democratic Socialist revolution was the Soviet myth: if people outside still thought that that particular form of revolution could succeed without betraying its goals, nothing new could be accomplished. The final note of Orwell's letter is optimistic: if people mistook his message for a conservative one, it was precisely their problem. They had no confidence in the possibility of an alternative to either capitalism or dictatorship. In a sense, they would be like those animals who, when forced into making a choice between a false set of alternatives by Squealer—either the return of Farmer Jones or unquestioning obedience to the rule of the pigs—failed to consider the possibility of a third choice, a democratic Socialist society. For although Orwell was prepared to provide a fairly detailed explanation of his animal story for his friend Macdonald, his letter makes it quite evident that the burden of understanding *Animal Farm* still lay with its reader.

Given the striking congruity between the text and Orwell's political commentary about it, it would be rash to argue that he had lost control of his allegory in *Animal Farm.* If it takes time and effort to expose the political intricacies behind the stark prose of his animal fable, this must have been partly his intention: the lesson of democracy was not an easy one to learn, and the next revolutionary move towards democratic Socialism could surely not be allowed to repeat the mistakes of Old Major. Still, we may wonder if the grain of hope provided by the final scene of the book is not, in this light, too insubstantial to feed a new generation of revolutionaries. Yet if Orwell had presented an easy political resolution to the horrors of totalitarianism, his warning would lose its force. His reader could remain complacent, detached from the urgent need for personal involvement in political change so emphasized by the animal allegory. If he had designed a political solution for the other beasts, furthermore, he could be accused of hypoc-

risy: his whole argument both inside and outside the text rested on the proposition that the people had to make and retain control of the revolution themselves if they wanted it to remain true to its goals. The deceit of the pigs was not the only failure on Animal Farm, for the foolish simplicity of the other animals and, indeed, of Old Major's naive idea of revolutionary change were as much to blame for the dictatorship which ensued. Orwell had to warn his readers that their apathy and thoughtlessness were as dangerous as blind admiration for the Stalinist regime. Only when all members of society saw the essential need for individual responsibility and honesty at the heart of any struggle for freedom and equality could the basic goals of Socialism, as Orwell saw them, be approached more closely. Meanwhile, no single revolutionary act could create a perfect world, either for the animals or for the humans whom they represent in the story. Acceptance of the notion of class struggle could not lead to an instant transformation of society unless those who would transform it accepted also the difficult burden of political power, both at the time of and after the revolution. While the most corrupting force on Animal Farm was the deception practiced upon the other animals by the pigs, the greatest danger came from the reluctance of the oppressed creatures to believe in an alternative between porcine and human rule. Yet it was in the affirmation of dignity, freedom, and equality tacitly provided by the nobler qualities of the presumed lower animals that Orwell saw the beginnings of such an alternative. So it is that, in the last moment of the book, he leaves open the task of rebuilding the revolution on a wiser and more cautiously optimistic foundation.

Michael Peters

SOURCE: "*Animal Farm* Fifty Years On," in *Contemporary Review,* Vol. 267, August, 1995, pp. 90-1.

Few books are as well-known as *Animal Farm.* Published fifty years ago, in August 1945, as the Cold War was about to begin, the novel with its mixture of simple fairy-tale and historical allegory, still has the power to charm and provoke, even though that war now seems to be part of a previous age. The novel, while frequently taught in schools to thirteen and fourteen year olds, is rarely to be found in sixth form or university syllabuses. Like the author, the book occupies an ambiguous place in the literary world. Yet its fame amongst the reading and, to an extent, the non-reading public is indisputable; the slogan, 'All animals are equal, but some are more equal than others,' is one that has become part of the language.

Orwell was very clear about his intentions in writing the book. During the Spanish Civil War, he had seen the effects of the repressions and deceptions of Stalinism at first hand. He wished to open people's eyes to the reality of the Soviet regime 'in a story that could be easily understood by almost anyone, even when that regime had become an ally to Britain and the USA in the fight against German fascism.' Such an exposure was essential, Orwell believed, if a true and democratic form of socialism was to be created. Working in London, first as a BBC journalist, and then as the literary editor of *Tribune, Animal Farm* was written whilst the bombs dropped; one bomb even damaged the manuscript when it fell on the street where Orwell and his wife lived. Certainly the process by which the book saw the light of day was a tortuous one, with publisher after publisher finding reasons for refusing or delaying publication. For Gollancz, who had first option, and Faber, in the person of T. S. Eliot, the novel was too much of an attack on Russia, which had suffered so hugely at Stalingrad. Cape first consulted the Ministry of Information, who were concerned that the Russian leaders would take offence at their depiction as pigs, before turning the book down.

At the other end of the spectrum, even the Anarchist, Freedom Press, took exception to the novel. In America, the Dial Press thought it 'impossible to sell animal stories.' When, eventually, Warburg agreed to take the book, publication was delayed for almost a year, until the end of the European War. The question of whether this was due to a shortage of paper—the official explanation—or to political necessity, is still unresolved. From Paris, to which he travelled in February 1945, to report the War for *The Observer* at closer quarters, Orwell checked the proofs, making one last change. When the Windmill is attacked Napoleon stays standing, instead of dropping to the ground, as a tribute to Stalin's courage in remaining in Moscow during Hitler's advance; even to his enemies Orwell is determined to be fair.

Inevitably *Animal Farm,* when it was finally published, created controversy, although not of the kind originally envisaged. With the end of the struggle against fascism, a new conflict had begun to develop—the Cold War. Once effectively banned because of its politics, the book started to become an instrument of propaganda in the West's campaign to claim the moral high ground. Many new translations were produced, some with the assistance of the US State Department, and were circulated in places where Soviet influence prevailed—for example, the Ukraine and Korea. In 1947 the 'Voice of America' broadcast a radio version to Eastern Europe. The success of the novel in propaganda terms may be gauged by the Soviets' fear and loathing of the book, expressed by the seizure of copies in Germany, as well as by the cancellation of proposed radio dramatisations in Czechoslovakia. This occurred just before Soviet crackdowns in 1948 and again in 1968 on regimes which seemed to be dangerously libertarian.

Whilst Orwell was happy to see his book used to attack the Soviet myth, he did become increasingly worried about the way it was being used by the Right as a means of demonstrating that all revolutionary change was bound to fail. Picking out as central the moment when the pigs keep apples and milk for themselves, he makes the point that if 'the other animals had had the sense to put their foot down then it would have been all right.' Major's dream could have been realised. The masses should be 'alert', ready to 'chuck out their leaders as soon as they have done their job.' This is rather a different message than that found in the anti-Communist propaganda which so frequently surrounded, and surrounds, the novel.

For Orwell personally, *Animal Farm* marked his entry into the halls of literary fame. With the first impression of 4,500 copies soon sold out, sales in the UK reached 25,000 within five years, and over half a million in the US within four years. From being a marginal left-wing figure, Orwell became one of the most celebrated writers of the day, with periodic radio and television adaptations of both *Animal Farm* and *Nineteen Eighty-Four.* In 1954, the first animated version of a literary text—a cartoon of *Animal Farm*—was made. However, in the last few years of his life, with a newly adopted son to bring up alone after his wife's unexpected death, and with his tuberculosis becoming increasingly serious, the success of what Orwell called his 'little squib' may have been some small comfort.

George Orwell, as many readers have done, recognised that the book's great achievement was to 'fuse political purpose and artistic purpose into one whole'. For this reason, fifty years on, in spite of the collapse of the Soviet system, in spite of the dilution of democratic socialism into liberalism, and in spite of the habit of literary critics to favour complex texts for deconstruction, *Animal Farm* may still be read with pleasure and profit, inside and outside the classroom, as one of the most imaginatively compelling satires on what Orwell called, in another of his fine phrases, the 'gramophone mind'.

Katharine Byrne

SOURCE: *"Animal Farm,"* in *Commonweal,* Vol. 123, No. 10, May 17, 1996, p. 14.

Although he was a respected novelist and journalist in England during the '30s and early '40s, George Orwell (1903-50) had a hard time getting *Animal Farm* into print. He finished it in 1944 and sent or carried it from one publisher to another, but no one would take it. World War II was in progress. Russia was our ally and Britain's. A book that satirized the betrayal of Russia's revolution by its leaders was regarded, at the very least, as an affront to a friend. Moreover, an American publisher told him you just can't sell an animal story to adults.

Not until the end of the war in 1945 and the customary reshuffling of friends and enemies was a publisher willing to invest enough precious paper to produce 450 copies. These were sold out within weeks. The Queen dispatched an emissary to her bookseller-by-appointment, but his shelves were bare; an anarchist book shop offered the Queen a complimentary copy. The book has never been out of print since then, read by millions in dozens of languages. Nineteen ninety-six marks its fiftieth anniversary of publication in the United States.

If you were in high school at any time since the 1950s, you probably read *Animal Farm,* a story of the revolt of Farmer Jones's livestock against their brutal, drunken owner. The venerable boar, Old Major, is the philosopher of the revolution. His ringing words to the clandestine assemblage of animals remind them that their lives are "miserable, laborious, and short," with no share in the fruits of their labor. While ascribing all their troubles to "man," his speech ends with the warning: "Above all, no animal must ever tyrannize over his own kind. Weak or strong, clever or simple, we are all brothers. All animals are equal."

The barnyard is roused to revolution. Led by the pigs, the animals rout Jones and take possession; "Jones's Manor" is now called "Animal Farm." Morale is high. Victory is sweet for the liberated animals but also brief. At first they gambol in joy at the prospect of living out their lives in dignity, sharing in the prosperity their labor produces. Each works hard to sustain the revolution.

But then, inexorably, methodically, equality and freedom are stripped away as the pigs, under Napoleon, a ruler as brutal as Jones was, develop a ruling elite that abrogates all privilege to itself at the expense of the "lower" animals. (The wily pigs explain that they really don't like the milk that they refuse to share with the other animals; they drink it only to keep up their strength so that they can pursue the welfare of all.)

Lies and terror now rule "Animal Farm." In the ultimate reversal of Old Major's words, "all animals are created equal, but some animals are more equal than others." One form of repression has been replaced by another. In the end, the wretched animals are looking in the window at an economic summit between Men and Pigs, "Looking from pig to man, and from man to pig they observe that there is no difference between them."

John Halas and Joy Batchelor, in their animated cartoon film of the book (1954), apparently could not bear this ending. In their version of the book, "the animals, united, came on relentlessly" and a brick was thrown through the window, "shattering Napoleon's magnificent portrait under the impact of yet another revolution." Understandably, students like this version better than the original.

But as Orwell tells it, the fable ends with all the brave hopes in ruins. Virtue is crushed and wickedness triumphs. What went wrong? Orwell lays out the story and asks us to look at it. He does not moralize. This is what happened, but we know it is not right. We are left morally indignant at the injustice suffered. Are we to believe that this is the inevitable fate of rebellion? Or that other political systems are better than Stalinist communism?

As to that, Orwell does not uphold the political systems of the West. The men who come to deal with the ruling pigs, Pilkington from capitalist England and Frederick from Nazi Germany, commiserate with the pigs: "You have your lower animals and we have our lower classes." From his earliest years as a policeman for the British Empire in Burma—an "unsuitable career," he called it—Orwell always spoke out against oppressors of the poor and helpless: returning to England he spoke for the rights of tramps, hop-pickers, or coal miners.

A self-defined democratic Socialist, Orwell had a hard time with other members of the Left. An episode in Bellow's *Mr. Sammler's Planet* describes the situation succinctly. Addressing a Columbia University seminar, Mr. Sammler is attempting to defend Orwell's position, but he is interrupted by one of the bearded and unwashed students with "Orwell was a counter-revolutionary shit, and you're an old shit too." With this declaration, the meeting is ingloriously ended.

Maligned by the Left, Orwell has often been appropriated by the Right. In the flurry of interest that coincided with the year 1984, Norman Podhoretz, editor of *Commentary*, claimed that Orwell would, if he had lived, subscribe to the conservative magazine and to the principles of its editor. In fact, *Animal Farm* had earlier entered the canon of required reading in most high schools for some of the wrong reasons, its author would say—and he did say Orwell was distressed to find his *Animal Farm* and *Nineteen Eighty-Four* being used, especially in the United States, as cold-war weapons, purportedly the work of a repentant Communist who saw the light and wanted to warn the world of the inevitable fruits of revolution. When he saw the issue of Henry Luce's *Life* magazine expounding this idea, Orwell insisted that he had not written a book against Stalinism to deny the right of revolt by oppressed people, nor to advance American foreign policy. "My books," he said, "are about the perversions that any centralized economy is liable to."

In a letter to Dwight Macdonald, editor of *Politics,* Orwell further explained, "Revolutions led by power-hungry people can only lead to a change of masters. . . . Revolutions only effect a radical improvement when the masses are alert and know how to chuck out their leaders as soon as the latter have done their job. . . . You can't have a revolution unless you make it for your self; there is no such thing as a benevolent dictatorship."

Should *Animal Farm* be read during the next fifty years? Of course, but for the right reasons: setting up as it does, with crystal clarity, the price paid when we do not safeguard our freedoms. The hard-working wretches of the world contribute to their own fate in their ignorant loyalty and apathy. In the book, the huge cart-horse, Boxer, a faithful, unquestioning worker ("I will get up earlier; I will work harder . . . Napoleon is always right") is sent to the knackers as soon as his usefulness is over. As he is carried off to his death, the weak protest of his hooves against the side of the van sounds the dying hope of the animals betrayed. The tendency of power to corrupt must always be recognized; people's hold over their own fate must prevail: an alert, informed, and wary electorate.

Is *Animal Farm* out of date since the Soviet Socialist Republics, as constituted, have failed? Only if it is read for the wrong reasons. The tale about independence won but lost continues to remind us that freedom is fragile and precious. Power corrupts, and there are forces at work seeking to wield it.

I have spoken to ten or twelve English teachers, from Highland Park, Illinois, to Highland Park in Dallas, Texas, about the continuing relevance of *Animal Farm.* I was glad to hear one of them say, "I'd hate to lose it as required reading. It is such a great story, told with precious touches of humor." Another added, "It's a rare classic that students really enjoy." A thoughtful teacher told me, "The book is talking about any concentration of power. Last year a bright student suggested that 'the story warns us not to fight for our rights as students and then let class officers impose their ideas on the rest of us.'"

After a lecture, Bernard Crick, one of Orwell's biographers, was asked by a listener, "If Orwell were alive today, what would he be?" Crick's answer sidestepped the questioner's effort to pull Orwell politically to the right or to the left and put a tag on him. "If Orwell were alive today," Crick said, "he would be a very old man; he would probably be counting the marbles in his head and hoping they were all there." Indeed, if Orwell were alive and well and had all his marbles he would be fighting as he did all the days of his brief life, writing against oppression and corruption wherever it exists, glad to know that the young are still reading and learning from *Animal Farm.*

Anthony Kearney

SOURCE: "Orwell's *Animal Farm* and *1984*," in *The Explicator,* Vol. 54, No. 4, Summer, 1996, p. 238.

The famous slogan in *Animal Farm,* "All animals are equal but some are more equal than others," is more ambiguous than it has usually been taken to be. The slogan has invariably been read as meaning that some animals (the pigs) are more equal (are better) than others. If being equal is a good thing, then the more equal you are the better. This is what we might call the obvious meaning of the slogan, a meaning authorized by popular usage over half a century and so deeply embedded in everyone's mind that advertisers, among others, can use it to trigger our desire to be better than everyone else. In the novel *1984,* for obvious reasons, the phrase was used often. "Are you more equal than others?" asked *The Welding Journal,* "This is your chance to become one who is more equal than others, more expert in the welding field. . . . " Being "more equal" means excelling in certain ways and being superior to others, just as the pigs in *Animal Farm* claim to be more equal than, and superior to, the other animals.

Although not disputing that this is the obvious way to read the slogan (nearly all readers have taken it to mean just that), I suggest that in the Orwellian context of *Animal Farm,* as opposed to that outside Orwell's text, the slogan can also bear quite another meaning, one which fits even better than the obvious one the issues raised by that work. If "equal" can mean something desirable and good, it can also in a primary sense mean no more than "identical" or "same." It is this meaning, I believe, that predominates in the slogan. The slogan should read, "some animals (not the pigs) are more equal (are more the same) than others (the superior pigs)." In this reading the pigs want less equality, not more; being "more equal" means that you belong to the common herd, not the elite. In the end this may lead to much the same conclusion as in the popular reading of the slogan—the pigs in both readings are marking themselves off from the other animals—but what is at issue here is the way equality is being defined, by the pigs and of course by Orwell himself. In the obvious reading of the slogan, equality is a desirable state of affairs, with the pigs claiming more of it for themselves; in the second reading it is distinctly undesirable, and the pigs want nothing to do with it. Lower animals are equal, the higher ones decidedly unequal. The slogan allows different readings due to the exploitable ambiguities of its key term, "equal."

Orwell's own view of equality approximated that of R. H. Tawney in [*Equality*] his classic work on the subject. For Tawney, promoting the ideal of human equality did not entail a belief in "the romantic illusion that men are equal in character and intelligence" but did entail a belief that social and economic inequalities were harmful to society. In the early 1940s, at the time he was writing *Animal Farm,* Orwell also wrote approvingly of "a growing wish for greater equality" among English people, hoping that some of the worst inequalities on the social, economic, and educational fronts would be removed after the war. This ideal of greater equality was obviously a basic tenet of his democratic socialism. However, his concern for the progress of equality made him extra sensitive to the unpleasant fact that the notion of equality was vulnerable to cynical manipulation by politicians. In **"Politics and the English Language"** (1946) Orwell lists "equality" as one of those "words used in variable meanings, in most cases more or less dishonestly." In *1984* he reveals even sharper anxieties about the term: Here not only has the ideal of equality as understood by the best political thinkers been totally abandoned, but the actual word itself has been reduced by "Newspeak" to mean no more than "identical." As Orwell phrases it in his appendix, **"The Principles of Newspeak,"** its former associations no longer exist:

For example, All mans are equal was a possible Newspeak sentence, but only in the same sense in which All men are redhaired is a possible Oldspeak sentence. It did not contain a grammatical error, but it expressed a palpable untruth—i.e. that all men are of equal size, weight, or strength. The concept of political equality no longer existed, and this secondary meaning had accordingly been purged out of the word equal.

To reinforce the point, Orwell cites the passage from the American Declaration of Independence containing the phrase "all men are created equal" and adds, "It would have been quite impossible to render this into Newspeak while keeping to the sense of the original."

This brutal purging of time-honored meanings of the term equality can already be seen occurring in *Animal Farm,* where the pigs themselves form an embryonic party. The pigs with their "some are more equal than others" idea begin the process—completed in the world of *1984*—whereby "equal" starts to lose its libertarian meaning and comes to mean no more than "identical." The term "equal" may, at the beginning of *Animal Farm,* hold its revolutionary connotation intact, but by the end of the book it carries a drastically reduced and sinister meaning.

If, as I think, this reading accords more convincingly than the more obvious and popular one with Orwell's main preoccupations in *Animal Farm* and *1984,* it is both ironic and appropriate that the slogan should have engendered such misreading and misapplication; it has all the appearance of a statement deliberately designed by its author to create problems of interpretation in a context where the manipulation of language is an essential part of the political process.

Robert Pearce

SOURCE: "Orwell, Tolstoy, and *Animal Farm,*" in *The Review of English Studies,* Vol. 49, No. 193, February, 1998, p. 64.

Leo Tolstoy and George Orwell are sometimes contrasted as two figures with totally opposite attitudes to life, the one an other-worldly believer and the other a this-worldly humanist. In a celebrated essay, published in 1947 [**"Lear, Tolstoy and the Fool"**], Orwell defended Shakespeare's King Lear against the Russian's intemperate attack and, moreover, also criticized his whole outlook on life. Tolstoy, he wrote, was an imperious and egotistical bully, and he quoted his biographer Derrick Leon that he would frequently 'slap the faces of those with whom he disagreed'. Orwell wrote that Tolstoy was incapable of either tolerance or humility; and he considered that his attack on the artistic integrity of Lear arose partly because it was too near the knuckle. Lear's 'huge and gratuitous act of renunciation' bore an uncomfortably close resemblance to Tolstoy's similarly foolish renunciation in old age of worldly wealth, sexuality, and other ties that bind us to 'the surface of the earth—including love, in the ordinary sense of caring more for one human being than another'. But this, according to Orwell, was what love was all about, and he characterized Tolstoy—and other would-be saints like Gandhi—as forbiddingly inhuman in their attitudes. He himself cared strongly about 'the surface of the earth' and was with Shakespeare in his interest in the 'actual process of life'. The main aim of the puritanical Tolstoy, Orwell believed, was 'to narrow the range of human consciousness', a process which he himself, in *Nineteen Eighty-Four* and other later writings, was struggling valiantly to counteract. It is very easy therefore to see the two men as polar opposites, in both their temperament and their artistic aims.

Yet this view is quite mistaken. Orwell's criticisms have sometimes been misunderstood; Orwell and Tolstoy had far more in common than is generally realized; and indeed the Russian influenced this peculiarly English writer in several important ways, not least in that—almost certainly—he furnished him with material for one of the most significant episodes in *Animal Farm.* The parallels between this book and Russian history are well known, but the debt owed to Tolstoy's *What I Believe* has never been acknowledged.

In his biography of Tolstoy, A. N. Wilson praises Orwell's image of Tolstoyas-Lear but insists that this unforgettable depiction of 'the reason' for the attack on Lear is misleading because it distracts our attention from Tolstoy's more deep-seated motivation, which Wilson sees as an 'unconscious envy'. But this is a misreading of Orwell's essay. The likeness between Tolstoy and Lear was, according to Orwell, only one reason for the diatribe against Shakespeare; and towards the end of his essay he pointed to another source of inspiration, the rivalry which the great Russian novelist felt towards perhaps his only rival in world literature. Elsewhere, Orwell referred directly to Tolstoy's jealousy of Shakespeare. Wilson has therefore stolen Orwell's clothes. Indeed too often Orwell's views on Tolstoy have been treated superficially. In fact he felt tremendous admiration for Tolstoy, and his 1947 attack was unrestrained only because he had found an 'opponent' worthy of his mettle. Hence it was, in many ways, a sign of re-

spect. In a broadcast in 1941, he insisted that if 'so great a man as Tolstoy' could not destroy Shakespeare's reputation, then surely no one else could.

Orwell read *War and Peace* several times, first when he was about 20. His sole quarrel with the book, despite its three stout volumes, was that it did not go on long enough. Its characters, he later recalled, 'were people about whom one would gladly go on reading for ever'. He judged that Tolstoy's creations had international appeal and that therefore one could hold imaginary conversations with figures like Pierre Bezukhov. Such men and women seemed to be engaged in the process of making their souls, and therefore Tolstoy's grasp was 'so much larger than Dickens's'. This was high praise indeed, and even when criticizing Tolstoy's attack on Shakespeare he paid a passing tribute to *War and Peace* and *Anna Karenina.* Nor was Orwell familiar only with these classics. He also read *The Cossacks, Sebastopol,* and other works, including the later short stories, written with parable-like simplicity. Indeed, such was his regard for Tolstoy that he went to considerable trouble to read several of his more obscure works. He even judged that Tolstoy would still be a remarkable man if he had written nothing except his polemical pamphlets, for no one could read him and still feel quite the same about life.

There is no evidence that Orwell read all of Tolstoy's translated writings. We do not know, for instance, whether he read a compendium of Tolstoy's religious writings translated by Aylmer Maude and published by Oxford University Press in 1940 as *A Confession: The Gospel in Brief and What I Believe.* Certainly there was no copy among Orwell's books at his death. Yet this is the book which, I wish to argue, influenced *Animal Farm.* It may be that Orwell came to it second-hand, by the extracts quoted in Derrick Leon's biography of Tolstoy, which Orwell read on publication early in 1944, referred to in his 'As I Please' column in the *Tribune* and reviewed for the *Observer,* describing it as 'an outstanding book'. He was reading it just as he was working hard to complete *Animal Farm.*

Everyone is familiar with the parallels between Russian history and the plot of *Animal Farm.* Perhaps indeed we are over-familiar with them, for the details of the book had a wider totalitarian relevance than to any one country, and Orwell borrowed from Italian history ('Mussolini is always right'—) and from German, as well as from Russian. But there is one issue in the book for which there seems no real-life equivalent: this is the rewriting of the original revolutionary aims, the principles of Animalism. Admittedly revolutionary idealism in Russia and elsewhere was betrayed and perverted, but there was no outward repudiation of Marxist rhetoric. Although Stalin ignored such theory in his actions and imposed his will by force of arms and propaganda, he never ceased to pay lip-service to the original ideals. Even when he was arraigning the Old Bolsheviks in the Show Trials of the 1930s, he was at pains to assert that it was they—not he—who had sinned against the holy writ of Marxist-Leninist ideology. So what inspired Orwell's brilliant and hard-hitting reformulations?

First, we must look at the precise ways in which the Commandments of the first chapter of *Animal Farm* were perverted in the course of the book. 'No animal shall sleep in a bed' became 'No animal shall sleep in a bed with sheets'. 'No animal shall drink alcohol' changed into 'No animal shall drink alcohol to excess'. 'No animal shall kill any other animal' became 'No animal shall kill another animal without cause'. Most famously of all, 'All animals are equal' became 'All animals are equal but some animals are more equal than others'. In short, each commandment received a coda, a reservation which effectively reversed its meaning.

There is no parallel to this in Russian political history. But Leo Tolstoy had observed a very similar perversion, in Russian religious history, as Leon recounts in his biography. What Tolstoy considered the essential precepts of the Sermon on the Mount had become almost their opposites in the mouths of Russian Orthodox clerics. The original 'do not be angry' had become 'do not be angry without a cause'. The phrase 'without a cause' was, to Tolstoy, the key to an understanding of the perversion of scripture. Of course everyone who is angry justifies himself with a cause, however trivial or unjust, and therefore he guessed, correctly as he soon found, that the words were a later interpolation designed to devalue the original injunction. Similarly the instructions not to promise anything on oath, not to resist evil by violence, and not to judge or go to law had all been overturned, and had become their opposites, when the church had sought accommodation with the civil power.

Orwell's reading of the extracts from Tolstoy in Leon's biography, as detailed above, may well have inspired his rewriting of the principles of Animalism. This, of course, is not to denigrate Orwell's achievement. It was he who had, first, to see the appositeness to his own work of the banal—but contextually

brilliant—'without a cause' and, then, to invent similar reservations. But it is to insist that the provenance of the details of *Animal Farm* is far wider than the painful period of history through which Orwell lived. It is also to contend that Tolstoy was an important influence on Orwell.

Although this may be considered more speculative, it is quite possible that Orwell actually read the original Tolstoy, either before Leon's book was published or as a result of seeing its brief extracts. We do know that Orwell was prepared to search 'all over London' to track down a Tolstoyan quarry; and as a bibliophile he was always well aware of new material being published, even in the dark days of 1940. The fact that, for effect, Orwell italicized his codas as did Tolstoy, though Leon's quotations were all in roman script, is added evidence for this. If he did consult the original translation by Aylmer Maude, Orwell would have found other neat reformulations by Tolstoy which may well have influenced his own. To say 'do not be angry without a cause', Tolstoy decided, was like urging someone to 'Love the neighbour whom thou approvest of'. He also drew attention to the 1864 edition of the Catechism which, after quoting each of the Ten Commandments, then gave 'a reservation which cancelled it'. For instance, the commandment to honour one God had an addendum to the effect that we should also honour the angels and saints, 'besides, of course, the Mother of God and the three persons of the Trinity'. The second commandment, not to make idols, was perverted into an injunction to make obeisance before icons; the third, not to take oaths, became a demand to swear when called upon to do so by the legal authorities. The command to honour one's mother and father degenerated into a call to honour also the Tsar, the ministers of the church, and all those in authority—specified on three long pages! 'Thou shalt not kill' was interpreted ingeniously. One should not kill 'except in the fulfilment of one's duties'.

The similarity between the methods employed in the relevant passages of Tolstoy and Orwell is astonishing. The most obvious way of accounting for this is by direct influence. There are indeed other indications that Orwell's reading and rereading of Tolstoy left its mark on his work. May not the character of Boxer in *Animal Farm* have been influenced by the long-suffering talking horse who was carried off to the knacker at the end of Tolstoy's short story 'Strider: The Story of a Horse'? Orwell's concept of Doublethink may also have owed something to a superb example from Vronsky's code of principles, in *Anna Karenina,* 'that one must pay a cardsharper, but need not pay a tailor; that one must never tell a lie to a man, but one may to a woman; that one must never cheat anyone, but one may a husband; that one must never pardon an insult, but may give one, and so on'. The arresting opening of *Homage to Catalonia* may also owe a debt to Tolstoy. Orwell took an 'immediate liking' to an unnamed, tough-looking Italian, whose face somehow deeply moved him. This episode, whose authenticity historians must doubt, bears a close resemblance to the passage in *War and Peace* where Pierre and Davout gaze at each other and, in so doing, see each other's essential humanity. Similarly the execution, in the same book, contains details resembling those Orwell included in '**A Hanging**'. Orwell's Burmese prisoner steps aside to avoid a puddle, despite the fact that he will soon be dead. In the same way, Tolstoy's Russian prisoner adjusts the uncomfortable knot of his blindfold just before the execution squad put an end to his life. Finally, Tolstoy is undoubtedly relevant to the nightmare world of *Nineteen Eighty-Four*. The Russian wondered when the priests would understand 'that even in the face of death, two and two still make four'; Orwell knew that some priests would never admit any such thing and that, after Room 101, even Winston Smith might accept that '2 + 2 = 5'.

Of course it may be merely a coincidence—or a series of coincidences—that Orwell's rewriting of the Seven Commandments bears such a strong resemblance to Tolstoy's exposure of the perversion of the Ten Commandments, and that there are, in addition, other parallels in their writings which seem best explained by direct, if perhaps unconscious, influence. But if so, then this is good evidence that the two men had far more in common than anyone has ever pointed out. Certainly their self-presentations were similar. Tolstoy once called himself 'a quite enfeebled, good-for-nothing parasite, who can only exist under the most exceptional conditions found only when thousands of people labour to support a life that is of no value to anyone'. Orwell did not go quite as far as that; but he was the British equivalent. 'I am a degenerate modern semi-intellectual who would die if I did not get my early morning cup of tea and my *New Statesman* every Friday.' On the surface, the two men seem so different, but the fact is that there were many similarities between them. (Who realizes, without looking up the dates, that their deaths were separated by only forty years?) Orwell may have castigated Tolstoy as other-worldly, but both men seemed essentially puritanical to others. Whereas the one insisted on making his own shoes, the other would try to make his own furniture, and both went to considerable pains to grow their own food. Each was an enemy of the machine age.

Both were dedicated writers, both moralists and humanitarians, and both polemicists. After writing discursive books early in their careers, each of them was an 'engaged' writer later in life. They needed a mission, or purpose, in life and shared the opinion that man could not live by hedonism alone. In addition, they berated mere intellectuals. Neither would passively accept what he was told: each had to work ideas out for himself, displaying great intellectual self-confidence—and considerable unorthodoxy—in the process. Should we compare them as religious thinkers? Certainly there are religious aspects to Orwell's thought. Should we, as George Woodcock argues, even compare Orwell's repudiation of his education and his quitting of his career in the imperial civil service with Tolstoy's renunciations, or his migration to Jura with Tolstoy's flight from Yasnaya Polyana to Astapovo? If so, then Orwell's criticisms of Tolstoy in 1947 were similar to Tolstoy's of Shakespeare in 1906, in that both were motivated by 'a half-recognized similarity'. Obviously such comparisons may be pushed too far. What does seem clear, however, is that the connections between these two figures are worth recognizing, and also worth further study.

James Arnt Aune

SOURCE: "Literary Analysis of *Animal Farm*," in *Understanding Animal Farm: A Student Casebook to Issues, Sources and Historical Documents,* edited by John Rodden, Greenwood Press, 1999, pp. 1-18.

THE MEANING OF *ANIMAL FARM*

A literary work is an act of communication, just like a political speech or an advertisement. It is composed by an author or group of authors. It consists of a message embodied in a set of linguistic and social conventions shared by a target audience in a particular time and place. The average American, for example, can make sense of a billboard containing a picture of a cowboy and the slogan, "Come to Marlboro Country," because an association between the macho cowboy and the smoking of Marlboro cigarettes has been built up in the public mind since the company decided to stop marketing Marlboros as a "women's" cigarette in the 1950s. Other English speakers who are not familiar with the Marlboro-cowboy association will find the billboard incomprehensible. Americans who visit England will sometimes see a billboard consisting of a torn piece of purple fabric. Someone has to explain to them that the advertisement is for Silk Cut cigarettes.

Like the cigarette advertisements, *Animal Farm* was composed by an author—George Orwell, the pen name of Eric Blair. Its message is an indictment of the communist betrayal of the ideals on which the Soviet Union was founded, told in the form of a fairy story (Orwell's original subtitle for the book) or allegorical fable. Unlike the Marlboro or Silk Cut advertisements, however, *Animal Farm* lives beyond its immediate context and target audience. Works that do that become "art" or "literature"; we might look at cigarette ads in a history book a hundred years from now, but we will look at them more as an amusing documentation of unhealthy habits than as art. Since ancient Greece and Rome, students of human communication have given the label "rhetoric" to messages that have a primarily persuasive purpose, and "poetic" to messages that have a primarily imaginative or literary purpose.

In his book on the art of rhetoric, Aristotle argued that persuasive speakers and writers accomplish their goals by using three kinds of strategies: *Logos,* or logical appeal, uses the basic beliefs and values of audiences to lead them to a conclusion desired by the persuader. *Ethos,* or ethical appeal, refers to the persuader's ability to create in the mind of the audience that he or she is a credible person with good character and with the audience's best interests in mind. *Pathos,* or emotional appeal, works by connecting an argument with the audience's passions—anger, affection, fear, and so on.

As persuasion, *Animal Farm* is a powerful argument against the delusions of Soviet Communism and the dishonesty of Western intellectuals sympathetic to the Soviet Union. Its logical appeal works by reducing the argument to the level of a fairy story, something so simple and obvious that perhaps intellectuals cannot understand it. Orwell creates an omniscient narrator in the novel who tells the story simply and plainly, as if representing the character of England itself, where "such concepts as justice, liberty, and objective truth are still believed in." *Animal Farm* connects with our emotions by relying on conventional identifications of animals with certain human characteristics.

A literary-rhetorical analysis that identifies persuasive strategies in a literary work needs to begin with the work's immediate context. Some literary works refer to a political or social context that no longer makes much sense to the average reader. Swift's *Gulliver's Travels* and Shakespeare's history plays are good examples. Although some background historical knowledge may aid our appreciation of these

works, we can usually appreciate them today for their purely "literary" rather than "persuasive" qualities. *Animal Farm,* on the other hand, is a rare example of a great work in which the timeless literary qualities are fused perfectly with the time-bound persuasive qualities. Like all other human communication, however, *Animal Farm* has communicated meanings to audiences in different social contexts, some of which were intended by the author and some of which were not.

THE ORIGINAL MEANING OF *ANIMAL FARM*

George Orwell wrote *Animal Farm* between November 1943 and February 1944. His unpublished preface to the book explains his intentions. He was angered by the fact that "the prevailing orthodoxy" in England in 1943 was "an uncritical admiration of Soviet Russia." This orthodoxy had been promoted by the English intelligentsia for many years, and the World War II alliance between England and the Soviet Union had extended this orthodoxy to the mainstream national press as well. It was easier, Orwell wrote, to criticize Winston Churchill, the British Prime Minister, than to criticize Stalin.

Orwell's efforts to get the novel published confirmed his insight. Three prestigious English publishers of varying political views (Gollancz on the left, Cape in the center, and Faber & Faber on the right) rejected the manuscript. Secker & Warburg, an obscure left-wing publisher with a history of accepting anti-Stalinist works, accepted it.

Orwell was not only what Americans today call a "liberal." He was a democratic socialist. He was convinced that an unrestrained free market leads to widespread poverty and degradation and that it also corrupts the integrity of the democratic process. Like others on the left wing of the Labour Party, he supported a generous welfare state with free health care and education, as well as support for children, the disabled, and the aged. He believed that basic industries such as energy and transportation should be owned by the people, and not run for profit. Unlike Communists, however, he believed that freedom of speech and a free press were not incompatible with the quest for greater economic equality.

Orwell's experiences as a scholarship boy in the most exclusive English public school—Eton, what Americans would call a prep school—as well as his experiences as a policeman in colonial Burma had led him to a lifelong sympathy with the underdog. When the Republican government in Spain was overthrown by Franco's fascists (allies of Hitler and the Nazis), Orwell, like many other radicals in England and the United States, went to Spain in 1938 to fight for the Republican cause. His book **Homage to Catalonia** chronicles his discovery that the Communists fighting on the Republican side were not interested in liberating Spain, but in promoting Communism at all costs. Orwell fought in an organization (Partido Obrero de Unificación Marxista [POUM]; Workers' Party of Marxist Unity) sympathetic to Leon Trotsky (the Russian revolutionary who was defeated by Joseph Stalin in the battle to succeed Lenin as leader of the Soviet Union), and the Communists seemed more interested in destroying the Trotskyists than in defeating Franco. Orwell and his wife barely escaped Spain alive.

There was plenty of evidence by 1943 that the Soviet Union's leaders had betrayed the promise of the October Revolution of 1917. The problem was that many of the most intelligent and influential figures in England either denied the evidence or refused to examine it. The October Revolution had promised to improve the standard of living of the people, especially the peasants and the working class. It had promised to create a radical democracy by placing political and economic decision making in the hands of "soviets," or local, representative councils. It promised to eliminate class privilege, promoting a truly equal society. None of these things happened. In fact, by most measures, the people were far worse off than they had been under the rule of the Czar. Millions of people died as the result of famine due to failed economic policies or from the direct order of Joseph Stalin. Freedom of speech and political dissent in any form were punished with exile to prison camps, torture, or execution. The Soviet leaders were not content just to kill opponents; they paraded them in public before the eyes of the Western press, forcing them to confess to crimes against the state. They provided a higher standard of living for Communist Party members and bureaucrats than for the ordinary workers and peasants whom they professed to make "equal." They made a deal with their archenemy Adolf Hitler.

The problem was that many intelligent people refused to see these things. This fact probably explains why George Orwell decided to point them out in the form of a fairy story, or allegorical fable. Much like the fairy tale about "The Emperor's New Clothes," **Animal Farm** tells the reader that the truth about Communism is so simple that perhaps *only* a child can see it.

The literary form of the animal fable has been used perhaps from the beginning of recorded literature.

Aesop's *Fables* dramatized simple, moral points for the edification of the reader. In the educational system of ancient Rome, which was designed to teach future orator-statesmen, the very first writing and speaking exercise was to paraphrase one of these fables. Later, more complex forms, called *allegories,* developed complex correspondences between fictional characters and real-life political events or moral dilemmas; Edmund Spenser's *Faerie Queene* and John Bunyan's *Pilgrim's Progress* are perhaps the two best-known examples of allegory in English. But **Animal Farm** also harkens back to a famous English satire, Jonathan Swift's *Gulliver's Travels,* a book that on the surface was a combination of travel story and animal fable, intended to express outrage at ridiculous political and philosophical attitudes popular among the English intelligentsia of his time. For most readers today, the targets of Swift's satire are unfamiliar, and the book can still be read as a commentary on the human condition as well as an entertaining story.

Orwell's allegorical satire has more direct reference to real-world people and events than these earlier examples. Part of the pleasure in reading the story, as well as educational usefulness, lies in the reader's detective work in tracking down the allegorical correspondences.

CHARACTERS AND EVENTS

Chart I: Characters

Animal Farm	Historical Figures
Farmer Jones	Czar of Russia
The Pigs	The Bolsheviks
Major	A combination of Marx and Lenin
Napoleon	Stalin
Snowball	Trotsky
Boxer	The working class— "Stakhanovite"
Mollie	White Russians
Moses	The Russian Orthodox and Roman Catholic church
Squealer	*Pravda;* Soviet propagandists
Napoleon's dogs	The secret police
Pilkington	England/Churchill
Frederick	Hitler (after Frederick the Great, admired by Hitler)
Minimus	Mayakovsky

| Whymper | Western businessmen and journalists |
| Wild animals | The peasants |

Chart II: Events

Animal Farm	Soviet History
The Rebellion	October Revolution (1917)
Battle of the Cowshed	The Civil War (1918-19)
Snowball's leadership	Trotsky leads Red Army
Rebellions on nearby farms	Hungarian and German communist rebellions (1919, 1923)
Revolt of the hens	Kronstadt rebellion (1921)
Napoleon's dealings with Whymper/Wellington markets	Treaty of Rapallo (1922)
Snowball's defeat	Trotsky's exile (1927)
Snowball and the windmill	Trotsky's emphasis on heavy industry
Napoleon's opposition	Stalin's emphasis on agriculture
Snowball's desire to send pigeons to nearby farms	Trotsky's "Permanent Revolution"
Napoleon's opposition	Stalin's "Socialism in One Country"
Demolition of windmill	Failure of First Five-Year Plan
Starvation	Ukraine famine (1933)
Confession of animals to aiding Snowball	Purge Trials (1936-38)
Deal with Frederick	Nazi-Soviet Pact of 1939
Battle with Frederick	German invasion (1941)
End of the novel	Tehran Conference (1943)

Other Parallels

Animal Farm	Soviet Union
Hoof and horn	Hammer and sickle
Order of the Green Banner	Order of Lenin
"Beasts of England"	"The Internationale"
Animalism	Marxism-Leninism or dialectical materialism

Mr. Jones, the cruel and drunken owner of Manor Farm, treats his animals badly. The old boar Major, shortly before his death, has a dream in which he imagines a world in which animals have overthrown their human masters. He teaches the animals a song, "Beasts of England," which expresses this yearning for a better world. He also teaches them seven commandments, warning them not to adopt human habits such as living in a house, sleeping in a bed, wearing clothes, drinking alcohol, smoking tobacco, touching money, or engaging in trade. Above all, all animals are equal.

Major has characteristics of both Karl Marx and V. I. Lenin. Karl Marx (1818-83) called for workers of the world to unite against their capitalist oppressors. He taught that the capitalists' downfall was inevitable because of inherent flaws in the capitalist economy, but it was possible for a unified working class to overthrow them now. Marx was influential on both communist and socialist parties. He never really specified how revolutionary change was to take place, and his interpreters continue to debate if his writings were responsible for the evil uses to which they have been put in communist countries.

Lenin (1870-1924) was the leader of the Bolshevik Party in its successful October 1917 revolution against the Czarist regime. He provided a theory of political change and revolution to supplement the basic Marxist indictment of the capitalist economy. His insight, first expressed in his book *What Is to Be Done?* (1902), was that the masses would never revolt on their own. The most they would ever do by themselves is organize trade unions. Only a rigidly disciplined "vanguard party" composed of the intelligentsia and "advanced" members of the working class would be able to engage in the subversive activity necessary to bring about radical social change. Lenin was skeptical about the achievements of liberal democracy: freedom of speech and press, freedom of religion, and free elections. He died relatively young, disappointed in the results of his Revolution and concerned about the growing distance between Communist Party leaders and the people.

The early death of Lenin, like the death of Major, led to a power struggle between his successors: Leon Trotsky (1879-1940) and Joseph Stalin (1879-1953), who correspond to Snowball and Napoleon, respectively. Trotsky was the leader of the Red Army in the Civil War of 1918-1919, when anti-Bolshevik armies, aided by Western capitalist countries, tried to overthrow the Bolshevik regime. Like Snowball's heroism in the Battle of the Cowshed, Trotsky's leadership in the civil war made him extremely popular.

Trotsky was in favor of rapid industrialization, a program symbolized in the novel by the plan to build the windmill. Stalin, however, emphasized agricultural policy, as does Napoleon. Trotsky was in favor of exporting revolution worldwide (sometimes called Trotsky's theory of "Permanent Revolution"), while Stalin was more interested in protecting the Soviet Union from outside forces (often summarized as "Socialism in One Country"). In 1927, Stalin defeated Trotsky at the Communist Party Congress, encouraging his followers to shout Trotsky down to prevent him speaking, much as the sheep do to Snowball before he is driven off the farm. Stalin had gained control of the secret police (Napoleon's guard dogs), who continued to work against Trotsky after his exile abroad. Trotsky was finally killed (with an ax) by a Soviet agent in Mexico City in 1940.

Animal Farm was originally published in England by the firm of Secker & Warburg, which had previously issued works sympathetic to Trotsky. Orwell himself had fought with the Trotskyist POUM during the Spanish Civil War, but it is clear from his other writings that he opposed Trotsky's willingness to suspend civil liberties. The fact that the pigs (Bolsheviks) hoard all the milk for themselves early in the novel is perhaps a sign that Orwell believed that the "animalist" philosophy itself, not just the personality of Napoleon, was responsible for the defeat of the animals' hopes. One commentator on the novel, Sanford Pinsker, argues that the reader does not need to know anything about Soviet history in order to appreciate the novel; Major's original division of the world into man versus animal led to the horrors inflicted by the pigs. Any system that is based on systematic hatred of one group for another will lead to oppression.

One event in the novel seems out of historical sequence: the revolt of the hens against the order to increase egg production. The event parallels the rebellion of Soviet sailors at Kronstadt in 1921, which Trotsky brutally repressed (although there are also some parallels to the peasants' revolt against forced collectivization of their farms in 1929). Still, Napoleon is directly responsible for the evils that follow, and the events have close parallels in Soviet history up to 1943: the widespread starvation that occurs during the first winter after the rebellion corresponds to millions of deaths by starvation in the Ukraine in 1933.

The public trial at which animals confess to various crimes is similar to highly publicized purge trials of 1936-38. Kryuchkov confessed to a crime similar to that of the sheep who murdered an old ram "by chasing him around and around a bonfire when he was suffering with a cough." He had purposely arranged long walks and bonfires that affected Maxim Gorky's (a Bolshevik writer) weak lungs.

The pile of corpses at Napoleon's feet, though shocking to the animals, is eventually accepted by them as a necessary defense of the revolution. Squealer, the archetypal Soviet propagandist (perhaps corresponding to the newspaper *Pravda*), makes the case for Napoleon. Minimus, a poet who corresponds to the Bolshevik writer Mayakovsky, writes a poem honoring Napoleon. Journalists who should have known better widely covered the show trials in the American and European press, in terms largely sympathetic to the Stalinist side, although the great American philosopher and socialist John Dewey organized an inquiry that exonerated the victims.

The various dealings with neighboring farms parallel first the Treaty of Rapallo in 1922, which led to the recognition of the Soviet Union by the Western powers. Frederick clearly represents Adolf Hitler, who greatly admired the German Emperor Frederick. Although for many years Hitler had been identified as the chief opponent of the Soviet Union, in 1939 Stalin arranged for a mutual nonaggression treaty between Germany and the Soviet Union. This startling turnabout disillusioned many Communists in the West, but once Hitler attacked the Soviet Union in 1941, Stalin became an ally of both England and the United States, and there was little criticism of him or his policies, even by conservatives. Pilkington, the other nearby farmer, is rather lazy and aristocratic, preferring hunting and fishing to active management of his farm. This portrait of Winston Churchill is distinctly negative, but fits the distaste Orwell and Labour Party supporters felt for Churchill's upper-class values.

The ending of the novel takes the reader up to the Tehran Conference in 1943, where Stalin, Churchill, and Roosevelt held a joint meeting. It is impossible, finally, to tell the difference between pig and man. This conclusion is no more flattering to Churchill and Roosevelt than it is to Stalin, but it fits Orwell's persuasive purposes as an independent socialist critic of both the Western capitalist countries and the Soviet Union. In his preface to the Ukrainian edition of the book, Orwell writes,

> A number of readers may finish the book with the impression that it ends in the complete reconcilia-

tion of the pigs and the humans. That was not my intention; on the contrary I meant it to end on a loud note of discord, for I wrote it immediately after the Teheran Conference which everybody had thought had established the best possible relations between the USSR and the West. I personally did not believe that such good relations would last long; and, as events have shown, I wasn't far wrong.

Orwell's sympathy for ordinary workers comes out most clearly in the portrait of Boxer, whose death is the saddest moment in the novel. (Boxer is also similar to the figure of Stakhanov, who was featured in Soviet propaganda as the "ideal" worker.) Orwell's dislike for religion is expressed in the figure of Moses, the tame raven who preaches to the animals that they will go to Sugar Candy Mountain (heaven) when they die. The reappearance of Moses late in the novel parallels the effort of Stalin to reach out to the Roman Catholic church in order to gain support for his policy toward Poland.

There are some other symbolic correspondences in the novel that are worth noting: the hoof and horn flag is like the Soviet flag with the hammer and sickle (symbolizing the workers and the peasants); the Order of the Green Banner is like the Order of Lenin; and the song "Beasts of England" is like the Communist hymn "The Internationale."

The general strategy of personification Orwell uses relies on a number of commonsense associations we have with certain animals. For example, a raven is a fairly sinister bird, but tameable by human beings in authority—an appropriate personification of religion, at least in Orwell's rather hostile view. A horse is a noble beast, one of humanity's oldest animal helpers, and Boxer and Clover are the most pleasant of the characters. Clover's effort to warn Boxer to escape from the knacker's van is probably the saddest moment in the novel. A knacker buys old horses and grinds them up for dog food or glue. At first, one might be inclined to note the "human" characteristics of Boxer and Clover, but it is really the pigs who are the most human creatures in the novel. Orwell's choice of the pig to personify the Communists' works on several different levels. Pigs are among the most intelligent barnyard animals. They do no useful labor (like horses do). They are greedy and vicious. Anyone who has lived on a farm or in a rural area has heard stories of pigs devouring small children who wander into their pens. For medical purposes, there are aspects of the pig's physiology that are very close

to humans'. (Some insulin, for instance, is derived from pigs.) The vicious, greedy, and nonproductive qualities of pigs make them the ideal personification of the Marxist intellectuals who profess to speak in the name of the workers, but do nothing productive themselves except spout propaganda and engage in murder.

But it is above all the smooth development of the plot of the novel that keeps the reader's attention. There seems literally not a wasted word. A historian might have required a thousand pages to write an accurate account of twenty-seven years of Soviet history. Orwell does so in fewer than a hundred pages, and in language understandable even by young children. The simplicity of language is essential to Orwell's overall persuasive point: the Soviet Communists' actions are so obviously evil that even a child can understand them. Why cannot everyone in England and the United States see that?

OTHER AUDIENCES

Even Orwell's publisher seemed to worry about the impact of the novel. Accepted for publication in 1944, it was not actually published until August 1945, when the war in Europe had been over for three months. The book was an immediate success. It was a Book-of-the-Month Club selection in the United States. The Signet paperback edition, published in 1956, has sold several million copies. *Animal Farm* appeared as a radio play and as a cartoon (with the animals defeating the pigs at the end!). Eventually it became a school text in both England and the United States.

Orwell died in 1950, at the relatively young age of forty-six, from tuberculosis. He was poor for his entire life and did not live to see the full extent of his fame and influence. His other novel about totalitarianism, *1984,* continues to be read as a powerful indictment of Communism, as well as a prophetic warning about technological invasion of privacy. As John Rodden documents in his book *The Politics of Literary Reputation,* there has been considerable debate about what would have happened to Orwell's political beliefs had he lived longer, with conservatives and radicals both claiming his legacy.

What got lost in the American reception of *Animal Farm* was the sense that Orwell was criticizing both Communism and capitalism. The Signet Classics edition, still the most widely read version, quoted Orwell's statement: "Every line I have written since 1936 has been written, directly or indirectly, against totalitarianism." What American readers did not get was the rest of Orwell's sentence: "and for democratic Socialism, as I understand it." The Everyman's Library edition by Alfred A. Knopf (1993) contains more useful background information, as well as a corrected text. Just as acts of communication sometimes live beyond their immediate historical purpose and context, their actual understanding by audiences is framed by their dissemination in the mass media or in educational institutions. It was not politically safe to talk about anti-communist socialism in the 1950s in the United States—a fact that Orwell no doubt would have deplored as much as the silence about Stalin in the British press in the 1940s.

Finally, if *Animal Farm* became an instrument of Cold War propaganda by Western capitalist countries, what will future audiences with a limited historical memory of Communism make of the novel? Does it contain the seeds of the current call for animal rights? Orwell based the details of the novel on his own experience as a farmer from 1936 to 1940 (when he kept a goat named Muriel). Does the novel, as Sanford Pinsker writes, make a much more general statement about the consequences of polarizing rhetoric such as Major's? Or is it a meditation on the theme that power, no matter who wields it, is inherently corrupting? If so, the enduring message of the novel would subvert Orwell's own political purposes: all efforts at radical change are doomed to fail; one should not tamper with the natural order of things. Despite the simplicity of the novel, these questions remain in the audience's mind, serving as the basis for continued meditation on the relationship between morality and politics.

TOPICS FOR WRITTEN OR ORAL EXPLORATION

1. Define the *rhetorical* and *poetic* functions of literature and communication in your own words.

2. If the rhetorical elements of a literary work outweigh its poetic elements, does that mean that a work is unlikely to survive past its immediate context?

3. Why did Orwell write *Animal Farm* in the form of an animal fable? Do his intentions matter in answering that question?

4. Should schools continue to assign *Animal Farm* as an important work of literature now that the Cold War is over?

5. Do you think that your teachers and other planners of your curriculum have political purposes in mind when they assign particular books for you to read?

6. Some people have criticized Orwell for being pessimistic. Is it fair to read *Animal Farm* as cautioning against any attempt to make society more just?

7. What is the saddest moment in the novel? What is the scariest? What tools of language does Orwell use to help us feel those feelings?

8. In the 1950s there was a cartoon version of *Animal Farm* that ended up with the animals rising up against the pigs, and everyone living happily ever after. Would the book be better with a happy ending? Why or why not?

9. Learn how to use the *Reader's Guide to Periodical Literature.* Select some examples of discussions of the Soviet Union in 1938, 1943, 1953, and 1989, and compare and contrast them.

10. Is Major "responsible" for what happens later?

11. After 1989, the countries under Soviet control gained their freedom very quickly. If you were writing a new ending for *Animal Farm,* how would you discuss the 1989 events in allegorical terms?

12. Does reading *Animal Farm* make you think differently about animals? Most people eat pigs, chickens, and cattle. Most Americans do not eat horses, although our pets and Europeans do. Where did your lunch today come from?

13. Why does the novel end where it does?

14. How would you sing "Beasts of England"? Find a recording of the "Internationale." (The English popular singer Billy Bragg sings it on a recent recording.)

15. Find a copy of the Signet edition of *Animal Farm,* the recent Everyman edition, and, if possible, the original Secker & Warburg edition and translations into other languages. What are similarities and differences in packaging?

16. Define the terms "liberal," "conservative," "Left," "Right," "Socialist," "Democratic Socialist," and "Communist." Where did the terms originate? Are their meanings different in the United States and in Europe? Have their meanings changed since the publication of *Animal Farm?*

17. Look up the terms *allegory, fable,* and *satire* in the Glossary and analyze why the terms are appropriate labels for *Animal Farm.*

18. Would things have turned out differently if Snowball had won the power struggle with Napoleon? Are there any clues in the novel itself about this issue?

Mitzi M. Brunsdale

SOURCE: "All Animals Are Equal, but . . . : *Animal Farm*," in *Student Companion to George Orwell*, Greenwood Press, 2000, pp. 121-22, 127-31.

Animal Farm has become Orwell's best-known and best-liked work. When he looked for a publisher for it in February 1944, though, he almost immediately encountered difficulties. The buildup for D-Day was underway, the "Second Front" that Stalin had been demanding from the Allies since 1941. Most British intellectuals wholeheartedly supported the Soviet Union, whose Red Army was diverting Hitler's attention from the Western Front. Gollancz and other British publishers rejected *Animal Farm* because they felt it played into the Nazis' hands by criticizing the Soviets, who, Gollancz told Orwell, had just saved the Allies' necks at Stalingrad. Some publishers also shunned *Animal Farm* because of Orwell's contractual obligations to Gollancz. In 1949, Orwell discovered that the Soviets had tried directly to block the publication of *Animal Farm* through a mole (secret agent) in the British Ministry of Information.

After a V-1 rocket destroyed his flat in 1944, Orwell managed to dig the "blitzed" manuscript out of the rubble and took it to T. S. Eliot at Faber and Faber. Eliot missed the book's point completely. Eliot told Orwell that the book didn't need more communism, it needed more pigs with public spirit. The American Dial Press turned it down because they thought it was an animal story for children. By this time Orwell was so desperate he considered publishing *Animal Farm* himself. He eventually submitted it to Fredric Warburg, who had published *Homage to Catalonia* and *The Lion and the Unicorn*. Warburg was delayed by the wartime paper shortage, so *Animal Farm* did not appear in England until August 17, 1945, after Hitler had been defeated and Stalin's usefulness as a British ally had diminished.

Once published, *Animal Farm* was immediately and astonishingly successful. The British edition sold over 25,000 copies in its first five years, ten times the sales of any of Orwell's previous books. When the American edition appeared in 1946, the start of the Cold War, it sold 590,000 copies in four years and became a popular selection of the U.S. Book-of-the-Month Club. Edmund Wilson praised *Animal Farm* as "absolutely first-rate," declared Orwell a major author, and insisted readers should pick up his earlier, neglected works.

The American success of *Animal Farm* depended largely on its being read simply as anticommunism, but Orwell insisted that his aim had been much broader, not just Soviet Communism but the general corruption of socialist ideals caused by the lust for power. Since the 1930s, fascism and communism were widely considered polar opposites, but Orwell was one of few observers to see that these systems were actually more similar than different, especially in achieving goals through propaganda. He also fleshed out their fearsome common denominator of authoritarian autocracy in four-footed form as the ruling swine of *Animal Farm*. Eventually, due largely to George Orwell, the world came to know such systems as totalitarianism.

Animal Farm has enormous literary merit. It is totally different from any of Orwell's previous works, the only one in which he did not insert himself as a narrator or a principal character or a commentator on the action. On the surface, the story of barnyard beasts who revolt against their cruel master in order to run their own society is so simply told that it can be enjoyably read by youngsters, who respond enthusiastically to Orwell's obvious affection for animals, but it can also be read as a clever and powerful political satire of Stalinism and as a sophisticated allegory warning against the dangerous abuses of political power and the necessity of placing limits upon it. Orwell's fluent, easygoing, highly approachable style is enriched by sly, generally good-natured humor influenced by his wife Eileen, who listened and commented delightedly each night as Orwell read his day's work to her. The humor here is mostly good-natured, which makes the scenes in which the ruling pigs reveal their ruthlessness and treachery even more shocking. Overall, Orwell claimed that *Animal Farm* was the first book in which he tried, knowing exactly what he was doing, to fuse political and artistic purpose into one literary entity. . . .

Orwell said that he had sweated hard to achieve *Animal Farm*. In this book, he unabashedly revealed his love for animals and meticulously portrayed their personalities. This was a culmination of a lifelong tendency to use animals and imagery about them in his works. In his posthumous autobiographical essay **"Such, Such Were the Joys,"** he indicated that most of his good memories up to about the age of twenty were related in some way to animals. He also used a great deal of animal imagery in his novels, describing many characters, especially the unpleasant ones, as beasts. Conversely, he was able to endow animals with convincingly human emotions. The animal characters of *Animal Farm* are not just cartoon figures but completely credible individuals.

Animal Farm also continues the character structure Orwell had been portraying from the start—a group of underprivileged and abused protagonists and a group of their own kind who betray and prey upon them. Both groups are trapped by the implacable lust for power, which encourages exploiters to misuse the exploited and debases the masters far more than the honest beings they dominate. Orwell's revolutionary animal society corresponds perfectly to the socio-political structure of the Soviet Union.

Manor Farm: the Soviet Union, the "workers' paradise"

Mr. Jones: Tsar Nicholas II, whom the Communists drove from the throne and killed

Major: Karl Marx, whose theories sparked the Communist revolution

Boxer: the Soviet workers, largely illiterate and thus easily manipulated

Napoleon, the only Berkshire boar on the farm: Stalin, a scheming Georgian who dominated the Russian Communists

Snowball: Trotsky, who insisted on "snowballing" the worldwide Socialist revolution and who was accused of vast anti-Stalin plots

Squealer: *Pravda* ("Truth"), the official Communist newspaper, preaching the Party line

Minimus: Mayakovsky, a poet who prostituted his art for Party purposes

The Pigs: the Bolsheviks who launched the October Revolution

The Dogs: the Soviet secret police (successively the Cheka, OGPU, NKVD, KGB)

Moses the crow: the Russian Orthodox Church, promising its followers paradise while allying itself with the Communists to stay alive

Mollie, the pretty mare: the Tsarist White Russians who drained Russia for their own luxury

Farmer Pilkington: capitalistic Churchill/Britain, which the Russians distrust

Farmer Frederick: militaristic Hitler/Germany, which the Russians fear and hate

Benjamin the donkey: cynical Jewish philosophers

The farm house: the Kremlin, where plots are hatched to corrupt Marxist aims

The Rebellion: the Bolshevik Revolution

The Battle of the Cowshed: the anti-Communist invasion of Russia in 1918-19

The windmill: Stalin's Five-Year Plans, designed to industrialize the Soviet Union

The Battle of the Windmill: the German invasion of 1941

"Beasts of England": the rousing Communist anthem "l'Internationale"

Orwell's friend Hugh Kingsmill noted that Orwell "only wrote sympathetically about human beings when he regarded them as animals." His most sympathetically-drawn animal protagonists in *Animal Farm* were Boxer, the powerful draft horse, and Clover, a stout motherly mare. Though Boxer was not very bright, he was widely respected for his good nature, his dependability, and his willingness to work harder and harder, qualities which the ruling pigs constantly abused. Smitten by the simple socialistic ideals of "Beasts of England"—freedom from cruel human masters, enough barley, hay, oats, and sweet water for all—Boxer takes on the heaviest labor of building the new society, aware that he should learn to read but putting it off until too late. Under his personal mottoes, "I will work harder" and "Napoleon is always right," he hauls stone until his mighty lungs collapse, going blindly to his death because he cannot read the letters spelling out the butcher's name on the van that carries him away.

Orwell completely avoided sentimentality, the usual pitfall of animal stories, by depicting Boxer's own shortcomings unsparingly. Boxer is a round character with the capacity to surprise, not just a stupid hardworking slave. He feels remorseful when he thinks he killed a stable boy in the Battle of the Cowshed, and he puzzles over Napoleon's reshaping of history to defame Snowball, who, Boxer knows, had led the animals bravely against Farmer Jones in the same confrontation. Boxer's great failing is the lack of sufficient intelligence and education to sift truth from Napoleon's propaganda. His female counterpart Clover, who can read a little, distrusts the pigs' distortion of Animalism, but she lacks the strength, imagination, and daring to act on her suspicions. She saves herself from liquidation by keeping quiet, but she dooms herself to slavery.

Clover remains silent, Benjamin the donkey philosophically grieves for his friend Boxer, Mollie the pretty carriage mare defects to Mr. Pilkington for a few ribbons and lumps of sugar, and the sheep are too stupid to do anything but bleat out the slogans the pigs teach them. Moses the black raven, absent during the early period of the animals' revolt, suddenly returns, preaching a Sugar Candy Mountain afterlife for all animals who believe in Napoleon's creed and meekly accept Napoleon's selfish leadership. The few who dare to rebel, like the black Minorca pullets, are savaged by the new generation of hounds Napoleon separates from their parents and raises to be loyal to himself alone.

Orwell treated Boxer and Clover with relatively gentle humor, but he poured out his most scathing satire on Napoleon and his hoggish hangers-on. Significantly, Napoleon is the only Berkshire boar on Manor Farm. The Berkshire, a dish-faced long-bodied black hog with white face and feet, is named for the English county where the breed was developed, a prime swine-raising area also home to Windsor, the British Royal Residence, so the Berkshire is known throughout Britain as the Royal Swine—a clear indication of Napoleon's aims. Conspicuous by his absence from the Battle of the Cowshed, the fierce-looking Napoleon is not a military strategist but a corrupt politician, distorting language in order to manipulate all the other animals through his clever literate fellow pigs. Napoleon shapes the younger pigs' selfish personalities and makes them his closest associates, putting one, Squealer, in charge of circulating Napoleon's plans and pronouncements through the animal ranks and "explaining" them to poor puzzled Boxer. At the outset, if Boxer had only realized the difference between what Napoleon was saying and what really was so, he could easily have kicked the Berkshire bully to Sugar Candy Mountain.

Napoleon also shrewdly sniffed out real or imagined plots against himself and his regime. When Boxer defends Snowball's heroic conduct at the Battle of the Cowshed and a few daring pigs protest Napoleon's abolition of the animals' Sunday Meetings, Napoleon enacts a swift, terrible vengeance. At his shrill squeal, his loyal dogs fall upon four of the pigs while others assault Boxer, who easily pins one hound down with his enormous hoof. Then, looking to Napoleon for guidance, he lets the dog go. First the four unfortunate pigs, then the three rebellious hens, a greedy grain-stealing goose, and several empty-headed sheep confess to crimes they might or might not have committed—all allegedly under Snowball's long-distance direction. The dogs slay them on the spot, "And so the tale of confessions and executions went on, until there was a pile of corpses lying before Napoleon's feet and the air was heavy with the smell of blood, which had been unknown there since the expulsion of Jones." In this fearsome passage, Orwell interrupts the gentle tone of his narrative to shift into bitter realism.

Snowball, who had masterminded the Battle of the Cowshed and fought bravely, bears the brunt of Napoleon's envious wrath. Snowball was more lively than Napoleon and he had a greater facility with language, but he did not seem to have the same strength of personality. He tirelessly tries to organize the animals into Committees which Napoleon rejects in favor of training the young, especially the submissive dogs, according to his own principles. Some of Snowball's initiatives, like the Re-education of Wild Comrades, fail because they contradict the nature of the animals they were supposed to "improve," but some of his other ideas, particularly his literacy campaign, succeed dramatically. Snowball also reduces the original Seven Animal Commandments to one principle: "Four legs good, two legs bad," which the silly sheep bleat mindlessly all day long.

Squealer the propagandizing pig and Benjamin the elderly donkey represent the two extremes of the animals' involvement with the revolution. Squealer opportunistically uses his glib tongue and gift for writing to revise the theory and history of Animalism according to Napoleon's wishes. Benjamin, on the other hand, keeps his distance from the revolution, working slowly and obstinately but not risking anything by openly taking a position. Benjamin's invariable comment is, "Donkeys live a long time"; he has seen everything and survived by keeping his furry nose clean. He does try to save his friend Boxer from the butcher's wagon, but his efforts prove too little and too late.

Orwell made the humans in his story just as reprehensible as the swine who exploited their fellow beasts. The drunkards Farmer Jones and his wife bring their difficulties on themselves. Neighboring Farmer Pilkington of Foxwood connives with Napoleon against wily Mr. Frederick of Pinchfield Farm, who sadistically misuses his animals and even cheats the cunning Napoleon. Pilkington hypocritically praises Napoleon while they drink up the profits of Animal Farm, insisting that Pilkington and his friends have their own lower classes to exploit, just as Napoleon has his lower animals. Humans and pigs share a lust to dominate the less fortunate that makes the two groups virtually indistinguishable. Malcolm Muggeridge suggested to Orwell that at the end of the novel, a herd of British fellow travelers (Communist sympathizers), like "the infamous 'Red Dean' of Canterbury and writer Kingsley Martin should come on the scene on all fours." Orwell laughed, but he didn't use the suggestion.

Additional coverage of Orwell's life and career is contained in the following sources published by the Gale Group: *Concise Dictionary of British Literary Biography,* 1945-1960; *Contemporary Authors,* Vols. 104, 132; *Dictionary of Literary Biography,* Vols. 15, 98, 195; *DISCovering Authors; DISCovering Authors,* Version 3.0; *DISCovering Authors: British; DISCovering Authors: Canadian; DISCovering Authors Modules: Novelists; Major 20th-Century Writers; Novels for Students,* Vol. 7; *Short Stories for Students,* Vol. 4; *Something about the Author,* Vol. 29; *Twentieth-Century Literary Criticism,* Vols. 2, 6, 15, 31, 51; *World Literature Criticism.*

How to Use This Index

CLR Cumulative Author Index

Scott, Jack Denton 1915-1995 .... **20**
See also CA 108; CANR 48, 86; MAICYA; SAAS 14; SATA 31, 83

Sebastian, Lee
See Silverberg, Robert

Sebestyen, Ouida 1924- **17**
See also AAYA 8; CA 107; CANR 40; CLC 30; JRDA; MAICYA; SAAS 10; SATA 39

Sefton, Catherine
See Waddell, Martin

Selden, George 8
See also Thompson, George Selden
See also DLB 52

Selsam, Millicent Ellis 1912-1996 .... **1**
See also CA 9-12R; 154; CANR 5, 38; MAICYA; SATA 1, 29; SATA-Obit 92

Sendak, Maurice (Bernard) 1928- **1, 17**
See also CA 5-8R; CANR 11, 39; DLB 61; INT CANR-11; MAICYA; MTCW 1, 2; SATA 1, 27, 113

Seredy, Kate 1899-1975 .... **10**
See also CA 5-8R; 57-60; CANR 83; DLB 22; MAICYA; SATA 1; SATA-Obit 24

Serraillier, Ian (Lucien) 1912-1994 .... **2**
See also CA 1-4R; 147; CANR 1, 83; DLB 161; MAICYA; SAAS 3; SATA 1, 73; SATA-Obit 83

Seton, Ernest (Evan) Thompson
1860-1946 .... **59**
See also CA 109; DLB 92; DLBD 13; JRDA; SATA 18; TCLC 31

Seton-Thompson, Ernest
See Seton, Ernest (Evan) Thompson

Seuss, Dr.
See Dr. Seuss; Geisel, Theodor Seuss

Sewell, Anna 1820-1878 .... **17**
See also DLB 163; JRDA; MAICYA; SATA 24, 100

Sharp, Margery 1905-1991 .... **27**
See also CA 21-24R; 134; CANR 18, 85; DLB 161; MAICYA; SATA 1, 29; SATA-Obit 67

Shearer, John 1947- **34**
See also CA 125; SATA 43; SATA-Brief 27

Shepard, Ernest Howard 1879-1976 .... **27**
See also CA 9-12R; 65-68; CANR 23, 86; DLB 160; MAICYA; SATA 3, 33, 100; SATA-Obit 24

Shippen, Katherine B(inney) 1892-1980 .. **36**
See also CA 5-8R; 93-96; CANR 86; SATA 1; SATA-Obit 23

Showers, Paul C. 1910-1999 .... **6**
See also CA 1-4R; 183; CANR 4, 38, 59; MAICYA; SAAS 7; SATA 21, 92; SATA-Obit 114

Shulevitz, Uri 1935- **5, 61**
See also CA 9-12R; CANR 3; DLB 61; MAICYA; SATA 3, 50, 106

Silverberg, Robert 1935- **59**
See also AAYA 24; CA 1-4R, 186; CAAE 186; CAAS 3; CANR 1, 20, 36, 85; CLC 7; DAM POP; DLB 8; INT CANR-20; MAICYA; MTCW 1, 2; SATA 13, 91; SATA-Essay 104

Silverstein, Alvin 1933- **25**
See also CA 49-52; CANR 2; CLC 17; JRDA; MAICYA; SATA 8, 69

Silverstein, Shel(don Allan) 1930-1999 ...... **5**
See also BW 3; CA 107; 179; CANR 47, 74, 81; JRDA; MAICYA; MTCW 2; SATA 33, 92; SATA-Brief 27; SATA-Obit 116

Silverstein, Virginia B(arbara Opshelor)
1937- **25**
See also CA 49-52; CANR 2; CLC 17; JRDA; MAICYA; SATA 8, 69

Simmonds, Posy 23

Simon, Hilda Rita 1921- **39**
See also CA 77-80; SATA 28

Simon, Seymour 1931- **9, 63**
See also CA 25-28R; CANR 11, 29; MAICYA; SATA 4, 73

Singer, Isaac
See Singer, Isaac Bashevis

Singer, Isaac Bashevis 1904-1991 .... **1**
See also AAYA 32; AITN 1, 2; CA 1-4R; 134; CANR 1, 39; CDALB 1941-1968; CLC 1, 3, 6, 9, 11, 15, 23, 38, 69, 111; DA; DAB; DAC; DAM MST, NOV; DA3; DLB 6, 28, 52; DLBY 91; JRDA; MAICYA; MTCW 1, 2; SATA 3, 27; SATA-Obit 68; SSC 3; WLC

Singer, Marilyn 1948- **48**
See also CA 65-68; CANR 9, 39, 85; JRDA; MAICYA; SAAS 13; SATA 48, 80; SATA-Brief 38

Sis, Peter 1949- **45**
See also CA 128; SATA 67, 106

Sleator, William (Warner III) 1945- **29**
See also AAYA 5; CA 29-32R; CANR 46, 83; JRDA; MAICYA; SATA 3, 68, 118

Slote, Alfred 1926- **4**
See also JRDA; MAICYA; SAAS 21; SATA 8, 72

Small, David 1945- **53**
See also SATA 50, 95; SATA-Brief 46

Smith, Dick King
See King-Smith, Dick

Smith, Jessie Willcox 1863-1935 .... **59**
See also DLB 188; MAICYA; SATA 21

Smith, Lane 1959- **47**
See also AAYA 21; CA 143; SATA 76

Smucker, Barbara (Claassen) 1915- **10**
See also CA 106; CANR 23; JRDA; MAICYA; SAAS 11; SATA 29, 76

Sneve, Virginia Driving Hawk 1933- **2**
See also CA 49-52; CANR 3, 68; SATA 8, 95

Snyder, Zilpha Keatley 1927- **31**
See also AAYA 15; CA 9-12R; CANR 38; CLC 17; JRDA; MAICYA; SAAS 2; SATA 1, 28, 75, 110; SATA-Essay 112

Sobol, Donald J. 1924- **4**
See also CA 1-4R; CANR 1, 18, 38; JRDA; MAICYA; SATA 1, 31, 73

Soto, Gary 1952- **38**
See also AAYA 10; CA 119; 125; CANR 50, 74; CLC 32, 80; DAM MULT; DLB 82; HLC 2; HW 1, 2; INT 125; JRDA; MTCW 2; PC 28; SATA 80

Souci, Robert D. San
See San Souci, Robert D.

Southall, Ivan (Francis) 1921- **2**
See also AAYA 22; CA 9-12R; CANR 7, 47; JRDA; MAICYA; SAAS 3; SATA 3, 68

Speare, Elizabeth George 1908-1994 .... **8**
See also CA 1-4R; 147; JRDA; MAICYA; SATA 5, 62; SATA-Obit 83

Spence, Eleanor (Rachel) 1928- **26**
See also CA 49-52; CANR 3; SATA 21

Spencer, Leonard G.
See Silverberg, Robert

Spier, Peter (Edward) 1927- **5**
See also CA 5-8R; CANR 41; DLB 61; MAICYA; SATA 4, 54

Spinelli, Jerry 1941- **26**
See also AAYA 11; CA 111; CANR 30, 45; JRDA; MAICYA; SATA 39, 71, 110

Spykman, E(lizabeth) C(hoate)
1896-1965 .... **35**
See also CA 101; SATA 10

Spyri, Johanna (Heusser) 1827-1901 .... **13**
See also CA 137; MAICYA; SATA 19, 100

Stanley, Diane 1943- **46**
See also CA 112; CANR 32, 64; SAAS 15; SATA 37, 80, 115; SATA-Brief 32

Stanton, Schuyler
See Baum, L(yman) Frank

Staples, Suzanne Fisher 1945- **60**
See also AAYA 26; CA 132; CANR 82; SATA 70, 105

Starbird, Kaye 1916- **60**
See also CA 17-20R; CANR 38; MAICYA; SATA 6

Staunton, Schuyler
See Baum, L(yman) Frank

Steig, William (H.) 1907- **2, 15**
See also AITN 1; CA 77-80; CANR 21, 44; DLB 61; INT CANR-21; MAICYA; SATA 18, 70, 111

Steptoe, John (Lewis) 1950-1989 .... **2, 12**
See also BW 1; CA 49-52; 129; CANR 3, 26, 81; MAICYA; SATA 8, 63

Sterling, Dorothy 1913- **1**
See also CA 9-12R; CANR 5, 28; JRDA; MAICYA; SAAS 2; SATA 1, 83

Stevenson, James 1929- **17**
See also CA 115; CANR 47; MAICYA; SATA 42, 71, 113; SATA-Brief 34

Stevenson, Robert Louis (Balfour)
1850-1894 .... **10, 11**
See also AAYA 24; CDBLB 1890-1914; DA; DAB; DAC; DAM MST, NOV; DA3; DLB 18, 57, 141, 156, 174; DLBD 13; JRDA; MAICYA; NCLC 5, 14, 63; SATA 100; SSC 11; WLC; YABC 2

Stine, Jovial Bob
See Stine, R(obert) L(awrence)

Stine, R(obert) L(awrence) 1943- **37**
See also AAYA 13; CA 105; CANR 22, 53; JRDA; MTCW 2; SATA 31, 76

Stone, Rosetta
See Dr. Seuss; Geisel, Theodor Seuss

Strasser, Todd 1950- **11**
See also AAYA 2; CA 117; 123; CANR 47; JRDA; MAICYA; SATA 41, 45, 71, 107

Streatfeild, (Mary) Noel 1895(?)-1986 ...... **17**
See also CA 81-84; 120; CANR 31; CLC 21; DLB 160; MAICYA; SATA 20; SATA-Obit 48

Stren, Patti 1949- **5**
See also CA 117; 124; SATA 88; SATA-Brief 41

Strong, Charles
See Epstein, Beryl (M. Williams); Epstein, Samuel

Suhl, Yuri (Menachem) 1908-1986 .... **2**
See also CA 45-48; 121; CANR 2, 38; MAICYA; SAAS 1; SATA 8; SATA-Obit 50

Sutcliff, Rosemary 1920-1992 .... **1, 37**
See also AAYA 10; CA 5-8R; 139; CANR 37; CLC 26; DAB; DAC; DAM MST, POP; JRDA; MAICYA; SATA 6, 44, 78; SATA-Obit 73

Swift, Jonathan 1667-1745 .... **53**
See also CDBLB 1660-1789; DA; DAB; DAC; DAM MST, NOV, POET; DA3; DLB 39, 95, 101; LC 1, 42; PC 9; SATA 19; WLC

Tarry, Ellen 1906- **26**
See also BW 1, 3; CA 73-76; CANR 69; SAAS 16; SATA 16

Tate, Eleanora E(laine) 1948- **37**
See also AAYA 25; BW 2, 3; CA 105; CANR 25, 43, 81; JRDA; SATA 38, 94

Taylor, Cora (Lorraine) 1936- **63**
See also CA 124; SATA 64, 103

Taylor, Mildred D. 9, 59
See also AAYA 10; BW 1; CA 85-88; CANR 25; CLC 21; DLB 52; JRDA; MAICYA; SAAS 5; SATA 15, 70

Author Index

CLR Cumulative Nationality Index

Nationality Index

CLR Cumulative Title Index

Title Index

Title Index

Title Index

Title Index

Title Index

ISBN 0-7876-4574-5

90000

9 780787 645748